Affectivity in Interaction

Volume 215

Affectivity in Interaction. Sound objects in English
by Elisabeth Reber

Affectivity in Interaction

Sound objects in English

Elisabeth Reber
University of Würzburg

John Benjamins Publishing Company
Amsterdam / Philadelphia

The paper used in this publication meets the minimum requirements of
the American National Standard for Information Sciences – Permanence
of Paper for Printed Library Materials, ANSI z39.48-1984.

Library of Congress Cataloging-in-Publication Data

Reber, Elisabeth.
  Affectivity in interaction : sound objects in English / Elisabeth Reber.
      p. cm. (Pragmatics & Beyond New Series, ISSN 0922-842X ; v. 215)
Includes bibliographical references and index.
  1. Grammar, Comparative and general--Phonology. 2. Emotions. I. Title.
P217.R36   2012
421'.5--dc23   2011039790
ISBN 978 90 272 5620 1   (Hb ; alk. paper)
ISBN 978 90 272 8165 4   (Eb)

John Benjamins Publishing Co. · P.O. Box 36224 · 1020 ME Amsterdam · The Netherlands
John Benjamins North America · P.O. Box 27519 · Philadelphia PA 19118-0519 · USA

Table of contents

Acknowledgements

The present study is a revised version of my doctoral thesis which was originally submitted to the Faculty of Arts, University of Potsdam, in July 2008. A lot of people have supported and contributed to the project at various stages and I wish to give them due acknowledgement.

First and foremost I wish to thank Elizabeth Couper-Kuhlen, my supervisor, mentor and friend, for her inspiration, guidance and support throughout the entire enterprise. I would also like to express warm thanks to Marja-Leena Sorjonen, my second supervisor, for her invaluable comments, enthusiasm and timely advice.

The data examined for this study were discussed in numerous data sessions at the "Linguistisches Kolloquium", University of Potsdam. I am particularly indebted to Margret Selting, Elizabeth Couper-Kuhlen and all other members of the colloquium for their sharp analytical ears and eyes and constant encouragement, which have substantially promoted the project. I also owe my thanks to the members of the study group G 405, Ulrike Bohle, Irene Forsthoffer, Cordula Schwarze, Doreen Siegfried and Silka Martens, to the members of the DAAD-STINT project "Interactional Linguistics in Crosslinguistic Perspective: Swedish-German-English", most noticeably Jan Anward, Elizabeth Couper-Kuhlen, Per Linell, Niklas Norén and Margret Selting, and to Richard Ogden for sharing their analytic expertise in discussing data examples of sound objects with me.

Dagmar Barth-Weingarten, Ulrike Bohle, Friederike Kern, and Sebastian Kürschner read single chapters of the book. I am most grateful for their insightful criticisms and confidence in me. Thanks are due to Elizabeth Couper-Kuhlen, Laura McKee and Guy Thornton for their meticulous proof-reading of the current manuscript in the final stages of production. The proofreading was supported by Gesprächsforschung e.V., whom I sincerely thank for their generous grant. I also thank Graham Huggan who encouraged me as a student at the University of Munich to pursue an academic career in the first place.

A big thank you to the series editor of the "Pragmatics and Beyond New Series", Anita Fetzer, for her great support and efficient handling of the project, two anonymous reviewers for their careful reading and thoughtful comments, and Isja Conen at John Benjamins for her patience and guidance.

And last, heartfelt thanks are owed to my friends and family and above all to my husband for his enthusiasm, humor and patience throughout all these years.

PART I

Introduction

General interest and scope of study

The present study was instigated by a general interest in how affectivity is displayed, claimed and accomplished in talk-in-interaction and what practices are deployed to these ends in English talk-in-interaction. Taking an interactional linguistic perspective, it is concerned with how such affective displays may be described in terms of their sound pattern, sequential placement and sequence-organisational and interactional functions.[1]

This general interest in affectivity in English talk-in-interaction is explored on the basis of so-called affect-laden sound objects, that is, prosodic-phonetically distinct objects with minimal semantic content, such as *oh, ooh, ah*, which have traditionally been termed 'primary interjections', and other objects of this sort which have become known as paralinguistic objects, such as clicks or whistles.

The starting point of the present study was the observation that participants in conversation may respond to affect-laden informings (Heritage 1984) with sound objects. Affect-laden informings may implement all kinds of conversational actions in addition to informing: They may function as e.g. news announcements, troubles tellings, complaints, repairs etc. A data analysis of British English interactions showed that affect-laden sound objects are most frequently used as responsive actions. The hypothesis to be explored in this study is that sound objects can represent a recipient practice to respond to affect-laden informings (or informings which were elicited through an affect-laden action) in an affect-laden fashion. More specifically, the present study will concentrate on objects which form an independent prosodic contour and are treated as forming an independent action:[2]

---

1.   The special relevance of the methodological paradigm of Interactional Linguistics to the study of sound objects will be illustrated in Chapters 1 and 2, cf. particularly Section 2.2.2, point *h*.

2.   Alternatively, sound objects can be integrated in a larger intonation phrase. In this case, they are usually produced in initial position and form part of an emerging action.

A: affect-laden informing
B: affect-laden sound object

In addition, the responsive turn may be expanded in systematic ways on post-production, i.e. after the production of the sound object.

In his seminal study on response cries, Goffman (1978) describes how speakers use "exclamatory interjections which are not full-fledged words", such as *Oops!* (ibid: 800), in order to respond to some event or communicative action. His point is that although these response cries appear to be a "flooding up" of emotion (ibid: 800), their production is actually constrained by social norms. Although the study has been widely received among linguists and conversation analysts, it has scarcely inspired any large-scale empirical work. It seems that only with the rising interest in emotion and affect in interactional studies (and on the scientific landscape in general) are his observations being gradually validated on empirical conversational grounds.

In the present study, four major empirical sections will present a selection of affect-laden sound objects which exemplify different aspects and issues relevant in the study of affectivity and sound objects.

The most frequent affect-laden sound objects identified in the data are types of *oh* (segmental substance [əʊ]), *ah* ([aː]) and *ooh* ([uː]), produced with context-specific prosodic-phonetic packages. In addition, they are almost exclusively deployed in responsive, turn-initial positions. To put the analyses of vocalic sound objects into perspective, two 'paralinguistic' objects found in the same sequential position were considered: Recreational whistling constitutes a particular noticeable resource, whereas clicks are especially minimal.

The present study touches on three topical fields: (1) linguistic domains, (2) minimal response forms in English talk-in-interaction, and (3) affectivity in talk-in-interaction.

First, in terms of linguistic domains, the study is situated at the interface between lexis and phonology in conversation. Treated as communicative resources specific for talk-in-interaction, vocalic sound objects will be analysed as lexical items whose meaning is constructed through its specific prosodic-phonetic packaging and sequential placement. It will be argued that – as for all kinds of meanings signalled by prosodic-phonetic cues – the affective meaning of the sound object is highly context-specific and constrained by the linguistic design, sequential position and action type of the turn the sound object responds to. Furthermore, it will be shown that affect-laden recipient responses of this kind serve to organise the sequential structure in specific ways and manage interactional relevancies of e.g. affiliation and commitment. Furthermore, including clicks and whistles into the analysis and subsuming them under the same class expands our understanding of oral communication. Clicks rarely have any prosodic prominence, which also leads to interesting questions for turn construction.

Secondly, by analysing affect-laden sound objects on the formal and functional levels, the study aims to deepen our understanding of minimal response forms in English. A decade ago, Sorjonen (2002) pointed to a gap in research with regard to recipient responses across languages: "There is a need for systematic studies of response forms in their particular sequential, epistemic, affective, and grammatical contexts in different languages as a topic of their own" (ibid: 190). In this vein, the present study attempts a contribution for English with a focus on affectivity. Moreover, it expands the scope of this type of research by showing that the prosodic-phonetic shape of sound objects, as well as turn expansions subsequent to the production of sound objects, may be formally and functionally systematic as well.

Thirdly, by combining a linguistic interest in the use of communicative sounds with a socio-cultural concept, affectivity, the study investigates language as a vehicle and tool for socio-cultural processes in talk-in-interaction. In this fashion, the present study approaches affectivity from an interactional linguistic angle and complements previous sociological, psychological, and (neuro)biological research on affectivity.

Some remarks on methodology

As stated in previous paragraphs, the method employed for the present study will be Interactional Linguistics (IL). Taking such an approach means that the analysis is empirically grounded, based on naturally occurring talk-in-interaction. It further involves affectivity being examined as an outward phenomenon, which is made visible, i.e. displayed, through linguistic contextualisation cues. For this reason, we will adopt a definition of affectivity which operates on the linguistic "surface" and considers affective expressions as socio-cultural constructs.

Furthermore, affectivity is analysed as a sequentially generated product, which is made relevant in specific sequential slots (Couper-Kuhlen 2009, Selting 1996). Thus, affectivity is treated as a conventional, interactionally achieved phenomenon which is signalled through linguistic (and paralinguistic) resources, e.g. sound objects.

Outline of the analysis

The study links up to previous conversation analytic/interactional linguistic research on affectivity. It provides empirical evidence for Goffman's claim that participants use sound objects to make affective displays in accordance with certain displays rules, and describes the systematics of their prosodic-phonetic form, sequential placement and sequential and interactional functions.

The study will take an interactional linguistic approach to affect-laden sound objects, one which combines linguistic concepts and categories with the sociologically informed study of talk-in-interaction, Conversation Analysis (CA), and an anthropological theoretical framework, Contextualisation Theory: This interdisciplinary perspective allows the examination of an object of study whose analysis requires a linguistic level of description (with regard to the form of the sound object), a conversational (with regard to the use of the sound object) and a socio-cultural one (in terms of its affective nature). A motivation for this method along with its central theoretical assumptions and methodological principles will be presented in Chapter 1.

Since sound objects correspond to what have been traditionally called primary interjections and paralinguistic sounds, Chapter 2 will outline definitional features of interjections and issues of debate, reviewing the most relevant literature from various backgrounds, including English grammars, Cognitive Linguistics, Discourse Analysis and Computational Linguistics, and then summarise major findings and results on such objects from research in Conversation Analysis/ Interactional Linguistics. It will become clear that the forms and functions of sound objects are best described in their natural habitat, naturally occurring talk-in-interaction, according to spoken language standards.

Two aspects contextualise the meaning of sound objects: Their prosodic-phonetic design and the sequential environment in which they are deployed. For this reason, Chapter 3 is concerned with prosody and affectivity. The chapter briefly addresses fundamental assumptions of prosody in conversation before summarising and discussing the major findings of prosody and affectivity in the field. Prosodic-phonetic clusters are taken as contextualisation devices for affectivity.

Chapter 4 gives an overview of previous research on conversational activities where affectivity is constructed and outlines major results and issues. Here activities in which affect-laden sound objects were found are described at some length in order to furnish the reader with the background knowledge needed for the analyses in the empirical part. Activities of this sort include troubles talk, news delivery sequences, complaints, assessments and repair. It is pointed out that an affect-laden activity is associated with specific affective dimensions, which are made relevant by participants. Recipients are invited to affiliate with these displays, which provides a methodological tool as to what kind of affective displays may be expected in recipient responses.

Chapter 5 shortly describes the data basis and transcription techniques and conventions used in the present study. An outline of the methodological procedure pursued for this study will be provided and issues of quantification will be discussed.

The empirical part comprises analytical accounts mainly of the following affect-laden sound objects: 'high and pointed' *oh*; *ooh*s of different prosodic-phonetic shapes; 'low-falling and tailed' and 'flat-falling and low' *ah*s; clicks and whistling. All form independent contours,[3] being used as initial responsive actions to different sorts of informings.

Chapter 6 presents the sound object *oh* [əʊ:] with 'extra high and pointed' prosody. Following a formal description of the prosodic packaging of this variant of *oh*, its uses with and without turn expansion will be presented in two sequential environments: repairs and news delivery sequences. Comparing the form and use of 'extra high and pointed' *oh* to another variant of *oh*, it will be argued that the interpretation of the former as a display of 'surprise' is a matter of degree. Finally, the interactional pay-off of ' extra high and pointed' *oh* will be discussed in terms of the question whether 'surprise' may be considered as an emotion.

Chapter 7 examines variants of *ooh* ([u:]). One focus is on *ooh* in high pitch register and a rising-falling contour, which is used to receipt, i.e. respond to, positive, unqualified assessments in radio phone-ins. Here it treats the prior assessment as exceptional and inviting heightened involvement, which is labelled as 'enthusiasm'/'positive excitement'. It is argued that these kinds of affective displays are staged for specific relevancies of radio interaction. In addition, midrange pitched variants of *ooh* in repair sequences in radio-phone-ins are examined. Finally, high pitched *ooh* is described in response to highly detailed informings in complaint sequences and troubles talk. Here the objects may be associated with displays of 'shock'.

Chapter 8 deals with the prosodic packagings of *ah* ([a:]), which are rather stable and clear-cut in contrast to the variants of *ooh*. First, 'low-falling and tailed' *ah* is examined as an affect-laden recipient response in troubles talk, where it is linked to affective dimensions such as 'sympathy'. The turn expansion systematically performs a closure-implicative move. The object may furthermore be used for mock displays. Coming with the same packaging, 'low-falling and tailed' *ah* also functions as a news response to bad-news announcements where the *teller* is the consequential figure in the scenario. Here, the turn is commonly expanded

---

3.   This does not apply to clicks because they do not tend to have prosodic prominence.

in terms of an idiomatic expression of 'sympathy', which solicits more talk related to the bad news. Finally, 'low-falling and tailed' *ah* is compared to 'flat-falling and low' *ah* in rejection contexts and a news sequence with the *recipient* as the consequential figure. It is argued that these similar shapes of *ah* may be exploited for conversational goals in contexts where the boundaries between functions and forms become blurred.

In order to show that sound objects beyond linguistic boundaries functionally form one class with these vocalic sound objects, we will present analyses of *clicks* and recreational *whistling* in the final empirical Chapter 9. The findings may only be regarded as tentative and must be inspected for a larger sample in further research. Clicks are examined as responsive actions at the boundaries of both narrative and non-narrative complaint sequences, seemingly affiliating with the 'moral indignation' displayed by the complainant. Finally, recreational whistling is presented as a news response, which appreciates informings (which make reference to a definite figure) with heightened involvement. At the same time, the sound object *whistle* does not take a valenced stance to that figure.

By way of conclusion, a summary of the main findings and a discussion of some of the theoretical and methodological implications of the study will be offered.

PART II

Background

This section aims to provide a background on the methodology adopted for the present study. In what follows, we will first introduce definitions of the two key concepts used and examined, affectivity and sound objects (Chapter 1), and outline the methodological approach of this study: Interactional Linguistics (Section 1.1) combines the descriptive tools of linguistics with the sociologically informed, methodological approach of Ethnomethodological Conversation Analysis (Section 1.2) and Contextualisation Theory (Section 1.3).

We will then come to a brief review of the previous linguistic literature on so-called interjections, discourse markers and vocalisations, which is relevant to the object of our study (Chapter 2). In this review, we will discuss core definitional features and issues of debate in English grammars and from the perspectives of Cognitive Linguistics, Discourse Analysis and Computational Linguistics (Section 2.1), before coming to an outline of the main assumptions and results for objects of this kind in Conversation Analysis and Interactional Linguistics (Section 2.2). A minor section will then deal with studies on communicative, so-called paralinguistic sounds (Section 2.3).

Chapters 3 and 4 will be concerned with affectivity in talk-in-interaction. The literature review reveals that from an interactional linguistic perspective, the prosodic packaging of a sound object and the type of interactional activity in which it is deployed are crucial for the analysis of the affective dimension of a sound object. For this reason, we will first take stock of the assumptions and findings in Prosody-in-Conversation in general and with respect to the contextualisation of affectivity in particular (Chapter 3). Finally, we will review previous findings on affect-laden activities in talk-in-interaction, particularly with regard to those which are subject to analysis in the present study (Chapter 4).

CHAPTER 1

Preliminaries

Affectivity and sound objects in an interactional linguistic perspective

Affectivity has attracted the interest of linguistic research from various angles, e.g. Syntax (Fries 1996), Lexical Semantics (Durst 2001), Cognitive Linguistics (Kövecses 1987, 1990, 2000), Pragmatics (Arndt and Janney 1987, Caffi and Janney 1994) and Neurolinguistics (Battacchi et al. ²1997). In contrast to this kind of research, the present study is about the use of so-called sound objects for displays of *affectivity in talk-in-interaction*.

To this end, the present study follows Ochs and Schieffelin (1989), who set out to investigate "the conventional displaying of affect through linguistic means" (ibid: 7). To indicate this perspective, we will use the term *affect* and adopt the definition of affect by the authors:

> We take affect to be a broader term than emotion, to include feelings, moods, dispositions, and attitudes associated with persons and/or situations. […] We are not concerned with issues of speakers' actual feeling states or the extent to which their affective expression is sincere. Such relations between inner states and outward expression are culturally variable […]. (ibid: 7)

Consequently, affect is regarded as a culturally learned display, which is performed in social interaction (cf. further ibid: 11). In this sense, the present study takes a socio-constructionist view of affectivity in talk-in-interaction (Hochschild 1979): Displays of affect are performed in orientation to conventional rules, which constrain the actual feeling of affective states, how they are displayed and the processing of displays by others. Consequently, they constitute social actions (Fiehler 1990b).

The following excerpt, taken from a British English radio phone-in on divorced fathers and their relationship to their children, reflects how the conceptualisation of affect as a social action may be observed as a lay concept as well. Here the in-studio presenter (Pres) asks the divorced father (C), who has left his wife because he discovered he was gay, about his reactions when his children broke off contact.

(1)   "do any anger" [Vanessa Feltz]

```
1        Pres:  ↑did you express i'm HURT-
2               i'm devastated you don't SEE me-=
3               =how can you do this to your FAther;
4               how could you not SEE me (**)
5     →         did you do any Anger and any hUrt (or pAin) or NOT.
6     →  C:     i resisted the temptation to D(h)O that;=
7        Pres:  yeah cause it's HUGE;
8               <<l>isn't it> [to DO that.
```

The use of the verb *do* in the expression *do any Anger and any hUrt* in line 5 indicates that expressions of anger and hurt are treated as actions which can be performed in social interaction with others. This way of conceptualizing affect is taken up and confirmed by the interlocutor in line 6.

Based on a general interest in how affectivity is organised, negotiated and made relevant in talk-in-interaction, we will examine the use of so-called affect-laden sound objects. To give a first, general definition, *sound objects* are described as conversational objects with minimal semantic content. Here the label *sound object* aims to reflect the fact that these objects are spoken language resources for which the sound pattern and its context-specific use are distinctive for the meaning. They include so-called 'primary interjections', such as e.g. *oh*, *ah* and *ooh*, and non-lexical sounds such as clicks and whistling, which have been found to function similarly in talk-in-interaction. More specifically, we will examine the use of affect-laden sound objects in response to affect-laden informings (and informings which were elicited by an affect-laden action).

A method which lends itself well to such an undertaking is Interactional Linguistics (Selting and Couper-Kuhlen 1996, 2000, 2001) – a methodological approach which combines conversation analytic and linguistic methodological tools with Contextualisation Theory in order to analyse linguistic structures in talk-in-interaction. In the following sections, we will outline the basic assumptions and concepts of the above traditions and highlight how they relate to the topic of the present study.

1.1   Interactional Linguistics

The method employed in the present study is oriented towards that of Interactional Linguistics (Selting and Couper-Kuhlen 2000), which stands for an approach as it was developed by scholars in the tradition of *Prosody-in-Conversation* (Couper-Kuhlen and Selting 1996a) in collaboration with the fields of *Phonology-for-Conversation* (e.g. Kelly and Local 1989, Local et al. 1986, Local and Walker

2005)[4], *Discourse-Functional Linguistics* (e.g. Ford et al. 2002) and *Conversation Analysis* (e.g. Sacks et al. 1974, Schegloff 2007).

Interactional Linguistics is concerned with language in a two-fold fashion: it investigates

i. what linguistic resources are used to articulate particular conversational structures and fulfil interactional functions? and
ii. what interactional function or conversational structure is furthered by particular linguistic forms and ways of using them?

(Couper-Kuhlen and Selting 2001: 3)

Furthermore, Interactional Linguistics "takes an interdisciplinary and a cross-linguistic perspective on language" (ibid: 3). While the cross-linguistic aspect of the approach is reflected only marginally in the present study, its interdisciplinarity is crucial for the questions investigated here. This interdisciplinarity derives from its combining "individual strengths of [three] discipline[s] – technical description in linguistics, research methodology in conversation analysis and cultural breadth in anthropology" (ibid: 1). Hence it is this combination of disciplines which is particularly well-fitted for the purposes of this study:

a. Linguistic tools of description: Sound objects are resources of spoken, embodied interaction. By using linguistic terms of description we can describe their segmental composition and prosodic-phonetic shape.
b. Sociological method for the analysis of talk-in-interaction: The methodology of Ethnomethodological Conversation Analysis (e.g. Sacks et al. 1974, Schegloff 2007) allows us to analyse affect-laden sound objects as communicative resources as they are deployed in talk-in-interaction in order to accomplish social actions and goals. In doing so, the study examines their use on the micro level of social interaction.
c. Grounding in linguistic anthropology: Contextualisation Theory and its concept of contextualisation cues offer a theoretical frame for understanding how participants interpret vocal (and visual) signals to arrive at meaningful inferences and deploy them to construct social interaction (Eerdmans et al. 2003b: vii).

In addition, Interactional Linguistics has a strong record of research with respect to prosody in conversation, which is particularly valuable since prosody plays a major role as regards the affective meaning of sound objects. Although its original and principal interest was the analysis of prosodic structures in interaction (cf. e.g. Couper-Kuhlen and Selting (1996a), Couper-Kuhlen and Ford (2004),

---

4. Cf. Szczepek Reed (2006) for a detailed review of *Phonology-for-Conversation*.

Selting and Couper-Kuhlen (2001), the scope of Interactional Linguistics includes linguistic resources on all levels (cf. e.g. Hakulinen and Selting (2005) on lexis and syntax). Selting (1995) points out the benefits of a comprehensive analysis of linguistic devices in interaction:

> Es resultiert die weitergehende Perspektive einer Linguistik der Konversation, in der linguistische Strukturen und Systeme als Signalisierungsmittel und als Ressource der Organisation der konversationellen Interaktion beschrieben werden. In dieser Perspektive wären analog zur interaktionalen Prosodie der Konversation auch segmental-phonologische, morphophonemische, syntaktische, lexikalisch-semantische u.a. Signalisierungssysteme als interpretativ relevante Kontextualisierungshinweise in der Alltagskommunikation zu untersuchen. Diese Analysen können z.T. durchaus an bisherige linguistische Analysen anschließen. Denn die mithilfe linguistischer Analyse- und Beschreibungsverfahren beschriebenen Systeme und Regeln sind als kognitive Orientierungsschemata die Basis und die Voraussetzung unserer Konstitution und Interpretation von konversationellen Aktivitäten.[5]   (Selting 1995: 366)

Because of this socio-anthropological approach to language, Interactional Linguistics lends itself particularly well to the analysis of affectivity as conveyed through linguistic resources. Affectivity does not form a linguistic category in itself but is a highly social construct which may be displayed, managed and negotiated through diverse communicative means.

As was mentioned above, a major concern of Interactional Linguistics in previous research has been the study of Prosody-in-Conversation, a research interest which – among others – led to the establishment of this field in the first place. In their seminal volume, Couper-Kuhlen and Selting (1996b) propose a set of methodological principles for Prosody-in-Conversation (cf. also Local and Walker (2005: 121–122) for a similar methodological catalogue). Since prosodic analysis is central in the present study and the methodological principles defined for Prosody-in-Conversation may be applied to interactional linguistic study in general, they are listed in what follows:

---

5.   This results in the further perspective of a Linguistics for conversation, in which linguistic structures and systems are described as signalling devices and as an organisational resource for conversational interaction. In this perspective, segmental-phonological, morphophonemic, syntactic, lexical-semantic etc. signalling systems would – by analogy to the interactional prosody of conversation – also have to be examined in terms of their role as interpretively relevant contextualisation cues in everyday communication. These analyses can to some extent align well with the linguistic analyses which have been performed to date. This is the case since the systems and rules which represent cognitive orientation schemes and which have been described with linguistic methods of analysis and description are the basis and precondition of our constitution and interpretation of conversational activities. (my translation, E. R.)

1. Give priority to the analysis of naturally occurring talk.
2. Treat the data as an integral part of the context in which [they occur].
3. Treat the data as emergent in the real time of ongoing interaction.
4. Ground analytic categories in the data [themselves by considering]:
    a. The relationship of the device to just prior turns,
    b. Co-occurring evidence within the turn,
    c. Subsequent treatment of the interactional device in question,
    d. Discriminability of the interactional device,
    e. Deviant cases in the use of the device.
5. Validate analytical categories by demonstrating participants' orientation
    to them.   (cited from Couper-Kuhlen and Selting (1996b: 25–39)

Because of this interdisciplinary approach to language, Interactional Linguistics lends itself particularly well to the analysis of affectivity conveyed through linguistic resources and beyond.

1.2   Conversation Analysis

The methodological principles of Conversation Analysis, which treats conversation as the orderly product of diverse systems of organisation including turn-taking, sequence organization, repair, etc. (Section 1.2.1), and which takes a participant's perspective in linking practices with actions (Section 1.2.2) are of general relevance to the present study. Furthermore, the following two assumptions are of particular importance to the analysis of affectivity from a conversation analytic perspective (Section 1.2.3): (a) affective expressions are social displays and (b) affectivity represents members' knowledge.

1.2.1   *The turn–taking system*
Conversation Analysis is concerned with the organisation of social interaction, first and foremost in mundane conversation, which is regarded as the primordial, primary locus of language use. Conversation Analysis works strictly empirically in the sense that its analyses are data-driven, i.e. based exclusively on recordings of naturally occurring interaction, and inductive.

The basic assumption of Conversation Analysis is based on the assumption that talk-in-interaction is orderly ("order at all points", Sacks (1984: 22). One system of organisation regulates turn-taking and provides for the fact that as a rule only one participant speaks at a time. Another system concerns actions and their sequencing in talk. The "basic, minimal" (Schegloff 2007: 22) sequence consists of an adjacency pair, two turns comprising a first pair part (initiating action) and a second pair part (responsive action), e.g. question – answer, greeting – return of greeting (cf. Schegloff (2007: 13–27) for an introductory discussion). In addition to the ordering of actions in sequences of action, conversational order is accomplished through participants' orientation to the systematics of the turn-taking system, which includes two components: (1) The turn-constructional component and (2) the turn-allocation component (Sacks et al. 1974: 702–703).

(1) The turn-constructional component refers to the observation that turns may be built in terms of various types of turn-constructional units (TCU). They may have the form of a word, phrase, clause or sentence (ibid: 702). It is central that units of this kind "allow a projectionof the unit-type under way, and what, roughly, it will take for an instance of that unit-type to be completed" (ibid: 702). The point where a TCU is possibly complete represents a transition-relevance place (TRP), a place where turn-taking may (but need not) occur (ibid: 703).⁶ TCUs constitute the basic blocks of turns and consequently are central to the turn-taking system.

(2) The turn-allocation component includes the methods by which speakers, on possible turn completion, nominate next speakers, yield the floor to incoming self-selecting speakers or, barring this, continue to talk themselves (ibid: 703).

As regards the present study, the basic assumption that participants organise talk methodically through turn-taking, sequence organisation and repair helps the analyst to understand the function(s) of affect-laden sound objects, that is, conversational objects whose meaning is rarely made explicit or accounted for in interaction.

---

6. The question how the projection of possible unit completion and potential TRPs is signalled is left unanswered by Sacks et al. (1974: 703, footnote 12) and has not been resolved in a satisfactory manner since. Syntax has been identified as a main resource for TCU construction (e.g. Schegloff 1979). For this reason, the issue becomes particularly difficult for syntactically minimal TCUs composed, e.g., only of single words. Here syntactic projection may be replaced by prosodic resources. Wells and Macfarlane (1998) offer the following prosodic definition of TRPs in English: "It is the stretch of talk between the final major accented syllable of the current turn and a point one or two beats following the onset of the next utterance (whether or not the next utterance is spoken by the same speaker or a new speaker)" (ibid: 280). On these grounds we may assume in a positive sense that sound objects with prosodic prominence generally create a TRP and therefore constitute a TCU. Alternatively, the question may be decided in a negative fashion: If a sound object is treated by the other speaker as having created a TRP, it must form a TCU (cf. Couper-Kuhlen (2001b: 20) for such a way of describing TCUs). Since the former approach (positive definition of TCU) is not fully concordant with the methodological approach of the present study, next-turn proof procedure, we will apply the latter analytic procedure (negative definition of TCU).

1.2.2   *A participant's perspective*

Participants signal their understanding of and orientation towards a prior turn and its action in their next turn (Sacks et al. 1974:728). In this way, participants make sense of what is being said/has been said in the following manner: On the one hand, they come to an understanding of the current turn as it is unfolding in real time and on the other hand, they create their next turn on the basis of this understanding (Schegloff 2006), i.e. next speakers display their understanding of an ongoing co-participant's turn in their subsequent turn. On the basis of the shape and sequential positioning of these next turns, analysts can reconstruct the way actions were understood from the participant's perspective (Sacks et al. 1974:729). In this sense, analysts' description and interpretation of conversational actions relies on what is displayed and made relevant by the participants themselves. By applying such a 'next-turn proof procedure' (Sacks et al. 1974:728–729, Hutchby and Wooffitt [2]2008: 15), the analyst seeks to reconstruct the participants' understandings of turns and actions through adjacency pairs and sequences (cf. Sacks et al. 1974, Schegloff 2007).

Analysts' strict reliance on the next speaker's display of understanding in his/her next turn has been, however, criticised for failing to acknowledge the signalling potential of a first speaker's turn (cf. the discussion in Schegloff 1996a). That is, the linguistic design of a turn may prompt or even project a specific next action, although that action or turn may never materialise. Furthermore, a strict analytic reliance on the next turn as a key to what a first speaker's turn was doing makes it impossible to account for misunderstandings between two speakers. For this reason, more recent accounts back away from the assumption that the next-turn proof procedure provides ultimate evidence for the analysis of turns at talk. Instead, this methodological tool is assumed to account for the prior turn "to be *possibly* doing the proposed action(s) or that [next speakers] are oriented to that possibility" (Schegloff 1996a: 172, my emphasis, E. R.). Accordingly, it is accepted that there is a link between the turn *shape* and the proposed *action* accomplished by that turn, that is, that the turn may have an "'objective' import" on formal grounds (ibid: 173, footnote 6). It is to be noted that this constraint on the applicability of the next-turn proof procedure converges with the interests of Interactional Linguistics: By acknowledging the relevance of the turn shape, i.e. of the linguistic design of a turn, for the interpretation of social actions, Conversation Analysis widens its scope from purely sociological considerations one to include linguistically informed ones.

1.2.3   *Conversation Analysis and affectivity*

Two basic assumptions are particularly relevant when examining affectivity from the perspective of Conversation Analysis: (a) Affective expressions are social displays and (b) affectivity represents members' knowledge. The following account will outline the implications of these assumptions.

a.   Affective expressions are social displays.
The CA view of affective expressions as social displays is heavily influenced by Goffman's (1978) seminal article on "response cries".[7] Response cries represent conventional, ritualised displays of inner states that the speaker attributes to him/herself and that he/she makes publicly available. The production of such displays does not presuppose any correspondence between the displayed emotion and the inner state of the producer (ibid: 806). What is crucial is the function of affective displays for "impression management" (Goffman 1959: 208) in social interaction. Affective displays can form responses to both extralinguistic events (as e.g. when the producer is served a large crepe with ice cream and nuts, Goffman (1978: 804–805), and to verbally conveyed events, which can concern the recipient him/herself, the speaker or a third party (ibid: 805). Most importantly, Goffman's observations concerning response cries, namely that they are "conventionalized as to form, occasion of occurrence, and social function" (ibid: 814), can be applied to affective displays in general.

For a 'pure' conversation analytic study, which relies solely on the observable behaviour of participants for its evidence, the implications of Goffman's findings are that it cannot determine whether inner states, i.e. affect-cognitive states and processes, are actually present when socially displayed or not. Instead, a conversation analytic study can only describe what is made relevant on the interactional surface of talk and in this way becomes publicly available (cf. e.g. Goodwin p.c. in Couper-Kuhlen 2009: 96, footnote 6): i.e. (1) what is conveyed in talk about some affect-laden or affect–implicative event, situation or state-of-affairs, (2) what is made lexically explicit and stated by reference to specific emotion terms, and/or (3) what is implicitly conveyed through prosodic-syntactic resources and thus contextualised through affect-laden talk. The various strands of Conversation Analysis which have dealt with affectivity have, however, adopted the notion of affectivity as social display in more or less extreme ways. At one end of the spectrum, Discursive Psychology strictly rejects the investigation of implicit affective displays as 'cognitivism'. Consequently, the main interest of scholars in this field is confined to the use of explicit emotion and cognition terms for specific actions in talk-in-interaction (e.g. Edwards 1999, Locke 2003, Potter 2006). At the other end of the spectrum, larger, interdisciplinary projects have been able to expand the methodological scope of Conversation Analysis, by including psychological

---

7.   Cf. Drew and Wootton (1988) and Bergmann (1991) for the general connection between Goffman's work and Conversation Analysis.

and physiological dimensions of affectivity into their research agenda. For instance, the research conducted within the Bielefeld based project *Kommunikative Darstellung und klinische Repräsentation von Angst* [Communicative description and clinical representation of anxiety] on patients' tellings of their pathological anxiety disorder was able to provide evidence for a relationship between these patients' linguistic and visual choices in their tellings and their particular type of disorder (e.g. Egbert and Bergmann 2004).

The present study will take a position in between these two extremes: It will analyse the contextualisation of affect through primarily phonetic-prosodic and lexical resources in situated interaction and thus consider both more implicit and more explicit forms of doing affectivity. Given that the interactional linguistic approach of this study cannot identify psychological or physiological processes going on in speakers' minds and bodies, an analytic focus will be placed on the question how participants, and more specifically, recipients, construct affect-laden actions in order to engage with the on-going interactional project, i.e. how affectivity is relevant to action formation in specific sequential slots, when participating in conversational activities such as news telling, complaining, etc. Furthermore, this means that affect-laden actions may not necessarily correspond to inner or bodily states but are performed in order to serve specific, situated communicative goals in the evolving interaction.

b.   Affectivity represents members' knowledge.
The methodological principle of a participant's perspective in Conversation Analysis is closely linked to the conceptualisation of affective displays as members' resources. By displaying affectivity, members accomplish social actions and create social order through them (cf. Firth 1995: 270).

The notion of 'member' in Conversation Analysis has an ethnomethodological origin and goes back to work by Garfinkel (1967) and Garfinkel and Sacks (1970), who use the term as an abstract concept. In their use of the term, being a *member* means having

> the capacities or competencies that people have *as* members of society; capacities
> to speak, to know, to understand, to act in ways that are sensible in that society
> and in the situations in which they find themselves.
>
> (ten Have 2002: paragraph 17, emphasis in the original)

Consequently, membership includes knowledge about the norms and conventions held in a society and how to act according to them. With reference to this work, Sacks (1995) makes the observation that speakers organise members' knowledge about their social interactional partners in different sets of categories, such as age, sex, race, religion, etc. (ibid: 40). To Sacks, this way of classifying interactional partners is fundamental to social organisation. Sacks goes on to point out that the inferences evoked by such category knowledge can be modified (ibid: 45). For instance, members' knowledge about the category 'age', namely that "someone who is 48 is past their prime" can be treated as not being valid by a current speaker who produces a modifying formulation of the sort "I'm 48 but I look and feel younger" (ibid: 44). Linking this kind of work to the study of affectivity in interaction, Wilkinson and Kitzinger (2006) argue that displays of 'surprise' may signal a shared category membership. The creation of so-called 'surprise' sources, that is, turns which are "designed precisely to elicit the surprise duly performed in next turn" (ibid: 156) and subsequent 'surprised' responses are seen as an indication of "social judgments about what is to be expected and what is not" (ibid: 173) and thereby as a speaker's resource to make normative member knowledge relevant.

We have seen that it is one of the basic assumptions of Ethnomethodological Conversation Analysis that interactants draw on members' knowledge in their construction and interpretation of social activities. However, the concept of members' knowledge is not only limited to the participants in the social activities analysed. It also includes the analysts of such interactions through what is known as 'common sense' or 'intuition'. Ten Have (2002) convincingly argues that membership knowledge presents an "[i]nevitable [r]esource" (ibid: heading to Chapter 5) not only in our everyday lives but also in all questions of research (ibid: paragraph 27). In this way, conversation analysts have adopted the use of membership knowledge from Ethnomethodolgy and operationalised it as a starting point in the analytic procedure (e.g. Sorjonen and Hakulinen 2009). Extending the definition of the term, Heritage (1995) expands the social notion of membership to that of membership in a linguistic community in his description of the initial step of conversation analytic study:

> As competent language users, analysts develop more or less conceptually informed 'hunches' about the uses and organizational properties of particular conversational practices.[8] At this point, the work normally begins with an inductive search for instances of the practice under investigation using as wide a range of data as possible.   (ibid: 399)

By emphasising the role of the analyst's language competence, Heritage thus integrates an interactional linguistic perspective into an otherwise conversation analytically informed methodological procedure.

In order to counter-check their subjective members' intuitions, analysts furthermore have two tools available. Firstly, data sessions: In data sessions researchers jointly listen to (and – if video material is available – watch) data and discuss it

---

8.   Note that Heritage speaks of competent, not of native language users.

either freely or guided by specific research interests. Here the recording presents a "'given object', while all subsequent re-workings of it – transcription, understanding and analysis – are open to intersubjective scrutiny" (ten Have 2002: paragraph 43). In this way, the analyst is able to test whether intersubjectivity can be established in terms of his/her understanding of the data and object of study (ten Have 2002: paragraph 43).[9] Secondly, next-turn proof procedure: Ten Have (2002) makes a strong case in arguing that CA's next-turn proof procedure presents a neat tool for checking and verifying these intuitions by virtue of a data-driven procedure (ibid: paragraph 29). Next-turn proof procedure can thus be understood as an analytic tool to avoid circular analysis. In the present study, both practices (repeated data sessions and next-turn proof procedure) have laid the foundation for the analytic procedure. Nevertheless, the analytic reconstruction of the recorded interaction is still based to some extent on interpretation, which cannot be fully detemined by nor entirely inferred from the conversational processes examined (Deppermann 2001: 56). It is our task as analysts to become aware of these interpretive processes and to lay them open as part of our analytic work.

To conclude, it has been shown that the conversation analytic method deployed by interactional linguists allows an empirical, data-driven account of affectivity as displayed by members of – in the best sense – socio-linguistic communities. In the present study, affectivity is seen as a resource for attending to local interactional relevancies and accomplishing conversational actions. In this way, affective displays are treated as social in nature and as constructed potentially independently of the actual presence of inner states.[10] They are considered to be expressions of members' knowledge, which is displayed and made relevant in specific interactional environments to achieve specific communicative goals.

1.3   Contextualisation Theory

Contextualisation Theory is bound up with the name and work of the interactional sociolinguist John Gumperz (Gumperz 1982, 1992, Auer and diLuzio 1992, Eerdmans et al. 2003a). Gumperz' main concern is to come up with a theoretical framework that explains the processes of conversational inferencing, that is, participants' sense-making of what is going on in time beyond the machinery of turn-taking when engaging in social interaction (Gumperz 1992: 231). In this

---

9.   Cf. also Kehrein (2002).

10.   This is furthermore concordant with the general orientation of CA to analyse the social organisation of actions without taking psychological dimensions into account (Heritage 1995: 396).

way, the framework accommodates knowledge about how both linguistic *and* so-cio-cultural knowledge come into play in interaction. For instance, culture-bound contextualisation conventions in different (sub)cultures may lead to miscommu-nication between members of different (sub)cultures which generally speak the same language.

Central to Gumperz' theory are the notions 'contextualisation', 'contextualisa-tion cues' and 'conversational inference'. *Contextualisation* is defined as

> speakers' and listeners' use of verbal and nonverbal signs to relate to what is said at any one time and in any one place to knowledge acquired through past ex-perience, in order to retrieve the presupposition they must rely on to maintain conversational involvement and assess what is intended.   (ibid: 230)

In this sense, contextualisation refers to the interpretive processes that partici-pants permanently have to manage and accomplish when engaging in interaction. The verbal and nonverbal signs that prompt such contextual presuppositions are so-called contextualisation cues. They include all linguistic signals that serve such a function (Gumperz 1982: 131). The notions of contextualisation and contextu-alisation cues were taken over by interactional linguists (e.g. Auer and diLuzio 1992) and further adopted by Selting (1995), who introduced the terms signal-ling devices and signalling systems (*Signalisierungsmittel, Signalisierungssysteme*, cf. Section 3.1).

Although conveying meaning, contextualisation cues are 'implicit' (Gumperz 1982: 131). They are "basically gradual or scalar" and "do not take the form of discrete qualitative contrasts" (ibid: 132). In this way contextualisation cues are classified as indexical signs.[11] Contextualisation cues work and affect inferential processes on three levels: First, on the level of vocal and visual perception, second on the level of sequencing and third on the level of activity (Gumperz 1992: 233). Furthermore, conversational inference involves "the situated or context-bound process of interpretation, by means of which participants in an exchange assess other's intentions, and on which they base their response" (Gumperz 1982: 153). A main interest of Gumperz' lies in the role of prosodic resources as contextuali-sation cues in conversation. It comes therefore as no surprise that his theory was welcomed by the pioneers in Interactional Linguistics whose original concern was the study of Prosody-in-Conversation, with their research programme being designed to meet the purposes of such study.

To conclude, Contextualisation Theory offers an explanatory framework for the way participants make sense of and understand conversational actions and

---

11.   Note that this use of the term indexicality departs from the definition of indices in Charles Peirce's semiotic theory of signs.

processes beyond what is explicitly conveyed through words. With respect to the present study, such a framework is especially useful for an account of non-referential conversational signals such as sound objects, whose meaning is prismatic and primarily signaled through sound packaging and situated placement in talk-in-interaction.

1.4   Summary and conclusions

The present study adopts a socio-constructionist perspective on affectivity, which treats affect as socio-cultural learned displays and analyses these displays independently of inner states and feelings. In this sense, sound objects are deployed as communicative resources for affect-laden displays in social interaction. The methodology employed in the present study follows that of Interactional Linguistics, whose background in the school of Prosody-in-Conversation, the method of Conversation Analysis and the framework of Contextualisation Theory offer a well-tailored approach for the analysis of affect-laden sound objects. In this way, the forms and functions of affect-laden sound objects can be described from a participant's perspective, as social actions performed in situated contexts in naturally occurring interaction, embedded in sequences of turns at talk and constrained by local placement in social activities.

CHAPTER 2

Approaching sound objects

Previous research on interjections, discourse markers and vocalisations

Because of the linguistic background and interest of the study, the following section will provide an overview of past linguistic research on what will be referred to as sound objects in the present study. In Linguistics, sound objects have been treated as so-called interjections, vocalisations, non-lexical conversational sounds or 'grunts', discourse markers or discourse particles. The abundance of terms nicely reflects a certain difficulty as to how to classify these entities (cf. Eckert and Barry (²2005: 246–249) for an especially impressive example), but is also a sign of the variety of linguistic traditions which have dealt with the issue.[12] The outline will first begin with a review of the definitional features and main issues in such research (Section 2.1), followed by a summary of the core assumptions and findings from conversation analytically/interactional linguistically informed studies (Section 2.2), with a short excursus on paralinguistic sounds (Section 2.3). The section will be closed off with final conclusions (Section 2.4). Due to the interests of the present study, a focus will be placed on accounts made for English.

2.1 Interjections – what are they?

A fundamental distinction shared by most linguistic scholars is that between 'primary' and 'secondary' interjections,[13] which are generally regarded as expressions of emotions (Nübling 2001: 21). The latter ('secondary') are interjections derived from syntagms, such as e.g. *blimey* < *God blind me*, or proper or common nouns, such as e.g. *gee* < *Jesus*. The former ('primary') constitute "prototypical" interjections (ibid: 20, also Nübling 2004), such as e.g. *oh*, *ah*. They differ from secondary interjections with respect to the following four properties: lexical opacity, lack of formal

---

12. Due to the synchronic angle of the present study, the literature review does not include diachronic studies. For historical surveys cf. e.g. Brinton (1996), Gehweiler (2008).

13. Cf. Ehlich (1986), Reisigl (1999) for comprehensive historical outlines of the term 'interjection'.

lexical integration (i.e. transparency), lack of meaning (motivationality) and lack of any concrete referential potential (motivation) (Nübling 2001: 24–25). According to this classification, sound objects largely relate to primary interjections.[14]

As per a minimal definition, interjections can be characterised by five constitutive features (Nübling 2004: 13): (1) expression of a spontanenous emotion, (2) absence of referential meaning, (3) lack of inflection, (4) syntactic autonomy and (5) possible onomatopoeic structures. With the exception of feature 3, these are also widely found in the descriptions of English interjections in grammars and within semantic/pragmatic, discourse analytic and computational linguistic frameworks.

Going back to Bühler's Theory of Language (*Sprachtheorie*) of 1934, the notion that interjections serve as expressions of a spontanenous emotion (1) is closely associated with the idea of the absence of referential meaning (2). Interjections are thus linguistic signs which do not have a representative, i.e. referential function, but serve an expressive function (*Kundgabefunktion*, Bühler 1999: 311) and are in this sense symptoms, that is, signs which express the inner states of the speaker (ibid: 28). English grammar books, for example, agree that interjections are words which have expressive, emotional meaning.[15] The emotional meaning of interjections is illustrated by proposing fixed form-meaning relations, e.g. *ugh* as an interjection for disgust (Quirk et al. 1985: 853, Biber et al. 1999: 1085) or as a "negative reaction to unpleasant sensations" respectively (Carter and McCarthy 2006: 224), or *wow* for "great surprise" (Quirk et al. 1985: 853, cf. also Carter and McCarthy 2006: 225). This kind of form-meaning pairing may lead to the conclusion on the reader's part that interjections have clear-cut denotations. Only Biber et al. (1999: 1082) clearly state that "[s]emantically, they have no denotative meaning: their use is defined rather by their pragmatic function".

Arguing along the same lines, Schourup (1982), in his study on discourse particles, which subsumes interjections such as *oh* and *ah*-like discourse particles under the functional class of the 'evincive' (ibid: 14–15),[16] states that the latter is

---

14. For this reason secondary interjections have been excluded from the literature review. In terms of particles, only discourse particles in the sense of discourse markers are considered (as opposed to e.g. modal, scalar or focus particles, which are not typical of English anyway, Abraham (1991).

15. A detailed account of dictionary entries will be given in the empirical chapters on the respective sound objects. For a further overview of interjections in English grammar books see Jovanović (2004).

16. Studies in Discourse Analysis approach interjections from a discourse-functional perspective, i.e. interjections are examined in terms of so-called discourse markers or discourse particles. That means that interjections such as *oh* and *ah* are categorised along with adverbs (e.g. *well, just, now, actually*), connectives (e.g. *and, but, or*) and phrases (e.g. *y'know, I mean*) in the

a linguistic item that indicates that at the moment at which it is said the speaker is engaged in, or has just been engaged in, thinking; the evincive item indicates that this thinking is now occurring or has just occurred but does not completely specify its content.

(ibid: 14)

The production of the evincive thus co-occurs with the mental processes which it expresses (ibid: 15). In this way *oh* and *ah* are treated as indices of the speaker's on-going cognitive processes and as being opaque in terms of what precisely these processes are.

This view is later disputed by Schiffrin (1987), who claims that discourse markers do not constitute "simply windows into a person's mind" (Aijmer 2002: 151) but are used as a discourse structuring device. They are defined as "sequentially dependent elements which bracket units of talk" (Schiffrin 1987: 31). In that view, discourse markers relate to longer passages of talk and not to "a more finely defined unit such as sentence, proposition, speech act, or tone unit" (ibid: 31). They function in "both [a] cataphoric and anaphoric [fashion] whether they are in initial or terminal position" (ibid: 31). Nevertheless, the assumption that interjections give an insight into the brain of a speaker still prevails even in more recent work: For example, Fischer (2000) in her investigation of discourse particles (including the German and English interjections *ja*, *äh/ähm* and *oh*) for the purposes of human-machine interaction defines discourse particles "as lexemes with under-specified meanings that disclose mental processes specified by reference to aspects of the communicative situation" (ibid: 284).

Although it is a widely shared assumption that interjections have non-referential meaning, the work done within the framework of natural semantic metalanguage (NSM)[17] also tacitly suggests that interjections have as much semantic

---

same functional class. This class includes lexical items which have been grammaticalised as discourse markers. Some of the most influential works and volumes on discourse markers/particles which consider interjections have been Schourup (1982), Schiffrin (1987), Aijmer (2002), Fischer (2006), Montes (1999). The major concern is to find the functional core meaning of a discourse marker as it is implemented on different discourse levels or planes.

17. In the cognitive semantic method of 'natural semantic metalanguage' (NSM) (e.g. Wierzbicka 1992, 1996, 1997), language universals, i.e. so-called semantic primes such as good, bad, do, happen, etc., are used for the 'semantic decomposition' of words. It is claimed that the semantic primes used are based on natural languages but at the same time are independent of them. Thereby they lend themselves for the description and comparison of lexical meanings across languages. Since the analysis of lexical meaning is understood as a key to cultural concepts, cross-linguistic analyses of e.g. emotion words at the same time constitute cross-cultural investigations of emotion concepts. Such analyses are informed by the scholar's or native informant's intuitions and literary or made-up examples.

content as other lexical items.[18] For example, the frame (i.e. the explanatory semantic paraphrase) of the English interjection *wow* is as follows:

> *wow!*
> I now know something
> I wouldn't have thought I would know it
> I think: it is very good
> (I wouldn't have thought it could be like that)
> I feel something because of that
>
> (Wierzbicka 1992:164, cf. Wilkins 1992:150, 151
> for an alternative description)

Accordingly, the meaning of *wow* implies some (change in) cognitive state, the attribution of positive valence to something and some affective state. On the basis of this
frame, it can be concluded that interjections may have a fixed, clear-cut and context-
free meaning (for a criticism of NSM in general see Pawlowska et al. (2002).

As to feature 4), syntactic autonomy, English grammars agree that interjections stand outside the sentence structure (Biber et al. 1999:1083, Carter and
McCarthy 2006:113, 493, Huddleston and Pullum 2002:22, 1361, Quirk et al.
1985:67, 853). As Kryk (1992:194–195) rightly observes, this kind of description goes back to Jespersen (1922, 1924) and has only been slightly altered since.
As to the syntactic position of interjections, it is stated that they are placed
at the beginning of utterances (Quirk et al. 1985:853), or in front of clauses
(Carter and McCarthy 2006:493, Huddleston and Pullum 2002:1361). This lack
of syntactic integration makes it very hard for grammarians to assign them a
place in the syntactic system, since parts of speech are classified according to
syntactic functions.[19]

While admitting that interjections, which are classified as inserts, a word
class which comprises non-clausal units consisting of single words (Biber et al.
1999:1082), cannot be grammatically integrated, Biber et al. (1999) expand on the
notion of integration, pointing to a possible *prosodic* integration of interjections

---

18.   This kind of work has found widespread circulation due to its publication in the Special
Issue on Interjections in the *Journal of Pragmatics* (Ameka 1992a).

19.   Deppermann (2006) refers to this as a 'sentence premise' ('Satz-Prämisse'), i.e. one of the
typical characteristics of mainstream grammars, which causes problems for the description of
conversational language structures. He states: "Vollständige syntaktische Einheiten sind Sätze;
sie drücken eine Proposition aus und bestehen mindestens aus Subjekt und Prädikat" ("Complete syntactic units are sentences; they express a proposition and consist of at least a subject
and a predicate" (ibid:44), my translation, E.R.).

into conversational speech.[20] "[T]hey may appear attached (prosodically, or, in the transcription, by absence of punctuation) to a larger structure, which may be a clausal unit or a non-clausal unit." (ibid: 1082).[21] While it will be shown in the present study that the prosody of interjections contributes to their meaning-making and works on the levels of turn-construction and sequence organisation, this aspect has been largely neglected in previous research.

Possible onomatopoeic structures (5) are taken as a criterion for the semiotic classification of interjections: Although it is not disputed that interjections are conventional and language-specific (Ameka 1992b: 269, Wierzbicka 1992: 160), it is pointed out that the phonetic make-up of e.g. interjections of disgust, such as German *pfui*, English *phew/pooh* or Polish *fe* may be iconic "of a 'natural' oral or nasal gesture" (Wierzbicka 1992: 178, cf. also Nenova et al. (2001) for an assumption of a physiological/cognitive motivation for the sound structure of interjections). This may possibly explain why interjections are related to onomatopoeic words and categorised as icons by some scholars: For example, Kryk (1992: 199, 200) considers onomatopoeic words as interjections with the lowest degree of conventionalisation (cf. also Wierzbicka 1992: 164, 165). In this sense, interjections are considered to be iconic, at least to some extent, by some scholars (Kryk 1992, Wierzbicka 1992). Others, however, reject this by claiming that interjections are indexical (Kockelman 2003: 471 with reference to Peirce (1955), Wilkins (1992); see also Aijmer (2002: 14–16).

The discussion about the sign relation of interjections shows that interjections are not regarded as fully arbitrary but rather as iconic by some scholars. In our view, interjections are distinct from onomatopoeic words because they cannot be connected to any concrete "natural sounds" as e.g. *cock-a-doodle-doo*, which is taken to imitate the sound a cock makes. Moreover, a crosslinguistic comparison (cf. German *kikeriki*, French *cocorico*) shows that even onomatopoeic words are conventionalised, language-specific signs. The idea of interjections being natural signs has been criticised as a mindset "still in the grip of binaries such as emotion versus convention" (Wilce 2003: 485). Others claim that interjections are indices, because the emotional expression signaled by the interjection is always linked to the speaker in the here and now. This seems more convincing but is still

---

20. Apart from interjections, inserts include so-called 'greetings and farewells' (*hi*, *hello*), 'discourse markers' (*well*, *right*), 'attention signals' (*hey*), 'response elicitors' (*eh*, *right*), 'response forms' (*yeah*, *yep*, *yes*), 'hesitators' (*er*, *um*), 'polite speech act formulae' (*please*, *thanks*), 'expletives' (*goddammit*, *geez*) (Biber et al. 1999: 1085–1095).

21. Biber et al. (1999: 1076) do not have the prosodic transcripts of the discourse (excerpts from the LSWE Corpus) analysed available and are – as they admit – unable to do exact prosodic analyses. They take punctuation marks as indicators of prosodic breaks.

problematic, since such an analysis may presuppose that the emotion expressed is actually felt by the speaker.

In addition to the features named above, (1) expression of a spontanenous emotion, (2) absence of referential meaning, (3) lack of inflection, (4) syntactic autonomy and (5) possible onomatopoeic structures, which represent recurrent definitional criteria for interjections in the literature, interjections are typically discussed under the following notions (cf. Reber and Couper-Kuhlen 2010): (6) (expressive) speech acts, (7) monologicity, (8) phonological and prosodic anomalousness and (9) graphemic restriction.

The question whether interjections may constitute (expressive) speech acts (6) is a controversial pragmatic issue, which e.g. studies within NSM aim to resolve. The discussion centres around the question whether interjections may have an illocutionary force and a proposition (cf. Ameka 1992b, Wierzbicka 1992, Wilkins 1992). Wilkins (1992) is in favour of such a view:

> The illocutionary purpose of emotive interjections is to show how the speaker feels at the exact moment of speaking (in a fashion that is conventional and appropriate to the situation at hand). On these grounds it is possible to say that emotive interjections are exclamative speech acts and are to be treated like exclamatory sentences.   (ibid: 152)

On the other hand, Wierzbicka (1992: 163) takes the opposite stance, in that she claims that interjections do not contain the component *I say …*, which would indicate a proposition, in their frames. Comparing the frames of the interjection *Yuk!* and the sentence *I feel disgusted!*, she argues that the interjection lacks an illocutionary component:

> *Yuk!*
> I feel disgusted
>
> *I feel disgusted!*
> I say: I feel disgusted
> I say this because I want to say what I feel.   (ibid: 162)

Ameka (1992b) and Wharton (2003) occupy a position inbetween in that they propose that interjections may qualify for speech acts, depending on certain factors: Wharton (2003) argues that interjections may constitute expressive speech acts in Searle's terms,[22] if "there appears to be an attitude, emotional or otherwise, being conveyed toward the proposition expressed" (Wharton 2003: 55).

---

22. In Searle's classification of speech acts, the illocutionary point of expressive speech acts "is to express the psychological state specified in the sincerity condition about a state of affairs specified in the propositional content" (Searle 1979: 15).

The discussion as to whether interjections may perform (expressive) speech acts seems to be motivated by the fact that interjections do not form sentences. For this reason it is subject to controversy whether they may have a proposition, which is a sentence-based concept. The problem is that in spite of this, interjections seem to be somehow performative. The application of speech act theory reflects a perspective which views interjections as (intentional) social acts in a speaker-centered (cf. monologicity, 7) and context-free fashion (or on the basis of an invented context). Furthermore, the controversy about whether interjections have a proposition nicely reflect the Cartesian dichotomy between reason and emotion, which commonly penetrates Western linguistic frameworks. Here language is viewed as "a means for representing and elaborating thought, rather than feeling" (Linell 2005:100). In this way, emotional expression is opposed to rational proposing. Linell (2005) objects to such a take on language, arguing that "[m]any communicative acts cannot be regarded only as regarding thoughts" (ibid:100). This may be the reason why speech act theory fails to account for interjections.

Generally, all the studies mentioned above – even the corpus-based ones – stand for approaches to interjections which are marked by graphemic restrictions (9), that is, they concentrate on interjections that have written lexical forms. In that sense they reflect a written language bias (Linell 2005). Ward's (2006) study on so-called non-lexical, conversational sounds or 'grunts' in American English represents a notable exception: In contrast to e.g. Fischer (2000) and others concerned with the use of discourse markers/particles in spoken corpora, Ward (2006) is interested in all sounds which appear to be non-words and yet fulfil some kind of conversational function. Accordingly, he describes his method as data, and not transcript, based (ibid:133):

> To avoid missing anything that might be relevant, the initial definition was made inclusive. Specifically, all sounds which were not laughter and not words were labeled as non-lexical items. A 'word' was considered to be a sound having (1) a clear meaning, (2) the ability to participate in syntactic constructions, and (3) a phonotactically normal pronunciation. For example, *uh-huh* is not a word since it has no referential meaning, has no syntactic affinities, and has salient breathiness. Although the distinction between words and non-lexical items is not clear-cut, as will be seen, this gave a reasonable way to pick out an initial set of sounds to examine. To keep the scope manageable, attention was limited to sounds which seemed at least in part directed at the interlocutor, rather than being purely self-directed. This ruled out stutters and inbreaths.   (ibid:133–134)

To some extent, this methodic procedure to uncover non-lexical sounds can be seen as exemplary. Unfortunately, the study is limited in that it categorises the non-lexical sounds on the basis of their segmental substance and does not rely on sound methodolgy in its description of prosody: While it is acknowledged that prosody may add further meaning, analytic interpretations are, as the author admits, "speculatively attributed" (ibid: 167). The same goes for the meaning of sounds as such. By contrast, the present study will provide evidence from a participant's perspective that the communicative meaning of a sound object is composed of its sound pattern and contextual factors, following an interactional linguistic approach.

In general, we can conclude from the discussion above that frameworks which aim to analyse interjections as objects with full semantics and regardless of their use in spoken discourse are not fully able to account for what they are. Interjections are entities which must be analysed in terms of their potential prosodic relations and integration instead of their syntax. From this it can be followed that first and foremost, interjections represent a spoken language phenomenon. Describing their forms and functions must thus be understood as an endeavour to work towards conversation linguistics.

2.2   Vocalisations in Conversation Analysis and Interactional Linguistics

Conversation-analytically informed work takes an interactional functional approach to objects with minimal lexical content in conversation, on the premise that everything which participants do in talk-in-interaction follows and at the same time constructs the interactional order and is potentially meaningful for the conduct of that interaction. In this vein, Atkinson and Heritage (1984) state in one of the earliest collected volumes in the field:

> Phenomena like the particle "oh," laughter, and applause (…) are by no means random interjections or exclamations that can simply be inserted at any point in the course of any interactional sequence, but are deployed in a variety of quite systematic ways for the accomplishment of particular local purposes. (ibid: 297)

At the same time, they "warn" that the investigation of single words is not in line with proper conversation analytic research. This might be at least one explanation why the use of interjections and similar minimal response tokens in talk-in-interaction is still to a great extent unexplored. In the following sections, we will first present the implications of the foundational studies on the use of vocalisations as continuers, assessments and displays of a change-of-state, which have furthermore proven to be relevant for the present study, and point to more recent developments (Section 2.2.1). We will then summarise the major findings and assumptions made for vocalisations in Conversation Analysis/Interactional Linguistics and related fields (Section 2.2.2).

2.2.1   Foundational studies

The conversation analytic body of research includes objects in a range of languages such as e.g. English (Goodwin 1986, Heritage 1984, Jefferson 1978a, 1985a, 2002, Schegloff 1982, Wiggins 2002), Finnish (Sorjonen 2001, 2002), French (Drescher 1997, 2003), German (Golato and Betz 2008), and Japanese (Endo 2007).

It has been shown that vocalisations of this kind occur in a systematic order and in a context-sensitive fashion in the same way as other conversational objects. They are functional in that they are deployed by participants as systematic resources to accomplish conversational actions. To date, the focus of research has been on sound objects accomplishing *responsive* actions. Most recently, work in the traditions of Interactional Linguistics and Phonology-for-Conversation has provided evidence that such particles are not only deployed systematically in terms of sequential organisation but also with regard to their prosodic-phonetic packaging (cf. e.g. Barth-Weingarten (in print a, b) for German, Couper-Kuhlen (2009, in print), Gardner (2002), Local and Walker (2008), Reber (2009), Reber and Couper-Kuhlen (2010) for English, Müller (1996) on Italian).

Generally, the terminology orients towards both formal and functional aspects and – aside from using terms from Conversation/Discourse Analysis (response particles/tokens) – relies on linguistic (particle, interjection) and sociological (vocalisation, response cry, adopted from Goffman 1978) traditions. Seminal studies discuss response tokens with regard to their sequence-organisational function and can be summarised as follows:

Schegloff (1982) calls items such as *uh huh*, *mm hmm* and *yeah* "vocalizations" (ibid: 73). They may serve the same interactional functions as visual cues, e.g. nods (ibid: 74). In his study of *uh huh*, he observes that *uh huh* is deployed at potential transition relevant places in order to signal recipients' "understanding, when appropriate, that an extended turn is under way, and to show their intention to pass the opportunity to take a turn at talk that they might otherwise initiate at that point" (ibid: 81). It is for this usage that he classifies them as 'continuers' (ibid: 81). Schegloff (1982) further reports that continuers may be responses alternative to "markers of surprise ('Really?'), assessments ('oh my', 'wow', 'you're kidding', 'isn't that weird', 'wonderful', etc.), and the like" (ibid: 85), which may be noticeably absent, i.e. withheld by recipients. He concludes:

> It may be suggested that the mechanism by which a series of same continuer tokens displays incipient disinterest involves the availability of tokens of surprise, special interest, assessment etc., the nonproduction of which shows the recipient not to be finding in the talk anything newsworthy, interesting, or assessable.[23]   (ibid: 86)

---

23. In the remainder of the article, Schegloff (1982: 87–88) further suggests that continuers and repair initiators specifically represent alternative options for responding to possible turn completions.

In a follow-up study to Schegloff (1982), Goodwin (1986) examines "alternative sequential treatments of continuers and assessments". He observes that continuers solicit turn extension after possible turn completion (ibid: 207–208). In contrast, assessments are treated as turn-terminating. These functional differences become visible in the positioning of the two resources: While continuers "bridge" (ibid: 207) two units in that they occur at the transition from one unit to the next, assessments are always brought to an end before the beginning of the next unit (ibid: 207–214). Continuers are typically vocalised as *uh huh*, constitute short units and serve – unlike assessments which can be produced both by speaker and recipient – as a recipient resource (ibid: 215). In contrast, assessments may be achieved through a range of resources:

> [T]hough assessments can take the form of talk with clear lexical content (for example 'Oh wow' and assessment adjectives such as 'beautiful'), they can also be done with sounds such as 'Ah:::' whose main function seems to be the carrying of an appropriate intonation contour, as well as gesturally (cf. M. Goodwin 1980).
> (ibid: 214)

While it may be disputed that *oh wow* and *ah* actually implement assessments (see below), it must be noted that recipients have alternative choices as to how to treat the current turn and thus to co-construct the on-going sequence. These alternative recipient actions have different functions that are systematically linked to formal aspects.

Heritage (1984) examines yet another alternative recipient action to the production of continuers and assessments, namely that of the change-of-state-token *oh* in response to informings (see also Schegloff 2007). Change-of-state tokens treat the prior informing as informative and complete and signal that a change in the recipient's cognitive state has occurred. Although possible affective dimensions of *oh* are not discussed in detail, reference is made to this possibility in passing. Adding to Heritage's (1984) analysis of the sequential positions and functions of *oh*, Local (1996) investigates some of the phonetic forms *oh* may take (cf. Chapter 6 for more detailed accounts of Heritage (1984) and Local (1996). In later studies on *oh*, Heritage explores its use in *oh*-prefaced responses to enquiry (1998) and in *oh*-prefaced assessments (2002). *Oh*-prefaced responses to enquiry signal "that a question has occasioned a MARKED SHIFT OF ATTENTION" (Heritage 1998: 294, emphasis in the original) in that the question's appositeness, relevance or presupposition are treated as problematic (ibid: 295). *Oh*-prefaced assessments, on the other hand, index epistemic independence in terms of the assessment performed by the second speaker. That means that the second speaker claims that their evaluation is based on a judgment made on independent grounds from the first speaker (Heritage 2002). Central to Heritage's work is the basic assumption that *oh* has an inherent, cognitively rooted 'change-of-state-semantics' (Heritage 1998: 327), which is evoked in the contexts described in different ways. This perspective is in accordance with the view adopted in Discourse Analysis that discourse markers such as *oh* have some kind of core meaning which is actualised in a context-dependent way (e.g. Aijmer (2002), Schiffrin (1987). Another basic assumption which is maintained throughout this work is the distinction between 'freestanding' or 'stand-alone' tokens and 'prefaced' units. While the former ('freestanding') form an independent intonation contour and therefore build an independent action unit, i.e. a TCU (Heritage 1998: 292, 293), 'prefacing' means that *oh* is produced turn-initially and is integrated with further elements in one single contour (ibid: 292).[24] The turn-initial placement is regarded as crucial for the function of *oh*:

> It is this placement that allows *oh* to qualify the entire turn-constructional unit that follows, and to provide a coloring or propositional attitude for that unit's response to the question that preceded it. While *oh* may be additional to, and not part of, the syntax of sentences as traditionally understood (Ochs et al. 1996), it is surely part of the grammar of the turn-constructional unit – a grammar for units of action (Schegloff 1979, 1996b) within which the sentence (among other units) is housed.   (Heritage 1998: 327)

Sorjonen (2001) studies the differences in use of the Finnish particles *joo* and *nii* in responses to the following turn types: yes/no questions, directives, affiliation-relevant utterances in A-event environments, affiliation-relevant utterances concerning a mutually known issue and informings. Interestingly, she finds that the respective choice of particle is related to the grammatical shape of the action the particle responds to (ibid: 31). Her data analysis shows the following aspects to be relevant for the alternative uses of the two particles: affiliation vs. neutral registering, disaffiliation, shared information vs. new information, foregrounded information vs. backgrounded information, non-compliance vs. compliance and continuation relevant vs. closure relevant (ibid: 280). Similarly, Endo (2007) on Japanese *a:::* adds to the discussion between Schegloff (1982), Goodwin (1986) and Heritage (1984). She argues that speakers may use the Japanese vocalisation as a sequence closing third (SCT) (Schegloff 2007) in the same way as the English change-of-state token *oh* (Heritage 1984) in e.g. repair sequences (cf. also Golato and Betz (2008). Secondly, she claims that *a:::* can function as an "aligning-continuer" (ibid: 12), which implies understanding, agreement and sympathy in response to negatively valenced tellings (Endo 2007: 16). This function straddles

---

24. In spite of this, it is still a matter of debate whether 'vocalisations' can be treated as full turns at talk. Schegloff (1982: 92) on *uh huh* proposes to treat this as an empirical question.

Goodwin's (1986) distinction between continuer and assessment and thus suggests that the functions may not always be so clear-cut.

According to Couper-Kuhlen (2009), conversational objects such as *ah, oh, oh I see, oh not to worry*, etc., with "subdued prosody" (ibid: 100), implement displays of 'disappointment' in response to a rejection. The rejection finalisers *ah* and *oh* are, on the other hand, treated as signalling 'surprise' when produced with a "dynamic" tone of voice (ibid: 103).

2.2.2   *Major findings and assumptions*
In essence, the major findings and assumptions on vocalisations in Conversation Analysis/Interactional Linguistics and related approaches can be summarised as follows:[25]

a.   Vocalisations perform specific, situated actions.
b.   Vocalisations are used in specific sequential positions and have specific interactional and sequence-organising functions
c.   The displayed meaning of vocalisations may comprise a continuum of 'cognitive' and 'affective' processes.
d.   Vocalisations may convey some kind of immediacy, spontaneity, and vagueness.
e.   Vocalisations may often be followed by standardised elements.
f.   The lexical status of vocalisations is controversial.
g.   Vocalisations may respond to visual and linguistic actions and events.
h.   The use of vocalisations not only orients towards a sequential order but also follows a formal systematics in terms of prosodic-phonetic properties.

These points will be elaborated as follows:

ad a. In general, vocalisations perform specific, situated actions.

For example, they can function as continuers (*uh huh*) or assessments (*oh my, wow*) (Schegloff 1982).

ad b. Vocalisations are used in specific sequential positions and have specific interactional and sequence-organising functions.

However, recipients may use a range of resources in the same sequential position. And by co-participants orienting towards theses alternative recipient responses in different ways in what follows, a different sequential and interactional development is achieved (e.g. Couper-Kuhlen 2009, Schegloff 1982, Sorjonen 2001).

---

25.   In the following sections, we will use the term vocalisation as an umbrella term.

ad c. The displayed meaning of some vocalisations may comprise a continuum of 'cognitive' and 'affective' processes.

A prime example – since it represents the best researched object in English – is *oh*: Depending on sequential context and prosodic-phonetic design, it can be deployed to signal a 'change-of-state'/disappointment'/'sympathy' (Heritage 1984), 'surprise' (Local 1996, Couper-Kuhlen 2009), and 'surprise' or 'disappointment'/ 'sympathy' (Couper-Kuhlen 2009). Similar observations have been made for the English *ah*. Meaning dimensions include a 'change of state', 'disappointment' (Couper-Kuhlen 2009), sympathy (see Chapter 8) and pleasure.[26] Depending on the context, the Japanese particle *ah* can display sharedness of stance (i.e. alignment) or of information, but the two functions may overlap (Endo 2007: 17).[27] In addition, the Finnish *nii* (and in a more complex way *joo*) is used to handle issues of epistemic stance taking (Sorjonen 2001) (cf. also Golato and Betz (2008) for German *ach/ach so*).

ad d. Vocalisations may convey some kind of immediacy, spontaneity, and vagueness (Wiggins 2002).

In her study on so-called gustatory *mms*, Wiggins (2002) states that their "vagueness and generality [...] afford [them] rhetorical strength" (ibid: 328) because they cannot be challenged or rebutted by the other speaker.

ad e. Vocalisations are often followed by standardised elements.

More specifically, vocalisations are commonly followed by assessments but they do not have to be (cf. e.g. (Heritage 1984). Wiggins (2002) reports that 'gustatory *mmms*' occur most frequently as freestanding items. If further elements are added, this is done in terms of *mmm*-plus-evaluation constructions (ibid: 320). Deviant cases, where the evaluation precedes *mmm*, make it visible that the turn-initial position is iconic of the immediacy and spontaneity conveyed by *mmm* (ibi: 325).

ad f. The lexical status of vocalisations is controversial.

In line with linguistic approaches, there is great uncertainty as to the lexical status and semantics of such conversational objects in interactional oriented studies. In the tradition of Goffman (1978) such items are commonly considered as "non-word vocalizations" (ibid: 810), which do not have full word status (cf. e.g. (Schegloff 1982). Couper-Kuhlen (2009) treats *ah* and *oh* as particles,

---

26. So far no interactionally informed study has been made, but e.g. Aijmer (2002) suggests that *ah* may fulfil similar but not the same functions as the change-of-state *oh*.

27. The view that cognition and emotion are two interactive, integrated mental systems is supported by recent findings in the cognitive sciences (Schwarz-Friesel 2008).

that is, as lexical items (ibid: 117), yet with "minimal lexical content" (ibid: 96). Goodwin and Goodwin (2001: 247) point to the indexical nature of words such as *oh*. More so than with proper lexical items, they acquire meaning locally and indexically by the precise sequential location where they occur. Heritage (1998) is one of the few sources proposing a full 'semantics' when describing the meaning of the change-of-state token *oh*. The position taken in this study is that objects such as *oh* and *ah* represent lexical items with minimal lexical contents. The word status can be evidenced by the fact that some words of this kind have entered the word formation process, e.g. the zero derivations from *ah* to *to aah* (Interjection → Verb), *wow* to *to wow* (Interjection → Verb) or the derivation of *yucky* from *yuck* (Interjection → Adjective). That still some minimal lexical contents must be left is indicated by the fact that even out of context, *ah* and *wow* or *ah* and *ooh* are not considered synonymous. In the present study, we will call such objects 'sound objects'.

ad g.   Vocalisations may respond to linguistic and visual actions and events.

To illustrate the latter (visual actions and events), in a famous example by Goffman (1978), a speaker uses *Oops!* to respond to a sudden trip when walking on the pavement (cf. also. e.g. Goodwin and Goodwin (1987, 2001).

ad h.   Interactional linguistic studies have enriched these results by showing that e.g. the use of vocalisations not only orients towards a sequential order but also follows a formal systematics in terms of prosodic-phonetic properties.

"Short tokens, long prosody" (Müller 1996: 133): In his study on Italian talk-in-interaction, Müller (1996) observes that acknowledgement tokens "display their particular 'fit' to the contingent speech object they acknowledge in placement and prosodic design." (ibid: 133). On a general note, he appreciates the relevance of prosody for response tokens, stressing that "[p]rosody opens up new possibilities for studying the fine-grained calibration of speaking and listening in conversation." (ibid: 164). The implications of the prosody-phonetics of vocalisations will be discussed in a more comprehensive and in-depth fashion in Chapter 3.

All in all, interactionally informed studies make it clear that vocalisations may be described in terms of their forms and uses in talk-in-interaction in a systematic fashion. Taking this insight as a starting point for the analysis of affect-laden sound objects, the present study will aim to contribute to this body of research.

2.2.3   *Communicative "paralinguistic" sounds*

Research on communicative "paralinguistic" sounds such as e.g. Jefferson (1984b, 1985b, 2004), Jefferson et al. (1987), Hepburn (2004), Heath (1989) has shown that even sounds made in laughing, crying, sobbing and expressions of pain are systematically embedded in interaction and can be oriented to as meaningful communicative actions. From this, it can be concluded that vocalisations and so-called paralinguistic sounds should not only be seen on a formal continuum, as suggested by Pompino-Marschall (2004: 73), but also on a functional continuum.

2.3   Summary and conclusions

The position adopted in this study is that interjections are not referential and may therefore not have a proposition associated with them. Consequently, the study of interjections must question the traditional understanding of language signs and their mainly referential nature. Semiotically, the sign relation of interjections is often described as iconic – because of their being seemingly "natural signs" – or indexical. From the spoken language perspective followed in this study, all signs used in conversation, including interjections, are indexical.

Conversation Analysis and Interactional Linguistics are quite clear about the categorisation of vocalisations: Having minimal semantic content, vocalisations serve to structure and organise conversational interactions and may signal cognitive/affective states and processes. While both approaches point to the relevance of prosody in relation to interjections, Interactional Linguistics is the only one which describes the prosodic packaging which accompanies interjections in a data based and systematic fashion. In addition, interactional linguistic work provides evidence for the systematic link between an object's prosody, sequential position and contextual meaning, that is, the object's use for sequence organisation and affective/cognitive displays. This has the following consequences for the present study: Because of the relevance of the sound shape of interjections for meaning construction, we will refer to conversational objects with minimal semantic content, which have traditionally been described as primary interjections, as sound objects. Since paralinguistic sounds such as clicks and whistling have been found to fulfil similar functions in talk-in-interaction, such objects are also classified as sound objects. Since prosody has been found to be relevant for the interactional and sequential functions of the instantiations of *oh*, *ooh* and *ah*, we now outline major findings in the field of Prosody-in-Conversation and then concentrate on prosody and affectivity in the next section.

CHAPTER 3

Approaching affectivity in talk-in-interaction I
Previous research on prosody

Prosody has always been ascribed major significance for the contextualisation of cognitive-affective dimensions in interactional settings. This is reflected from early on: In a seminal paper based on data originating in a dialect survey of Tyneside English, Kelly and Local (1989) study recipient responses to the interviewer's word proffering for recognition. They find three types of responsive actions which are performed with different kinds of prosodic-phonetic resources: (1) 'display of recognition', (2) 'understanding check', and (3) 'mulling over'. At least two of the labels (1, 3), if not all, can be said to involve cognitive processes with 'mulling over' perhaps even implying an affective dimension. Even if such aspects are not addressed in the study, cognitive (-affective) processes are treated as adequate descriptions of what recipients convey through their prosodic-phonetic choices. Some years later, Selting and Couper-Kuhlen (1996, see also Schegloff (1998: 243) began their introduction to the first collected volume in the field of Prosody-in-Conversation by pointing out the link between prosodic cues and a particular "'tone of voice', a 'feeling' about the way our partner spoke, the 'atmosphere' of a conversation" (Selting and Couper-Kuhlen 1996: 1). These examples show that cognitive-affective dimensions in and of talk-in-interaction have been treated as an object of study in Prosody-in-Conversation from early on. What is more, prosody is assumed to play a *key* role in the contextualisation of such dimensions.

In the present section, we will first make some preliminary remarks on the field of Prosody-in-Conversation (Section 3.1) before coming to a review of the literature on prosody and affectivity in conversation (Section 3.2).

3.1   Preliminaries: Prosody-in-Conversation

The field of Prosody-in-Conversation is closely connected to the general research programme of Interactional Linguistics.

Prosody, which is concerned with suprasegmental sound patterns, is subsumed under the domain of phonetics, which expresses a general interest in "all audible aspects in and of speech that are produced by the human vocal apparatus"

(Ford and Couper-Kuhlen 2004: 3). According to Ford and Couper-Kuhlen (2004), the umbrella term "phonetics" further includes phonetics (segmental sound patterns), and paralinguistics. In this way, the term "phonetics" can be used as both a hyperonym (of phonetics, prosody and paralinguistics) and a hyponym (of phonetics). In the present study reference will be made to single terms in the sense of hyponyms of phonetics or to combinations of them (e.g. prosodic-phonetic) if we wish to narrow our focus onto one subcategory (cf. ibid: 21, footnote 2). Representatives of Phonology-for-Conversation usually use phonetics in the sense of the hyperonym.

Central to the approach of Prosody-in-Conversation is that prosodic properties "can be reconstructed as *members' devices*, designed for the organisation and management of talk in social interaction" (Couper-Kuhlen and Selting 1996b: 25). The view of prosody as a members' device is complemented by a perspective on prosody as a signalling system deployed in talk-in-interaction: Prosody is treated as only one among various autonomous linguistic 'signalling systems' (*Signalisierungssysteme*, Selting 1995: 266) available in talk-in-interaction, which mutually serve as 'contextualisation cues'. They indicate how participants' actions are to be taken both from participants' and analysts' perspectives.[28]

Prosody-in-Conversation thus views prosody not as a part of grammar or fulfilling the task of information structure;[29] instead it represents what Couper-Kuhlen (2001b: 16) calls a "prosody-as-contextualization cue" approach: It understands prosody as a linguistic resource, which provides a frame of reference for the interpretation of activities and other units of action.

It has been suggested that prosodic cues actually *constitute* actions. This represents a rather strong claim, which prioritises cues of this kind over lexico-semantic or grammatical ones, for example. However, e.g. in the interpretation of repair initiations as doing 'astonishment', prosody may be constitutive for the 'astonished' display (Selting 1996).

Since prosodic signalling systems represent *linguistic* resources, their forms and functions must be treated as language and context specific. A prosodic cue can fulfil different functions and signal different meanings dependent on context (cf. Couper-Kuhlen (2001b) for a state-of-the-art of prosody and intonation). Thus, the nature of prosodic resources is both context-bound and context-free. The view of prosodic resources as contextualisation cues, which are interpretable only when embedded in context, means that they are – as are all other linguistic

---

28. The works by the Goodwins (e.g. Goodwin and Goodwin 2001) complement this approach by providing an empirical account of the interplay of prosody with visual 'semiotic resources' for meaning construction in interaction.

29. Cf. Couper-Kuhlen (2001b) for a discussion of these two alternative approaches.

signs in a spoken-language view – indexical (cf. Gumperz (1982), Linell (2005). Along these lines, prosody is regarded as "by its very nature nonreferential, gradient and evocative" (Couper-Kuhlen 2001b: 16).

Prosodic contextualisation cues often come in bundles, with each cue adding a single specific aspect to the meaning signalled (Selting 1995: 231) (cf. Section 3.2 on the implications of this observation for the analysis of prosody as a contextualisation device for affectivity). This observation has theoretical consequences for how the relationship between phonetics and prosody should be conceptualised. Whilst a division between phonetic and prosodic properties is traditionally made, Local (2004) argues for a more holistic treatment:

> One theoretically interesting result of this work is the recurrent demonstration that in structuring their talk-in-interaction speakers systematically draw on bundles of phonetic features which cut across the traditional classification of phonetic parameters into 'prosodic' on the one hand *versus* articulatory (or 'segmental') on the other. This suggests that phonetic parameters are best treated as falling into functional bundles or clusters, irrespective of their 'prosodic' or 'segmental' characteristics, on the basis of how speakers deploy them to achieve particular interactional goals. If the analysis is conducted in these terms, it becomes possible to document systematically the ways in which speakers and listeners manipulate phonetic parameters in managing the moment-to-moment flow and interpretation of ordinary conversation.   (ibid: 396)

To sum up, in the view of Prosody-in-Conversation, prosodic properties are members' devices, which are deployed for the organisation of talk-in-interaction. Prosodic cues constitute indexical signs, which often come in bundles. They constitute only one amongst other linguistic signalling systems which contextualise actions in conversation.

3.2   Prosody and affectivity in conversation

The body of research on affectivity from the perspective of Prosody-in-Conversation shows the following tendencies: To begin with, it is subject to controversy whether phonetic properties of speech should generally be associated with specific labels of affect. In the following section we will first outline the studies which make a case that phonetic bundles cannot be ascribed any affective quality: They claim that data analysis does not allow any systematic correspondence between the phonetic contextualisation and the kind of affect made explicitly relevant by participants through lexical resources (Section 3.2.1). Secondly, we will continue with a review of studies which establish a link between certain phonetic properties of a conversational unit and an affect label, either because participants provide an explicit indication of specific inner states or because participants show an implicit understanding that a display of such an inner state has been performed. This strand of research comprises studies of narrative and non-narrative sequences involving affectivity (Section 3.2.2).

This literature review will serve to single out the theoretical and methodological implications for the analysis of affectivity as signalled by prosodic-phonetic cues in the present study. As to the discussion as to whether there is an "'affect phonetics'" (Local and Walker 2008: 734) or not, we will first and foremost take the position that "prosodic patterns [which are heard as affect-laden] serve a *double* function in that they are not functional in the management of [...] stance-taking alone" but also fulfill sequence structuring tasks (Reber 2010b: 300, my emphasis).

Secondly, it is not the vocal design of an action turn alone which may be treated as performing an affect-laden display. Instead, it is the interaction of all kinds of contextual cues prior to the turn, within the turn and subsequent to it, which may indicate that specific affective dimensions have been made relevant by the speaker. To treat an action turn as performing this or that affect-laden display may thus be treated as a shorthand to capture a certain contextual interpretation. To reflect this, we will use scare quotes for affective labels in our analysis (cf. Couper-Kuhlen (2009: 96, footnote 7) for a discussion of the use of scare quotes with respect to affect labels).

3.2.1   *The non-affect phonetics approach*

In recent work in Phonology-for-Conversation (but see Local (1996) below), the claim is made that phonetic clusters cannot be directly linked to claims and displays of specific affective states: Local and Walker (2008) ground their argument in a study on other-attributions on the affective quality of the other speaker's talk. They find that when participants make a so-called 'explicit lexical formulation' in the form of e.g. *you sound happy, don't sound so depressed*, etc.) about their interlocutor's state, this may be motivated in the interlocutor's talk: especially through "voice quality, turn design, and sequential organization" (Local and Walker 2008: 733). However, no one-to-one relationship between the phonetic make-up of the talk and the attribution delivered by other speaker could be identified (ibid: 741). The authors conclude that speakers' ascriptions of affect may not be "good indicators of 'affect phonetics'" (ibid: 734) but such formulations should be treated as a recipient's resource to solicit talk about their interlocutor's state.

The study on *wow*, when deployed as a "[s]tandalone non-lexical [response] to informings" (ibid: 735) follows a similar argument: The phonetics of *wow* does not correlate to the affective valence and weight of the prior informing.[30] Hence, it cannot be linked to a particular affective stance (ibid: 739). Their data examplify two kinds of realisations of *wow*: The first one receipts informings of positive and negative valencies. In terms of its phonetic design, it has the same loudness as the same and other speakers' talk and "approximately level pitch, just below mid in the speaker's range, with a narrow pitch span (excursion)" (ibid: 736–737). It is delivered with voicing and audible breathy voice quality, can be creaky and has initial and final labiality and final velarity (ibid: 737). The second kind of *wow* is deployed in response to neutrally or positively valenced informings with varying weight (ibid: 739). As the first kind of *wow*, it has equal duration (neither longer or shorter than other instances of *wow* in the sample) and the same loudness as the same and other speaker's talk. However, the second kinds of *wow* come with a rising-falling contour (rise and fall by approximately four semitones). The pitch peak can be done on mid-production time and with maximum loudness and they are done in modal voice quality. The initial consonant is labialvelar. While such instances of *wow* have final labiality and velarity, they are "closer and backer" at the end (ibid: 739).

As a basis for discussion, we find the first case study on explicit lexical formulations convincing. Similar findings from a discursive psychological perspective (e.g. Locke 2003, Potter and Hepburn 2003) have shown that emotion words are linked to specific action types and thus may be instrumental for the achievement of conversational goals rather than merely serving to make reference to affective states. As regards the second case study, we feel that the observation that the production of *wow* is not linked to the valence of the prior turn does not necessarily provide evidence for its non-affective nature. Without knowing the data which was analysed for this study, *wow* may be one of the response tokens which do not ascribe any valence to the action they receipt. This does not mean, however, that there are not any affective dimensions at all at stake.

3.2.2   *Prosody as a contextualisation device for affectivity*

Assuming the interaction between sequential, prosodic and other contextualisation cues for the interpretation of communicative acts, the studies to be presented in this section describe prosodic clusters which help to contextualise affectivity. This kind of research falls into two groups: Those which are concerned with prosody and affectivity in storytelling and others which examine non-narrative sequences. Although storytelling forms only a small part of the data analysed for the present study, we will give a short review of some of the major findings (Section 3.2.2.1) before coming to prosody and affectivity in non-narrative sequences (Section 3.2.2.2).

---

30. 'Weight' is defined as the "the significance for the interactants of the information being given" (Local and Walker 2008: 735).

3.2.2.1 *Prosody as a contextualisation device for affectivity in storytelling.* In her seminal paper, Selting (1994) describes the linguistic construction of 'heightened emotive involvement' with a focus on story climaxes in German multi-party face-to-face interaction. Heightened emotive involvement is signalled through the use of so-called 'marked prosody', which "is recognizable as more noticeable and salient than in the surrounding units" (ibid: 381). This kind of emphatic speech style is principally characterised by a "[m]arkedly high density of accentuated syllables" and a "rhythmic organization with markedly short isochronous cadences". In addition, "pitch accents with markedly higher pitch peaks or greater loudness than in the surrounding units" and lexico-syntactic cues ("intensifying lexical items" and "ellipses and/or syntactic parellelisms") may be deployed (ibid: 404, cf. also (ibid: 392). Prosodic resources are thus rated over lexico-semantic cues for the constitution of emphasis. Emphatic speech style further provides a speaker resource for inviting alignment on the part of the story recipient (ibid: 403).

In association with storytelling, many studies show a great interest in the use of prosodic and other vocal resources for displays of affective stance in narrative reported speech. Reported speech in storytelling is organised on more than one affective level since it serves both to convey the voice of the story character and the storyteller's stance towards the utterance quoted (cf. Couper-Kuhlen (1998: 21), Günthner (1997: 268). In this way, the affectivity signalled in reported speech is enacted and dramatised for narrative purposes: Vocal resources are exploited in order to animate the characters' voices. Although these studies contain multiple detailed prosodic analyses of reported speech, they do not, however, offer any systematic prosodic patterns for single types of affect. An explanation for this might be that narrative and 'quoted' contextualisations of affect are achieved in a different fashion than affective displays performed in non-narrative, 'unquoted' actions and action sequences: In contrast to non-narrative diplays in the here and now, affect-laden displays in storytelling are performed when reconstructing and talking about past actions and events.

Couper-Kuhlen (1998) shows that for English everyday interactions shifts in 'vocal deixis', i.e. deviations from a speaker's prosodic-paralinguistic common idiosyncratic properties, are treated as 'shifted deixis' and can create a second deictic center (ibid: 6) to the effect that this talk is heard as indexing another voice. At the same time, this shift in voicing is exploited to display the speaker's affective stance towards the other voice. Even though these cues are implicit and non-referential, recipients can be successful in interpreting the nature of this stance in situations where explicit 'verbal' cues are absent or even misleading (ibid: 26).

In conclusion, prosody works in two ways in the narrative reconstruction of past actions and events: Storytellers may use prosodic devices in order to contextualise sequence-organisational moves, e.g. the climax of the story, as well as to make their affective stance visible, e.g. in and towards reported speech and to cue different voices.

3.2.2.2 *Prosody as a contextualisation device for affectivity in non-narrative sequences.* In the investigation of affectivity in non-narrative sequences, prosodic formats which can be heard as cueing affective displays are either analysed in relation to certain types of actions and activity or in relation to specific lexical items associated with a specific function. The overview begins with the former sort of studies (actions and activities) and is then concerned with the latter (lexical items in a specific function):

Selting (1996) is concerned with the prosodic contextualisation of 'normal' vs. 'astonished' repair initiations in German talk-in-interaction. Here the author abandons the notion of emphatic *speech style* to describe the linguistic practices deployed for displays of 'astonishment'/'surprise' (but see Selting (1994: 391). The distinction between 'unmarked' and 'marked' prosodies to signal 'normal' (that is, 'unastonished') and 'astonished' initiations of repair respectively, is, however, maintained (Selting 1996: 233). Two prosodic clusters for the 'marked' choice are identified: (1) "high global pitch and greater loudness" or (2) "the combination of at least one of the global parameters, high pitch or increased loudness, with at least one locally marked accent constituted by a larger pitch range or markedly greater loudness in an accented syllable" (ibid: 239).

Günthner (1996) examines whether there is empirical evidence for what can be heard as a 'reproachful voice' (*vorwurfsvolle Stimme*) in German everyday interactions. She finds that in *why*-formatted reproaches a specific bundle of prosodic features together with negatively valenced lexical resources cue such a tone of voice. As does Selting (1994, 1996), she identifies a hierarchy of prosodic cues present: In this sense, "falling terminal pitch, rising-falling (falling-rising) pitch movements, narrow or verum-focus" are uncovered as constant properties in the *why*-formats, while others can be found in 'most' cases ("global increase of loudness, lengthening, and glide on the verb, primary accent placement on the verb") or only 'on occasion' ("increase of tempo, staccato accentuation", Günthner (1996: 292).

Schegloff (1998) analyses aspects of pitch for doing affect in the opening of an American English telephone interaction. He labels the deployment of high absolute pitch on a return greeting *hi* as 'pleased surprise'/'enthusiasm' (ibid: 245). The acoustic analysis provided additionally shows a wide ranging rising-falling contour on the syllable (ibid: 244). He observes that the distribution of affective displays is linked to the speaker's interactional role and to the sequential position in the interaction: In the example discussed, it is the party called which can perform a display of 'pleased surprise' upon recognition of the caller's voice. In contrast to the caller, she could not anticipate who she was going to talk to when responding to the summons (ibid: 245, footnote 12).[31] Schegloff further notes that an adjustment of pitch in the conversational opening may indicate alignment with the current interlocutor's stance (ibid: 246).

Freese and Maynard's (1998) study of good and bad news (cf. also Maynard (1997) is concerned with two central questions: What is the systematics of prosody in conversational news deliveries? How do prosodic and lexical resourcess interactively accomplish the valence of news? (Freese and Maynard 1998: 195–196). Their prosodic analysis comprises pitch, intonation, loudness and speech rate and is complemented by the investigation of what they call a paralinguistic feature, voice quality. On the basis of 100 news delivery sequences from British and American telephone conversations they find a systematic use of distinctive and characteristic prosodic designs related to the positive and negative valencing of news both in news tellers' and recipients' turns (ibid: 197–198). Table 1 provides a summary of the prosodic formats which the authors associate with displays of 'enjoyment' and 'sorrow' respectively.[32] In news sequences of these kinds, the explicit lexical evaluations and the prosodic cues signal a concordant stance, while in "bright side sequences" (Holt 1993), that is, in news sequences about the death of a third party, they are discordant: Positive lexical ascriptions of valence are delivered with 'negative' prosody (Freese and Maynard 1998: 210–212).

Couper-Kuhlen (1993) states that rhythmic delay, being a feature of surprised responses, can constitute the preferred way to time news responses:

> Whereas *delaying* the onset of a second [pair part] contextualizes something akin to stunned surprise and for this reason can be thought of as the preferred way to respond to some kinds of news, rhythmic *integration* contextualizes by contrast little or no surprise and may thus actually be out of place following putative 'news-y' turns, where it would be interpreted as cueing 'nothing to get excited about'.
>   (ibid: 262, emphasis in the original)

---

31. A display of this sort by the caller, on the other hand, would be accountable only when the participants may have not been in touch for a longer period of time or when something significant (and usually positive) may have happened to the called party (Schegloff 1998: 245, footnote 12).

32. For reasons of time and space, we cannot outline a detailed account of the prosodic format of each sequential step of the news delivery activity. Reference to these findings will be made when required for the purposes of the analysis in the empirical part of the present study.

Table 1. Characteristic prosodic structures of good and bad news. Table taken from Freese and Maynard (1998:198) (slightly modified)

Prosodic parameters	Good news ~ 'enjoyment'	Bad news ~ 'sorrow'
pitch level	high	low, excepting displays of 'surprise' at the start of announcement responses
pitch range	increased, wide	narrow
contour	frequent, sharp, and often abrupt steps-up and rises; announcement responses sometimes produced with a high onset and with a sustained high contour	stretched vowels with pronounced falling pitch
voice quality	normal	often breathy or creaky
loudness	very loud on key words	key words sometimes quieter
speech rate	fast; tending to speed up as the utterance progresses	slow; tending to slow down as the utterance progresses

In conclusion, the outline suggests that pitch, volume, duration, rhythmic timing, and voice quality may be deployed as resources for the contextualisation of affect in social interaction. For this reason, these cues will be paid special attention to in the present investigation. Furthermore, what the studies above have in common is that they all connect prosodic cues which *depart* from the prior prosodic setting in some way or the other with signals of affect. For instance, the pitch may have become noticeably high or low, the pitch range, loudness and speech rate may have noticeably increased or decreased, or the rhythmic timing of the next turn may be delayed, etc. All prosodic contextualisations are done in terms of clustered cues. This means, it is not one cue alone which makes some stretch of talk hearable as affect-laden. In addition, it is not prosody alone which is treated as doing affect: Analyses always take concurrent lexical (and to some extent syntactic) resources into account, which together constitute what is heard and understood as an affective display. It follows that the use of prosodic cues for the contextualisation of affect does not seem to be organised in a manner different from their use for other signalling tasks in conversation: Their meaning must be interpreted relative to what went before and in relation to concurrent cues of other contextualisation systems.

3.2.2.3 *Key findings for prosody and affectivity in interaction.* We have seen in this review of the literature review that prosodic contextualisations of affect can be observed for a range of actions and activities. It it is central to these studies that they treat these affective displays as products of context-bound inferential processes.

The following list summarises primary findings and assumptions made in these studies, which – apart from the first item – also constitute generalisable aspects of prosody and affectivity in interaction. Following this list, we will provide brief explanations of each point.

a.   Prosody may set the affective tone of an action/activity.
b.   Prosody is implicit, non-referential and therefore non-accountable.
c.   Prosodic bundles are indexical.
d.   Prosodic cues may be iconic.
e.   Prosodic contextualisations of affectivity are associated with specific action and activity types and not with sentence types.
f.   Prosodic properties are hierarchic.

ad a. Prosody may set the affective tone of an action/activity.

Prosody can "add [...] emotive 'overtones'" (Selting 1994: 380, cf. also Selting (1996: 264) to the ongoing action or activity and thus guide the recipient's perception of how lexico-semantic cues may be interpreted (cf. e.g. also Freese and Maynard (1998: 212). Prosody is thus treated as 'setting the tone' of an action or activity. When it accompanies lexical material with minimal semantics (and syntax), such as idiomatic routines in conversational openings (e.g. *hi, how-are-you*) (Schegloff 1998: 244), the prosodic design can become the key resource for the interpretation of their affective meanings. The prosodic framing may mark a contrast to the semantics of the lexical resources used: For instance, the production of a positively valenced adjective like *fine* with a "'downbeat'" prosody in response to a how-are-you enquiry can be heard as a "negative response" (Schegloff 1998: 244, footnote 11, cf. also e.g. Couper-Kuhlen (2004a: 234–235) on the prosodic contextualisation of *never mind* and respective affective meanings).

In the case of *sound objects*, English may rely more heavily on different prosodies than on lexical choices for marking affective differences. This becomes evident in comparison to particle languages such as German (Couper-Kuhlen 2009: 117) and Swedish (Aijmer 2004: 107).

ad b. Prosody is implicit, non-referential and therefore non-accountable.

Being implicit, non-referential and therefore non-accountable, prosodic cues can provide a particularly powerful resource for the signalling of affect in socially delicate situations, where overt evaluations could be risky (cf. Günthner (1996), Günthner (2000: 149–151) on reproaches).

ad c. Prosodic bundles are indexical.

Prosodic signals are organised in fine detail and must be interpreted in a context-specific fashion, i.e. their meanings are situatively embedded (e.g. Couper-Kuhlen (2009), Freese and Maynard (1998: 207), Local (1996), Selting (1996: 239).

ad d. Prosodic cues may be iconic.

The idea of an iconic correlation between pitch levels and the emotion and attitude signalled was first proposed by Bolinger (1986), who applies the up-down metaphor (Lakoff and Johnson 1980) to the description of pitch levels (Bolinger 1986: 202). Scholars in the tradition of Prosody-in-Conversation adopt this idea by arguing for an iconic sign relation between certain prosodic cues and affective meanings: For instance, Freese and Maynard (1998) suggest that 'faster pitch rate' and 'increased pitch range' may be iconic of the speaker's eagerness and excitedness when delivering good news. In contrast, bad news are produced with 'reduced speech rate' and 'constricted pitch range' which may point to the speaker's reluctance and difficulty in accomplishing their task (ibid: 198–199). Couper-Kuhlen (2009) describes the prosody of 'disappointed' *ah* as being iconic of the producer's "turning inward" (ibid: 99) (cf. also Selting (1995: 230), Couper-Kuhlen (2004a: 235) for additional examples).

ad e. Prosodic contextualisations of affectivity are associated with specific action and activity types.

For example, Selting (1996) makes the link between the prosodic packaging of next turn repair initiators and 'astonishment', whereas Freese and Maynard (1998) identify different prosodic clusters in terms of every sequential step in bad and good news delivery sequences.

ad f. Prosodic properties are hierarchic.

In the prosodic clusters found, there may be cues that are more important than others to index affectivity. This means that some cues are obligatory for a cluster to be interpreted as signalling affectivity, while others are optional in the sense that they are not always present (Günthner 1996: 292, Selting 1996).

3.2.3 Summary and conclusions

Approaches which examine prosody in interaction, that is, Prosody-in-Conversation and Phonology-for-Conversation, are divided in terms of whether to relate indexical, non-referential, prosodic-phonetic cues to displays of concrete affective dimensions. There are good reasons for each position: While representatives of 'non-affect phonetics' argue that there is no necessary link between the prosodic bundles identified and the type of affect made relevant, other students of prosody and affectivity in interaction point out that there are *context-bound* correspondences between specific prosodic clusters, action types and affective qualities made locally relevant by participants in conversation. In the present study, labels, that is, emotion words, for the nature of affective displays will be used if they are warranted by the data. However, they are only to be treated as shorthand for the potential cluster of affective dimensions displayed.

In addition, we have seen that prosodic cues for the contextualisation of affectivity are interpreted in terms of the affective involvement and the valence signalled.[33] Even though affective involvement and valence are not relevant for all affect-laden sound objects in the same way, these two concepts allow us to note differences and commonalities between them.

Since it is one of the basic assumptions of this study that affective displays are locally constructed social products that are generated by sequences of actions, we will now briefly present the activities which were found to generate affect-laden sound objects in the corpus examined.

---

33. These two dimensions (involvement and valence) correspond to two of the three dimensions, which are commonly used by psychologists, psycholinguists and linguists for the description of affectivity (Caffi and Janney 1994).

CHAPTER 4

Approaching affectivity in talk-in-interaction II
Previous research on conversational activities

Research on talk-in-interaction has shown for a number of languages such as e.g. German, English, French, Finnish and Japanese that there are social activities where the displaying and labeling of affect are part and parcel of their emergent structure and may be accomplished through multimodal practices in both formal and everyday contexts. Not only do these studies illustrate the interactional resources deployed by participants in order to signal or to refer to various affective states, they also provide evidence that actions involving affect are sequential products and may occur in multiple sequential positions.

In the following Section 4.1 we will first summarise the main findings on affectivity in interactional activities. In Section 4.2 affect-laden activities which have been identified as loci for affect-laden sound objects are described in more detail.

4.1   Common findings and assumptions

The following common assumptions and findings are shared by scholars taking a conversation analytic/interactional linguistic view on affectivity in talk-in-interaction. Further implications and explanations of the points listed will be given subsequently.

a. Affective expressions are treated as displays.
b. Affective displays are 'situated practices'.
c. Affective displays can be made relevant.
d. Affective states are interactionally generated: They are products of interaction, which may become visible as (a) displays or (b) manifestations in specific sequential places.
e. Affective displays can be dealt with in the subsequent talk.
f. Affective displays or dealing with affect can be resisted.
g. Affective displays can constitute dispreferred actions.
h. Affective displays can perform 'mock emotions'.
i. Affective displays can be deployed for the construction of affiliation/disaffiliation.

j.   Affective displays are embodied.

k.   Affective displays are culture-bound.

ad a. Affective expressions are treated as displays.

Affective expressions are treated as displays, i.e. they are analysed inde-pendently of whether they mirror actual inner states (cf. Section 1.2.3). In this sense, affectivity is made interactionally and publicly available (e.g. Goodwin p.c. in Couper-Kuhlen (2009:96, footnote 6), Sandlund (2004:324), Wilkinson and Kitzinger (2006:152). Similarly, Schegloff (1991) argues that speakers' cognitive states can only be treated as *claims* that are made relevant through linguistic and other communicative practices in social interactions. They are not treated as *re-flections* of such states (ibid:157).

ad b. Affective displays are 'situated practices' (Goodwin and Goodwin 2001:239).

A view of affective displays as situated practices means treating them as con-text-sensitive, recipient designed and interactional achievements. Their presence as well as their relevant absence is consequential for the subsequent development of the interaction. Affect is not seen as something that merely accompanies an ac-tion but is treated as being produced by the preceding context (see point *d* below) and in the same way shaping what comes next.

ad c. Affective displays can be made relevant.

Affective displays can be made relevant by prior actions (e.g. Sandlund (2004:324) and by "the structure of *practices for performing*" a specific action, e.g. an out call (Goodwin and Goodwin 2001:246, emphasis in the original).[34] This observation is closely connected to the next point:

ad d. Affective states are interactionally generated: They are products of interac-tion, which may become visible as (1) displays or (2) manifestations in specific sequential places.

> (1) Affective displays are generated as products of the prior context.
> Affective displays are analysed as products of specifically designed prior contexts (i.e. contexts with particular actions, contents, linguistic formats, participation frameworks). However, this does not mean that there is a deter-ministic relation between prior context and the quality of the affective display produced. Moreover, non-displays of affect are prepared for in the same way as displays:

---

34. Here Goodwin and Goodwin (2001) refer to an example of two girls playing hopscotch where one girl reacts with an affect-laden *OUT!* to the other girl's violation of rules.

In her pioneering work, Selting (1996) is able to systematically show that 'astonished' repair initiations are prepared for by different interactional settings than non-astonished ones: 'Astonished' repair initiations (and more specifically, those that are implemented in other-initiated repair sequences, ibid: 233) "signal problems of expectation" (ibid: 233) and are based on inferences made in terms of the previous talk (ibid: 264).[35] 'Normal' repair initiations, on the other hand, indicate problems of hearing or understanding (ibid: 233) (cf. also Wilkinson and Kitzinger (2006) on 'surprise'). Goodwin (2007: 68) shows on the basis of an interaction between a father and his 11-year-old daughter that anger can be the product of failing alignment to the participation framework.

Couper-Kuhlen (2009) qualifies the display-as-product view in that she shows that so-called "rejection contexts" (ibid: 105) can bring about different kinds of affective displays in response. In the English data, either displays of 'disappointment' or 'surprise' on the part of the recipient of the rejection were identified (ibid: 105). A contrastive study of German data further revealed displays that can be labelled as 'annoyance' or 'frustration' in comparable contexts (ibid: 112).

Likewise, the *non*-showing of affect has been found to be generated in interaction by the format of the prior context. In a study on bad news in doctor-patient interactions, where the doctor conveys to the patient that he is terminal,[36] Lutfey and Maynard (1998) note (with reference to Maynard 1997) that the stoicism with which the patient receives the news is "very much an interactional product" in that it "may reflect the matter-of-fact or 'reporting' fashion (Drew 1984) by which a physician delivers bad news and avoids stating the upshot". What is achieved by stoic displays is that they "do not elicit further unpackaging of the gloss" (Lutfey and Maynard 1998: 333). This means that stoic responses block the doctor's delivery of the news or topical talk related to it.

---

35. Selting (1996: 239) offers yet another definition of 'astonishment'/'surprise':

> 'Astonishment' or 'surprise' is used as a label for a context-sensitive interpretation of bundles of prosodically marked cues in certain types of repair initiation, either explicit problem signaling or securing of understanding. The same cues may trigger quite different inferences in other sequences and contexts, inferences such as 'emphasis', 'indignation', etc. (ibid: 239).

She points out that "the prosodic cues high pitch plus locally marked accents" can signal 'emphasis' (Selting 1994) and 'indignation' (Günthner 1996) in other sequential environments.

36. In this study all patients were male.

(2) Affect becomes manifest in actions which show an orientation to a mental state.

Drew (2005) seeks to delimit himself from the kind of display-as-product view reported on above, in that he makes a subtle argument for a manifestation-as-product-view:

Drew (2005) argues that "[a] cognitive state is not made visible or manifest in [a] display" (ibid: 171) (and thus not deployed as a resource) but is shown through an action that *orients towards* this state. He exemplifies this point with a study of repair initiations, an action, where – in Drew's (2005) view – 'confusion' may become "particularly visible" (ibid: 174).[37] In such actions, participants thus do not claim or show a particular state of mind (in order to achieve particular actions) but this state of mind is rather expressed/ surfaces in specific participant actions. Being generated by the other speaker's prior conduct in the interaction, it only surfaces in a position where the speaker needs to come in (ibid: 177–79).

While it sounds convincing that specific actions may be prone to make inner states manifest, the example given in the text suggests that the repair initiation is two-partite by consisting of a display *plus* a manifestation of 'confusion' (cf. Excerpt 4 below). It is thus arguable whether the interpretation of the repair initiator as a manifestation of 'confusion' was inferred from the display that preceded it or is actually based on the repair initiator itself.

ad e. Affective displays can be dealt with in the subsequent talk.

The point that affect displays are dealt with in what follows is related to the concept of affectivity as situated practice and it being generated as a product of prior talk. Other speakers' orientations to affective displays are used as a methodological tool in order to provide evidence of the affective quality of a display from a participant's perspective. A systematic analysis of how such affective displays are treated by participants is offered by Selting (1996: 247, cf. also e.g. Couper-Kuhlen (2009), who identifies an orientation to 'astonished' repair initiations in two respects: (1) Subsequent actions orient towards the 'astonished' quality of the repair initiation, which becomes visible by a preference for agreement and alignment, and (2) address the content of the repair initiaion, by dealing with it in terms of clarification and repair.

It must be added that a participant orientation of this kind, which includes both the affective and the action levels, provides evidence that affect-laden actions

---

37. Drew (2005) defines 'confusion' as a "collision between what they (previously) know or expect, and some new and contradictory information – something which occurs in the interaction and runs counter to what they were expecting" (ibid: 174).

are indeed treated as action turns. Here the affective loading of an action offers a key as to how to interpret that action interactionally. In the present study, the subsequent treatment of the sound object either by the same or other speaker provides a major methodological tool to access and gives evidence for their affect-laden nature. This is especially so, since sound objects are inherently implicit and vague in meaning.

ad f. Affective displays or dealing with affect can be resisted.

When a specific display of affect is expectable in a specific sequential position, it can be 'resisted' by the participant: Sandlund (2004: 185–194) suggests that laughter is used for embarrassment resistance (cf. also Haakana (1999) on laughter in doctor-patient interactions).[38]

ad g. Affect displays can constitute dispreferred actions.

Affective diplays can constitute dispreferred actions in some types of interaction. For instance, Ruusuvuori (2005) makes this observation for 'empathy' (preferred) and 'sympathy' (dispreferred) in Finnish doctor-patient-interactions. Similarly, Sandlund (2004) shows on the basis of institutional talk-in-interaction that displays of 'frustration' on the part of students are dispreferred actions in feedback activities in American classroom interaction. Observing that students are told by the instructor not to show such responses, she takes the rare occurrence of frustrated responses in feedback activities as an indication of their dispreferred status.

ad h. Affect displays can perform 'mock emotions'.

The term 'mock emotions' was coined by Sandlund (2004, 2005).[39] She finds that participants can enact mock displays in order to achieve certain interactive goals (Sandlund 2005: 183), e.g. teasing, topicalising social transgression or exaggeration (ibid: 187). The "non-genuine" nature of these displays (e.g. of surprise, embarrassment, annoyance) and other participants' understanding of them as such is hereby crucial for the accomplishment of situated actions (ibid: 184). However rare in the present data, an instance of a mock display performed through 'low-falling and tailed' *ah* is discussed in Section 8.4.3.

---

38. A related example for cases where recipients avoid joining in an interactional modality is Drew (1987) on po-faced responses to teases.

39. Mock emotions are defined as follows: "A mock state-of-being [...] is the means through which a speaker *pretends* to be experiencing a particular state-of-mind or emotion, while making it clear that the display is an enactment and not something that is actually felt or experienced at that moment." (Sandlund 2005: 184, emphasis in the original)

The observation that affectivity can be performed in a non-serious mode provides valuable insights into the social nature of affectivity. It can be inferred that participants must have some kind of meta-communicative knowledge of how and when to display affect as well as when to treat affective displays as genuine or not.

ad j. Affect displays can be deployed for the construction of affiliation/disaffiliation.

That affectivity is deployed to construct and organise affiliation represents a widely shared view in the literature. In this sense, affectivity is deployed by recipients to signal that they are putting themselves into the same position as the speaker, that they are siding with the speaker. However, affiliation involves a non-affective dimension as well: For instance, Sorjonen (2001) understands affiliation as the recipient's signalling "'I recognize the logic of what you are talking about; I know what you are talking about; I see your point'" (ibid: 132, see also Jefferson (2002: 1343) for similar paraphrases). Both authors observe that some kinds of utterances may make affiliative responses on the part of the recipient relevant:[40] Sorjonen (2001) observes that such turns can occur in a speaker's "my-side telling", that is, talk about "some events or states of affairs in her or his life to which the recipient does not have direct access" (ibid: 132). Here utterances which display the teller's stance to their ongoing telling invite an affiliative response. Jefferson (2002) further suggests:

> [S]ome or many 'negatively framed utterances' might be 'affiliation implicative'; utterances to which a recipient relevantly not only shows hearing-understanding of what was said, but gives (or recognizably withholds) support, agreement, sympathy, etc.   (ibid: 1349)

Lack of affiliation does not necessarily mean disaffiliation but is a mere claim of understanding of what the other speaker said, a claim which can be described as 'non-affiliative' (Jefferson 2002: 1343). Disaffiliation, on the other hand, implies a negative stance: For instance, booing may be seen as a prototypical disaffiliative display (Clayman 1993).[41]

Formally, prosodic resources such as e.g. 'prosodic orientation' (Szczepek Reed 2006) and rhythm (Couper-Kuhlen 1993, Müller 1996: 160) represent

---

40. In general, participants tailor their turns in a context-sensitive and recipient-designed fashion to meet specific interactional goals (cf. Goodwin (1996) for informings and announcements in and from the operations room at an airport).

41. Cf. also Müller (1996), who distinguishes between "three basic semantic values", which can be "neutral, affiliating and disaffiliating in relation to current talk." (ibid: 133)

implicit resources for the contextualisation of responding actions as dis-/affilia-tive.[42] Similarly, Müller (1996: 156) shows for Italian conversation that affiliative acknowledgement tokens may be "'attuned'" to the prior unit, while disaffiliative ones may be "'out of tune'".

To sum up, recipient responses can accomplish affiliation, non-affiliation and disaffiliation with the prior action. Affiliation comprises aspects of understanding, support, and agreement on both affective and non-affective levels. Non-affiliation refers to a mere display of understanding on the part of the recipient, which does not involve any stance-taking. Disaffiliation, on the other hand, means the display of a negative stance toward a co-participant's action. All three interactional dimen-sions can be inferred from formal aspects of the recipient's talk. In the present study, we will use affiliation, non-affiliation and disaffiliation in the way summa-rised (In quotations, the terms will be used according to the author cited).

A concept often related to affiliation is alignment, for which one finds conflict-ing definitions in the literature: Heritage (1984) treats alignment as co-operation/ agreement between participants as to the formal aspects of the current and emerging communicative project, that is, its sequential organisation (ibid: 320) and the speaker roles which come with it (ibid: 315) (cf. also Goodwin (2007) for such an approach). This kind of view on alignment goes back to Goffman (1981). Yet, it is acknowledged that such accomplished alignment does not only work on the formal level but also on an interpersonal/social level (Heritage 1984: 320). In Heritage (1985: 108), alignment is distinguished from affiliation, which is defined as "agreeing with or endorsing [a] position on [one's] own".[43]

To sum up, alignment in the Goffmanian sense means co-operation/agree-ment between participants in terms of the sequential organisation and the par-ticipation framework of the on-going and emerging communicative project. We will adopt this notion for the present study. (In quotations, the terms will be used according to the author cited.) Furthermore, the literature suggests that the ac-complishment and organisation of affiliation/alignment seems to be a pervasive dimension of responsive affective displays. Thus affective displays of that sort can be regarded as special practices for such tasks.

---

42. Couper-Kuhlen (1993) shows that speakers can time their seconds such that they signal affiliation on the prosodic level, while carrying out a dispreferred action otherwise: "[O]ne plau-sible account for rhythmic integration in such situations [denials of assertion and other dispre-ferred activities] is that it is being used to smooth over a potentially face-threatening activity or to lend an affiliative note to an action which is otherwise socially disaffiliative." (ibid: 256)

43. Cf. further Du Bois (2007) for a discourse analytic perspective, which makes an association between 'alignment' and 'resonant' linguistic structures.

ad k. Affectivity can be contextualised through vocal and visual cues, that is, it can be displayed without words.

Nonverbal contextualisations of affect analysed include visual and vocal signalling systems: A key assumption of Goodwin and Goodwin (2001: 241) is a view of "Emotion as Embodied Performance" (cf. Goodwin and Goodwin (2001: 243): "affect is lodged within embodied sequences of action").

4.2   Sequences and practices

This chapter is concerned with sequences of actions where affect is used as a practice for accomplishing specific actions in talk. A basic assumption of the present study is that the form and function(s) of an affect-laden sound object depend on its sequential placement in a specific activity and on the shape and action type of the prior action. We will therefore describe the sequential structures of the affect-laden activities, which contain affect-laden sound objects in the data and the actions which are constitutive for these activities. Furthermore, if specified in the literature, we will make a short reference to affective dimension(s) typically connected with a specific activity. This will give us hints as to the type of affect that may be expectable with regard to recipient sound objects. In this way the following section provides the analytic background knowledge for the discussion of affect-laden sound objects in the respective activities.

As stated in Chapter 5 below, the corpus compiled for this study also includes recordings from radio phone-ins, which will be treated as semi-institutional interactions. Activities or actions exclusively performed in interactions of this sort will be briefly introduced in the respective chapters. Otherwise we maintain the position that affect-laden actions and activities as found in (semi-)institutional interactions constitute adjustments of the ones practiced in mundane contexts. This means that these affect-laden actions and activities, which have their primordial habitat in mundane interaction, are performed in ways which are sensitive to the (semi-)institutional context in which they are used.

Apart from the activities identified as providing a possible environment for the production of sound objects in the data examined for the present study and as described in the following subsections, other activities have been shown to be settings where participants make affectivity relevant. They include e.g. therapeutic interactions (e.g. Edwards (1999), Egbert and Bergmann (2004), Fussell and Moss (1998)), academic class-room interaction (e.g. Sandlund (2004)), emergency calls (e.g. Whalen and Zimmerman (1998)), and story telling in everyday interaction (e.g. Günthner (1997), Selting (1994)).

In the following outline we will proceed from activities which tend to form "big packages" (Sacks 1995: 354) to ones which tend to be more constrained in the number of turns taken. Accordingly, the structure of this section will be as follows: troubles talk (Section 4.2.1), news delivery sequences (Section 4.2.2), complaint sequences (Section 4.2.3), assessments (Section 4.2.4), repair (Section 4.2.5).

4.2.1 *Troubles talk*

The term 'troubles talk' was first introduced in the work by Gail Jefferson (1980, 1984a, b, 1988), where the notion of trouble is understood in an everyday sense as an event, situation or state-of-affairs which constitutes a cause of concern, discomfort or worry for the teller. Characteristic of troubles talk is a permanent tension between "attending to a trouble" and "attending to business as usual" (Jefferson 1988: 419). Two types of sound objects examined in the present study were found to be deployed as affect-laden recipient responses of different sorts in mundane troubles talk: While both recipient types perform affiliative actions, 'high' *ooh* (Section 7.8.2) can be characterised as a display of 'horror' or 'shock' and 'low-falling and tailed' *ah* as a display of empathy (Section 8.4). The sound objects are embedded in sequential structures which resemble the "Candidate Troubles-Telling Sequence", as proposed by Jefferson (1988: 420). It is organised as follows: (A) Approach, (B) Arrival, (C) Delivery, (D) Work-Up, (E) Close Implicature, (F) Exit. Each sequential step comprises several turns at talk, in which a specific sequence of actions is achieved by participants; for reasons of space, these actions are not outlined in detail here but will be made reference to in the analytic section when identified in the data. At the same time, Jefferson points out that no instance of troubles talk actually follows this sequential order, i.e. incorporates all these moves (ibid: 419). What is important, both the opening and closing of troubles talk are carefully managed interactional projects: By implementing 'trouble-premonitory responses' to how-are-yous and inquiries about the recipient's well-being, potential troubles tellers can signal orientation to a trouble (Jefferson 1980). Likewise, trouble recipients frequently use methods to move out of the activity which enable them to affiliate with the teller and yet to bring the activity to a close (Jefferson 1984a). The activity of troubles talk further culminates in mutual displays of affectivity: In (C) Delivery, the trouble recipient is invited to affiliate with the trouble. In response, the troubles teller may produce emotionally heightened talk by "'letting go' and/or turning to or confiding in the troubles/recipient [sic!]" (Jefferson 1988: 428). Interestingly, Jefferson notes in a footnote (ibid: 430, footnote 2) that such so-called affiliation responses were found in the American sample only (and not in the British one). We will see in the analysis of sound objects below that troubles tellers in the present British English data at least show an affect-laden orientation to the recipient's affiliation, which would qualify Jefferson's observation.

Finally, the notions of 'troubles resistance' and 'troubles receptiveness' are of importance when analysing the role of affect-laden sound objects in troubles talk: Stemming from Jefferson's work on laughter in troubles talk, they are used to describe the stance participants are locally taking towards the trouble: By laughing, the troubles teller constructs him-/herself as 'troubles-resistant' (Jefferson 1984b: 351), that is, as taking a light-hearted stance to it. In response, there is a tendency for troubles recipients not to chime in with the teller's laughter (Jefferson 1984b: 350), which deviates from the relevancies otherwise found in everyday interaction. In this way, the recipient displays 'troubles-receptiveness' (ibid: 351), that is, an orientation to attending to the trouble. In the rather infrequent opposite setting (production of laughter on the part of the recipient but not on the part of the teller), the troubles teller indicates troubles-receptiveness, whereas the recipient claims troubles resistance (ibid: 358).[44] In the present study, the production of affect-laden sound objects in troubles talk is generally treated as a display of 'troubles receptiveness'.

In addition to these observations made for mundane interaction, e.g. Edwards (1995), ten Have (2001), Jefferson and Lee (1981), and Pudlinski (2005) account for troubles talk in institutional settings.

To summarise, troubles talk follows a specific sequential structure, which is, however, highly variable with regard to the sum of its moves. The trajectory of troubles talk is characterised by a constant tension between an orientation to 'business as usual' and to 'attending to a trouble'. For both teller and recipient, laughter is described as a resource for managing this tension between 'trouble resistance' and 'trouble receptiveness'.

We will now turn to our next affect-laden activity, news delivery sequences, comprising both good- and bad-news reports.

4.2.2   News delivery sequences
The notion of news delivery sequences is associated with the seminal work carried out by Maynard and colleagues (e.g. Freese and Maynard (1998), Maynard (1997), (2003).[45]

We will first give a short summary of the sequential structure of the news delivery sequence and then come to aspects of valence and the construction of

---

44. It is only in so-called 'time-outs' or 'buffer topics' that the troubles recipient is found to accompany the teller in laughter (ibid: 351).

45. Due to the analytic focus of the present study on affect-laden sound objects in everyday interaction, the following outline will not consider the extensive body of research on news telling in institutional interaction (e.g. Lutfey and Maynard (1998), Maynard (2003).

news as 'good' or 'bad' and implications following therefrom. Maynard (1997:99) describes the structure of the news delivery sequence as the following:

A: announcement
B: announcement response
A: elaboration
B   assessment

Key to the present study, Maynard stresses the notion that structures of this type are not prefabricated but interactively achieved by participants (ibid:99–100). One consequence is that news delivery sequences can be telescoped such that they are curtailed after the announcement response and take on the following form:

A: announcement
B: response
C: confirmation

Furthermore, news announcements can be anticipated by participants using specific 'occasioning practices': 'Pre-announcements' constitute a deliverer's resource. In return, recipients can either block or solicit the news announcement through a 'go-ahead token/phrase'. Potential news recipients on the other hand can elicit an announcement through 'news inquiries' (Maynard 1997:95). Another sequential position where the development of a potential news delivery sequence can be curtailed or promoted, that is where recipients display whether they treat the announcement as "news-for-them" (Terasaki 1976:7 in Maynard (1997:104) or not, is the position in which an announcement response is made relevant. Possible options in this slot include: 'news receipts' (Maynard 1997:107), 'news marks' (ibid:108) and standardised 'oh-prefaced assessments' (ibid:109). Each type of announcement response brings different contingencies about:

News receipts are implemented in terms of freestanding *oh*s, *oh really*s and non-syntactical queries (*she did?*). Such news receipts "show a retrospective orientation, primarily acknowledging an announcement as news while discouraging development of the news" (ibid:107), to the effect that they "may elicit a confirmation in next turn but no elaboration and sometimes may mark the end of an informing sequence altogether" (ibid:107). This means that the sequence may emerge in the telescoped form as shown above. When the news receipt is performed through an *oh*, the sequence can be retrospectively analysed in terms of an informing sequence (Heritage 1984). This shows that stand-alone sound objects may put constraints on the further development of the sequence.

News marks furthermore "both receive an announcement as news and promote development or elaboration of that news" (Maynard 1997:108). They have the form of 'oh-plus partial repeats' (*Oh do they*), 'freestanding but query-intoned objects' (*really?*) and of 'syntactical queries' (*did she?*). Standardised oh-prefaced assessments such as e.g. *oh dear, oh lovely* (ibid:109), on the other hand, function in more ambiguous ways. They can be oriented to as either news receipts or news marks and are in this sense weak, because they do not unequivocally solicit sequential termination or expansion (ibid:109). However, they may represent a strong rhetorical resource in that

> both *oh good* and *oh dear* are standardized, having an abstract and laconic quality that endows them with a utility for responding to very diverse kinds of good or bad news. Therefore, recipients can use them to align to announced good or bad news without being overly committed or distanced in displaying their appreciation of the newsworthiness and valence so far displayed.
>
> (ibid:109, emphasis in the original)

The interactive nature of news delivery sequences, as outlined above, is depicted in Figure 1:

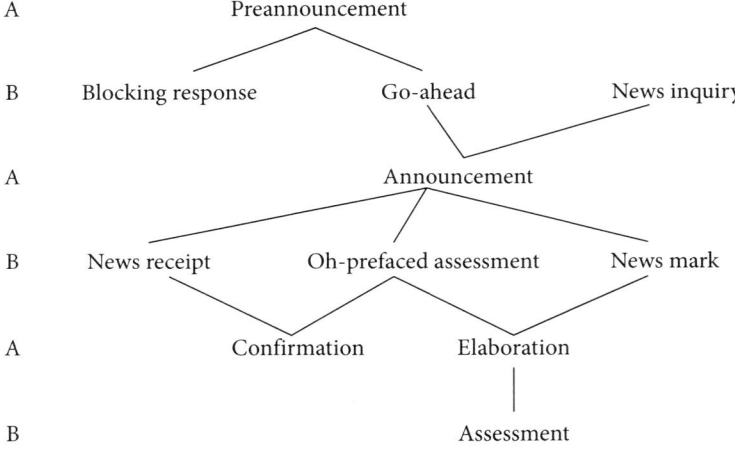

Figure 1. Interactive construction of news delivery sequences

In the present study, the affect-laden sound objects in news tellings generally serve as announcement responses, showing different affective dimensions and occasioning different sequential developments in what follows (cf. Section 6.5 on 'extra high and pointed' *oh*, Sections 8.5, 8.6.2 and 8.7 on two variants of *ah* and Section 9.2.2 on *whistle*).

Another notion central to the present study is that of the valence of news. It is – like the newsworthiness of an event (which can even be disputed by recipients) (Maynard 1997:105) – interactively constructed in conversation. Events are not good or bad as such but their valence is achieved by participants in their talk (ibid: 101). Valence may be signalled through lexical and/or prosodic means (ibid: 100, cf. also Freese and Maynard (1998). Negative valence is linked to displays of 'sorrow' and 'frustration', while positive valence is indicated by displays of 'enjoyment'. There is a tendency for speakers to align with the consequential figure in terms of valence and sound objects are powerful resources to manage such relevancies. Here the term "consequential figure" is of special importance: Coined by Maynard (1997: 94), it refers to the character affected by the consequences of the events, state-of-affairs or situation, referred to in a news delivery sequence. If consequential figures perform the news telling, they construct the valence of news in the pre-announcement, the announcement and elaboration. In the interactional slots subsequent to the announcement and elaboration turns, recipients can co-accomplish the newsworthiness and valence of a telling (ibid: 101). As found in the present study, the question whether the news teller or recipient are consequential figures of the news telling is of special importance because it has consequences for the type of affect displayed by the recipient in response to bad news (cf. the discussion of this observation in Section 8).

To summarise, fully-fledged news deliveries are structured in terms of four-turn-sequences: announcement-announcement response-elaboration-assessment. The trajectory of the activity is collaboratively constructed between teller and recipient and may be curtailed and even entirely blocked through alternative recipient actions. Similarly, the valence of news deliveries is not pre-assumed but co-constructed in the course of the activity through primarily lexical and prosodic resources.

In this sense, bad-news reports and talk about troubles are of course closely related: It is only in time that a sequence emerges in terms of one or the other through the interactional work performed by participants.

4.2.3   Complaint sequences

Like troubles talk and bad-news deliveries, complaining in mundane interaction is an activity involving displays of negatively valenced affective dimensions.[46] A first general distinction has to be made between complaints against a present party in the here and now and those about non-present third parties or more general complainable matters. For example, Günthner (2000) distinguishes between reproach activities (*Vorwürfe*) and teasing/pestering (*Frotzeln*) in the here and now (cf. also Dersley and Wootton (2000), Monzoni (2008) on *in situ* complaint sequences) and complaint stories (*Beschwerdegeschichten*), which deal with

---

46. For complaint activities in institutional interaction, cf. Heinemann (2009) and Vöge (2010).

"past reproach activities" ("vergangene [...] Vorwurfsaktivitäten", ibid: 203). As the sound objects analysed for the present study are exclusively deployed in complaint sequences which contain complaints about non-present third parties or more general complainable matters the following literature review will focus on the description of activities of this kind.

Unlike troubles talk and bad-news deliveries, the kind of affect associated with complaining, and more specifically, complaints about non-present third parties in mundane conversation is (moral) 'indignation' (Drew 1998, Günthner 2000).[47] This means further that the affective quality made relevant by complainants is 'indignation' and that complainants invite their interactional recipients to perform co-displays of this affect (Günthner 2000, Drew 2003). According to Drew (1998),

> [t]hat moral work consists of activities such as describing another's conduct as manifestly having been at fault, condemning that person for his or her behaviour, expressing indignation about their behaviour or treatment, and seeking the recipient's support for and affiliation with that sense of indignation with the 'wrongness' of the other's conduct. (ibid: 312)

In the present study, variants of the sound objects *oh*, *ooh* and *click* are analysed as recipient resources in different sequential positions in complaint activities, which involve both narrative and non-narrative complaints about non-present third parties or more general complainable matters. Most importantly, it is shown that these different kinds of sound objects are not equally functional in performing the affiliative moral work, that is, the affective treatment required by the recipient.

As regards their formal aspects, complaint sequences about so-called 'moral transgressions' of non-present third parties have the following characteristic properties in everyday English conversation (Drew 1998):

(1) Complaint sequences have clear sequential boundaries ("bounded sequences" (ibid: 304): They are initiated by e.g. "a story introduction or an announcement" (ibid: 304), with their closing being accomplished by "topically terminal summaries followed by disjunctive openings of new topics" (ibid: 305). (2) Moral transgressions are expressed in a plain manner ("explicit formulations" (ibid: 306). (3) 'Moral indignation' is made openly manifest ("overt expressions of moral indignation" (ibid: 310).[48] Just as with troubles talk and news deliveries, potential recipients of complaints may, however, anticipate that such an activity

---

47. Interestingly, Schnieders (2002) on German *in situ* customer complaints finds irritation (*Verärgerung*).

48. For the interrelation between linguistic structures and interactional practices in complaining cf. further Haakana (2007) on Finnish and Yoon (2007) on Korean.

is about to be occasioned by potential complainants and forestall such a communicative project: This is shown by Schegloff (2005), who is concerned with the analysis of participants' orientations to "possible complainable[s]" (ibid: 452), i.e. complaints which might be about to be issued by other speaker. He discusses how recipients treat such contexts in such a way that they may not even be actually performed. We can thus state that complaint activities may be performed in terms of stories, in and through which (moral) 'indignation' towards a third party's misconduct is constructed. Characteristically, concordant displays of affect on the part of the recipient are made relevant by the complainant.

4.2.4   Assessments

In all the affect-laden activities described in the sections above (i.e. troubles talk, news deliveries, complaining), speakers make use of evaluations, in that they ascribe a quality on a negative-positive scale to the subject of their topical talk. In contrast, the technical term of assessments commonly refers to assessment-assessment adjacency pairs, as discussed in the seminal work by Pomerantz (1984) and in follow-up studies, for instance Auer and Uhmann (1982) and Ogden (2006) (cf. further Heritage (2002) and Sorjonen and Hakulinen (2009) on assessment responses). Here, a special analytic focus is placed on second assessments which express a stance towards the same referent as the first (Pomerantz 1984: 59). Such adjacency pairs are organised as follows:

A: first assessment
B: second assessment

The preference organisation of adjacency pairs of this kind is of special interest to the present study. Pomerantz (1984) observes that first assessments make alternative actions relevant in second position: either agreements, usually achieved by upgrades, or disagreements, usually achieved by downgraded assessments, with agreement being the preferred response.[49] Extending Pomerantz's findings, Auer and Uhmann (1982) show that upgrading second assessments are sequence-terminating, while downgrading second assessments are sequence-expanding. Independently of Pomerantz's (1984) approach, the work on so-called 'high-grade assessments' provides further evidence for the sequence-terminating nature of *strong* assessments: Antaki et al. (2000) identify high-grade assessments, such as e.g. *brilliant, smashing*, to be functional at sequential completions in therapeutic interviews. High-grade assessments are shown to be produced by the interviewer in a sequential structure of the following shape: [answer receipt] + ["ok" or "right"

---

49. This preference organisation is reversed in the case of self-deprecatory first assessments: Here disagreement is the preferred second pair part.

etc] + [**high-grade assessment**] + [next item] (ibid: 239, emphasis in the original). In this position, they do not orient towards the content of the interviewee's answer (ibid: 241) but "project [...] curtailment of the respondent's turn and a move to next business in the series administered by the interviewer" (ibid: 245). In a follow-up study on everyday telephone conversation, Antaki (2002) finds that the high-grade assessment *lovely* projects the *resumption* of interactional closings. Thus, upgraded and strong assessments (two classes which may principally fall together) can achieve sequence termination, while downgraded ones yield sequence expansion.

Importantly, assessments have been closely linked to expressions of affectivity in the literature: According to Fiehler (1990a, b, 2002), participants accomplish two communicative tasks in conversation, namely to communicate factual information and to evaluate it. Displays of affect constitute a communicative practice for making evaluations in talk. Making a point similar to Fiehler's, Goodwin and Goodwin (1987) claim that "[a]ffect displays are not only pervasive in the production of assessments, but also quite central to their organization." (ibid: 9). Going even further, they regard such affect displays as "resources for the interactive organization of c o –experience [sic!]" (ibid: 9) (cf. also Goodwin and Goodwin (2001: 253) for the same argument). From the perspective taken in the present study, Goodwin and Goodwin's (2001) treatment of affectivity and assessments is problematic in two respects: First of all, to describe the outcome of mutual affective displays as 'co-experience' suggests that the parties involved actually *feel* the same. Since we think that this is contradictory to a social constructionist view that treats affectivity as situated displays, we would rather speak of 'co-affiliation'. Secondly, these and other studies by the authors (especially Goodwin (1986), Goodwin and Goodwin (1987) suggest that affective displays constitute *per se* assessments. It is true that affective displays and assessments may function in the same way, insofar as both practices signal a speaker's stance. In addition, idiomatic expressions for the display of affective states may be lexically/syntactically shaped in terms of evaluations, e.g. *oh that's a pity* (our data), *it's really sad* (Goodwin and Goodwin 1992: 162). Yet when it comes to vocal displays of affect (prosody, phonetics) – and of course visual ones – the matching of assessments and affectivity is not so clear. As will be argued with respect to the interactional pay-offs of sound objects, it is the very forte of such signals that they do not make the speaker's stance explicit as would fully lexical assessments. In contrast to this, Goodwin and Goodwin's and Fiehler's conceptualisations of the relationship between affectivity and assessments seem to be rooted in verbal concepts of language and communication. In a similar vein, Endo (2007) criticises Goodwin's (1986, also Goodwin and Goodwin (1992) analysis of English *Ah:::* as an assessment. She states in her study on Japanese *a::::*

"*[A]*::: does not on its own reveal what the recipient thinks about the current unit. Rather, it reveals that the recipient feels the same way about the subject of the current unit that the speaker does." (Endo 2007: 16)

On the grounds of these considerations, affective displays and assessments/evaluations will be treated as separate practices in their own right in the present study although there are cases where they can overlap. An example of the latter can be found in Peräkylä and Ruusuvuori (2006) on assessment responses to storytelling in face-to face interaction: They find that story recipients display their affective stance by facial cues prior to the production of lexical assessments. What is more, the stance shown through facial expressions can deviate from the one verbalised through lexical means.

4.2.5 *Repair*

Repair is usually not considered as an activity in which affective dimensions are made relevant. Nevertheless, next turn repair initiators have been connected to cognitive-affective states of various kinds. What is more, in the present study it will be shown that repair receipts, that is, responses to repairs, are loci for affect-laden sound objects such as 'extra high and pointed' *oh*, midrange and pointed *ooh* and 'low-falling and tailed' *ah*.

Repair sequences probably belong to the best-researched interactional activities from a conversation analytic/interactional linguistic-perspective (e.g. Jefferson (1974), Sacks et al. (1974), Schegloff (1979, 2000), Schegloff et al. (1977), also Curl (2004). Their common definition describes them as treating "troubles or problems of speaking, hearing, or understanding" (Schegloff 2007: 100, cf. also Schegloff et al. (1977) in talk-in-interaction. The two basic parameters of analysis address aspects of repair initiation and performance of repair, on which basis the following four repair types are defined: self-initiated self-repair, self-initiated other-repair, other-initiated self-repair and other-initiated other-repair. The distribution of these types is biased, with Schegloff et al. (1977) suggesting a preference for self-repair in mundane conversation.

What is important for the present study, more recent research suggests that *other*-initiations of repair can be functional for other communicative purposes than merely soliciting repair for problems in hearing and understanding: They can be deployed to display an epistemic and/or affective stance towards what the other speaker said. For example, other-initiation of repair can foreshadow an epistemic stance such as potential disagreement with a prior base first pair part and function as so-called 'pre-disagreement' (Schegloff 2007: 102). Consider the following example:

(2) [TG, 1:16–21] (Schegloff 2007:102)

```
1   Bee:   Fb     → =[W h y  ]whhat'sa mattuh with y-Yih
                      sou[nd HA:PPY, ] hh
2   Ava:                 [ Nothing.  ]
3   Ava:   Fins   → u I sound ha:p[py?]
4   Bee:   Sins              [Yee]uh.
5                     (0.3)
6   Ava:   SB     → No:,
```

Sequentially, the repair is embedded in an adjacency pair sequence, building a post-first sequence expansion. The repair initiation forms the first pair part, while the repair turn forms the second pair part (lines 3–4). In what follows, disagreement is signalled (line 6). The disagreement turn forms the second pair part in the base sequence (Schegloff 2007:103).

Furthermore, other-initiations of repair can enact a 'display of ritualised disbelief' (Heritage 1984:339–340). Repair initiations of this kind function as news marks in that they treat the other speaker's turn as news and solicit a development of the news. Wilkinson and Kitzinger (2006) adopt the notion of ritualised disbelief, by claiming that such displays serve as 'surprise responses': "These displays of ritualized disbelief do not so much 'ask questions' as convey a stance: that news in the prior turn is unexpected in some way and needs confirmation before it can be otherwise receipted and reacted to." (ibid:169)

Since such repair initiations not only work on the informational level but also express a stance, Selting (1996:265) in her study of German 'astonished' repair initiations proposes to distinguish between two analytic levels: the affective aspects and the content of the next turn repair initiator. Adding a further angle to this work on 'surprise', Drew (2005) points out that other-initiated repair initiations are actions where participants' 'confusion' about some incongruity in the prior talk can become manifest (in American and British English telephone interactions).

We can conclude that beyond being functional in the clarification of speaking, understanding, and hearing problems, other-initiations of repair can serve to display an epistemic stance to the effect that they foreshadow disagreement and affective stances such as 'astonishment'/'surprise' and 'confusion'. The latter can be ritualised in the sense that they are deployed as practices to solicit the expansion of a news delivery sequence.

4.3   Summary and conclusions

We have presented a review of sequential structures and practices in affect-laden activities as analysed in the previous conversation analytic/interactional linguistic literature. The review was selective in that it covered the range of major activities where affect-laden sound objects were found in the present study: Troubles talk, news delivery sequences, complaint sequences, assessments and repair. The rather long list of core findings and assumptions across activity types and language communities provides evidence for a shared systematics concerning how affectivity is accomplished and deployed in talk-in-interaction. Apart from the work on troubles talk and assessments, all studies linked the activity examined to specific affective dimensions: A crucial aspect of how affectivity is managed in troubles talk, news delivery sequences, complaint sequences and assessments is that the first speaker invites the recipient's affiliation with the affective stance displayed by him/her. This means that the first speaker makes concordant affective displays relevant on the part of the recipient. It may thus be expected that the set of recipient responses in such activities is constrained in terms of their affective quality. Another key finding is that affect displays are implemented in specific sequential positions. This means that some action turns are more prone to affective contextualisation than others. In addition, there may be differences in terms of the involvement and quality between affect-laden turns in one and the same activity. These two main findings, relevance of concordant affective appreciation on the part of the recipient, and specific placement of affect-laden turns can be exploited for the analysis of affect-laden sound objects. First of all, they allow assumptions about the nature of affectivity made relevant in the respective activities. At the same time, we can form the hypothesis that different affective qualities and degrees of involvement are accomplished by different linguistic resources.

Furthermore, the literature review reflects general tendencies and developments in the study of affectivity in talk-in-interaction. While early work like that on troubles talk was primarily concerned with the sequential organisation of the activity and was less interested in the linguistic shape of turns at talk and the type of affectivity signalled, more recent literature like that on news deliveries by Maynard (1997), Freese and Maynard (1998) and that on complaints by Drew (1998) aims to examine the two aspects crucial to an interactional linguistic study of affectivity: sequential organisation *and* the use of specific linguistic resources.

PART III

An analysis of responsive affect-laden sound objects in talk-in-interaction

CHAPTER 5

Affectivity and sound objects

An interactional linguistic perspective

The following sections will provide an overview of the data on which the present study is grounded, briefly describe the transcription techniques and conventions used (Section 5.1), and outline the methodological procedure followed (Section 5.2).

5.1 Data and transcription

The British-English corpus consists of more than 16 hours (16:22 h) of naturally occurring data from all kinds of conversational settings. They include recordings of everyday interactions (telephone conversations – and to a minor extent *face-to-face* interactions – between friends and family) and radio phone-ins (cf. Table 2).

Table 2. Overview of British English database*

Type of interaction	Name of corpus	Length of corpus
telephone interactions (largely) between friends and family	Holt corpus, other	7:04 h, 0:17
face to face interactions between family	Wally and friends	3:49 h
radio phone-in	Brain teaser	1:12 h
radio phone-in	Sadie Nine BBC Radio Essex, 9 June 2007	2:38 h
radio phone-in	Vanessa Feltz – Saturday – 8Sept2007BBCLondon94.4	2:02 h

*I am greatly indebted to Elizabeth Couper-Kuhlen and Elizabeth Holt for their permission to use their data.

The data analysed are transcribed according to GAT (Selting et al. 1998, 2009). In some cases (the HOLT corpus, Wally and Friends, Brain Teaser) transcripts prepared according to different transcription conventions were already available. Here the excerpts analysed were re-transcribed, which meant that new transcripts were made by repeated listening to the audio recordings and then compared with the original transcripts at hand. When the quality of the audio recordings was especially poor, e.g. due to repeated copying of the original tapes, the version of the original transcript was given priority over the author's own hearing. The study furthermore includes rhythmic analyses by the author which are also transcribed in GAT.

In the transcripts, sound objects are represented in IPA symbols (cf. Pullum and Ladusaw (²1996) and in rough phonetic transcription. The reason for doing so is to stress the fact that they were retrieved from the data through auditory analysis and to emphasise that their form was not pre-conceptualised at the outset of the analysis.[50]

One of the major findings of this study is that the sound objects come with a rather fixed bundle of prosodic-phonetic properties. Here speakers' voice ranges, and more specifically the voice ranges of the producers of sound objects, served as reference points for the description of pitch contours. For this reason the pitch floor and ceiling values specified in the acoustic analyses provided correspond to the approximate bottom and top level of that sound object producer's voice range. In Figures 20–22, where the bottom of the other speaker's voice range is lower than that of the sound object producer, the bottom level of the latter is indicated by an extra horizontal dotted line the picture.

Table 3 summarises the voice ranges of the producers of sound objects in the excerpts cited in the present study.

To represent the prosodic-phonetic packaging of the sound objects in the conversational transcripts, the phonetic transcript will be complemented by GAT symbols. This merging of conventions combines the strengths of both systems. In the running text, verbal descriptions of supra-segmental properties will be used.

Most importantly, the prosodic-phonetic transcription is intended to give the reader an idea of what the object sounds like. This could not be ensured had graphemic representations been used, as they are not consistently conventionalised for sound objects. Thus, the prosodic-phonetic transcriptions are meant to give abstract representations of the sound quality connected to a sound object.

Since Interactional Linguistics takes a participant's perspective for prosodic analysis, the primary methodological imperative was "ears first". This means that analysis was primarily done auditorily, although it is backed up by acoustic measurements where feasible. In addition, the strength and usefulness of auditory analysis becomes particularly visible, considering that some prosodic phenomena, such as e.g. accent and rhythm, which have been shown to be interactionally functional, constitute cognitive entities but cannot be instrumentally measured.

---

50. The special need for this auditory method of analysis becomes particularly visible with regard of incorrect representations in ready-made transcriptions that came with some of the audio material used.

Table 3. Sound object producers' voice ranges in the excerpts cited*

Name of speaker	Voice range	Sex
C	ca 80–(300) Hz	male
C1	ca (212)–377 Hz	female
Gordon	ca 65–325 Hz	male
Hillary	ca 85–365 Hz	female
IN1	ca 70–(240) Hz	male
IN2	ca 110–505 Hz	female
Leslie	ca 115–600 Hz	female
Linda	ca 85–360 Hz	female
M1	ca 85–530 Hz	male
M2	ca 100–445 Hz	female
Mark	ca 75–335 Hz	male
Rep	ca 80–400 Hz	male
Robin	ca 85–580 Hz	female

* Due to the poor quality of the recordings available, no pitch values can be offered for speaker Mum. Figures in parentheses give values on the basis of a limited data sample only.

All acoustic analyses were done with Praat 5.2.03, courtesy of Paul Boersma and David Weenink (www.fon.hum.uva.nl/praat). The acoustic analyses serve to illustrate fundamental frequency, intensity (shown by the oscillogram) and time. In order to facilitate readability, the text shown in the Praat picture represents a simplified version of the transcript.

5.2   The methodological approach of the present study

The method used in the present study is informed by the research programme of Interactional Linguistics as outlined in Chapter 1. The methodological procedure used for the purposes of the present study can be described as follows:

To start with, by listening to the data, we identified interactional environments which could be heard as affect-laden on grounds of the analyst's intuition.[51] It was found that sound objects constitute a speaker resource in such affect-laden environments. The search was then limited to environments where sound objects were produced as recipient responses in order to investigate their interactional-functional role in affect-laden stretches of talk in general and to examine the affective meaning they display and accomplish in particular.

---

51. Cf. Kehrein (2002) for a similar analytic procedure.

The following sample of sound objects showed the highest frequency:

Sound objects
a. which are used in a sequential next turn following some kind of affect-laden informing,
b. which are deployed in turn-initial position in this turn, and
c. which implement a recipient action to that prior informing.

The position of most sound objects was exclusively restricted to this position.

It is for this reason that the scope of the present study was limited to this type of interactional-sequential context. It includes the structure of the turn-external (a) and turn-internal (b) environments and accounts for the interactional functions of the sound object and the affect-laden informing.

Furthermore, a first division between categories of sound objects was made according to segment structure, since the latter was treated as the most distinctive property. The sound structure could be strictly vocalic, e.g. [aː], [əʊ] etc., strictly consonantal, e.g. [!] etc., mixed e.g. [ʔʊːx], or paralinguistic ([ʍ]).

A first analysis of ca. 520 tokens revealed affect-laden sound objects with the following segmental substances (Table 4):

Table 4. Affect-laden sound objects in the present data

Segment	[əʊ]	[aː]	[uː]	[ɔː]	[ɜː]	['ʌha]	[hʌ]	[aɔː]	[haː]	[waʊ]
Total	340	55	32	7	1	7	6	11	2	2

Segment	[jʌk]	[həʊː]	[mː]	[ʔʊːx]	[!]	[⊙]	[ʍ]	sighing	coughing
Total	1	4	10	4	6	3	3	10	16

Since it was observed that the actions in what follows the production of a sound object display an orientation to that sound object, the analysis further addresses formal and functional aspects of this so-called post-production context of sound objects, both on the part of the same and other speakers. In this sense, the analysis of the post-production context was used to find evidence for the affective dimension of the sound object analysed (cf. Couper-Kuhlen (2009) for such a methodological approach in the analysis of the affect-laden rejection finalisers *ah* and *oh*).

Furthermore, it is assumed that a comprehensive analysis of formal (sequential, prosodic-phonetic, lexical, syntactic-grammatical) and functional contextual aspects (actions, activities) best captures the organisation of the sound objects analysed (cf. Sorjonen (2001: 31) for a similar view as to the analysis of the Finnish response particles *joo* and *nii(n)*).

The following questions were used as parameters for the analytic procedure, following the interactional sequence as it develops in time. Each point addresses first formal and then functional issues:

1. What formal (semantic/lexical, syntactic, prosodic) properties does the affect-laden informing have? What action does it implement (for example, a complaint, an account, a repair, etc.)? What kind of affective valence/involvement is displayed?

2. Does the sound object have a distinct prosodic-phonetic form and timing? If so, how can they be described? In what sequential positions is it forthcoming? What functions (sequential and interactional) does the sound object have? What action does it perform?

3. Is there other-speaker talk following the production of the sound object? If not, in what ways is the turn expanded? Is the turn constructional unit (TCU) extended, i.e. the sound object is integrated with other elements in one TCU, or does the sound object form an independent TCU and more units are added? What type of linguistic properties do these additional elements have? What actions do they perform?

4. Subsequent to the turn including the sound object, is the sequence expanded or terminated?

5. Does any participant orientation (by the same or other speaker) to the sound object become manifest? If so, in what terms can it be described?

Furthermore, the local informing sequence was examined in terms of the larger conversational setting:

6. What position and function does the local informing sequence in which the sound object is produced have in relation to the global structure of the interaction?

Finally, the analysis considered

7. deviant cases.

The findings gained through these analytic parameters allowed a more fine-grained analysis of sound objects: In addition to the segmental substance, the respective sound objects could be further characterised in terms of a number of specific prosodic-phonetic clusters accompanying them. Furthermore, the distribution of formal types could be matched to specific types of affect-laden informings (formal and/or functional) in particular activities. Thus, sequential patterns of a specific type of affect-laden informing plus a certain type of sound object could be uncovered. In addition, typical formal-functional structures in the post-production context of the sound object could be identified. These indicated an understanding of the sound object's cognitive-affective meaning, sequential and interactional function from a participant's perspective. The amalgamation of these factors created the basis of the interactional-functional description of the respective sound object and enabled an interpretation of the affective dimensions signalled by it.

The present, select study presents variants of the vocalic sound objects *oh*, *ooh* and *ah*. They were chosen for this study because they are exemplary in elucidating different aspects of the phenomenon:

The affect-laden sound objects *ah* with 'low-falling and tailed' and 'flat-falling and low' packagings are used in activities which invite displays of negatively valenced affect with heightened involvement on the part of the recipient, such as troubles talk, deliveries of bad news, rejections of proposals and complaints. The corpus revealed 55 instances of this segmental type, which showed the highest frequency in everyday interaction.

The variants of the affect-laden sound object *ooh* represent a type of recipient response which can be implemented in response to positively and negatively valenced informings, treating them as extreme. Thirty-two tokens of this segmental type were identified, with the majority being produced in radio-phone-ins.

The affect-laden sound object 'extra high and pointed' *oh* in response to unexpected or exceptional informings in repair or news sequences exemplifies a recipient resource which performs as-if affective displays (Wilkinson and Kitzinger 2006) showing high involvement. 30 instances of this type could be identified.

In order to put the findings on these vocalic sound objects into perspective, a small study of clicks (consonantal sound objects, 9 instances) in complaint sequences and whistling (non-lexical, 3 instances) was added. It aims to show that sound objects beyond the English language system can be used in response to affect-laden informings.

This overview shows that the study is not about a highly frequent phenomenon (cf. by contrast Finnish *joo* and *nii(n)* in Sorjonen (2001), which raises questions of generalisation and quantification:

The interactional linguistic orientation of the present study warrants a qualitative approach to its object of study. Qualitative studies often involve a limited amount of data, which leads to the question to what extent the results of this study are generalisable, given that generalisation is commonly linked to high frequencies.

The issue of quantification is approached from the following angles in CA- and also IL-informed work: Since it is one of Conversation Analysis' basic assumptions that participants orient towards each others' displays in systematic, orderly ways, even the absence of a phenomenon can give valuable insights with respect to the nature of the phenomenon. In fact, the observation of an 'official absence' provides an analytic tool for the investigation of the properties of the phenomenon in question

(Schegloff 1968). An appreciation of absences of this kind sheds an entirely different light on the significance of the actual occurrence of a phenomenon.

Also, even the analysis of single cases (see e.g. Schegloff 1987) can provide evidence for the existence of a practice. In this way, the notion of relevance is interpreted in a different way than in quantitative approaches:

> The best evidence that some practice of talk-in-interaction does, or *can* do, some claimed action, for example, is that some recipient on some occasion shows himself or herself to have so understood it, most commonly by so treating it in the ensuing moments of the interaction, and most commonly of all, next. Even if no quantitative evidence can be mustered for a linkage between that practice of talking and that resultant "effect," the treatment of the linkage as relevant – by the *parties* on *that* occasion, on which it *was* manifested – remains.
>
> (Schegloff 1993: 101, emphasis in the original)

Finally, it is subject to debate whether larger collections of samples should be precisely quantified or whether "informal quantification" (ibid: 99) as is commonly done in CA work should not be sufficient. Schegloff (1993) argues that there are good grounds for such informal quantification by problematising the notions and concepts of denominator (defined as "environments of possible *relevant* occurrence" (ibid: 103, emphasis in the original), numerator ("set of types of occurrences whose presence should count as events" (ibid: 103), and domain (type of activity/speech exchange system). In a review of CA methodology, Heritage (1995) replicates Schegloff's discussion with particular reference to the example *oh* (Heritage 1984). He raises some points that relate to the present study very well and can be summarised as follows: When embarking on a study, the denominator may not be clear from the beginning: The study itself serves to uncover what the nature of the denominator is (Heritage 1995: 402). On the other hand, CA-methodology in itself may be limited in assessing what may count as a denominator. As for the numerator, the following issues arise in terms of *oh*:

> Which intonations of 'oh' are to be counted for statistical purposes (cf. Local [1996])? What combinations of 'oh' with other turn components, such as assessments, newsmarks etc. are to be permitted as instances of the occurrence of 'oh' and so on.
>
> (Heritage 1995: 403)

Finally, the domain is a crucial factor in making adequate judgments of analyses and different domains may provide a richer environment for a phenomenon (ibid: 403–404).

Taking a more radical position, Golato (2003) argues that

> questions concerning generalizability of results are entirely misplaced since they mistakenly presuppose an approach to data collection and analysis used neither in CA, nor within many other qualitative research methodologies.   (ibid: 112)

In her view, the aim of quantitively oriented research to make "probability-based assertions" (ibid: 112) contradicts the core interest of CA-informed study in forming an understanding of the organisation of social interaction.

This shows that figures and frequencies do not have much significance *as such* in the qualitative approach taken for this study but are rather something "built on its back" (Schegloff 1993: 102). However, quantification can lead to interesting insights for studies like the present one: For example, although problems of comparability arise, the variety of domains used for the present study allows further characterisation of the phenomenon at hand. Furthermore, the low quantities of the objects examined can be treated as indicators that the use of affect-laden sound objects is restricted to specific domains, i.e. 'conversational' telephone interactions. What is more, the low frequency may indicate that non-referential, affect-laden action like those carried out by sound objects constitute a "marked" choice (cf. Selting's (1996) use of the term "marked" vs. "unmarked" for 'astonished' vs. 'non-astonished' repair initiators) in the domains examined. In this way, low frequency may be inherent to the object of study and a qualitative method like the one used may be especially suitable to exploring its nature.

CHAPTER 6

Affect-laden *oh* in repair sequences and news tellings

Oh is the best researched and most common sound object in English talk-in-interaction. Depending on its prosodic-phonetic form and the interactional and sequential contexts, it has been analysed to display a range of cognitive-affective processes, such as 'change-of-state' (Heritage 1984), 'disappointment' (Couper-Kuhlen 2009) and 'surprise' (Couper-Kuhlen 2009, Local 1996).

This section examines the form and uses of *oh* in repair and news delivery sequences, when orienting towards the unexpectedness or exceptionality of an informing. In particular, the section investigates *oh*s which can come off as 'extra high and pointed', located in two kinds of environments: (1) in response to repairs which are initiated in order to perform repair on a prior incongruent context and (2) in response to a piece of news which is set up as exceptional, i.e. in contrast to the regular case. In such environments, this 'extra high and pointed' tone of voice can be heard as doing so-called 'surprise', 'astonishment' or 'amazement'.

As regards affectivity, *oh* has probably most often been associated with dimensions of 'surprise' and 'astonishment' in previous research. Nevertheless, the following account will add further aspects to this kind of research in the following ways: First of all, it will be argued that an interpretation of 'surprise' cannot be linked to a rising-falling contour on the object alone but is cued by the interplay of prosodic signals especially such as pitch height, pitch movement and duration in particular, which can be heard as 'extra high and pointed'. Secondly, it will be shown that responses of 'surprise' not only reflect socio-cultural and category membership (Wilkinson and Kitzinger 2006: 173), but can be treated as products of the linguistic-rhetorical design of the sequence they receipt. Thirdly, by illustrating that prosodic contextualisations of responses to unexpected informings may vary in terms of involvement, an argument will be made for a conceptualisation of 'surprise' and related dimensions as a matter of degree. This will enable us on the one hand to further understand why the traditional association between the rise-fall and notions of 'surprise' has been criticised (cf. Local (1996) for a critical review of the literature) and on the other to integrate diverging interpretations with respect to the prosodic cluster of 'surprised' *oh*: For instance, Couper-Kuhlen (2009) labels instances of *oh*, whose packaging involves lower pitch as doing 'surprise' as well. This points to the fact that 'surprise' is used as an umbrella term for a range of formal and functional phenomena.

Although variants of *oh* are produced without prosodic prominence and integrated in a larger unit in the majority of cases found in the data, the analysis will deal with cases of *oh* which have prosodic prominence, i.e. responsive *oh*s in turn-initial position which are done on an independent contour (as in the other sections on vocalic affect-laden sound objects, i.e. on *ah* and *ooh*). This is for the following reasons: First, the major analytic interest lies in prosodically prominent instances of *oh*, since they are treated as single actions rather than merely framing the way an emergent action is going to be heard. This allows an analysis which concentrates on the sound object rather than on what is to come and therefore is rather unimpeded by considerations in terms of the elements which follow. Secondly, 'extra high and pointed' *oh* was exclusively found in turn-initial position.[52]

The following section will outline previous accounts of *oh* in the literature (Section 6.1) and summarise the work done on 'surprise' in talk-in-interaction (Section 6.2). Section 6.3 will be concerned with the prosodic packaging of 'extra high and pointed' *oh*. Further, Sections 6.4 and 6.5 will provide an account of the two uses of 'extra high and pointed' *oh* in repair and news delivery sequences. Serving as a repair receipt in the former sequential environment and as a news response in the latter, this kind of sound object is specifically generated in contexts which prepare for 'surprise'. Section 6.4 describes other-initiated self-repair sequences in which 'extra high and pointed' *oh* is produced as a 'surprised' repair receipt. The section further discusses the relationship between a rising-falling contour of *oh* and the notion of 'surprise' in this sequential environment. Section 6.5 deals with news delivery sequences which elicit 'extra high and pointed' *oh*s. Here the sound object serves as a 'surprised' news response. An additional section (6.6) will discuss what the interactional pay-off of such 'extra high and pointed' *oh*s is and whether 'surprise' is an emotion. By way of summary, Section 6.7 winds up the discussion of 'extra high and pointed' *oh*.

6.1   Previous accounts in the literature: *Oh* in English

6.1.1   *English* oh *in dictionaries*
Dictionary definitions of *oh* (or *o*, /əʊ/) give the impression that interjections convey emotions, inner states and serve discourse-organisational functions. The entry in the Longman dictionary of contemporary English (Mayor [5]2009:1212)

---

52.   When *oh* is found in non-initial turn position in the British English data, it is not accompanied by 'high and pointed' prosody.

can be considered exemplary for those in other dictionaries (e.g. Mayor (2002), Wehmeier (⁷2005), Sinclair (1995): *oh* is (1) "used when you want to get someone's attention or continue what you are saying", (2) "used when you are giving an answer to a question", (3) "used to make a slight pause when you are speaking", (4) "used to show that you are very happy, angry, disappointed etc about something", (5) "used to show that you are surprised about something".

Additional meanings mentioned in other dictionaries are "introducing something new", "showing you understand", "showing when you did not know something" and "introducing speech" (Mayor 2002: 984) or expressing fear or joy (Wehmeier ⁷2005: 1054). Providing no further information than single examples about these uses, these English monolingual learner's dictionaries thus give rather contradictory meanings for the interjection. Reber (2010a) criticises the fact that their entries do

> not include any information on prosodic properties which would potentially distinguish between the various kinds of 'oh', for instance, 'happy', 'angry' and 'disappointed' oh's would sound quite different from one another. In this way, such entries suggest a confusing polysemy of 'oh' without providing the learner with enough prosodic and contextual information on how (and when) to use the interjection in conversation.   (ibid: 4)

6.1.2   *English* oh *in interactional studies*[53]
In his seminal study, Heritage (1984) describes *oh* in response to informings as a 'change-of-state token' (cf. also Heritage 2005):[54] It signals that "its producer has undergone some kind of change in his or her locally current state of knowledge, information, orientation or awareness." (Heritage 1984: 299). Heritage suggests that *oh* has a full-fledged semantics (Heritage 1998: 327), even though the meaning of *oh* is highly context-bound.[55]

---

53. Because of the focus of the present study on responsive sound objects, work on sequence-initial uses of English *oh* (e.g. Bolden (2006) will not be considered in the discussion.

54. In later work, Heritage further examines "oh-prefaced turns in response to inquiry" (1998) and "oh-prefaced responses to assessments" (2002). Since these studies deal with *oh*-prefacing, i.e. instances where *oh* is integrated into larger units, findings from these studies will only be mentioned when relevant for a particular analysis.

55. The semantics of *oh* is simple indeed: The particle proposes that its producer has undergone some kind of cognitive 'change of state,' primarily either of attention or knowledge (Heritage 1984, Schiffrin 1987). In their use of *oh*, speakers rely on contextual aspects of their utterances as resources that permit hearers to determine the sense of the 'change of state' proposal being made. Thus variations in the sense of an oh-carried 'change of state' proposal are managed through sequential and contextual particularizations of the particle's placement, and they emerge through conversational inference.
                                                                (Heritage 1998: 327)

Four kinds of informing sequences involving *oh* are distinguished (Heritage 1984):

(1) Question-elicited informings (question – answer – *oh*), (2) Counter-informings (informing – counter-informing – *oh*), (3) Other-initiated repair (repairable – repair initiation – repair – *oh*) and (4) Understanding check (informing – understanding check – confirmation/disconfirmation – *oh*).

In contrast to continuers or "receipt-objects" like *yeah*, *yes* or *mm hm*, stand-alone *oh* receipts an informing as informative and complete to the effect that the informing sequence is terminated (ibid: 301–302, 305).

The prosodic-phonetic form of *oh* is only barely accounted for: Nevertheless, it is pointed out that a "stretched and rise-fall intoned" *oh* (ibid: 306) may have a slightly similar function to the default *oh*, in that it "foregrounds" a specific piece of information conveyed in the informant's prior talk (ibid: 306). It can thus be inferred that in context, prosody may add to or slightly alter the meaning of *oh*.

Although free-standing *oh* is assigned a sequence-terminating function, participants can expand their turn/TCU for "treat[ing] the local trajectory of the informing as complete (with assessments) or incomplete (with requests for further information)." (ibid: 305). Both stand-alone *oh* and 'oh-plus-assessment' thus treat an informing sequence as complete. However, there seems to be a division of labour between the two practices, an aspect not addressed in the article. As Heritage's data suggests (a low frequency of stand-alone *oh*), stand-alone *oh* may often be too weak a response for achieving sequence-termination.

In general, Heritage (1984) acknowledges that *oh* may have some affective quality, yet does not mention on what empirical grounds these descriptions are based. He mentions 'disappointed-sounding' and 'sympathetically intoned' *oh*s. The transcript suggests that the sympathetic *oh* is diphthongal, lengthened and has "final" intonation (ibid: 333).

"[D]isappointed-sounding" *oh*s can be treated as opaque in terms of their meaning by interlocutors, which becomes visible in the absence of a relevant uptake in the next slot (ibid: 326). In contrast to this, interlocutors may take their turn in overlap with the production of an *oh*-receipt in order to "forestall the possible production of [...] additional turn components in the service of retaining control over the future development of topical talk." (ibid: 327). This can be functional when emotionally loaded *oh*s, for example ones that are "sympathetically intoned", respond to an informing in a way not wished for by the informant (ibid: 345, footnote 21).

When *oh* is not followed by further talk by the same speaker (as is usually the case), it can be treated as withholding further talk. The examples given in Heritage's study include *oh*s which are heard affect-laden and ones which are not (ibid: 333–335).

Local (1996) examines stand-alone *oh* in the function of a news receipt, *oh* plus additional turn components, *oh* plus partial repeats of prior turn, freestanding *oh* in question-elicited informings and *oh* in relation to 'surprise'. His particular interest concerns the phonetic make-up of such *oh*s in these sequential environments. His analysis of so-called news receipt *oh* seems to describe the properties of the default change-of-state token: initial glottal stop possible, prominence, falling pitch movement even though with varying range and initial pitch height, variable duration, tense articulatory setting, possible creaky voice, typically diphthongal and with close back, delayed production (ibid: 182).

'Surprised *oh*' is accompanied by "high, wide-range rising-falling pitch" (ibid: 204). It can come with initial glottal closure and both as a monophthong or diphthong (ibid: 207). His examples exclusively comprise excerpts where the *oh*-producer makes "an explicit display of misinformedness or forgetfulness" (ibid: 205) on post-production of *oh*. This means he is only concerned with instantiations of *oh* plus turn expansion.

Couper-Kuhlen (2009) investigates the use of *oh* as a 'rejection finaliser' in British English telephone conversation; i.e. a rejection finaliser is described as a short response, which displays an acceptance of rejection in response to a request (ibid: 98). She finds that *oh* in this sequential position can be heard as either 'disappointed' or 'surprised'. These different affective qualities are achieved by different prosodic-phonetic forms: A 'subdued' prosody indexes 'disappointment', while a 'dynamic' prosody cues 'surprise'. The interpretation of *oh* as a display of 'surprise' is based on an analysis of the speaker's having been "under a different impression or […] misinformed" (ibid: 103) and a 'dynamic' prosody on *oh*. That means, *oh* "is shorter and stronger in articulatory force [than the subdued *oh*]. It has an upstepped pitch peak moving into a wide fall and ends in glottal closure" (ibid: 103). A 'subdued' tone of voice on *oh* (and further turn elements) indexes 'disappointment':

> [It is] produced with softer volume than normal; with breathy phonation and weaker articulatory force than usual; and with low, narrow and slightly falling pitch. The *oh* token undergoes some stretching and ends in a trail-off (Local and Kelly 1986). […] Overall, this combination of pitch, loudness, phonatory setting and timing creates a tone of voice which seems akin to a turning inward.[56]
> (Couper-Kuhlen 2009: 98–99, emphasis in the original)

---

56. Couper-Kuhlen (2009: 117) further points out that a comparable set of properties on German *oh* /oː/ can equally be heard as doing 'disappointment'.

The production of 'subdued' *oh* is also oriented to by specific interactional work in the post-*oh* context, such as a revision of the request (Couper-Kuhlen 2009: 105).

Discourse-analytic studies largely complement this picture: *oh* is analysed in terms of a discourse marker along with e.g. *well, now* or *I mean*. According to Schiffrin (1987), the general function of *oh* is "information management" in conversation (ibid: 100). It fulfils "cognitive tasks" with a "pragmatic effect" (ibid: 101). In addition to "recognition and receipt of the informational content of ongoing discourse" *oh* can be used to "display shifts in expressive orientation" (ibid: 95). This shift in expressive orientation is signalled through what Schiffrin (1987) calls "intensification", i.e. strong emotional responses which are due to "a shift in [the speaker's] evaluative involvement" (ibid: 96).

Aijmer (2002) states that *oh* can display a range of cognitive-affective processes in conversation. She points out that these multiple functions of *oh* are constructed in terms of "its collocations, position, prosody, text type and position in the text." (ibid: 151, cf. also Aijmer (1987).

We have seen that *oh* may display a range of cognitive-affective processes and states, depending on its prosodic-phonetic form and sequential context. Recipients use *oh* in order to indicate how they treat the other speaker's talk and this treatment is then consequential for how the interaction progresses. Beside its 'cognitive' function as a 'change-of-state token', *oh* can be deployed to display affect: Along with 'sympathy' and 'disappointment', 'surprise' was identified as a type of affect claimed by *oh*. Since *oh* doing 'surprise' is the general focus of this chapter, we will summarise the main findings on 'surprise' in talk-in-interaction before we proceed to our analysis.

6.2   'Surprise' in talk-in-interaction

Notions of 'surprise' or 'astonishment' are among the affective dimensions which have attracted the most attention among conversation analytically informed scholars. Here notions of 'surprise' or 'astonishment' have been related to "problems of expectation" (Selting 1996, Wilkinson and Kitzinger 2006) or to "displays of being misinformed and displays of forgetfulness" (Couper-Kuhlen 2009, Local 1996) and have been linked to a range of practices and activities.

Wilkinson and Kitzinger (2006) find that so-called 'surprise tokens', such as *wow, gosh, oh my god, ooh!, phew*, etc., occur in typical sequential positions, that is, following 'surprise source turns' (turns designed to elicit 'surprise') in everyday and institutional English interactions. Surprise source turns can be constructed in terms of "negative observations" and/or 'extreme case formulations' (ECF,

Pomerantz (1986), which can address numerical values (ibid: 157).[57] The authors
further identify a 'surprise sequence' with the following structure:

A: surprise source turn,
B: display of 'ritualised disbelief' (Heritage 1984, adopted by Wilkinson
    and Kitzinger 2006) (enacted for instance by a next turn repair initia-
    tors (NTRI)),
B: confirmation,
A: surprise token.

Displays of 'surprise' can thus be made relevant in specific sequential positions
and are generated by certain cues in the preceding talk (ibid: 156). "Nonlexi-
cal reaction tokens" such as *oh* are heard as 'surprised' through a "punched-up
prosody" (ibid: 154). Their definition of 'surprise' is similar to Selting's (1996).
It is defined as "the public display of finding something counter to expectation"
(Wilkinson and Kitzinger 2006: 152).

Selting (1996) examines the differences between 'normal' and 'astonished'
next turn repair initiators (cf. above for a description of prosodic aspects) in German talk-in-interaction:

> Unlike a prosodically *unmarked* configuration in repair initation, which is used
> to signal 'normal' problems of hearing and understanding, a prosodically *marked*
> configuration is used as an 'astonished' or 'surprised' signalling of a problem of
> expectation which requires special treatment.
>
> (Selting 1996: 231, emphasis in the original)

Recipients of 'astonished' NTRIs are found to show an orientation towards both
the affective aspects (made visible through the subsequent justification of the
trouble source) and the contents of the NTRI. Such subsequent justifications are
organised in terms of a preference for 'agreement' and 'alignment' (ibid: 265). In
contrast to Selting (1996) and Wilkinson and Kitzinger (2006), Local (1996) in
discussing 'surprised' *oh* overtly rejects the view that such uses of *oh* can be linked
to unexpectedness (Local 1996: 202).

---

57. Pomerantz (1986) describes 'extreme case formulations', that is, constructions with lexical markers such as "everybody", "forever", "no time", etc., as presenting the extreme case of a
scenario or state-of-affairs (Pomerantz 1986: 219). In this way they are "[o]ne practice used in
legitimizing claims" (ibid: 219), in particular in order

1. to defend against or to counter challenges to the legitimacy of complaints, accusations,
    justifications, and defenses;
2. to propose a phenomenon is 'in the object' or objective rather than a product of the
    interaction or the circumstances;
3. to propose that some behavior is not wrong, or is right, by virtue of its status as fre-
    quently occurring or commonly done. (ibid: 219–220)

As discussed in more detail in Section 3.2.2.2 above, Couper-Kuhlen (1993:261–262) furthermore finds that the rhythmic integration of news acknowledgement turns such as *what?* or *you wha-?* is functional as a marker of 'surprise' in English. Whereas a delayed production of news acknowledgements is heard as contextualising 'stunned surprise', a timing of such turns on the next beat signals "little or no surprise" (ibid:262).

As the above literature review on *oh* has shown, 'surprise' has on the one hand often been examined in connection with *oh* in Conversation Analysis/Interactional Linguistics. On the other, displays of 'surprise' have been associated with distinct bundles of prosodic-phonetic features (see Table 5).

Table 5. Prosodic-phonetic properties associated with displays of 'surprise' in English

Prosodic-phonetic properties	'Stunned surprise' in news acknowledgements (Couper-Kuhlen 1993)	'Surprise' in rejection finalisers *oh* (Couper-Kuhlen 2009)	'Surprise' in news receipts *oh* (Local 1996)	'Surprise' in greetings *hi* (Schegloff 1998)
pitch level	–	–	high	high absolute pitch
pitch movement	–	sharp rising-falling	wide-range rising-falling	wide-range rising-falling
duration	–	shorter than 'subdued *oh*'	–	–
loudness	–	–	–	–
rhythmic integration	delayed	–	–	–
articulatory force	–	stronger than 'subdued *oh*'	–	–
glottalisation	–	final glottal closure	initial glottal closure	–
vowel quality	–	–	monophthong or diphthong	–
auditive label	–	'sharp and dynamic'	–	–

The table reflects a homogeneous conception of "the prosody of surprise" in English. A rising-falling contour and high pitch are identified as common properties of what is heard as 'surprise' in specific contexts. What is more, the rhythmic integration of a recipient action serves as an additional contextualisation cue as regards the affective meaning of that action. However, the table makes it plain that the prosodic properties found for 'surprise' are not tied up with *oh* or any other sound object: They can accompany other elements such as *hi* as well. This observation bears heavy implications for the theoretical modeling of sound objects: It shows that the prosodic cluster which makes a particular sound object come off as "surprised" is somewhat separate from its segmental substance. This raises the question whether two objects which are packaged with a similar prosodic cluster may also be heard as signalling different things.

To summarise, a review of the main body of research shows that 'surprise' can be displayed in various interactional environments: news deliveries, repair sequences and rejection contexts. On post-production, participants may perform actions which are oriented towards the display, e.g. they may make accounts. Furthermore, prosody seems to be constitutive for the contextualisation of 'surprise'. In addition, *oh* seems to be a candidate resource for displaying 'surprise'. The present study will explore the implications of 'surprised' *oh* more fully: It examines instances of *oh* with 'extra high and pointed' prosody in the function of repair receipts and news responses and analyses the specific interactional settings which prepare for the use of such tokens, both with subsequent turn expansion and without.

6.3   The prosodic-phonetic packaging of 'extra high and pointed' *oh*

Oh with an 'extra high and pointed' contour can be used by recipients in order to receipt a repair or a piece of exceptional news.

As to its segmental substance, the sound object is realised in terms of a diphthong: Its quality can be described as a glide from an open-mid central unrounded vowel to a vowel in the region of cardinal vowel 8 ([u]).[58] Alternatively, the initial central mid vowel can be retracted and more open and thus close to cardinal vowel 14 ([ʌ]).[59] Despite these minor differences in vowel quality, these objects can be heard as the same type of sound object. Local's (1996) phonetic transcription of 'surprised' *oh*s shows similar variants (ibid: 213–214).

When performing a repair receipt or news response, this sound object can come in a prosodic-phonetic package which will be termed 'extra high and pointed': It includes a set of properties of which some are obligatory for the token to be heard as 'extra high and pointed', and others are facultative.

---

58. The 'cardinal vowel' system goes back to the British phonetician Daniel Jones (Jones 1917, 1918) and has been adopted by the IPA for its vowel chart. Cardinal vowels do not represent real vowels but serve as reference points for the phonetic description of vowel quality in languages.

59. This seems to be due to regional variation (I am indebted to Christian Mair for this comment).

Obligatory properties make up the prosodic design of the sound object which can be heard as 'extra high and pointed'.

(1) The sound object is noticeably lengthened. (2) Its pitch is not only higher than prior speech by the same speaker but is high in the speaker's range in absolute terms. (3) It has a rise-fall contour, starting on a high onset, rising to a peak at the top of the speaker's range and falling on a glide to mid (Figure 2 provides a stylised representation of the sound object's contour in tadpole notation).[60]

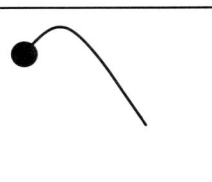

Figure 2. Pitch contour of 'extra high and pointed' *oh*

This set of prosodic properties (increased duration, high pitch in absolute terms and rising-falling contour) can be assigned specific signalling functions in the contexts of repair and news delivery sequences.

The set of facultative properties includes aspects of loudness and rhythmical timing, which add to the affective contextualisation of the sound object: As to the loudness of the object, it can be delivered in higher or slightly lower volume than prior talk by the same speaker. Furthermore, the sound object can be timed following micro or medium pauses, either on the next beat or not. 'Extra high and pointed' *oh* tends to come on the next beat when serving as a repair receipt, while it is delayed as a news response.

Finally, the sound object may be accompanied by two optional kinds of properties, whose presence is not related to one another: The vocalic sound object may but need not be produced with initial glottal closure and may be accompanied by breathy voice.

To sum up, the kind of sound object which will be referred to as 'extra high and pointed' *oh* comes with a set of obligatory, fixed properties in repair and news delivery sequences. This set consists of lengthening, high absolute pitch,

60. The term 'tadpole notation' refers to the 'interlinear tonetic' transcription system as used by e.g. Couper-Kuhlen (1986), Cruttenden (1986), and O'Connor and Arnold (1961). Here "the top and bottom lines represent the top and bottom of the speaker's pitch range" (Cruttenden 1986: xiii). The dots stand for accented syllables, that is, for syllables with pitch prominence, and the tails for pitch movement.

and a rising-falling contour. Additionally, the object is characterised by variant loudness and timing. Sometimes, initial glottal closure and/or breathy voice quality may occur.

The following sections are concerned with the use and functions of this kind of sound object in repair and news delivery sequences and the meaning signalled by 'extra high and pointed' *oh*. In Section 6.4 its use as a repair receipt is investigated: Here the *oh*-producer initiates repair in an affect-laden way because of some incongruency in the preceding talk. The repair offered is then responded to with an *oh* which displays 'surprise'. In Section 6.5 the function of *oh* as a news response will be described. Recipients use *oh* with 'extra high and pointed' prosody in orientation towards a news telling with a specific rhetorical pattern: Following a telling of the regular case, the exceptional case is presented in a contrastive construction. Section 6.6 offers a general discussion of whether 'surprise' can be considered an affective dimension.

6.4   Affect-laden *oh* in response to repair

Our corpus shows that participants may use 'extra high and pointed' *oh* to receipt repairs related to trouble in understanding in order to acknowledge them and to treat them as running counter to prior expectations or assumptions. Such repair sequences often form post-expansions of news delivery sequences, which contain some kind of incongruity. Repair receipts realised with an 'extra high and pointed' *oh* in such environments can be heard as doing 'surprise': In addition to acknowledging the repair the way change-of-state tokens do, their production occasions more talk related to the content of the repair sequence: On completion of the sound object, the *oh*-producer can expand her turn with talk seeking affiliation and agreement on repairable or the other speaker can elaborate further on the content of the repair (cf. Golato and Betz (2008) on German *ach* for a similar observation). We will first examine a case of 'extra high and pointed' *oh* plus turn expansion (Section 6.4.1) and then turn to a case where the use of 'extra high and pointed' *oh* is followed by other-speaker talk (Section 6.4.2).

6.4.1   Oh *as a repair receipt + turn expansion*
'Extra high and pointed' *oh* may implement repair receipts in response to other-initiated self-repair. *Oh*s of this type treat the content of the repair as running counter to their expectations. Repairs which are treated in this way are performed in order to clarify some problem of understanding due to incongruity in the previous talk.

Excerpt 3 provides an example of an 'extra high and pointed' repair receipt *oh* which is embedded in the wider context of a news delivery sequence. In the post-production context of the repair receipt, the implications of the repair are further dealt with in turn expansion. The repair receipt (line 41) is delayed in that the credibility of the repair proffered is challenged before the receipt is finally delivered.[61]

(3) [HOLT:M88:1:5] "allergies"

```
1    Les:   oh ↑how's MARy ↓kEEping;
2           cause uh her ALlergies;
3           are they (.) .h[hh
4    Rob:                  [well she ↑came in blotchy the other
5           DAY,=
6           =and they didn't (.) couldn't decide what it WAS. .hh
7    Les:   HM:.
8    Rob:   i mean i FEEL-
9    Les:   .hh
10          (-)
11   Rob:   UH::M: (-)
12          i mean she SEEMS very well,
13          she cErtainly lost some: WEIGHT;
14          and she looks !E!ver so nice;=
15          =she's gʔ obviously had some new: .hh ↓CLO:THES,=
16          which (.)↓you know (.) suit her very WELL,
17   Les:   oh GOOD;
18   Rob:   yes ↓so that (.) that's very NI:C[E,
19   Les:                                    [HM[:.
20   Rob:                                       [in fact we find
21          we're wearing more of the same COLours,
22          we have to be CAREful, .h[h
23   Les:                            [´`OH;
24   Rob:   ↑eh[hh ((high-pitched laughter particle))
25   Les:      [YES;
26          [cause=sh
27   Rob:   [(well) beige and NAVy,
28 → Les:   oh yes cause she can't wear BLUE:; h
29          (-)
30 → Rob:   she ↑CAN'T ↓wear blue,=
31 → Les:   =nO: that's one of the colours she's al↑LERGic to;
32          (-)
```

---

61. This nicely complements the observation made for the sound object *ah*, whose production may be delayed by similar strategies in request sequences.

```
33  →  Rob:    <<falsetto>well ↑THAT'S funny>,
34  →          <<falsetto>she was wearing ↑ALL blue the other DA[Y:>?
35  →  Les:                                                       [.hh
36  →          oh eh she has to wear a specific SORT of blue.
37  →          .hh one: (.)
38  →          eh she can only wear THIN:GS; .hhh
39  →          that dOn't have INdigo In them.
40  →          (.)
41  →  Rob:    <<h>´`[əʊː]>; ((extra high and pointed))
42  →          (---)
43  →  Rob:    <<hh>well and she[↑told me how this had suddenly:
44  →  Les:                     [((sniff))
45  →  Rob:    started over the last (.) year (.) two YEARS>?
46             [and
47     Les:    [YE:S,
48             (.)
49     Rob:    the SUN is another one,
50             ISn't it;
51     Les:    .hh WHO?
52             the sUn [YE:S;
53     Rob:            [the SUN;
```

The repair sequence is located in a news delivery sequence initiated by Leslie in line 1. The topical talk is about Mary, a mutual acquaintance of the interlocutors. In lines 20–22 Robin informs Leslie that she and Mary are wearing the same colours. This action can be heard as a subtle complaint. Robin's news is receipted by the change-of-state token *OH* in line 23. *OH* has a rising-falling contour to mid, with an onset and peak in the middle of the speaker's range and is no louder than the previous talk by same speaker. According to Heritage (1984: 306), the rise-fall signals that a specific aspect of the news is treated with heightened relevance.

Both the teller's and the recipient's subsequent talk show an orientation towards this treatment: The teller specifies her claim in that she details the types of colours she and Mary are wearing: beige and navy (line 27). The recipient, on the other hand, gives an account (indicated by the conjunction *cause*), claiming that Mary cannot wear blue (line 28). Given that navy is a shade of blue, the account shows disagreement with the implication of the news teller's earlier informing, namely that Mary is wearing blue clothes. The news teller next initiates repair on this (line 30): The animated pitch movements with which the repair initiator is delivered and the high contrastive pitch accent on the modal auxiliary contextualise the next turn repair initiator as affect-laden and full of disbelief. It can be interpreted as a pre-disagreement marker (Schegloff 2007: 102), in that it foreshadows lines 33–34.

In the repair which follows (line 31), the news recipient accounts for why Mary cannot wear blue by claiming that she is allergic to it. In what comes next, the repair is not ratified. Instead, the news teller challenges its credibility: The repair initiator first assesses the repair as funny, i.e. as strange, and then provides an evidential account which serves to refute the claim that Mary cannot wear blue (lines 33–34). The evidential account is formatted in terms of an extreme case formulation: The adverb *all* states that the referent wore nothing but blue clothes and therefore presents an extreme case. In argumentative contexts such extreme case formulations are deployed to strengthen and defend one's claims. Prosodically, the turn is marked through its production in a falsetto register. The interactional function of this type of voice quality is still to be explored in a systematic way, but here it makes the turn stand out and therefore serves as an additional vocal resource lending extra (affective) weight to the claim.

Leslie's response displays an orientation to this: Its *oh*-prefacing lends epistemic authority to the turn and thereby heightens its argumentative thrust (Heritage 2002). At the same time, it backs down, in a concessive formulation, from the previous unqualified claim that Mary cannot wear blue at all: In specifying the type of blue Mary can wear (indigo), the news recipient modifies her initial repair.

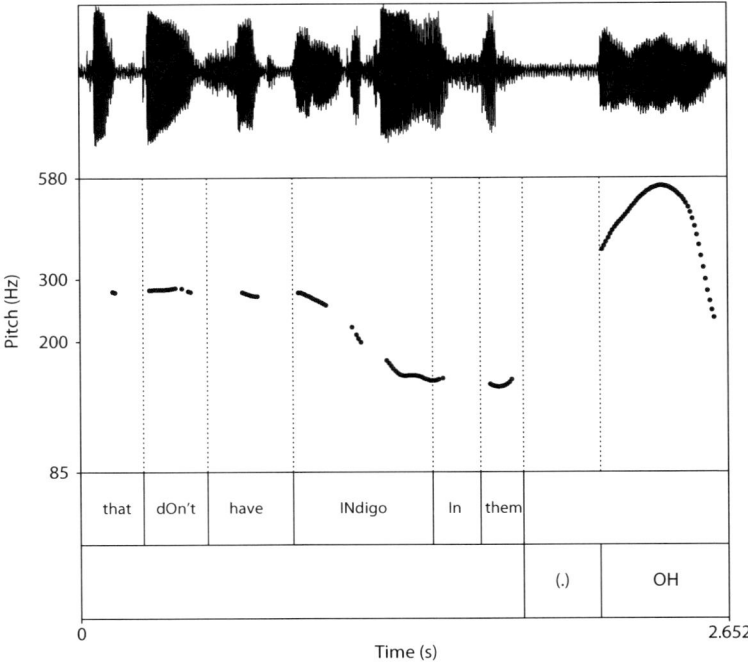

Figure 3. Acoustic analysis of Excerpt 3 ("allergies"), lines 39–41

It is this kind of modification which is responded to by Robin, the news teller, with an 'extra high and pointed' *oh*, which functions as a 'surprised' repair receipt.

To give a formal analysis, the initial vowel quality of the diphthong is open-mid central unrounded and glides to a vowel quality in the region of cardinal vowel 8. The prosody with which the sound object is delivered is heard as extra high and pointed: *Oh* has a lengthened, wide ranging rising-falling contour, with the speaker's pitch register reaching high values in absolute terms. The contour begins with a high onset (at 363 Hz), rises to an extra high peak (554 Hz) and falls on a glide to mid (280 Hz). This is illustrated in the acoustic analysis shown above (Figure 3).

In terms of loudness, the sound object is produced in a slightly softer fashion than previous talk by the same speaker. It occurs in a well-timed fashion, i.e. on the next beat, as can be seen in the analysis below (Excerpt 3').[62]

(3') Rhythmic analysis of Excerpt 3 ("allergies"), lines 38–42

```
1   Les:    eh she can only wear THIN:GS; .hhh
2           that
3           /dOn't have       /
4           /INdigo           /
5           /In them;
6                         (.)= /
7   Rob:    /=<<h>´`[əʊː]>;
8           (---)
```

As the long pause which follows the sound object indicates, the rhythmic structure breaks off thereafter.

The prosodic contextualisation of the sound object can be interpreted in the following way: The lengthened and rising-falling production can be seen as orienting towards the fact that the content of the repair runs against the recipient's assumptions: Even if the information conveyed has been prepared for beforehand and does not come completely unexpected (cf. Excerpt 3, line 36), it is treated as

---

62. For transcription conventions cf. the Appendix. The description of speech rhythm in the present study follows Couper-Kuhlen (1993):

> [W]e shall refer to perceptually isochronous sequences as *rhythmic structures*. They are structure-like due to their gestalt nature and they are rhythmic because of the temporal regularity which serves as their primary organizing principle. The prominent syllables which articulate them will be called *rhythmic beats*. The analogy to music is intentional: the perceptually isochronous syllables of a rhythmic structure establish a regular pulse which is not unlike the 'beat' in musical production. (ibid: 72, emphasis in the original, cf. also (ibid: 69–70) for a more detailed description of how perceptually isochronous sequences are organised)

requiring extra time to process. The high pitch maintains to some extent that the level of involvement displayed through the falsetto voice in lines 33–34, that is, the production of *oh* builds on the affect-laden delivery of the prior NTRI.

The rhythmic integration of the sound object can further be interpreted as an indication of a certain readiness to accept and acknowledge the repair (cf. (Heritage 1984). The fact that the rhythmic structure breaks off on the object's completion can be taken as contextualising the object's function as a repair receipt that locally closes down the repair sequence. The sound object ratifies the repair and at the same time treats it as running counter to previous assumptions. This epistemic orientation in combination with high affective involvement makes it come off as a 'surprised' repair receipt.

The long pause which follows marks an uptake by the other speaker as noticeably absent. We see that the *oh*-producer orients towards this silence by resuming with her talk in the next line (line 43). She offers more details concerning Mary's allergy and thus adds topical talk on the content of repair, which can be treated as a final alignment with and agreement to the repair (cf. Selting (1996) for a similar observation in post-astonishment contexts). Given that the talk prior to the repair was characterised by disagreement, the post-repair context shows interactional moves oriented towards seeking agreement and consensus (cf. also lines 49–50 with the tag question signalling an allocation of epistemic authority to Leslie).

To sum up, 'extra high and pointed' *oh* can serve as a 'surprised' repair receipt in response to repairs which clarify some kind of incongruity occurring in the other speaker's telling. It treats the repair as running counter to prior assumptions but accepts it readily and in an affiliative way. In retrospect, the affect-laden production of such *oh*s can further be interpreted as building on the affect-laden framing of the repair initiator.

In turn expansion, the repair initiator can make a move which further thematises the previous topical talk. This can be seen as re-establishing agreement on the content of the topical talk, which was disputed through the initiation of repair.

6.4.2   Oh *as a repair receipt + subsequent other-speaker talk*

Alternatively to the same speaker's expanding the turn subsequent to the production of a 'surprised' repair receipt, the other speaker can take over the floor instead. Here similar moves can be observed to the effect that the speaker who performed the repair orients towards the display of 'surprise' by adding more detail to the content of the repair.

Excerpt 4 exemplifies this: Here the *oh*-producer treats the news teller's description of the tops she bought as incongruous. This becomes manifest in her

delivery of a "confused" next turn repair initiator (cf. Drew's (2005) analysis),
which, as in Excerpt 3, deals with a trouble in understanding. After the repair has
been conducted, the speaker then responds with an 'extra high and pointed' *oh*,
which can be interpreted as a display of 'surprise'. The topical talk is about Leslie's
successful shopping tour. Skip is Leslie's husband.

```
     (4)    [HOLT:M88:1:2] "outer wear tops"
1          Les:    i got some nice cotton ↓TOPS:.
2                  i'm not gonna [↑TELL skIp;
3          Lin:                  [↑Oh DID [↓you:,
4          Les:                            [.hhh ´`YE::S;
5                  <<all>i mEAnt (.) only to get one or TWO>?
6                  .hhh but they're?
7                  (.)
8                  you KNO:W,
9                  <<all>i mEAn if i stOck up NOW>;
10                 then i dOn't need to do it aGAIN,=
11                 =DO i; hhe [he he he
12         Lin:               [<<p>yEAh (that's) RI:GH[T>,
13         Les:                                       [.hhh YES;
14         Lin:    Oh (**)
15    →            <<len>OU:ter wear: tops> you mEAn,
16    →    Les:    .hhh well NO:;
17    →            sOme i can wEAr underNEATH:;
18    →    (Les):  h
19    →    Lin:    <<h, breathy>´`[ʔʌʊː]>; ((extra high and pointed))
20    →    Les:    you SEE:,
21    →            (they're) agAInst my SKIN:; h[h
22         Lin:                                 [<<nasal>´`[əʊ[:]>;
23         Les:                                          [.hh and
24                 SOME ↓i can wear on tOp.
```

The NTRI in lines 14–15 expands the news delivery sequence in lines 1–13. In
the news delivery sequence, the news teller (Leslie) announces to her interlocutor
(Linda) that she bought *some nice cotton ↓TOPS:*, a purchase which she is not going to tell her husband about. The recipient marks line 1 as news, but does not pick
up on line 2. The news mark (line 3, Maynard (1997) is produced in overlap with
part of line 2. Leslie orients towards the news mark by doing a confirmation (line
4), which is followed by an elaboration in the form of an account (lines 5–11).
The turn-final tag question and the laughter on post-completion (line 11) invite
agreement and laughter on the recipient's side. Yet Linda only receives this with
weak acknowledgement (line 12), which signals disaffiliation (Drew 2005: 177):

Leslie's production of a "post-confirmation confirmation" (line 13) gives back the floor; she thereby creates a slot where the recipient's lack of understanding of the news telling becomes visible (ibid: 177–178). This lack of understanding arises from an apparent incongruity in Leslie's description of the tops. However, it is open to conjecture why Linda does not understand Leslie's telling. According to Drew (2005: 178) the incongruity of the telling can be attributed to the fact that one does not normally stock up on clothes such as tops, because one wants to go with the fashion. Another interpretation is that the news recipient finds it hardly likely that the teller's husband will not notice her having purchased new clothes (Mirka Rauniomaa, p.c.).

The slot is filled by a repair initiation (lines 14–15). The inarticulate sounds audible after *Oh* can be treated as iconic of the 'confusion' arising from the incongruent telling.[63] This observation is deviant from Drew's (2005) account, according to which it is the NTRI as such which makes a state of 'confusion' manifest. Done as a candidate understanding and thus indicating what her best guess is, the NTRI makes the news recipient's commitment to certain assumptions visible and expects a confirmatory response.[64] Similar to Excerpt 3, it is accompanied by the display of a cognitive, if not affective state of mind.

The dispreferred turn shape (Pomerantz 1984, Schegloff 2007) of the following, disconfirming repair (lines 16–17) shows orientation to this: It is delayed (by filled pausing, line 16) and hedged (by a *well*-preface, line 16). This further indicates that the NTRI is treated as signalling strong commitment to what it proposed.

After a filled pause, which is probably Leslie's, the repair is receipted through an *oh*-token (line 19). The vowel quality of the sound object is diphthongal, with a glide from a retracted and opened mid central vowel to a vowel in the region of cardinal vowel 8 ([u]). Its prosody can be heard as high and pointed: The object has a lengthened, wide range rising-falling contour done with high global pitch.

The contour begins on an upper middle level in the speaker's pitch range (201 Hz), rises to a peak at the top of the speaker's range (354 Hz) and falls to a lower level (122 Hz). In addition, it is louder and pitched higher than the previous turn by the same speaker (cf. the acoustic analysis in Figure 4).

---

63. The instantiation of *oh* in line 14 will not be considered in my analysis of sound objects because it does not have prosodic prominence.

64. Heritage (1984: 319) treats such offers of candidate understandings as as subtype of repair initiation, which he calls understanding checks. He observes that responses to such understanding checks can be receipted in terms of the change of state-token *oh*.

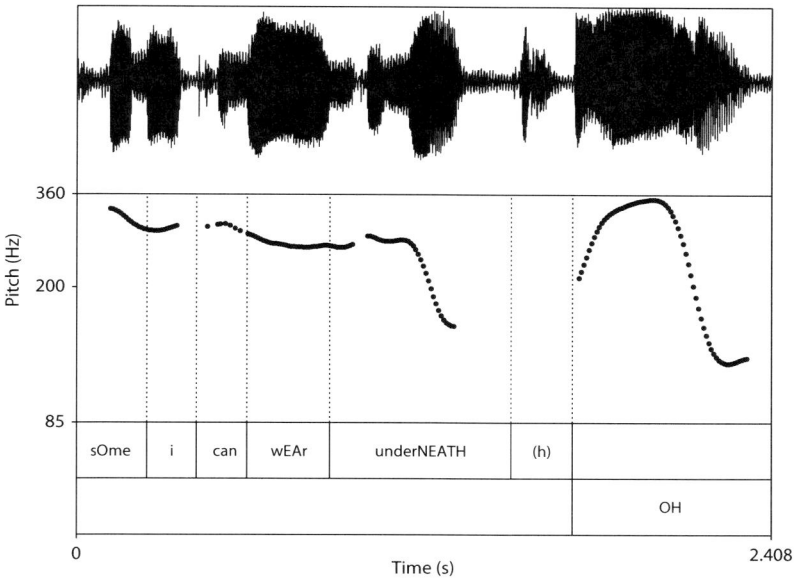

Figure 4. Acoustic analysis of Excerpt 4 ("outer wear tops"), lines 17–19

Further, the object is integrated in the rhythmic structure established from line 17 in Excerpt 4 as represented in Excerpt 4':

(4')   Rhythmic analysis of Excerpt 4 ("outer wear tops"), lines 16–22

```
1   Les:    .hhh well no:;
2           /sOme i can         /
3           /wEAr under         /
4           /NEATH:;=           /
5   (Les):  h
6   Lin:    /=<<h,breathy>´`[ʔʌʊ:]>; ((high and pointed))
7   Les:                    you/
8           /SEE:, (they're) agAInst my/
9           SKIN:; h[h
10  Lin:             [<<nasal>´`[əʊ[:]>;
```

Following the production of the *oh*-token in line 6, this rhythmic structure is terminated. This supports the view that the sound object serves as a repair receipt, ratifying the repair performed by other speaker.

Further, the diphthong is produced with an initial glottal stop. In terms of voice quality, the repair receipt is breathy, a property which is not regularly observed with such sound objects.

In sum, we can conclude that the object signals acknowledgement of the repair. On top of this, it orients towards the repair running counter to the speaker's original assumptions, which were made explicit in the NTRI (Excerpt 4, lines 14–15). Due to its unexpectedness, the information can be assumed to require more work processing and thus involves an increased level of information management. The lengthened, rising-falling contour can be taken as an indication of this. In addition, the high global pitch and the animated pitch movement can be understood as cueing heightened affective involvement on the part of the recipient. These two factors, a display of extra cognitive processing due to the unexpectedness of an informing, combined with a display of heightened involvement can be regarded as signals of 'surprise'.

Wilkinson and Kitzinger (2006) have found that surprise tokens are typically delayed. However, the sound object in the present example comes on the next beat, which constitutes the unmarked case of turn-transition (Couper-Kuhlen 1993: 126–127).

Further, lines 20–24 indicate that *oh* does not terminate the repair sequence. Instead, the news teller treats the repair receipt as signalling that more information is needed. After making an appeal to the recipient's understanding (lines 20), the news teller adds another piece of information which clarifies the nature of the tops in question (line 21). That the tops are meant to be worn against her skin may explain why Leslie has bought a larger quantity of them: She has skin problems and the tops she can wear may be hard to get. In line 22, another *oh*-token is delivered, however not with 'extra high and pointed' prosody. This instance will be discussed below.

Selting (1996) has shown that 'astonished' repair initiations can be oriented to by further interactional work on the affective display. We have seen that is what happens here as well: The repair sequence is further expanded and the display of 'surprise' is dealt with in that more detail concerning the repairable is provided.

To sum up, 'extra high and pointed' *oh* can be used to signal 'surprise' in repair receipts. Repair sequences of this kind are elicited through a NTRI which addresses some trouble in understanding, displaying a certain cognitive/affective state of mind. 'Extra high and pointed' *oh* acknowledges the repair but makes visible that the content of the repair runs counter to previous assumptions; it is treated with a display of heightened affective involvement. Unlike non-affect-laden change-of-state tokens, a 'surprised' repair receipt can invite a further work-up of what was claimed in the repair.

We have seen that *oh* with extra high and pointed pitch can implement an affect-laden repair receipt in response to a turn that repairs some incongruity in a prior news telling. On post-completion, either the *oh*-producer can expand the turn or the other speaker takes the floor. The structure of the sequence can be described as follows:

A: incongruent news telling
B: initiation of repair (dealing with a trouble in understanding and displaying a cognitive/affect-laden state of mind)
A: repair
B: affect-laden repair receipt
A/B: further addition to content of repair/news telling

The repair runs counter to the inferences that the *oh*-producer made on the basis of the incongruent news telling. She thus treats the repair as unexpected, requiring extra time to process and inviting heightened involvement. This cluster of cognitive-affective dimensions can be labelled as a display of 'surprise'.

In the analysis presented, we argued for 'surprise' being contextualised through a lengthened, extra-high, rising-falling contour on *oh* in response to a repair which was initiated due to some incongruity in the other speaker's telling. However, not all repair receipts with a rising-falling contour can be found to display 'surprise'. The next section shows that 'surprise' must be regarded as a matter of degree and that prosodic cues, because of their gradient nature, are particularly well suited to contextualise cognitive-affective dimensions because they may not always be so clear-cut.

6.4.3   *The rise-fall revisited: 'Surprise', a matter of degree*
The previous discussion has illustrated that recipients can use 'extra high and pointed' *oh* (pronounced as [əʊː] or its variant [ʌʊː]) in order to perform 'surprised' repair receipts. It was found that in sequential environments, where repair is initiated in orientation towards an incongruity in the news teller's talk, the prosodic shape of *oh* can be heard as lengthened, extra high and produced with a wide ranging rise-fall. These prosodic cues in connection to a specific context were interpreted as displaying 'surprise'.

We wish to argue, however, that it is a matter of degree whether an *oh*-object which serves as a repair receipt is perceived as a display of 'surprise': When a rising-falling *oh* has a lower onset and/or comes in a lower register, it is no longer heard as 'surprised' but as a slow registering of unknown, unexpected information. Moreover, the analysis shows that sound objects are not *per se* affect-laden but may, depending on their prosodic-phonetic packaging and sequential positioning, display a range of cognitive-affective processes.

Yang (2006) makes a similar observation for Mandarin Chinese *oh*:

Our data show that the high degree of uncertainty inherent in intense surprise causes a high rise in pitch, [...] whereas a sharper and narrower arch shape indicates the presence of surprise with co-occurring emotions, as [...] great amazement [...] and horror. A lower pitch range often reflects acceptance and registering of information, with a lesser degree of surprise [...], and a matter of fact acceptance of information that offers little challenge to the speaker's knowledge state causes the pattern of nearly flat pitch slopes [...]. Emotions that are closely related to acceptance, such as sympathy and approval, also tend to be expressed in a low pitch level.   (Yang 2006: 280)

The prosodic contour of the sound object thus represents a finely tuned tool to display subtle cognitive-affective dimensions. Similarly, Aijmer (2002) on English points to *oh* (and *ah*) indicating a speaker's "arriving at a realisation" (ibid: 113), without, however, making the link to the prosodic contextualisation of the display. She states that such *ohs* (and *ahs*) often come in overlap (ibid: 114).

Excerpt 5 is an example of a case where *oh* displays a slow registering of the repair turn it responds to. It sets in where Excerpt 4 ("outer wear tops") left off. Here Leslie complains that she could not get any cotton petticoats or slips on a recent shopping tour.

```
    (5)   [HOLT:M88:1:2] "polyester mostly"
1          Les:   .hh but the ↑thIng was i cOUldn't get uhm: ⊙
2                 i couldn't get a (.) cotton: (-) petticoat or (.)
3                 k? cotton SLIP;
4                 ↑ANywhere;
5    →    Lin:   COUL[Dn't you[:,
6    →    Les:       [.hhh     [NO;
7    →           they're all this polyESter mOstly,
8                 .h[hh
9    →    Lin:     [[!] ´`[ʌʊ[:].
10         Les:                  [so ↑in the end i bought a whIte hh
11                cotton SKIRT;=
12                =and i hOpe it won't be too FULL;=
13                i'll just have to SEE.h .hh
14   →    Lin:   ´`[əʊː];
15   →           ´`YES.
16   →           <<l>THERE's a point>,
17         Les:   YES. .hh
18                ↑ANYway;
19                (.)
20                SO:- hh
21                there we ↑ARE?
```

We find two instances of rising-falling sound objects in the example.

The first instance of *oh* receipts a repair which is embedded in a news tell-ing which implements a complaint: The complaint about not being able to get a cotton petticoat or a cotton slip (lines 1–4) constitutes the first turn in a new sequence. The high onset in line 1 contextualises the turn as a 'new beginning' (Couper-Kuhlen 2004b). It is responded to with a NTRI (line 5). Here the NTRI signals strong disbelief on the part of the recipient. In return, the complaint is confirmed and elaborated on by a specification of the complainable (lines 6–7).

This is receipted with an alveolar click (cf. Chapter 9 for the function of clicks in complaint sequences). The *oh*-token which follows acknowledges the com-plaint as informative, while at the same time treating it as running counter to the recipient's expectations. In terms of its prosodic-phonetic form, it is similar to instances of *oh* displaying 'surprise', except for its pitch: The object is extremely lengthened, has a rising-falling contour and is performed with slightly lower vol-ume than the preceding talk by the same speaker. In contrast to *oh* doing 'sur-prise', it is, however, produced with a remarkably lower register, which prevents the object from coming off as 'extra high and pointed': Its onset is located in the lower part of the speaker's voice range (at 164 Hz), followed by a long upwards glide to mid (peak at 233 Hz) and a long gliding fall to low (116 Hz) (cf. Figure 5 for an acoustic analysis of the sound object).

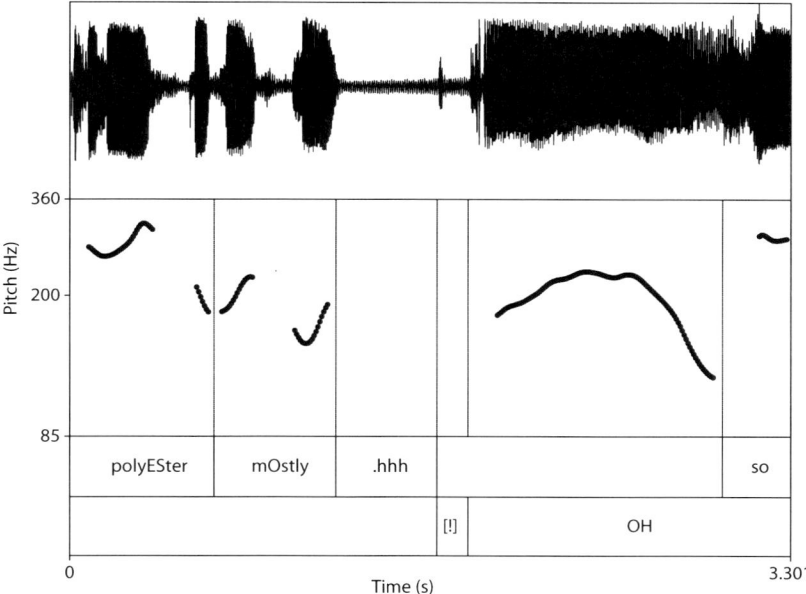

Figure 5. Acoustic analysis of Excerpt 5 ("Polyester mostly"), lines 7–10

Because of its location in the lower and mid parts of the speaker's voice range, and because of the long gliding rise, the token does not come off as signalling the same kind of involvement as 'extra high and pointed' *oh* but is perceived as performing something slightly different than 'surprise': It seems to be doing a kind of slow realisation and signalling that extra time is needed for processing this information. The display could be paraphrased as "I didn't expect what you told me but I see what you mean".[65] This kind of understanding is confirmed by the data: the complainer does not expand on the content of line 7 but moves on to the next event in her news report.

Further, just as in the instances of 'surprised' *oh* discussed above, the *oh* examined here does not signal affiliation in the sense that it appreciates the negative loading of the informing nor does it perform a co-complaint. Thus, instead of displaying 'indignation' as would be made relevant on the part of the recipient in complaint sequences, the repair simply ratifies the 'informational' side of the repair, namely that slips and petticoats are mostly made of polyester.

The complainer next delivers a concluding turn, conveying a solution to her shopping dilemma. Again the recipient responds with a rising-falling *oh* in lower pitch. It can be heard as a similar object to the one in line 9, yet with shorter duration (cf. Figure 6).

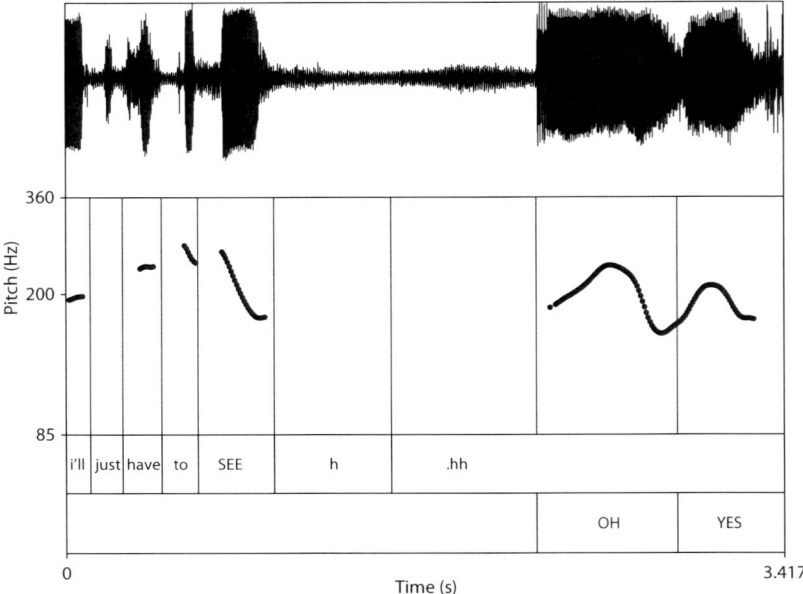

Figure 6. Acoustic analysis of Excerpt 5 ("Polyester mostly"), lines 13–15

---

65. In contrast, displays of 'surprise' as analysed in Excerpts 3 and 4 could be paraphrased as "I didn't expect what you told me and I don't see exactly what you mean".

Again, the object acknowledges the complainer's turn and signals a slow process-ing of unknown, newsworthy information.[66] The turn expansion is concordant with such an interpretation: The following idiom *<<l>THERE's a point>*, (line 16) once more makes the running cognitive process of understanding visible and thus provides a verbalised indication of the recipient's orientation to the referential information and of the absence of affective, affiliative involvement.

To conclude, recipients can receipt repairs with a low-pitched rising-falling *oh*, which displays a slow registering and realisation of what is treated as un-known, unexpected information. In activities such as complaining, where af-filiation is made relevant on the part of the recipient, such displays of cognitive registering can be used to avoid or defer actions of affiliation and agreement. The complainer's closing actions in lines 17–21 support such an interpretation: The 'frustration' signalled there can be taken as resulting from the recipient's lack of affective responses to her complaints. On the other hand, it can be argued that the sequential environment analysed in Excerpt 5 does not prepare for displays of 'surprise' because the repair sequence is not generated by an incongruous telling of the kind e.g. observed in Excerpt 4 ("outer wear tops").

As to the prosodic contextualisation of 'surprise', it can be concluded that a rising-falling contour alone does not accomplish 'surprise' but that it is a cluster of prosodic properties which cues such an interpretation. Thus, the controversy about the rising-falling contour and its association with 'surprise' seems to be grounded in the assumption that the rise-fall is a signal of expectation problems, which are then equated with 'surprise'. But as we have seen, problems of expecta-tion can be conveyed in a fashion which suggests the operation of cognitive pro-cesses rather than of affective states.

6.5   Affect-laden *oh* in response to news

The next sections will be concerned with the use of 'extra high and pointed' *oh* as a recipient response in a different kind of activity: news delivery sequences. We will first examine the case of 'extra high and pointed' *oh* plus turn expansion (Section 6.5.1) and then turn to sound objects of this kind with other-speaker talk following (Section 6.5.2).

6.5.1   Oh *as a news response + turn expansion*
News responses in the form of extra high and pointed *oh* which are followed by a turn expansion are rare in the corpus. The corpus contains a number of

---

66. Note that *oh* comes before the acknowledgement token *YES* in line 15.

cases of high pitched, *oh*-prefaced news marks in which *oh* forms a high pitched contour together with other elements following. However, *oh* on an *independent* 'extra high and pointed' contour plus a turn expansion is not as readily found in this position. One explanation for this may be that the sequential position of news responses is reserved for highly conventionalised recipient responses which are not usually characterised by a prosody signalling heightened affective involvement.

Excerpt 6 represents an example of a news response done in terms of an 'oh-plus partial repeat' (Maynard 1997). It comes in two units with *oh* coming first, forming an independent contour.

```
    (6)   [HOLT 1:8] "over long since"
1           Mum:   have you been busy this WEEK?
2           Les:   .hh yes i HAVE been busy;=
3     →            =katherine's had uh .h kEIth to STAY?
4                  (--)
5     →     Mum:   so oh is it KEiTH uh-
6     →     Les:   REDgrave,
7     →     Mum:   <<hh>^[əʊː]>; ((extra high and pointed))
8     →            DID she?
9                  (-)
10          Les:   Y[ES,
11          Mum:    [<<smile>i thought that was over ↑LONG since>;
12                 hi[hi
13          Les:     [<<hh> well yes but he's still a `FRIEN[D>?
14          Mum:                                          [yes GOOD;
15          Les:   he's got a girlfrien:d in uhm (.)
16                 EDinborough,
```

In line 1 the news delivery sequence is occasioned, which – after a confirmation (line 2) – leads to a news announcement in line 3. Because of some uncertainty regarding the object in the announcement turn, Keith, Mum initiates repair next (line 5). The repair is performed in line 6 by the news teller. It is receipted with a sound object *oh* which is delivered in an 'extra high and pointed' tone of voice and on an independent contour.[67] In the next line the recipient expands her turn with a 'partial repeat' (line 8). The syntactic shape of the pro-form makes reference to the content of the news announcement (Katherine had Keith to stay) and not to the wording of the NTRI (Is it Keith).

---

67. Due to the poor quality of the recording, no acoustic analysis is possible.

For this reason it can be argued that the turn is doing two things when examined in real time: first receipting the repair and then receipting the announcement as news. But the news teller responds only to the news receipt, with a confirmatory response in line 10 (cf. Wilkinson and Kitzinger (2006) on such minimal confirmations of surprise sources), ignoring the 'extra high and pointed' repair receipt. The *oh*-producer's account which comes next (line 11) provides evidence that the 'extra high and pointed' *oh* is produced in a position where conflicting assumptions must be dealt with. We can thus treat Mum's initial response (line 7, if not line 8) as a display of 'surprise'. As can be seen by the confirmation and account in lines 13 and the informing in lines 15–16, the news teller orients towards this account in what follows rather than elaborating on the news announced in line 3. This suggests that 'extra high and pointed' *oh* plus turn expansion may be an uncommon choice in response to news because the implications of a 'surprised' display override the sequential relevancies (i.e. an elaboration of the news) set up by the partial repeat in the turn expansion (see Section 6.5.2 for further evidence of this point).

This observation and the lack of other, more straightforward examples in this position may explain why extra high and pointed *oh* on an independent contour plus turn expansion is not a common practice when responding to news. On the other hand, the analysis makes the hybrid nature of news marks visible: '*oh* plus partial repeat' represents an *oh*-prefaced next turn repair initiator which forms a practice to encourage more talk on the news. If it is realised in two TCUs, two actions are formed, which may make different orientations relevant.

To come to the next section, the production of 'extra high and pointed' *oh* with subsequent other-speaker talk is more frequent in the present corpus. Its delivery can be elicited through the specific rhetorical design of the prior news telling. Here a regular case is contrasted with an exceptional one, which prepares for a 'surprised' response. The following section examines such instances.

6.5.2   Oh *as a news response + subsequent other-speaker talk*

Recipients can deploy *oh* with an extra high and pointed pitch contour in response to a news announcement which is presented as exceptional and unusual by the news teller. The news announcement is thus treated not only as newsworthy but as extraordinary.

According to Wilkinson and Kitzinger (2006), displays of 'surprise' in response to news of this kind constitute resources for "displaying cultural, subcultural, and category memberships" (ibid: 173): "These displays of surprise show what co-members treat as unexpected, exceptional, or unusual [...], and thereby what they take to be expected, unexceptional, or business as usual." (ibid: 173)

Our analysis adds an interactional linguistic angle to such a view: We agree that rather than merely being grounded in the *oh*-producer's cultural assumptions, their production shows an orientation to the rhetorical and linguistic design of the news which prepares for a 'surprised' uptake. The rhetorical pattern can be described as follows: First a general case is stated. Then an event or state-of-affairs is formatted as unusual or exceptional. In the data, this pattern is constructed in terms of a sequence including a pre-announcement (general case) and a piece of news treated as the announcement of the news (exceptional case). The response is done through the production of an 'extra high and pointed' *oh* whose prosodic form makes such an understanding interactionally available: Invited by the announcement of an exceptional piece of news, the sound object is interpreted as a 'surprised' response. Such a display is, however, treated as premature: the news teller deletes its implications by continuing with their previous activity in the post-production context, without dealing with the implications of the display of 'surprise' response, a practice that has been documented for recipients of 'surprised' news receipts (cf. Section 6.5). It will be argued that the news teller deletes the trajectory of the *oh*-receipt precisely *because* it makes an orientation to 'surprise' relevant and thereby potentially interferes with the conversational project undertaken by the news teller.

Alternatively, the rhetorical pattern (regular case – exceptional case) can be used to construct the point of a news telling. Here the 'extra high and pointed' *oh* is deployed in a position where the final evaluation and appreciation of the news sequence has been made relevant on the part of the recipient.

We will first examine two excerpts where the rhetorical pattern occurs in the pre-announcement and announcement (Section 6.5.2.1) and then turn to an excerpt where it builds up to the point of the news telling (Section 6.5.2.2).

6.5.2.1 *Pre-announcement – announcement – oh.* Excerpt 7 illustrates the use of 'extra high and pointed' *oh* as a news response particularly well: In this telephone conversation between Mark and his cousin's husband Dwayne, Mark is told that Dwayne's son sprained his hamstrings. Lines 1–2 close off an extended sequence of sequences about Mark's family, with line 2 finally soliciting talk about Dwayne's family.

```
    (7)   [HOLT:M88:2:1] "hamstrings"
1         Mar:   .hhh so uh ↑yeah we're All- (-)
2                <<all>pretty good> and your LOT? h
3    →    Dwa:   ↑yes uh [all are
4         Mar:          [.hhh
5                (--)
```

```
 6   →   Dwa:    very WELL,=
 7               =and UH:-
 8               (1.44)
 9   →   Dwa:    at the moment DONald's uh:
10   →           sprained a couple of uh
11               <<all,p>↓WHAT is it dOnald>?
12               (1.15)
13   →   Dwa:    HAMstrIngs;
14   →           and in[stEAd  of
15       (D's son):   [(pulled)
16   →   Mar:            [<<h>´`[ʔəʊː]>; ((extra high and pointed))
17               (-)
18   →   Dwa:    instead of straining ↓ONE,
19               he's he's done ↑BOTH of them:;
20               (-)
21       Mar:    [↑OH heck;
22       Dwa:    [(that's) why he's
23       Mar:    what was he DOing then; h
```

Here the *oh*-token (line 16) responds to the news that the Dwayne's son has sprained/strained his hamstrings (lines 9–10, 13). The announcement is solicited through a 'news inquiry' (Maynard 1997:95) (line 2). Again, the news receipted by the *oh*-token is working on a contrast to a previous conversational object: In lines 3 and 6, the news teller states that *all are very WE:LL* and then goes on to announce that his son sprained his hamstrings (lines 9–10, 13), an event which implies the opposite of well-being. Even if *very WE:LL* can be treated as a routine to the "how-are-you" enquiry in line 2, the announcement about the son's injury is still in contrast to the news recipient's positive concluding assessment about his own family (lines 1–2). In that sense well-being is opposed to being injured, and the news teller's family is opposed to a single member of it. It is thus a news announcement which presents the unusual case, which is receipted by *oh*.

The sound object has 'extra high and pointed' prosody. The token acknowledges the prior informing as informative, with the rise-fall indexing an orientation to it as unexpected. The animated pitch movement and extra high pitch are treated as displays of heightened involvement. The high volume is further taken as an additional cue for heightened involvement (cf. the acoustic analysis in Figure 7 below). Although produced in overlap, the F0 trace is clearly visible because of the intensity with which the object is delivered.

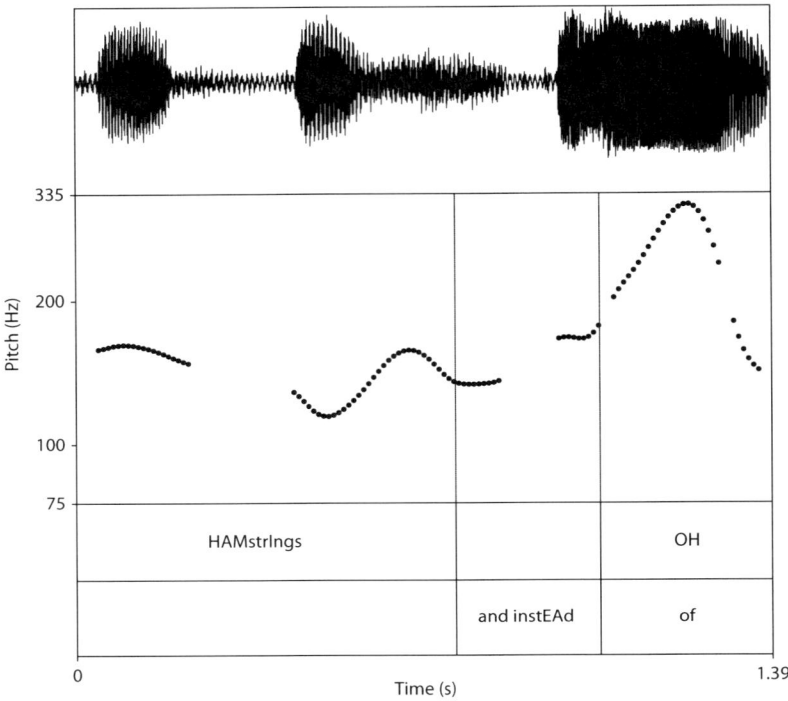

Figure 7. Acoustic analysis of Excerpt 7 ("hamstrings"), lines 13–16

The unexpectedness with which the news is treated, and the high involvement displayed, warrant an analysis of the object as showing 'surprise'.

Further, the news response comes rhythmically delayed. Consider Excerpt 7':

    (7')   Rhythmic analysis of Excerpt 7 ("hamstrings"), lines 9–17

```
1   Dwa:   at the ↑mOment Donald's uh:
2          sprained a couple of uh
3          <<all,p>↓WHAT is it dOnald>?
4          (1.15)
5   Dwa:   /HAM              /
6          /strIngs;    and in /
7          /[stEAd [of
8  (D):    /[(pulled)
9   Mar:          /[<<h>´`[ʔəʊ:]>;
10         (-)
```

The delay with which the *oh*-response is timed may be taken as iconic of the extra time needed for the processing of the news. Unlike in repair sequences, where the recipient may anticipate unforeseen contents in the repair turn, exceptional news may not be as readily accepted.

In addition, the news response comes in overlap with the next TCU produced by the news teller, with the TCU being briefly broken off on the production of the sound object. After a noticeable absence of talk (Excerpt 7, line 17), the news teller resumes the TCU on a restart in which parts of the TCU are recycled. In contrast to the repair sequences analysed above, the talk subsequent to the display of 'surprise' shows no orientation towards its affective quality. Instead, the activity is continued at the point where the news telling was disrupted by the 'surprised' display: This kind of sequence-expansion is not only displayed on the action level but also lexico-syntactically: On post-production of the sound object, the news teller returns to the syntactic point where the sound object came in and, recycling the lexical material he used, links up to where his TCU left off. What is more, the recycled version presents his son's injury in an even more dramatic fashion (lines 18–19). What was conveyed by the adjective *a couple* in line 10 is now emphatically formulated in a contrastive construction (note also the contrastive accent on *both* in line 19). In this fashion, the news teller deletes the trajectory of the 'surprised' display, which makes some kind of account or additional explication relevant. The deletion allows the teller to carry on with his news telling and keep his momentary rights as primary speaker.[68]

Excerpt 8 is another good example of such a sequence, which works in a similar fashion.

```
(8)  [HOLT:X(C)1:1:1] "export award"
1       Les:    it's ↑good that i've dOne most of my christmas
2    →          shopping cause poor old mark's wOrking
3               most SATurday[s,
4       Mum:                 [YES,
5               (--)
6       Mum:    HM;
7               (---)
8    →  Les:    .hh b[ut ↑nEx:t (-) THURSday,
9       Mum:         [(*)
10   →  Les:    he has to go to yeov uhm (-)BRIStol;
11              (--)
12   →  Les:    they've ↑pUt in: to wIn=uhm (1.38)
```

---

68. Line 21 shows another affect-laden recipient response, yet this time in terms of an *oh*-prefaced formula (see below for an analysis).

```
13  →           an ↑EXport awArd;
14              (-)
15  →  Mum:     <<h>´`[əʊː]>; ((extra high and pointed))
16     Les:     AND uhm:-
17              (-)
18              he's ↑bEEn invited to a dinner at the city HA:LL;
                ((turn continues))
```

The news teller initiates the news delivery sequence by making a 'pre-announce-ment' (Maynard 1997: 95) (lines 1–3). A continuer (line 4) in the function of a 'go-ahead token' (Maynard 1997: 95) yields the floor for further telling. After some silence (lines 5 and 7), the teller finally comes forward with a piece of news (lines 8–13). It links up to the pre-announcement in terms of the connective "but" and is thus framed as being in contrast to what was stated before. Mark's working most Saturdays is opposed to him going to Bristol for an export award. Business as usual is contrasted with an unusual event. 'Sympathy' for Mark ("poor old Mark") is contrasted with a more positive stance.

The recipient responds to this piece of news with the production of an instance of 'extra high and pointed' *oh*. As in the example analysed above (Excerpt 7), the news response comes in rhythmically delayed (cf. Excerpt 8'):

> (8')   Rhythmic analysis of Excerpt 8 ("export award"), lines 12–16

```
1   Les:   they've ↑pUt in: to wIn=uhm (1.38) an
2          /↑EXport a         /
3          /wArd;
4                            (-)/
5   Mum:              /<<h>´`[əʊː]>;
6   Les:   AND uhm:-
```

The prosodic design of the *oh*-token indicates that it treats the news as informa-tive and as unusual. Pitchwise, it, however, does not match the prosodic make-up of the informing it receipts, which is done in rather low register.[69] This suggests that the *oh*-receipt comes off as premature: It displays heightened involvement at a piece of news in a position where such an affective display occasions a tele-scoping or changing of the news delivery sequence. In the data, the display of 'surprise' seems to make a shift in topical talk relevant, which may not be desired by the news teller (cf. Heritage (1984: 345, footnote 21) for a similar observation with regard to 'sympathy' *oh*). Instead of allowing the teller to develop the news sequence, the display requires a specific kind of subsequent interactional work,

---

69. Due to the poor quality of the recording, no acoustic analysis can be provided for this excerpt.

that is, for example a more detailed account of the surprise source (i.e. Mark's firm having put in an export award).

As in Excerpt 7, the news teller does not respond to the 'surprised' nature of the news response in what follows: In not dealing with the 'surprise' the sound object displays, the news teller deletes the implication of such a recipient response. Instead, she resumes her current activity: Through *AND uhm:*, she signals a return to her news telling (Local 2004) and continues with the next point on her agenda (Excerpt 8, lines 16–18).

To sum up, news recipients can deploy 'extra high and pointed' *oh* in order to receipt an announcement which presents a piece of news, as opposed to the general case, as exceptional and unusual. In this sense, the news teller's contrasting of the regular case to the exceptional one generates a display of 'surprise' by the news recipient. The sequential structure is designed as follows:

A: pre-announcement: regular case
B/A: continuer/pausing
A: news announcement: exceptional case
B: affect-laden acknowledgement of the news
A: expansion of the news telling

The prosodic cluster with which the 'surprised' *oh* is produced when functioning as a news response is similar to the repair receipts we examined above. Rhythmically, the news response tends to be, however, delayed. Couper-Kuhlen (2007a) points out that the pause preceding the surprise token iconically indicates a relationship between the lengthened duration of cognitive processes and the production of speech. In addition, it can be analysed as iconic of the missing alignment (Couper-Kuhlen 1993) between the news teller's and the news recipient's actions, which were shown to become visible on the turn-constructional level as well.

On post-production of the sound object, the 'surprise' displayed is not dealt with. Instead, the news teller resumes their activity where it was left off, which amounts to a deletion of the trajectory of the 'surprised' display. It was argued that the news teller does not perform the extra interactional work made relevant because it may jeopardise her/his own conversational project. To ignore the *oh*-receipt allows the teller to keep primary speaker rights and to continue with their telling.

6.5.2.2 *News telling* – oh. 'Extra high and pointed' *oh* can not only be used in order to receipt an exceptional piece of news in the beginning of a news delivery sequence but also to respond to the point of a news telling. Again, the receipt appears somewhat inappropriate since it comes in a place where an evaluative appreciation of the news telling is invited.

Excerpt 9 presents an example of such a case: The excerpt contains a news delivery sequence between two cousins Hillary and Mark. In the talk prior to the excerpt, not shown here, Hillary has elicited talk about Mark's (grown-up) children. Following some talk about his elder daughter, Mark shifts to talk about his son Gordon, who is currently taking his A-levels. In line 1, Hillary asks about Gordon's study plans.

```
(9)    [HOLT:M88:2:4] "Portsmouth Poly"
1      Hil:   [(what does he want to do has he) any iDEA?=
2      Mar:   [((YAWN))
3             =AR:chitecture; h
4      Hil:   does he R[EALl[y;
5      Mar:            [.hh [YEA:H-=
6             =he's gOt a poSITion;=
7             =he's gOt a? .hhhh
8             If he gets the right GRADes this is-
9   →         he's got an ↑Offer in NEWcastle,
10            (---)
11  →         er: and an ↑Offer in SHEFfie:ld,
12            (.)
13     Hil:   yea:[h,
14     Mar:       [All my kids seem to wanna go NO:RTH,=
15            m:? (.) <<all>gO away as far as POSsible>;
16            <<all>(i wonder) what it IS>,
17            sOmething i SAID perhaps,
18            h[hh
19     Hil:    [ye(h)ah,
20     Mar:   A:ND=uh:-
21            OR:-
22            (.)
23  →         u? pOrtsmouth ↑POLy; h
24            (-)
25  →   Hil:  <<h>´`[əʊ:]>; ((extra high and pointed))
26            (--)
27     Mar:   SO: uhm:[:
28     Hil:          [you'd rAther like portsmouth POLy [of course?
29     Mar:                                             [.hhh NO:;=
30            =i don't KNOW, ((turn continues))
```

The news delivery sequence is occasioned by a news enquiry about Gordon's study plans, which are announced in line 3. The recipient responds with a display of ritualised disbelief (line 4): The news mark solicits an elaboration of the news. Following a brief confirmation, the news teller names the universities where his son has been offered a place in a list (lines 9, 11, 23). Lists usually come with a three-part structure and a typical 'list intonation' (cf. Couper-Kuhlen (1986), Jefferson (1990), Selting (2003) for list construction). It is the last item in the list, *portsmouth POLy*, that is receipted with a sound object (line 25).

The first two items in the list present universities situated in the North of England (lines 9, 11). This is thematised by the news teller in terms of a jocular parenthetical sequence (lines 14–17) in list expansion (cf. Selting (2003: 31), which is "inserted *between* TCUs in a multi-unit turn" (Mazeland 2007: 1819, emphasis in the original, for a turn-constructional classification of parenthetical sequences).

In this sequence, the news teller addresses the fact that his son – along with his elder daughter – seems to want go North, i.e. to accept an offer from a university located several hundred miles from his parents' home (lines 14–15). *NO: RTH* can be treated as an explicit summary of the commonalities between the first two list members *NEWcastle* and *SHEFfie:ld*. Lines 14–15 are further constructed in terms of two extreme case formulations. First, the use of the quantifier *All* in the NP *All my kids* relates the intention of going north with the maximum number of experiencers (here Mark's children) possible. Second, the meaning of *NO: RTH* is specified in terms of *as far as POSsible*, a phrase, which defines *NO:RTH* as being located at a maximum distance from Mark's home. At this point in the interaction, the jocular parenthesis is backward-looking, that is, it refers to the previous two list items. At the same time, it establishes a frame of expectation as to where the last item to be named is located. This frame of expectation can be paraphrased as "all of Mark's children go North and away as far as possible". The news teller next names the third item on his list, *pOrtsmouth ↑POLy* (line 23). In contrast to the other two towns, Portsmouth lies much closer. It is situated in the South of England and even south of the speaker's home. It is this Southern and close location which qualifies *pOrtsmouth ↑POLy* as an exceptional list member, whose contents run counter to the expectations set up by the news teller. Jefferson (1990: 79) observes that third list members are frequently used to solicit 'surprise': "Third list members may also be the locus of special work; e.g., the expectable sameness provided by the adequate representivity feature exploited to design for 'surprise', 'punchline', etc.".

Both aspects ('surprise' and punch line) are present here: First of all, the last list member is constructed as the point of the telling. Secondly, the recipient treats the last list member as counter to her expectations with an extra high and pointed *oh* (line 25). The object is accompanied by a prosodic cluster similar to that of the sound objects examined in Excerpts 7 ("hamstrings") and 8 ("export award"): It is slightly lengthened and has a rising-falling contour, which starts from a high onset, rises to extra high and falls to low (cf. Figure 8). Further, it comes with higher pitch and higher volume than the same speaker's prior talk. The lengthening can be seen as iconic of the extra time needed to process the last list item. The rising-falling contour is treated as orienting towards the unexpectedness of this piece of information, since the nature of the last list item deviates from what was made expectable in the list expansion. Furthermore, the extra high pitch signals heightened involvement. This analysis is further supported by the acoustic analysis shown in Figure 8.

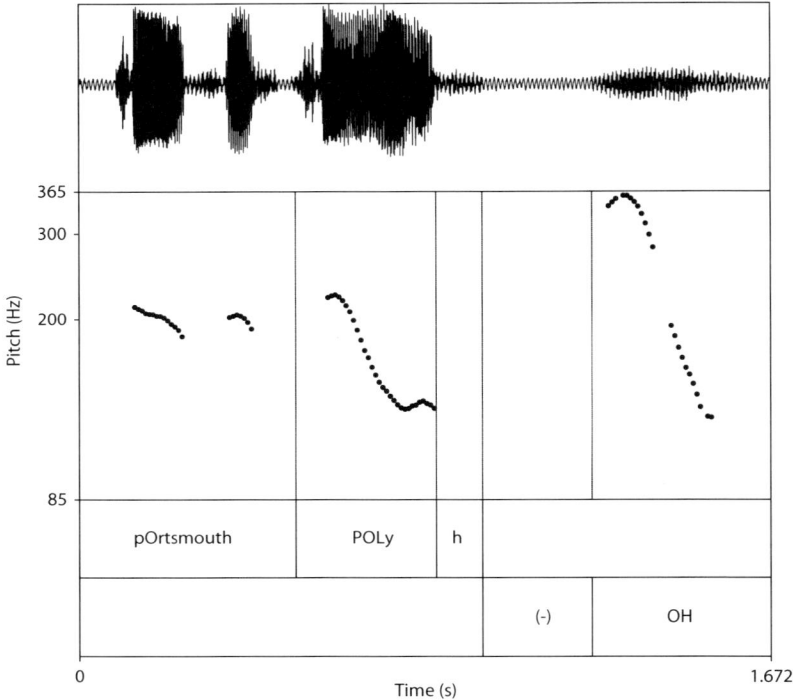

Figure 8. Acoustic analysis of Excerpt 9 ("Portsmouth Poly"), lines 23–25

In addition, the object is again produced with some rhythmic delay as is reflected in the rhythmic transcription below:

(9') Rhythmic analysis of Excerpt 9 ("Portsmouth Poly"), lines 23–25

```
1   Mar:       /pOrtsmouth    /
2              /↑POLy; h
3                          (-) /
4   Hil:          /<<h>´`[əʊː]>;
```

This can be seen as another indication of the unexpectedness with which the last list item was received. The bundle of prosodic properties described and the sequential positioning following a piece of news, which was rhetorically set up as exceptional and therefore comes unexpectedly, contextualise the *oh*-token as a display of 'surprise'.

In terms of its interactional function, the *oh*-receipt acknowledges the last list item. In addition, it takes an epistemic stance to the content of the TCU by treating it as exceptional. In this way, it marks a functional contrast to the 'neutral' acknowledgement tokens (Excerpt 9, lines 13 and 19). However, it does not do the evaluative work made relevant at the boundaries of news elaborations. According to Maynard (1997), news delivery sequences are terminated by the recipient's final assessment of the news. When we examine how the sequence develops, we see that unlike Excerpts 7 ("hamstrings") and 8 ("export award"), the news teller does not resume his activity: Following some silence, he produces a 'trail-off' (Local and Walker 2005) in line 27. Here the "postcompletion 'So'" (Jefferson 1978b: 246, endnote 13) proposes sequence-closing by making a "request for a recipient comment" (ibid: 231, cf. also Raymond (2004).

In line 28 an evaluation is still not forthcoming. Instead, the *news recipient* resumes with topical talk soliciting an evaluative work-up of the news sequence through the news teller (lines 29–30) (for further discussion see Section 6.6 below).

To sum up, news tellers can use the rhetoric pattern regular case – exceptional case to construct the point of their news telling and in this way occasion a display of 'surprise'. In terms of sequential position and action this rhetoric pattern implements the elaboration of the news. In this way, the responsive 'extra high and pointed' *oh* is placed in a slot where recipient assessment of the news is made relevant (Maynard 1997). The specific list structure in the example additionally makes an (affective) recipient response relevant.

The display of 'surprise' realised by the sound object further acknowledges and marks the news telling as exceptional but does not signal an evaluative stance to it: It does not ascribe a valence to the news teller's talk. For this reason, 'extra high and pointed' *oh* does not carry out a preferred recipient response in this position.

The next section discusses the implications of this finding in more detail: It is concerned with the interactional pay-off gained by using 'surprised' *oh*s as a recipient resource.

6.6   Interactional pay-off of 'extra high and pointed' *oh*: Is 'surprise' a full-fledged emotion?

The question why speakers use 'surprised' *oh* as a repair receipt and as a news response can best be approached when asking what such sound objects convey: As we have seen, 'extra high and pointed' *oh*s treat other speaker's repair or news as unexpected and/or exceptional and with heightened involvement: They can orient towards some kind of incongruity in the prior talk and/or to the exceptionality of the news presented. In terms of sequence-organisation, 'surprised' repair receipts acknowledge the repair, while inviting more talk on the contents of the repair and delaying a return to the base sequence. On the other hand, 'surprised' news responses, which receipt news announcements, are deleted and do not change the trajectory of the news delivery sequence. It follows that depending on the placement of the 'surprised' display, (other) speakers may orient towards the implications of the 'surprised' display or not.

What these kinds of *oh*s do not do, however, is orient towards the *affective valence* of the prior turn: In this sense, they respond to the unexpectedness and exceptionality of what the other speaker has said but do not ascribe any positive or negative valence to it. Thus, the display performed by 'extra high and pointed' *oh*s differs fundamentally from a sound object such as e.g 'low-falling and tailed' *ah* in response to troubles talk (cf. Chapter 8), which appreciates the affective loading of the troubles telling by treating it as negative and thereby signalling affiliation and commitment to it.

So what is the interactional pay-off for recipients to show a highly involved response without ascribing any valenced quality to what they have been told? Wilkinson and Kitzinger (2006) observe: "[T]he production of surprise [functions] as an alternative to some other action (such as an assessment, a co-complaint, or an expression of 'sympathy'), or as a means of deferring it" (ibid: 178). 'Surprise' may thus come in places where evaluative and/or affect-laden actions have been invited by the first speaker. We suggest that it is precisely the display of heightened involvement accomplished by 'extra high and pointed' *oh* which makes it a powerful tool for handling such relevancies: It does not take a valenced stance to the prior turn but still comes off as an affect-laden response. Given that valence has been considered an inherent aspect of affectivity (Caffi and Janney 1994), the view proposed here is to regard 'surprise' as doing 'pro forma' affect:[70] A display of 'surprise' treats the informing it responds to with heightened involvement but does not signal any valenced stance to it, i.e. it does not evaluate it as good or

---

70. The psychologist Paul Ekman indeed casts doubt on the concept of surprise as a basic emotion (Ekman 1999: 50, 55).

bad. Beyond psychological (cf. Colombetti (2005) for an overview of the notion of valence) and other linguistic approaches to affectivity, there seems, however, to be a broad consensus in the CA-/IL-informed literature that the ascription of a valenced stance to topical talk is one, if not, *the* major function of affect-laden displays (cf. e.g. Fiehler (1990), Freese and Maynard (1998), Maynard (1997).

A look into the present data disconfirms such a view for the use of 'extra high and pointed' *oh*: In some cases, the *oh*-producer withholds an assessment or affective display throughout the sequence, or when coming forward with one, produces a response in the form of questions or formulaic expressions. The following examples illustrate that 'extra high and pointed' *oh* can serve (1) to avoid affiliation, (2) to defer an explicit valenced uptake, and (3) to leave the evaluation of the news to the news teller, i.e. the speaker with the greater epistemic rights:[71]

1.   Recipients can deploy 'extra high and pointed' *oh* in order to avoid an affiliative response when made relevant.

Excerpt 4" illustrates this particularly well: It represents an extended version of Excerpt 4 ("outer wear tops"), which is reproduced in full length for convenience.

```
(4")   [HOLT:M88:1:2] "outer wear tops"
1       Les:    i got some nice cotton ↓TOPS:.
2               i'm not gonna [↑TELL skIp;
3       Lin:                  [↑Oh DID [↓you:,
4       Les:                            [.hhh ´`YE::S;
5               <<all>i mEAnt (.) only to get one or TWO>?
6               .hhh but they're?
7               (.)
8               you KNO:W,
9               <<all>i mEAn if i stOck up NOW>;
10              then i dOn't need to do it aGAIN,=
11              =DO i; hhe [he he he
12      Lin:               [<<p>yEAh (that's) RI:GH[T>,
13      Les:                                        [.hhh YES;
14      Lin:    Oh (**)
15  →           <<len>OU:ter wear: tops> you mEAn,
16  →   Les:    .hhh well NO:;
17  →           sOme i can wEAr underNEATH:;
18  →   (Les): h
19  →   Lin:    <<h, breathy>´`[ʔʌu:]>; ((extra high and pointed))
20  →   Les:    you SEE:,
21  →           (they're) agAInst my SKIN:; h[h
```

---

71.   Cf. also Betz and Golato (2008) on German *achja*.

```
22    Lin:                                    [<<nasal>´`[əʊ[:]>;
23    Les:                                         [.hh and
24           SOME ↓i can wear on tOp.
```

Remember that in lines 1–11, Leslie shares the "secret" with Linda that she bought a larger quantity of *nice cotton* ↓*TOPS:*, which she does not intend to tell her husband about. Drew (2005: 178) notes that the news telling "trades off a kind of marital joke: wives go shopping and don't tell their husbands what they've bought or how much they've spent, and husbands complain about how much their wives spend."

Leslie's telling thus invites an evaluative and affiliative recipient response in two respects: Firstly, the conversational tasks of news teller and recipient in news reports is to construct the delivery of news and its valence (Maynard 1997) in a joint project: "In and as their methods-in-detail (Garfinkel 1988) of inform-ing and responding, participants accord events-in-the-world their in-situ news-worthy status and their in vivo valence as good or bad." (Maynard 1997: 126). Co-constructing the newsworthiness and valence of the content of topical talk, participants further tend to align with the stance displayed by the consequential figure in the telling (ibid: 101). Secondly, jokes make an affiliative response rel-evant (Jefferson et al. 1987). On post-completion, recipients of a joke are invited to display their appreciation of it. As was discussed above, the recipient's weak acknowledgement (line 12) does not follow up on this relevancy. The subsequent recipient responses (lines 19 and 22) in the repair sequence, which forms a post-expansion to the jocular news telling, do not show any disaffiliation either: The use of a 'surprised' *oh* in line 19 makes the unexpectedness of the repair visible, without, however, orienting towards the positive implications of Leslie's getting herself some tops she can wear, i.e. the response does not share the news teller's pleasure at a successful shopping tour.

When the repair is further extended and detailed (lines 20–21), it is again receipted in terms of a sound object which orients towards the unexpectedness of the informing (line 22), yet in a more downgraded fashion. Like the sound object in line 19, it does not ascribe any valence to the content and possible implications of the repair and in this sense does not affiliate with it. In the next line, the news teller further expands on the repair in a concessive construction (lines 23–24).

To sum up, the example shows that the 'surprised' sound object is performed in a slot where an evaluative and affiliative recipient response would have been relevant. Such a response is heard as noticeably absent throughout the entire sub-sequent sequence. We can conclude that the 'surprised' *oh* can form a strategic resource to avoid an ascription of valence to and an affiliation with the teller's informings (cf. Wilkinson and Kitzinger (2006: 177–178) for a similar case).

The next example shows a case where a valenced response is forthcoming in the next recipient response subsequent to the production of a 'surprised' *oh*.

2.   Recipients can defer a valenced affective response through 'extra high and pointed' *oh*.

In Excerpt 7" (reproduced below for convenience), the recipient first treats the news about Donald's injury as surprising (line 16). When it is reformulated in terms of a punchline-like phrase, the recipient orients towards the affective loading of the news, using a formulaic expression.

```
(7")   [HOLT:M88:2:1] "hamstrings"
1        Mar:    .hhh so uh ↑yeah we're All- (-)
2                <<all>pretty good> and your LOT? h
3    →   Dwa:    ↑yes uh [all are
4        Mar:            [.hhh
5                (--)
6    →   Dwa:    very WELL,=
7                =and UH:-
8                (1.44)
9    →   Dwa:    at the moment DONald's uh:
10   →           sprained a couple of uh
11               <<all,p>↓WHAT is it dOnald>?
12               (1.15)
13   →   Dwa:    HAMstrIngs;
14   →           and in[stead [of
15     (D's son):       [(pulled)
16   →   Mar:                    [<<h>´`[ʔəʊː]>; ((extra high and pointed))
17               (-)
18   →   Dwa:    instead of straining ↓ONE,
19               he's he's done ↑BOTH of them:;
20               (-)
21       Mar:    [↑OH heck;
22       Dwa:    [(that's) why he's
23       Mar:    what was he DOing then; h
```

The news announcement is first treated as surprising (line 16): Following a restart, the announcement is redone in terms of a formulation which comes off as a punchline (lines 18–19): The unmarked declarative sentence *donald's sprained a couple of HAMstrIngs* (lines 9–10, 13) is replaced by a marked construction involving adverbial fronting *instead of straining ↓ONE, he's he's done ↑BOTH of them:;*. In response, the recipient delivers an affect-laden formula (line 21).[72] The

---

72. Note that "heck" is derived from the taboo word "hell": heck can thus be considered as semantically bleached and a weaker choice than "hell".

use of such a formula can be regarded as a resource for affect display, without being too personal and accountable (Drew and Holt 1988, Kitzinger 2000). In this way, the news recipient appreciates the negative valence of the informing without showing too much commitment.

It can be inferred that through the initial display of 'surprise', the recipient defers a valenced, affective receipt of the bad news. When the valenced display is finally forthcoming, it follows a marked syntactic construction which upgrades the negative affective loading of the news. The valenced, affective display has thus been interactively generated.

Excerpt 10 ("primulas") exemplifies a case where a more explicit assessment is deployed following the display of 'surprise'. Unlike all the other examples provided in this section, it is delivered in the context of troubles talk. It may be speculated that the activity generally prepares for more explicit and stronger affective displays than news sequences.

The excerpt sets in where Excerpt 3 ("allergies") left off. In talk prior to Excerpt 10 not shown here, the troubles teller, Leslie, has given a 'trouble-premonitory' response to an enquiry (Jefferson 1980). [73] In what follows, the recipient displays an understanding of the trouble connected to Leslie's house. In orientation to the troubles resistance shown by Leslie, the trouble is, however, not pursued. In Excerpt 10, lines 1 and 3 refer to the trouble-premonitory response made earlier. The troubles announcement (lines 4–5) which follows introduces a different kind of trouble than that anticipated by the recipient. This may be one reason why it is treated as unexpected. In addition, the announcement contains a contrastive construction (marked by the adversative connective *but*).

```
 (10)   [HOLT:M88:1:5] "primulas"
1          Les:    .h[h <<f>↑wEll (.) this is why i'm not QUITE so
2          Rob:      [hm:;
3          Les:    well at the moment>,
4     →            i'd thought i'd got to the: bottom of my ↑ALlergies;=
5     →            =but i came out a most ↑TERrible rash last week,
6                  .hh[h
7     →    Rob:       [<<h,f>``[əʊ[:]>; ((extra high and pointed))
8          Les:            [and i was tElling them all at school
9                  how much better i WAS,
10    →            but i ↑thInk it might have been: um priMULas i
11                 touched-
```

According to Jefferson (1980), such downgraded conventional responses to inquiry "need not project an immediately forthcoming report on a trouble, it may nevertheless mark the *presence* of a trouble." (ibid: 158, emphasis in the original).

```
12              (.)
13  →   Rob:    oh you poor ↑↑THI[NG;
14      Les:                 [´`hm:.
```

The troubles announcement is constructed in terms of an extreme case formulation, accomplished through lexico-grammatical resources. The noun phrase "bottom of my allergies" denotes the state of being free of allergic attacks and therefore constitutes an extreme case at the positive end of the scenario. It is contrasted with the worst case scenario: The superlative degree in *a most* ↑*TERrible rash* denotes the extreme case of an allergic attack. The extremely negative valence of the troubles announcement invites an affect-laden response.

The recipient response does not orient towards these relevancies, in that it does not respond to the negative implications of the telling. The prosodic design of the *oh*-token includes a lengthened rising-falling contour, starting from a high onset with a rise to an extra high pitch peak and falling to mid; it is louder than the same speaker's prior talk and comes rhythmically delayed. Figure 9 shows an acoustic analysis of this.

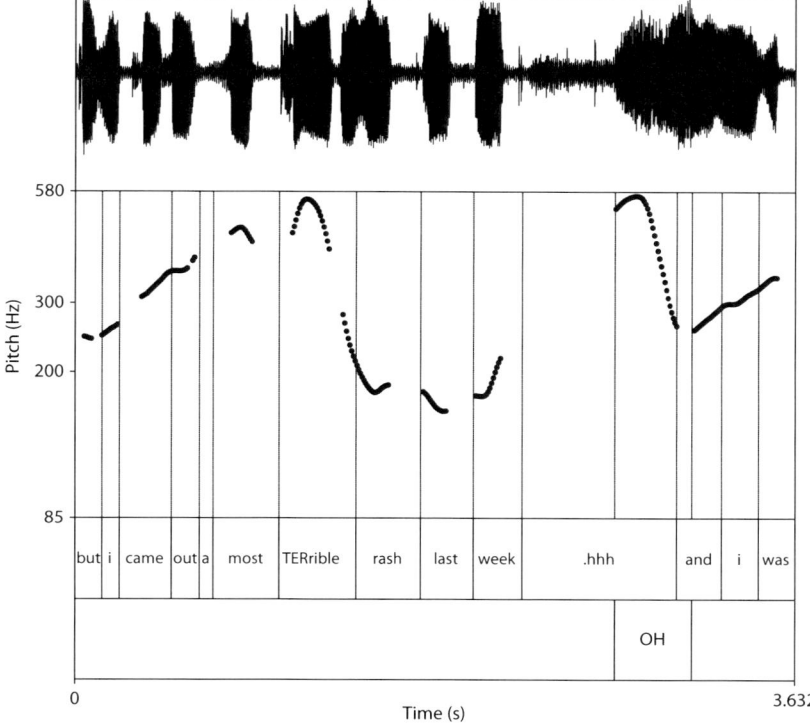

Figure 9. Acoustic analysis of Excerpt 10 ("primulas"), lines 5–8

Thus, the prosody with which the sound object is produced can be heard as extra high and pointed: Responding to a troubles announcement running counter to initial assumptions, the sound object treats the announcement as unexpected, requiring extra processing time and with heightened involvement.

In what follows, the troubles teller elaborates on the announcement by providing a more detailed report of her condition (lines 8–11).[74] Its contrastive structure is parallel to the teller's prior turn and is presented as a report of past speech and thought events (indicated by the use of a verbum dicendi in lines 8 and 10).[75] Note that she does not orient towards the recipient's display of 'surprise' but 'deletes' it in a similar way as was observed for the talk subsequent to 'surprised' news responses. In return, the recipient produces an *oh*-prefaced assessment which constitutes an idiomatic expression for 'sympathy' (line 13) and therefore can be treated as showing affiliation and commitment, in that it makes a negative, sympathetic stance relevant. As the affective formula in Excerpt 7" ("hamstrings"), it is, however, not accountable.

To sum up, the discussion of Excerpts 4" ("outer wear tops"), 7" ("hamstrings") and 10 ("primulas") has shown that recipients can use 'extra high and pointed' *oh*s in order to receipt informings which invite an evaluative, if not affect-laden response and affiliation without ascribing any valence to what the other speaker has said.

If a valenced affective display is delivered at a later point, it is achieved through a telling which specifically prepares for a valenced, affect-laden response. That means that the teller had to do extra interactional work to elicit a valenced recipient response. The valenced, affective displays found are, however, designed in terms of idiomatic formulae, which are typically non-accountable and less committing than more explicit, syntactically complete evaluative phrases.

Finally, recipients can deploy yet another strategy to avoid the straightforward assessment of a telling: They can leave the evaluative move to the teller her/himself:

3. 'Extra high and pointed' *oh* can be deployed to leave the evaluation of the news to the news teller, i.e. the speaker with the greater epistemic rights.

Excerpt 9" ("Portsmouth Poly") illustrates that the display of 'surprise' is not always a mere signal of disaffiliation. It can be deployed as a resource to handle

---

74. The delivery of detailed aspects is a rhetoric resource to prepare for affect-laden recipient responses. (cf. Section 7.8).

75. Couper-Kuhlen (2007b) argues that speakers can "substantiate and authenticate" (ibid:99) an assessment through presenting past utterances and thoughts in non-narrative reported speech.

topical epistemic rights in the ongoing interaction. The excerpt represents part of Excerpt 9, which is reproduced in short for convenience.

```
(9")   [HOLT:M88:2:4] "Portsmouth Poly"
1      Mar:        [All my kids seem to wanna go NO:RTH,=
2                  m:? (.) <<all>gO away as far as POSsible>;
3                  <<all>(i wonder) what it IS>,
4                  sOmething i SAID perhaps,
5                  h[hh
6      Hil:         [ye(h)ah,
7      Mar:  A:ND=uh:-
8            OR:-
9            (.)
10  →        u? pOrtsmouth ↑POLy; h
11           (-)
12  →  Hil:  <<h>´`[əʊː]>; ((extra high and pointed))
13           (--)
14     Mar:  SO: uhm:[:
15     Hil:          [you'd rAther like portsmouth POLy [of course?
16     Mar:                                            [.hhh NO:;=
17           =i don't KNOW, ((turn continues))
```

Here the news recipient first treats the point of the news telling in line 10 as surprising (line 12). After some negotiation for the floor (lines 13–14), she eventually addresses the affective implications of the telling in line 15. The turn is syntactically constructed in terms of a declarative statement but is prosodically cued as a question, which enquires about the news teller's preferences regarding the study places denoted in the list. Through the personal pronoun in the second person singular in subject position, the assessment of Portsmouth Poly is allocated to the news teller. The responsibilities of expressing an affective stance towards the news are thus handed over to the teller. Only the adverbial "of course" may index that the predicate presents the recipient's take on the news.

From the way the enquiry is performed it can be inferred in retrospect that 'extra high and pointed' *oh* in line 12 is not disaffiliative; rather, it can be viewed as a resource for paying respect to the news teller's greater epistemic rights, which are grounded in him being the father (cf. Raymond and Heritage (2006). In other words, the use of 'surprised' *oh* serves as a resource, in that instead of using the slot reserved for her to assess the news telling, the recipient invites an evaluative work-up of the news on the part of the news teller.

In sum, we have seen that 'extra high and pointed' *oh* represents a rhetorical resource for treating news with affective involvement but without ascribing a valence to it. Given that it is a commonly held view that affective displays have a positive or negative quality and are treated by participants accordingly, this sound object may therefore be described as doing a 'pro forma' display of affect. This means the *oh*-producer exploits the object in order to make the response look like a full-fledged affect-laden display; instead, using the object, they orient towards the unexpectedness of a prior informing and thus avoid or at least defer the action of affiliation where it is relevant. Further, by avoiding an assessment of the news, 'surprised' *oh* can be strategically deployed to allocate the assessment to the speaker with the greater epistemic rights.

Also, the analysis has shown that 'surprised' receipts can be generated through the linguistic design form the previous sequential environment, which can be specifically designed to elicit such a response. It is thus not the 'decision' of the recipient alone as to how to treat an informing but it also depends on the linguistic packaging of the actions performed by the first speaker. In this light the function of 'surprise' to "displace or defer other actions made sequentially relevant" (Wilkinson and Kitzinger 2006: 178) does not appear as a one-sided move accomplished by the recipient. On the contrary, its display reflects the recipient's analysis and understanding of the prior talk.

6.7   Summary and conclusions

The prosodic packaging and sequence-organisational and interactional functions of extra high and pointed *oh* can be summarised as shown in Table 6.

In sum, the bundle of properties identified for extra high and pointed *oh* in repair and news delivery contexts in the present data differs from the type of 'surprised' *oh* analysed in Couper-Kuhlen (2009) in rejection contexts in that the latter is shorter in duration and lower in pitch register. This suggests that 'surprise' is only a shorthand to label affect-laden displays which do similar things, yet surface in different (linguistic) forms and sequential contexts. Despite the association between 'extra high and pointed' *oh* and 'surprise' proposed, – and Couper-Kuhlen's study also supports this – *oh* does not have a static prosodic packaging: Our analysis has shown that by varying the pitch register of *oh*, speakers can convey different shades of cognitive/affective states. In this sense it was proposed that 'surprise' is a matter of degree. It will be a subject for further research to identify even more shades of meaning than 'surprise' evoked by rising-falling *oh*s (cf. Rasoloson (1994) for such results on the Madagascan interjection *M*, also Yang (2006) on Mandarin Chinese *oh*). 'Extra high and pointed' *oh* was further seen as a resource to provide an affective display without taking a valenced stance to what was said. Because it defers or comes in the place of an affective, valenced action, it can often also be treated as a disaffiliative move. Nevertheless, 'surprised' displays are as

Table 6. Forms and functions of the affect-laden sound object *oh*

Sound object		Extra high and pointed *oh*
obligatory prosodic-phonetic properties	segmental substance	diphthongal glide from an open-mid central unrounded vowel to a vowel in the region of cardinal vowel 8 (Alternatively, the initial central mid vowel can be retracted and more opened)
	duration	lengthened
	pitch register	absolute high pitch
	pitch movement	rise-falling: begins on a high onset, rises to a peak at the top of the speaker's range and falls on a glide to mid
	rhythmic integration	on the next beat / delayed
sequential placement		A: incongruent informing B: affect-laden next turn repair initiator (with respect to a problem of understanding) A: repair B: affect-laden repair receipt (extra high and pointed *oh*) A/B: elaboration of further details related to the content of the repair A: pre-announcement (regular case) B/A: continuer/pause A: news announcement (exceptional case) B: affect-laden acknowledgement of the news (extra high and pointed *oh*) A: expansion of the news telling
sequence-organising function		acknowledgement of repair (repair receipt) / acknowledgement of the news (news response)
interactional function		display of 'surprise': treats the contents of the repair as unexpected and with heightened affective involvement / display of 'surprise': treats the news not only as newsworthy but also as exceptional and in this sense as unexpected and with heightened affective involvement
if turn expansion		elaboration of further details related to the contents of the repair / –
if stand-alone		elaboration of further details related to the contents of the repair / expansion of the activity / deletion of the affect-laden response

much products of the prior interaction as valenced displays of affect. The disaffiliation accomplished though *oh* must thus be seen as interactively generated, not
as a one-sided process. Furthermore, 'surprise' can further serve to allocate the
evaluative treatment of what has been said to the speaker with the greater epistemic rights. Here it can be regarded as showing affiliation with other speaker.

CHAPTER 7

Affect-laden *oohs* in radio phone-ins and in mundane complaint sequences/troubles talk

The variants of the sound object *ooh* ([uː]) represent conversational objects which have hardly been documented. Not all dictionaries have an entry for *ooh*, and to our knowledge there are no other interactionally informed studies which have examined it. Formally, the prosodic shapes of the graphemic expression *ooh* are not as stable as those identified for *oh* or *ah*, in that they do not allow quite so straightforward a description of the relationship between sequential context and form. Similarly to the variants of *oh*, *oohs* can make gradable displays. For instance, the object may come with a rising-falling contour in different pitch registers. Interestingly, variants of *ooh* were found most frequently in radio phone-ins, where it represented an exclusive resource of the presenter. Here the object is used with varying prosodic packaging as assessment and repair receipts. On post-production, the turn is always expanded. The sound object allows the presenter to perform staged affective displays which treat the positively valenced, prior informing as intense in valence and exceptional. In mundane interaction, the sound object may receipt highly detailed negatively valenced informings, signalling heightened involvement.

The following chapter is structured as follows:

In Section 7.1 we will shortly summarise entries of *ooh* in dictionaries, which constitute the only available source on *ooh* to our knowledge, and then give a review of the previous literature on extreme and dramatic affect displays in talk-in-interaction (Section 7.2). Coming to our analytical discussion, we will first give a description of the prosodic-phonetic packaging of *ooh* (Section 7.3) and then present findings concerning 'high and pointed' *ooh* and turn-expansion as an affect-laden response to unqualified assessments in radio phone-ins (Section 7.4). Section 7.5 will examine 'mid-range' *ooh* and turn expansion as an affect-laden repair receipt. In addition, the sequential position of *ooh* within the global activity is discussed (Section 7.6). Section 7.7 contains a single case analysis of one of the rare cases of stand-alone *ooh*. The analytic account of *ooh* is wound up by a section on 'high' *ooh* as an affect-laden receipt of highly detailed negatively valenced informing in everyday complaint sequences and troubles telling (Section 7.8). Finally, Section 7.9 extracts in more detail what the specific meaning of *ooh* (e.g. in contrast to *oh*) is. Section 7.10 offers a summary and conclusions.

7.1   Previous accounts of *ooh* in dictionaries

When searching for previous accounts of an object with the segmental substance [u:] in talk-in-interaction, a first difficulty arises from the fact that it may be spelt in different ways. According to English dictionaries, *ooh* or *oo* are standard orthographic representations of the segment /u:/. Nevertheless, some transcribers of talk-in-interaction use these graphemic expressions to indicate lengthened forms of *oh* to the effect that the sound structure of the object remains unclear unless the sound file is available.[76] In fact, the lexeme /u:/ cannot even be found in all dictionaries. For instance, there are no entries in older editions such as Webster's Third New International Dictionary of the English Language, Unabridged (Gove et al. 1986), The Random House Dictionary of the English Language (Stein 1966), The English Oxford Dictionary (1933; 1970) and The American Heritage Dictionary of the English Language (Morris ²1973). Although this should be investigated in terms of a larger, diachronic corpus-based study, this might suggest that *ooh* is still emerging as a lexical item.

On the other hand, the Concise Oxford Dictionary of Current English (Sykes ⁷1983) lists *ooh* as a "natural excla[mation]", whose pronunciation is described as consisting of a vowel like the one in *boot* or symbolised by the IPA symbol /u/. It is characterised as "expr. surprised pleasure, excitement, pain, etc." (ibid: 712). Along the same lines, The Collins Cobuild English Language Dictionary (Sinclair 1987) classifies *ooh* or *oo* /u:/ as an exclamation with positive and negative affective meaning. The semantic-pragmatic description reads as follows: "People say **ooh** when they are surprised, looking forward to something, or find something pleasant or unpleasant; an informal word. EG *Oo* [sic!], *I like going swimming... Ooh, you are wonderful... Ooh, that feels nice*" (ibid: 1006, emphasis in the original).

The Cambridge International Dictionary of English (Procter 1995) provides the most comprehensive record. The entry includes *ooh* /u:/ as an exclamation, a noun (a count noun, usually in plural) and as an intransitive verb, with the latter two parts of speech (noun and verb) being treated as derivations from the former (exclamation). Used as an exclamation, *ooh* is again referred to as conveying both positive and negative emotions (surprise, pleasure, approval, disapproval) in addition to pain (ibid: 987). The meanings of the homonymous noun and the verb are not further explained but given in terms of example sentences only. Interestingly

---

76. Cf. Example 18, line 2, in Heritage (1984: 307): Here an instance of what is analysed as the change-of-state token *oh* is transcribed as *Ooh::*.

enough, the use of the noun is exemplified in a collocation with *aah*:[77] "*There was a chorus of oohs* **and aahs** *from her fellow MPs as she launched a vehement attack on the Prime Minister.*" (ibid: 987, emphasis in the original). The example leaves it open what kind of meaning *ooh* (and *aah*) expresses here. Depending on the perspective of the "fellow MPs", "a vehement attack on the Prime Minister" can be something to respond to with expressions of negative or positive emotion or even surprise. For the use of the verb, two examples are given, one again showing *ooh* in a collocation with *aah*: "*The crowed oohed when the skier lost his footing and tumbled down the slope. · Thousands of spectators oohed* **and aahed** *(= expressed admiration) as the pilots performed amazing stunts in their planes*". (ibid: 987, emphasis in the original). Here the first sentence seems to exemplify the verb *ooh* as meaning to show either surprise or negative emotions ('Disapproval' would not make sense in the light of the example sentence). "To ooh and aah", on the other hand, is an idiomatic expression for admiration.

To sum up, conversational objects with the segmental substance /uː/ have not been explored from an interactional perspective. Not even all dictionaries include the interjection *oo/ooh* among their entries. This may indicate that its form and meaning is still in the process of conventionalisation.

If the lexeme *oo/ooh* is listed, its sound structure is usually transcribed with a lengthened vowel /uː/. Syntactically, it is categorised as an exclamation. The example sentences further suggest that *ooh* occurs in the initial position of sentences. Semantically, *ooh* can express a range of various emotions which do not have much in common: surprise, surprised pleasure, pleasure, approval, excitement, anticipation, disapproval, displeasure. One dictionary consulted mentions two homonymous derivations of *ooh* (a noun and a verb), specifically in collocation with *aah*. E.g. "to ooh and aah" refers to an action through which admiration is conveyed.

As is usually the case with dictionaries, no information about conversational uses beyond the sentence level is provided nor do they contain any prosodic description. In this sense, the dictionaries reflect the same written language bias (Linell 2005) as English grammars.

---

77. According to the entry on *ah* in the same dictionary (Cambridge International Dictionary of English 1995), under which *aah* is subsumed, *ooh* and *aah* are partly synonymous: It states that *ah* (or *aah*) constitutes an exclamation which serves to convey "understanding, pleasure, pain, surprise or the fact that you have noticed something" (ibid: 28). Cf. further Section 8.1.1.

7.2   Extreme and dramatic affect displays in talk-in-interaction

The variants of the sound object *ooh* are deployed as an affect-laden recipient response to informings which are treated as being extremely positive or negative. To our knowledge, accounts of extreme, in situ affect displays in talk-in-interaction are rare: A seminal study is Whalen and Zimmerman (1998) on 'hysteria' in emergency calls, where callers are faced with real-life situations which may constitute a matter of life or death. 'Hysteria' is conceptualised as "an *account* of a kind of situational incompetence [on the part of the caller] – namely, the inability to co-operate appropriately in the work of the call" (ibid: 144, emphasis in original). Such instances of 'situational incompetence' are contextualised by extremely high volume, a distorted voice, sobbing or crying, gasping for breath, and exclamations (ibid: 146). Thus, the authors' point is that in cases of hysteria, physical arousal, affect-laden displays and sequentially organised actions fall together, forming a "social construction" (ibid: 158).

In contrast, the variants of *ooh* to be analysed here serve as a resource for making extremely positive or negative dimensions of affect visible in response to *verbal actions*, that is, unqualified assessments in semi-conversational advice-giving sequences in radio phone-ins and highly detailed statements in mundane complaint/troubles talk sequences. It will be argued that these displays are generated by the linguistic design of the prior action and the interactional relevancies at stake.

7.3   The prosodic-phonetic packaging of *ooh*

Before presenting a sequential and interactional analysis of forms and uses of *ooh* in advice-giving sequences in radio phone-ins and in complaint/troubles talk sequences in everyday telephone interactions, we will first give descriptions of the segmental substance and the prosodic-phonetic packaging which can accompany variants of the sound object. It will be argued that, generally, the variants of *ooh* treat the prior turn as conveying something extreme or dramatic in one way or another, beyond implementing an information receipt.

Like instances of *oh*, *ooh*s can be produced with varying degrees of prominence: Integrated into a TCU, they may preface the further elements of the unit. As prosodically prominent objects, they may form the first TCU in a multi-unit turn (i.e. they may be followed by turn expansion) or stand as a single unit (after which the other speaker resumes talk). The following analysis will concentrate on objects with prosodic prominence, since they are treated as implementing independent actions and were found most frequently in the corpus. More specifically, it will focus on variants of *ooh* with a high pitch accent. However, since instantiations of *ooh* are 'gradable' objects like those of *oh*, the discussion will also address the implications of other prosodic-phonetic clusters identified with *ooh*.

The segmental substance of all variants of *ooh* has a vowel quality close to cardinal vowel 8 ([u]). The vowel can be rounded, unrounded or even ingressive. Based on the current state of our knowledge, the phonetic variation reflected in the various articulatory modes for the back close vowel (rounded, unrounded, ingressive) does not create significant distinctions in meaning.

As regards the prosodic-phonetic clusters which accompany the instances of *ooh* examined, they can vary in terms of pitch register and contour, which can be a flat or wide ranging rise-fall.

The discussion will concentrate on so-called 'high and pointed' and 'high' *oohs*, i.e. objects done in high pitch register, as they are found most frequently. More marginally, midrange-pitched objects will be examined.

High pitched *oohs*, which are treated as displays of heightened affective involvement and appear most frequently in the data, are analysed as having obligatory and variant properties: Obligatory properties include lengthened duration and higher pitch than the same speaker's prior talk and a rising-falling contour. The object may come with a lengthened, wide-ranging contour ('high and pointed' *ooh*) or a flat rising-falling pitch movement ('high' *ooh*), with the former being found typically in radio phone-ins (cf. Figure 10).

Figure 10. 'High and pointed' and 'high' contours of *ooh*

The 'high and pointed' format to the left shows strong parallels with the cluster of prosodic properties examined for 'extra high and pointed' *oh*. Nevertheless, it will be shown that 'high and pointed' *ooh* may be deployed in different sequential slots and perform different actions than 'extra high and pointed' *oh*. This will be taken as evidence that the segmental substances and prosodic properties of these objects are two freely interacting contextualisation systems. In addition, such an *ooh* is typically accompanied by breathiness.

Variant properties of high pitched *oohs* include loudness and timing: In terms of loudness, they can be softer or slightly louder than the same speaker's prior talk. The timing can be on the next beat or not. Sometimes, such objects are produced with initial glottal closure.

On the other hand, *oohs* with increased duration and a midrange rise-fall may convey a different quality of affective involvement. Again they may come with either a wider ranging or flatter rise-fall (cf. Figure 11).

Figure 11. 'Midrange' contours of *ooh*

It will be argued that midrange objects of this kind are often deployed in positions where an orientation to progressivity is visible, e.g. in insert sequences.

7.4   'High and pointed' *ooh* + turn expansion as an affect-laden response to unqualified, positive assessments

In the radio phone-ins examined, 'high and pointed' *ooh* plus turn expansion is most frequently used to receipt unqualified, positive assessments in opinion-giving sequences. In such activities, callers are often doing being experts on a specific topic they have been asked to give their opinion/advice on. The Cambridge International Dictionary of English suggests that the concept of advice is tightly connected to that of opinion. It states that advice is "an opinion which someone offers you about what you should do or how you should act in a particular situation" (Procter 1995: 20).

Since the term "advice giving" is, however, heavily bound to an interactional framework which sees a professional expert as an advice giver and a lay person, the caller or the radio audience, as an advice seeker, we wish to speak of opinion-giving here, even if this opinion may sometimes function as advice. In opinion-sequences, the turns which the recipient receipts with 'high and pointed' *ooh* generally implement assessments, which often contain an affective dimension. These assessments are presented as first-hand knowledge on the part of the opinion giver, and who constructs himself/herself as an expert on the topic.[78] Furthermore, 'high and pointed' *ooh* is exclusively deployed as a presenter's resource in these sequential environments. We will argue that 'high and pointed' *ooh*

---

78. Cf. Hutchby (1996: 44, footnote 2) for a discussion of the analytic distinction between descriptions and evaluations.

serves as an affect-laden recipient response which acknowledges the assessment and takes some kind of affective stance to it. The affective dimensions signalled can be labelled as 'positive excitement', 'pleasure' and 'enthusiasm'. By taking this kind of stance, the recipient shows commitment to the truthfulness of the opinion stated, an action which is usually not observed with institutional representatives (Heritage 1985). Since this kind of display is performed in radio phone-ins with a split audience, i.e. an audience divided between the in-studio recipient and/or the caller and the public radio audience, the affectivity displayed by the presenter may be deployed as a strategic resource in order to raise the rate and degree of audience participation in the programme. For instance, Cantor (1994) reports that "entertainment and [emotional] arousal" (ibid: 227) are frequent reasons for consumers seeking mass media exposure.

Excerpt 11 illustrates a particularly good example of 'high and pointed' *ooh* plus turn expansion construction which receipts an unqualified assessment in an opinion-giving activity. In addition, it provides evidence that 'high and pointed' *ooh* comes in positions where heightened affective involvement is made relevant. The excerpt is taken from a radio phone-in where listeners are asked to give the presenter ideas as to where to go on her honeymoon. The caller's proposal for a honeymoon is Cape Town.

The sequence of [unqualified assessment – 'high and pointed' *ooh* + turn expansion], which we are concerned with occurs as the second item of a list (lines 22–26). The analysis will address aspects of the preceding sequence in order to account for how the sequence of interest is generated.

```
(11)   [Sadie Nine 5] "a little tip"
1              C2:    a lIttle TIP;
2              M2:    uHUH,=
3              C2:    =If you're GOing,
4                     .hh arRI:VE on a sAturday and SUNday;
5                     (--)
6              M2:    RI:GH[T,
7              C2:         [because in the ↑week DAYS-
8                     .hh the trAffic going into cApe town itSELF;=
9                     =<<all>because Everybody goes back to WORK;>
10                    <<rall>is: Absolutely horRENdous>.
11             M2:    <<p>[ у̣] DEAR>;
12                    (.)
13             M2:    <<p>[ у̣] [DEAR>;=
14             C2:             [( )
15             M2:    =<<p>RIGHT>;
16             C2:    <<all>i mean> thAt CAN be;=
```

```
17              =thAt (0.27) thAt's the ONly thing;=
18              =<<all>but i MEAN
19    →         .hh <<f>↑drIve on the same side of the road (as) US>-
20    →    M2:  ↑[ʔʉ] thAt sOUnds GOOD;
21              (.)
22    →    C2:  ↑pEtrol's chEAp,
23    →         fIfty pence uh: a ↑LIter;
24              (-)
25    →    M2:  <<h>´`↑[ʔʉ:]>;
26    →         sOUnds even BETt[er;
27         C2:                  [uhm
28              (.)
29              .h you can hIre a cAr and it comes in every liberty
30              hotel (* * * * * *) what we
31              which (-) is what we DO,
32              .hh uhm
33              (-)
34              and in ↑FACT,
35              i just <<staccato>cAn't (.) tAlk> highly enough about
36              the PLACE.
37              it is (.) sO: sO fanTAStic;
38         M2:  <<f>↑ANdrew>;
39              <<f>thank you v:Ery much indeed for yOUr CALL>; ((turn
                continues))
```

As regards vowel quality, we find clear instances of the sound object concerned in lines 20 and 25.[79] Their formal make-up is locally situated and sensitive to the local contingencies of the interaction. All sound objects respond to claims related to Cape Town as part of an opinion-giving sequence.

Lines 7–10, which constitute the first claim in the excerpt, serve as an account for the proposal in lines 3–4. In line 10, the assessment which the speaker began in lines 7–8 is completed. The syntactic structure of the assessment is [NP + be (copula verb) + AP]. The pre-modifying adverb "absolutely" functions as a booster, intensifying the negative meaning of the evaluative adjective. The assessment presents the traffic as as horrendous as possible, and thereby claims an extreme case. Pomerantz (1986) states that such extreme case formulations are "[o]ne practice used in legitimizing claims" (ibid: 219). It serves to strengthen the caller's position as an expert on Cape Town and to substantiate his tip for the presenter to arrive at the weekend (line 1).

---

79. The sound objects in lines 11 and 13 do not qualify so readily as members of the category since their vowel quality is more open. All sounds objects are products of their prior interactional contexts.

The presenter treats the extreme case formulation as having negative valence and making an affect-laden response relevant. The recipient TCU (line 11) has the structure [sound object + noun]. Maynard (1997:109) describes the phrase "oh dear" as a 'standardised *oh*-prefaced assessment' which forms a common response to bad news. The frequency of this idiomatic phrase in our data points in the same direction.[80] The initial sound object is prosodically integrated in the larger unit, that is, it prefaces the TCU and does not implement an independent action. In terms of its form, it has lower pitch and softer volume than the same speaker' prior talk and a level pitch contour (cf. Figure 12).

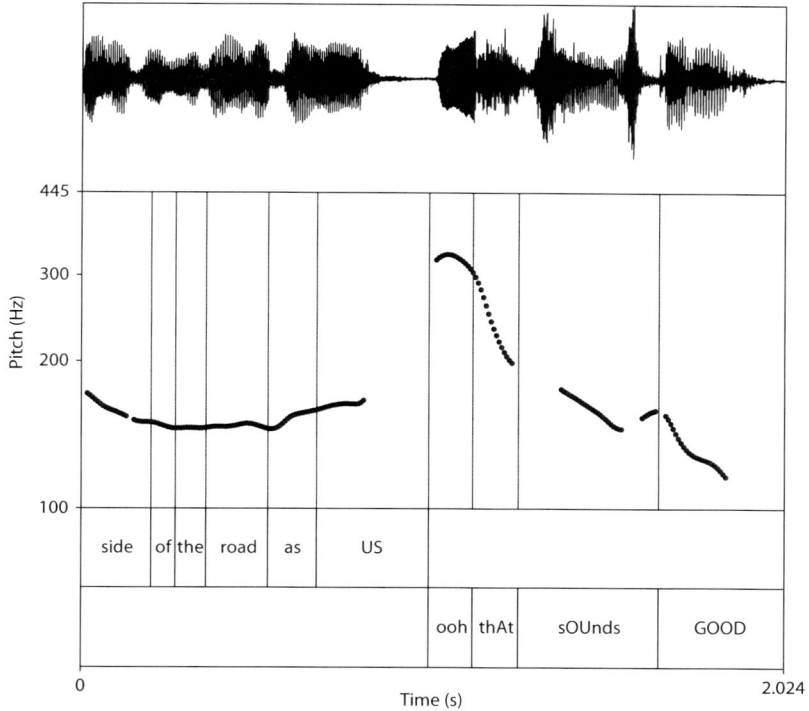

Figure 12. Acoustic analysis of Excerpt 11 ("a little tip"), lines 19–20

---

80. The silence after the first ocurrence of <<p>[u̞] DEAR>; and the following recycling of the phrase before the production of the discourse marker <<p>RIGHT>; may display an orientation to the functional ambivalence of *oh dear* in response to news announcements (Maynard 1997:109). Being ambivalent in terms of its interactional function as a news mark or a news receipt, it can both promote or discourage the further development of a news sequence.

In terms of vowel quality, it is between cardinal vowels 7 ([o]) and 8 ([u]). The choice of the sound object over a diphthongal *oh* can be taken as a non-routine production of the idiom and reflects the recipient's orientation to the extremeness with which the assessment is presented by the opinion-giver. Due to the non-routine vowel quality of the prefacing sound object, the standard phrase comes off as more affectively loaded. The recipient thus exploits the sound object to modulate the affective stance conveyed by the phrase. In addition, the speaker uses the repetition of the phrase (line 13) as an iconic resource to display increased affective involvement.

The further analysis of the sequence shows that the caller then makes two more claims in favour of Cape Town (lines 19, 22–23) which are receipted by sound objects. The concessive formulations in lines 16–17 indicate that they are constructed in orientation to the presenter's negatively valenced, affect-laden receipts. The discourse marker *i mean* (line 16) typically projects concession (Couper-Kuhlen and Thompson 2005, Imo 2005). The modal auxiliary *CAN* in the same line indicates a shift in epistemic stance; it recontextualises and qualifies the prior claim as a possibility, not as a general, unchanging scenario. The next line (17) downgrades the significance of the negative informing to a minimum and is then followed by a construction (line 18) which projects a reformulation of the initial claim (Couper-Kuhlen and Thompson 2005, Imo 2005). The caller next makes a claim which is in favour of Cape Town (line 19). The turn is syntactically structured in terms of a zero-subject construction. Its final rising pitch movement to mid points to an emergent list structure (Couper-Kuhlen 1986, Jefferson 1990). Again, the presenter treats the caller's claim as inviting an affective response. She responds with an *ooh*-prefaced turn (line 20). This turn-initial vowel has a quality close to the cardinal vowel 8 ([u]) and is unrounded. Produced on a level, unlengthened tone, it forms the first stressed syllable in the intonation phrase. It is higher pitched and louder than same speaker's prior talk. The more distinct vowel quality of the sound object in line 20 signals a greater extent of affective involvement than in lines 11 and 13. Similarly, the sound object does not perform an action on its own but "provide[s] a coloring" (Heritage 1998: 327) of the remaining unit as affect-laden and as treating the prior informing as extremely positive. At the same time it is backwards-looking, as it treats the caller's claim as inviting an affective response. The further turn elements implement a positive assessment. The full syntactic structure indicates less idiomacy and opacity than in lines 11 and 13. This greater explicitness nicely concords with the higher degree of affectivity signalled by the sound object. The assessment is followed by an expansion of the list.

The next list item, which presents another novel, positively valenced aspect of Cape Town (lines 22–23), is structured in a bipartite fashion. The first TCU contains a positive, generalising assessment of the form [NP + be + evaluative adjective] (line 22). In the second TCU, the evaluation is backed up with an evidential account which provides detail of the claim (line 23). Both TCUs are shaped as declaratives and, lacking softeners or any other modifiers or adverbials, have the format of lexically unqualified statements. These constitute a strong rhetorical resource in contexts where the speaker's task is to make a case for their standpoint – here Cape Town being a fantastic honeymoon destination. In contrast to extreme case formulations, however, they do not as easily become a target for critical comments which may question the point made by the opinion-giver (cf. Hutchby (1996: 65) on extreme case formulations in radio talk): Edwards (2000) argues that "although a nonextreme generalization is logically and semantically weaker than an ECF, it can be rhetorically and interactionally stronger." (ibid: 354). Also, Couper-Kuhlen and Thompson (2005) describe cases where speakers back down from their initial ECFs, a practice they call 'concessive repair'. They provide evidence for concessive repair following non-extreme statements. This substantiates the claim made in terms of our data that lexically non-extreme, yet unqualified assessments can be treated as having extreme interactional thrust and can be oriented to accordingly in the subsequent interaction.

In our example, the recipient treats the assessment (lines 22–23) as making a display of heightened affective involvement relevant: Again, she responds with a 'high and pointed' *ooh* in the initial position, yet this time under an independent contour (line 25). The object has a vowel quality close to the cardinal vowel 8 ([u]), yet is unrounded. The vowel is lengthened and is producd with a higher pitch than the same speaker's prior talk. Further, it has a wide ranging rising-falling contour, which begins in the midrange of the speaker's voice (281 Hz), rises to its top (440 Hz) and falls to low (131 Hz). It is produced slightly louder than the same speaker's prior talk and comes in neither early nor late (cf. Figure 13).

As regards the display made by the sound object, the high pitch is interpreted as a signal of heightened affective involvement, which is made relevant by the unqualified nature and the sequential positioning of the assessment it responds to. The interpretation for the wide ranging rise-fall is not so straightforward, since the sequential and rhetorical design of the prior interaction does not give any clues which would warrant an interpretation of the unqualified assessment as unexpected or exceptional. Nevertheless, we wish to argue that the rising-falling contour signals the recipient's *treating* the assessment as being exceptional and out of the ordinary. For this reason, it can be regarded as 'staged' display.[81] Such an analysis is further supported by the particular participant framework of radio phone-ins, which includes an in-studio presenter, the caller and the listeners.

---

81. Cf. Schmitt (2003) on staged displays of affect in mass media communication.

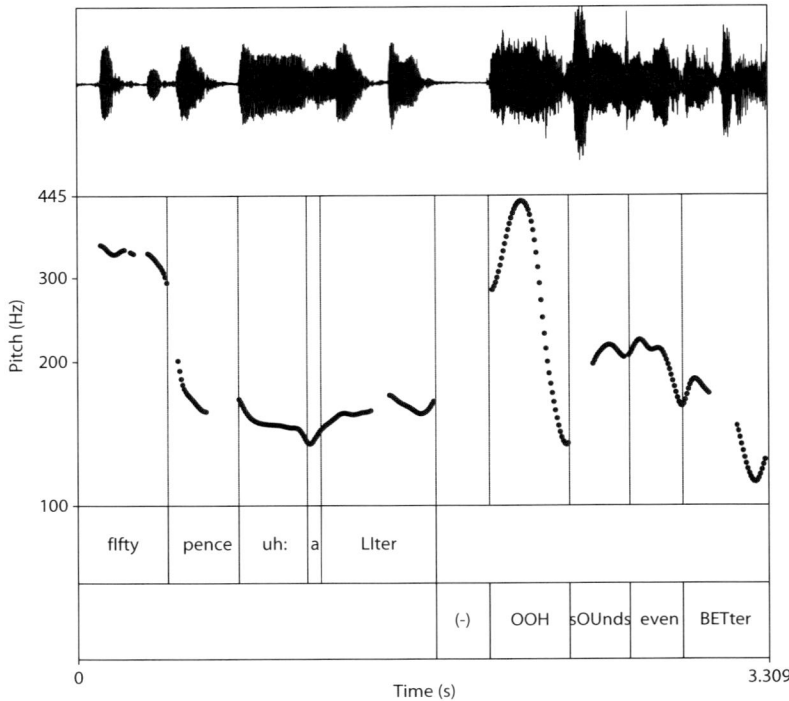

Figure 13. Acoustic analysis of Excerpt 11 ("a little tip"), lines 23–26

Since the presenter's actions must always be analysed as acting for a split audience, the presenter's recipient response, too, addresses both the caller and the radio audience: On the one hand, it appreciates the exceptional nature of the caller's advice in a highly affect-laden way and serves interactional relevancies, i.e. those of affiliation. On the other, the affect-laden response shows commitment to what was claimed by the opinion-giver. This finding deviates from Heritage (1985) on recipient responses in institutional frameworks, where he observes that unlike recipients in everyday interaction, the institutional representative refrains from responding to informings with "*mm hm, oh,* newsmark, or affiliative assessment" (ibid: 98, italics in the original) of any kind. In this way, they do not signal any "commitment" but a stance of "formal or official neutrality" towards the claims made by the interviewee (ibid: 98).

This display of commitment may be considered a strategic choice: By conveying to the listening audience that the caller has made an exceptional and extremely positive contribution, the presenter increases the entertainment value of the broadcast and encourages other listeners to phone in and provide even better advice. All in all, 'high and pointed' *ooh* ratifies the opinion-giver's assessment by treating it as exceptional and inviting heightened involvement.

In turn expansion, the recipient produces an assessment. The TCU recycles the positive evaluative adjective in line 20 in comparative degree and thus in a lexically upgraded fashion (line 26). Prosodically, the assessment comes in without delay and with noticeably lower pitch. The undelayed production points to the entire turn being perceived as a planned unit. Moreover, the lower pitch comes off as *non*-affect-laden. The TCU can be treated as making aspects of what the sound object was doing explicit and available: That means that interactionally, the sound object treats the assessment made by the opinion-giver with upbeat affective involvement, which can be paraphrased in everyday emotion words such as 'positive excitement', 'pleasure' and 'enthusiasm'.

In what follows, the opinion-giver resumes his talk after some delay. His turn implements the next item in the list and provides another argument for a honeymoon in Cape Town. By introducing a new list item, he expands on the sequence but does not add to the previous list item in terms of content. This indicates that the [*ooh* + positive assessment] turn treats the local list item as complete while encouraging an extension of the global list sequence.

To summarise, we have seen that the recipient responds to each informing with a sound object of increasing prominence. The prominence of the sound object can be seen as an iconic signal of the affective intensity conveyed. The increase of affective intensity is also reflected by the lexical and grammatical choices made in what follows: A non-syntactic idiomatic phrase is upgraded in terms of an assessment with full syntax. The assessment is, in turn, recycled in comparative degree, which again intensifies its meaning.

We can thus conclude that a prosodically prominent *ooh* which forms a single TCU and is followed by an assessment in turn expansion performs an action which signals more heightened affective involvement than a sound object which prefaces an assessment and is integrated with it in a single TCU.

Also, it can be argued that participants use the different prosodic designs of the sound object *ooh* to achieve different degrees of prominence and involvement and to display affective dimensions of different intensity. In doing so, *ooh*-producers can orient towards the local contingencies of the prior informing. Furthermore, the comparative degree of the evaluative adjective, which is used in the turn expansion following 'high and pointed' *ooh*, indicates that the affective dimension signalled by the sound object is more than average, i.e. extremely positive. Furthermore, the rise-fall on the object is treated as a staged orientation to the exceptionalness of the prior assessment. The staged nature of the display is context-sensitive and at the same time shapes the interaction as semi-institutional.

Excerpt 12 illustrates another case of a 'high and pointed' *ooh* which receipts an unqualified assessment in an opinion-giving sequence. The sequential structure is slightly different from that in Excerpt 11, with the assessment serving as a concluding summary. Here the turn introduced by *ooh* is expanded in terms of a metaphorical expression for cognitive processes. The example is taken from the same radio phone-in as Excerpt 11. As a follow-up to an earlier suggestion by a caller to go to the Amalfi coast, a co-presenter (CP) in the studio, who used to work for a tour operator in the region, gives her opinion about the coast.[82] She thereby constructs herself as as much of an expert as the callers.

In the talk prior to this excerpt, not shown here, the opinion-giving sequence is initiated through an enquiry about the Isle of Capri by the presenter. The adversative connective *but* in line 1 marks a contrast to the Isle of Capri as a holiday resort for the rich and famous.

```
(12)   [Sadie Nine 2] "scenery"
1        CP1:   but if you jUst go arOUnd the COAST line;
2               you've got what's cAlled the amalfi COAST;
3               and you've got uhm aMALfi,
4               raVELlo,
5               and posiTAno;
6               .h which are All sort of (-) clIff-built (-) TOWNS;
7               little VILlages;
8        M2:    YEAH?
9        CP1:   they've (STARted off) as vIllages;
10              NOW are tOwns;
11              and thEY are (.) BEAUTtiful;
12              .h <<all>so much> dOn't mind hairpin BENDS,
13              .hh there's abOUt
14              <<p,all>phEw i don't KNOW>-=
15              =<<p,all>about fifty hairpin bEnds to get ROUND
16              there>;=
17   →          =<<p>but the> SCE:nery>,
18   →          hh <<p>is fanTAStic>;
19   →   M2:    <<pp>´`[ʔu:]>;
20   →          i'm being SOLD here;=
21              <<all>you sEE>,=
```

---

82.   The presence of an in-studio expert is typical of the framework of advice-giving shows (as analysed in detail in Hutchby (2006: 102–117). However, as this expert's advice is not directed to a help-seeking caller but to the studio host in the present data, she cannot be characterised as acting in such a framework.

```
((ca. 8 secs praise for good advice directed at the callers omitted))
22  →          thanks ↑Ever so mUch;
23  →          well ↑kEEp those calls coming IN; ((turn continues))
```

The sound object *ooh* (line 19) responds to the unqualified assessment in lines 17–18, which summarises the point of a longer contribution by CP1.

As indicated by the initial adversative connector 'but' (line 17), the assessment is set in contrast to the prior talk (lines 12–16), which reports on the road along the coast having a lot of hairpin bends. Hairpin bends can be treated as a lexical item with potentially negative connotations, as this piece of information potentially weakens the speaker's claim of the Amalfi coast being a recommendable honeymoon destination. The summarising assessment (lines 17–18) is thus framed as being in contrast to a potentially negative aspect of the proposal.

The speaker assesses the scenery of the Amalfi coast with the evaluative adjective *fanTAStic*, which conveys highly positive meaning (lines 17–18). The evaluation has the syntactic structure of [X + be (copula verb) + adjective]. Lexically, it lacks modifiers and/or adverbials, which would limit or boost its scope and meaning. The evaluation thus comes off in an unqualified, generalising fashion. Prosodically, the evaluation is constructed in terms of two units, with the first one ending with a final rise to mid. The prosodic break following the subject serves to achieve a rhetorical effect (Couper-Kuhlen 1983:80): By keeping the listener in suspense as to what exactly will come next, it heightens the positive thrust of the evaluative adjective when it is eventually produced. Furthermore, this kind of prosodic contextualisation can be interpreted as signalling an affective stance, which makes an equally affect-laden response relevant. It accomplishes the local task to both name and "sell" a honeymoon destination, in explicitly assessing the referent in very positive terms.

The recipient next responds with a 'high and pointed' *ooh* (line 19). Like the sound object 'high and pointed' *ooh* in Excerpt 11, it is lengthened and higher pitched than the same speaker's prior talk. However, the peak of the rising-falling contour does not reach a maximum height. The contour begins at a low level of the speaker's voice range (196 Hz), rises to a peak in the upper range (331 Hz) and falls to low (116 Hz). The object is slightly louder than the same speaker's prior talk, timed not too early and not too late and is produced with breathy voice quality. Again, the object ratifies the assessment, while its lengthening and high pitch cue it as a display of heightened affective involvement. Further, the rising-falling contour indicates the recipient's treatment the prior assessment as conveying exceptional content. Although the assessment is delivered as part of a contrastive construction, the rise-fall orients towards this contrast as such, because the contrast does not put the regular vs. the exceptional case into opposition. Instead, the rising-falling contour reflects the recipient's strategy to appreciate the opinion-giver's advice as exceptional for the reasons discussed above. All in all, the sound object accomplishes an upbeat, affiliative response which acknowledges the summarising assessment and at the same time appreciates it affectively, signalling dimension such as 'pleasure', 'enthusiasm' and perhaps to a lesser extent 'positive excitement'.

Furthermore, the production of the sound object can be regarded as the recipient's specific orientation to the sequential position of the evaluative statement, an observation which will be discussed in more detail below.

When the presenter expands her turn (line 20), she indicates that she finds her interlocutor's proposal very convincing, using a metaphorical verb which stands for a cognitive process. The TCU makes visible that again, the presenter displays her "commitment to the truth or the adequacy" of the interlocutor's claim (Heritage 1985:99). This can be taken as further evidence that the sound object was indeed produced at a point where it is the recipient's task to show her appreciation and acknowledgement of the advice given. What the turn expansion also accomplishes in addition is that it manages the sequential development in the post-production space of the sound object. Here the turn expansion serves as a pivot, in that it is both backwards- and forward-looking. It both implements a response to the opinion-giver's assessment and leads to more appreciative talk on the part of the presenter.

To summarise, the analysis has shown that 'high and pointed' *ooh* plus turn expansion is deployed by the presenter to receipt unqualified assessments. The sound object acknowledges the assessment and at the same time signals an upbeat affective involvement, which can be paraphrased in everyday emotion words such as 'positive excitement', 'pleasure' and 'enthusiasm'. *Ooh* thus serves as an affective opinion-receipt, which makes the recipient's heightened affective involvement towards the opinion-giver's assessment visible. In addition, the content of the assessment is treated as exceptional. In this way, the recipient displays her commitment and accomplishes affiliation. This is not only achieved on an interactional level between presenter and opinion-giver. Rather, the affective dimension of the claim is also made "visible" and "available" for the public audience (cf. Hutchby (2006:68).

The turn expansion serves as a space for the management of the subsequent sequence. The turn expansion can either encourage the development of the sequence or lead up to the closing of the opinion-giving sequence.

To sum up, the sound object *ooh* plus turn expansion functions to receipt unqualified assessments with positive valence via an affect-laden token which orients towards both the great intensity of the assessment and its exceptional content.

7.5 'Midrange' *ooh* + turn expansion in response to repair

In addition to turns containing 'high and pointed' *ooh*, *ooh* may be accompanied
by increased duration and a rise-fall pitched in midrange. In the data, midrange
pitched objects of this kind are often deployed in positions where an orientation
towards progressivity is visible, as for example in side sequences, and followed by
turn expansion. Side sequences can be initiated in connection with other-initiated
repair. Excerpt 13 is an example of this. Here the caller's talk about a recommendable honeymoon destination shifts to talk about her own holidays.

```
(13)  [Sadie Nine 3] "get about"
1        C4:    so THIS year we're nOt uh actually GOing there;
2               =<<all,p>we're going to STRESa>;
3               .hh but I have[n't uh?
4   →    M2:                  [where's STRESa;
5               (–)
6   →    C4:    in:=uhm ↑lAke maggiORe;
7               (–)
8   →    M2:    <<all,p>´`[ʔu:]>;
9   →           <<all,p>´`[ʔu:]>=you
10  →           .h you get aBOUT;
11              dOn't you ↓JUdy-
12              (–)
13       C4:    an:d we've also been to GARda?
14              (– –)
15       M2:    <<p>´`↑[ʔu:]>;
16              (.)
17              S:EE:;
18              .h about sorRENto;
19              YOU'RE backing up as a [gOOd place
20       C4:                           [i LOVE sorrento;
21              for a hOney moon.
22              (.)
23       M2:    fanTAStic;
24              JUdy,
25              thank you SO: much- ((turn continues))
```

The sound object in line 8 is used to receipt a question-elicited claim which
emerges in the course of an other-initiated self-repair sequence. In line 2, the
caller refers to the name of a small Italian town, Stresa. Coming in in overlap
with the speaker's following TCU (line 3), the presenter produces a next turn
repair initiator (line 4) regarding the location of that town. After a short pause,

the caller repairs the trouble source by specifying the location of Stresa. The presenter responds after a short delay with a double production of the sound object
ooh (lines 8–9). With less lengthening than the high pitched variants, this variant
also has lower pitch and is produced on a rise-fall to mid. The contour begins
at 147 Hz, reaches a pitch peak of 290 Hz and falls to 140 Hz. Additionally, it is
softer than the same speaker's prior talk. The repeated sound object comes with a
similar contour but is slightly louder (cf. the Praat picture in Figure 14).

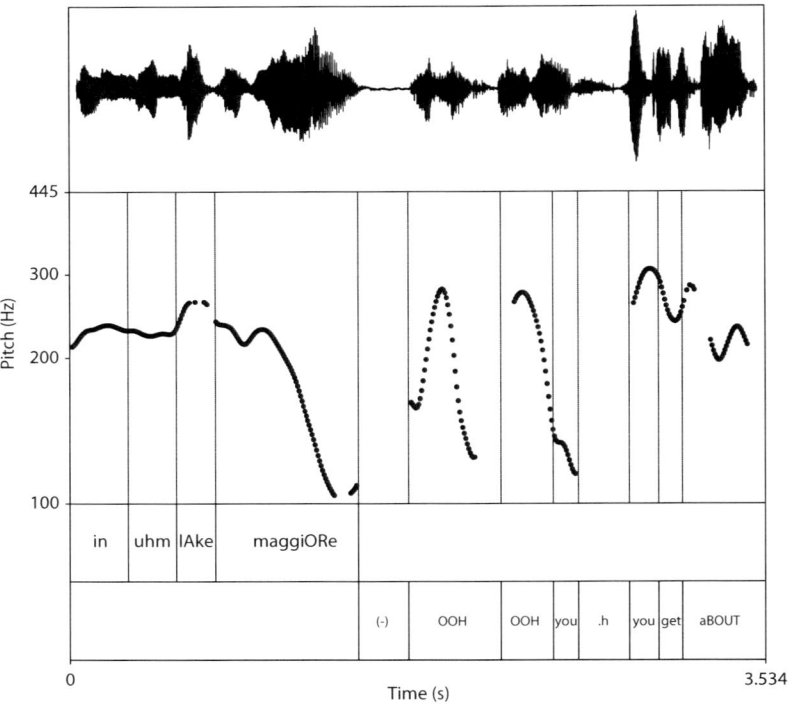

Figure 14. Acoustic analysis of Excerpt 13 ("get about"), lines 6–10

The sound object ratifies the repair, functioning as a repair receipt. Again, the
rise-fall is regarded as treating the content of the repair as exceptional. As in the
case of 'high and pointed' *ooh*, this treatment is not grounded in the way the repair has been set up but is staged in order to serve communicative goals related
to the constraints of interactions in radio phone-ins. The recycled repetition may
be iconic of an upgraded display. In turn expansion, the presenter produces an
other-attribution which can be interpreted as making the following two things
relevant (lines 10–11): First, it appreciates the expert knowledge displayed in the

repair.[83] Secondly, and perhaps only in a wider sense, it acknowledges the positive connotation of the referent Lake Maggiore as a holiday resort.

From this it can be followed that these *ooh*-objects are produced in a slot subsequent to a turn which invites appreciation of its extraordinary and exceptional nature. Unlike the unqualified assessments which are receipted by 'high and pointed' *ooh*, the repair is, however, not evaluative.[84]

Excerpt 14 exemplifies another instance of 'midrange' *ooh* plus turn expansion in a repair sequence. In contrast to Excerpt 13, the next turn repair initiator serves here as a display of ritualised disbelief.

Before the excerpt sets in, the presenter has asked the caller whether she in general likes men with hairy chests, which she has confirmed. The question is a kind of running gag in the programme. Asking all callers this question, the presenter is keeping a tally of which side (women who like men with hairy chests or those who do not) scores highest in the end.

```
(14)   [Brain teaser] "drooling at the lips"
1   →   M1:     .hh has your ↑HUSband got a hairy chEst.
2       C3:     <<breathy>oh he HAS>,
3               (.)
4       M1:     HAS he,
5   →   C3:     <<breathy>YE[AH>;
6   →   M1:               [[ʔu:];=
7   →           =↓you're drOOling at the LIPS- .h[hh
8       C3:                                      [I A[M;
9       M1:                                          [he[he
10      C3:                                             [hehehe[he
11      M1:                                                    [.hh
12              <<smile>one or two hellos to all your friends in
13              CHEAdle>.
```

The production of *ooh* in line 6 is generated in a sequence elicited by line 1. Here the presenter inquires whether the caller's husband has got a hairy chest himself. Given the interactional context of a public radio broadcast, this question can be regarded as intimate and done in a rather saucy style. It receives an *oh*-prefaced confirmation. According to Heritage (1998: 326), "*oh*-prefacing can be exploited to supply emphasis to a response". Thus, the use of *oh* in this sequential position can be taken as an implicit cue which signals the extra significance of the

---

83. In fact, such an analysis is quite ironic because the speaker pronounces the name of the lake in an 'inexpert', i.e. non-native, way.

84. The sound object in line 15 will be discussed in Section 7.6.

confirmation. The entire turn is produced with breathy voice quality, pointing to the sexual implications of the answer. After a micro pause (line 3), the presenter responds with a next turn repair initiator which enacts a display of 'ritualised disbelief' (Heritage 1984: 339) (line 4). It playfully challenges the caller's assertion, alluding to its sexual undertone. When the caller confirms her claim (line 5), this is again done in a breathy voice, once more alluding to the underlying sexual implications of her statement.

In overlap, the recipient responds with the sound object *ooh* (line 6). The lengthened vowel has slightly lower pitch and is slightly softer than the same speaker's prior talk.[85] It has a rise-falling contour to mid. Timed early, it comes with breathy voice quality. Like *ooh* in Excerpt 13, the sound object ratifies the repair. Furthermore, it can be heard as appreciating the sexual implications of the caller's claim, treating them as intense. We would like to argue that this choice of register is related to its sequential placement. The sound object receipts a turn which – when spelled out – can be paraphrased as: "yes, my husband has a hairy chest". It is the second time that a claim to that effect has been made in the sequence (lines 2 and line 5). Its repetition is solicited by the presenter's initiation of repair. In that sense the sound object occurs at a point after the 'progressivity' (Heritage 2007, Schegloff 2007) of the interaction has been suspended in order to perform extra interactional work on the caller's claim. The sound object thus responds to a recycled version of the claim, which is oriented to with a more down-toned, yet affect-laden, recipient receipt.

Next, the presenter extends his turn with a TCU which contains an other-attribution (line 7). It is constructed in terms of a bodily metaphor which visualises the caller's physical pleasure at her husband's hairy chest. This TCU is latched onto the turn-initial sound object, which can be interpreted as an iconic indication of a close conceptual relationship between the two units: While the sound object performs an implicit response to the sexual dimension of the informing, the subsequent other-attribution makes this sexual meaning lexically explicit.

We have shown that midrange *ooh* may be used as an affect-laden repair receipt in response to repair turns of various kinds. While it acknowledges the repair, it treats the content as extraordinary/intense and exceptional. In turn expansion *ooh*-producers may verbalise their stance towards the content of the repair. Such verbalisations occasion a transition to the base sequence.

---

85. Due to the overlap with which the sound object is produced, no reliable Hertz values can be given.

7.6   Global sequential position of variants of *ooh* in radio phone-ins

On a more global level of interaction the analysis of *ooh*-receipts plus turn expansion of the kind presented above is further illuminating with regard to their use in radio phone-ins. Irrespective of form, they are all deployed in the final stages of the interaction shortly before a (pre-)closing is initiated.

It will be argued that similar to the use of 'low-falling and tailed' *ah* in troubles talk (cf. Chapter 8), *ooh* plus turn expansion comes in positions where a maximal appreciation of the other speaker's affective stance is displayed. Subsequent to such a display, an orientation to the next item on the agenda and thus to next-positioned matters may be shown (cf. Beach (1993) for a similar observation with respect to *okay*). We do not argue, however, that the use of *oohs* of this kind projects such a sequential development. Instead, it is suggested that in the talk subsequent to the turn expansion, such a sequential development may be managed and negotiated. Hence the following observations have been made in retrospect, when taking a product-view on interaction. All examples will be reproduced for convenience.

In Excerpt 12', *ooh* plus turn expansion ratifies a summarising assessment, which closes off a longer stretch of talk.

```
(12')   [Sadie Nine 2] "scenery"
1       E1:    but if you jUst go arOUnd the COAST line;
2              you've got what's cAlled the amalfi COAST;
3              and you've got uhm aMALfi,
4              raVELlo,
5              and posiTAno;
6              .h which are All sort of (-) clIff-built (-) TOWNS;
7              little VILlages;
8       M2:    YEAH?
9       E1:    they've (STARted off) as vIllages;
10             NOW are tOwns;
11             and thEY are (.) BEAUTtiful;
12             .h <<all>so much> dOn't mind hairpin BENDS,
13             .hh there's abOUt
14             <<p,all>phEw i don't KNOW>-=
15             =<<p,all>about fIfty hairpin bEnds to get ROUND
16             there>;=
17 →          =<<p>but the> ↑SCE:nery>,
18 →          .h <<p>is fanTASti[c>;
19 → M2:                        [<<pp,h>´`[ʔu:]>;
20 →    i'm being S:OLD here;
```

```
21  →              <<all>you sEE>,=
((ca. 8 secs praise for good advice directed at the callers omitted))
22  →              thanks ↑Ever so mUch;
23  →              well ↑kEEp those calls coming IN; ((turn continues))
```

Here the turn containing *ooh* is followed by a metaphorical expression which is backwards-looking in the sense that it expands on the prior affective appreciation of the interlocutor's contribution. At the same time, it is forwards-looking by proposing a move to the next item on the agenda: The presenter's talk that follows is directed at both the in-studio interlocutor and the radio listeners (cf. Hutchby (2006:73) for this ambivalence of recipiency) and achieves an exit from the conversation as well as inviting further calls. It can therefore be noted that *ooh* plus turn expansion is produced *before* the transition to closing is managed.

The next excerpt illustrates another example of *ooh* plus turn expansion before the presenter engages in transitory moves towards an exit from the conversation.

```
    (14')  [Brain teaser] "drooling at the lips"
1  →  M1:    .hh has your ↑HUSband got a hairy chEst.
2     C3:    <<breathy>oh he HAS>,
3            (.)
4     M1:    HAS he,
5  →  C3:    <<breathy>YE[AH>;
6  →  M1:               [[ʔu:];=
7  →         =↓you're drOOling at the LIPS- .h[hh
8     C3:                                      [I A[M;
9     M1:                                          [he[he
10    C3:                                             [hehehe[he
11    M1:                                                    [.hh
12           <<smile>one or two hellos to all your friends in
13           CHEAdle>.
```

In what follows the sound object plus other-attribution (lines 6–7), the presenter makes a closing-implicative move (lines 12–13). The proposal to greet some friends serves to move to the next item on the agenda, which in this programme usually introduces a stepwise termination of the interaction proper.

Excerpt 13' shows that the transition to closure-implicative, next-positioned matters must sometimes be negotiated with the caller.

```
    (13')  [Sadie Nine 3] "get about"
1     C4:    so THIS year we're nOt uh actually GOing there;
2            =<<all,p>we're going to StRESa>;
3            .hh but I have[n't uh?
4  →  M2:                  [where's STRESa;
```

```
5                    (-)
6    →   C4:         in:=uhm ↑lAke maggiORe;
7                    (-)
8    →   M2:         <<all,p>´`[ʔu:]>;
9    →               <<all,p>´`[ʔu:]>=you
10   →               .h you get aBOUT;
11                   dOn't you ↓JUdy-
12                   (-)
13       C4:         an:d we've also been to GARda?
14                   (--)
15       M2:         <<p>´`↑[ʔu:]>;
16                   (.)
17                   S:EE:;
18                   .h about sorRENto;
19                   YOU'RE backing up as a [gOOd place
20       C4:                                [i LOVE sorrento;
21                   for a hOney moon.
22                   (.)
23       M2:         fanTAStic;
24                   JUdy,
25                   thank you SO: much- ((turn continues))
```

Following an *ooh*-receipt (line 15) in response to the caller's informing, the presenter initiates a closing of the interaction: In lines 17–19 the presenter performs a
concluding enquiry about the caller's stance toward Sorrento, the town initially mentioned as the place to go on a honeymoon. According to Heritage (1985: 100), "for-
mulating", that is, "summarising, glossing, or developing the gist of an informant's
earlier statements" constitutes a strategic tool for interviewers to steer the on-going
interaction (cf. also Drew and Heritage (1992b: 49). The caller's response (line 20)
can be understood as an upgraded confirmation (in the sense that "loving Sorrento"
lexically upgrades the meaning of "being a good place"). The presenter responds
with a 'high-grade assessment' (Antaki et al. 2000) (line 23) and then expresses her
thanks, the latter being a conventional way to proffer closings in radio-phone-ins
(Thornborrow 2001). The turn-initial *ooh*-receipt thus serves as a recipient response
in the final stages of that interaction,[86] before closing is proposed.

What are possible implications of the frequent co-occurrence of *ooh* receipts
plus turn expansion and interaction-closing moves? Antaki et al. (2000) observe
that in clinical questionnaire-based interviews, the interviewer may insert a

---

86. Given that a radio broadcast is subject to time constraints it is even possible that the presenter has been given a signal in the background to close down the interaction. This would
mean that the closing is occasioned by factors external to the interaction.

'high-grade assessment' such as "brilliant" or "terrific" both after completion of single question-answer pairs and of larger units, e.g. the first page or the entire questionnaire (ibid: 246–249). This kind of sequential pattern is described as [answer receipt] + ["ok" or "right" etc.)] + [high-grade assessment] + [next question] (ibid: 242). Such high-grade assessments do not relate to the content of the answer given by the patient; instead "they explicitly signal the previous material as having been successfully, indeed praiseworthily completed" (ibid: 246). According to Antaki et al. (2000: 238), high-grade assessments differ in this respect from answer receipts which orient simply towards the "informational or propositional content" of the patient's answer.

In the present data, presenters are introducing the final stages of an interaction before closing. These seem to be biased for the use of *ooh*-receipts in response to callers' claims. *Ooh* receipts are reserved primarily for the presenter, who is the institutional representative and therefore in charge of the interaction. This points to *ooh*-initial responses serving as a structural resource in a way similar to the 'high-grade assessments' of Antaki et al. (2000). Remember that the callers, claiming to draw on first-hand personal experience, construct themselves as experts concerning their contribution. In return, it is the presenter's task to appreciate the caller's contribution and their role as an expert and to *reward* them for their proposal. In contrast to 'high-grade assessments' *ooh*-objects operate in terms of sequential aspects *and* content: The sound object ratifies the prior action, while at the same time appreciating its affective implications. In this way the presenter can signal that the caller's reason for the call and therefore the business of the interaction has been achieved and completed. We do not argue that *ooh*-initial responses project a transition to the next stage the way 'high-grade assessments' do. Yet their sequential positioning can be analysed as strategically exploited in order to construct maximal appreciation before gradually moving to a termination of the conversation.

7.7   Stand-alone *ooh*+ subsequent other-speaker talk in radio phone-ins

The radio data contain only two instances of prosodically prominent *ooh*s followed by a next-speaker incoming. Moreover, the forms and uses of these two tokens are not fully compatible with the collection of *ooh*s plus turn expansion. Formwise, both tokens have different prosodic-phonetic packaging. The object presented below can be compared to the type of 'midrange' *ooh* but it is even lower pitched. In terms of use, both stand-alone *ooh*s in the radio data are deployed as recipient tokens of prepared speech in pre-arranged telephone interactions. Hence, they do not receipt spontaneous talk like those delivered in the interactions between caller and presenter. Interestingly enough, in both cases the sound object receipts the activity of "doing giving cooking tips" by radio chefs, that is, by experts. What the two tokens have in common is that they appreciate and affiliate with the positive valence of the expert's talk by signalling a kind of pleased satisfaction and that they make a sequence expansion and more topical talk relevant next. In contrast to the cases of *ooh* plus turn expansion, what follows does not introduce new aspects of the on-going topical talk (e.g. Excerpt 11 "a little tip") but extends the turn receipted by *ooh* in terms of content.

Excerpt 15 is taken from a pre-arranged telephone conversation between chef Ronnie and the in-studio presenter. Line 1 occasions the activity.

```
(15)   [Sadie Nine 3] "on your slab this morning"
1        M2:     .hh and whAt's on your slab this MORNing ronnie-
2                (--)
3    →   CR:     (well) on the slab this morning we've got some
4    →           <<len>wOnderful english grey MULlet>,
5                (---)
6    →   M2:     <<l>´`[?u[:]>.
7        CR:             [they're a vEry seasonal THING-
                 ((turn continues))
```

Line 1 elicits the cooking tips sequence. It asks about the dish the chef is going to recommend. The response is forthcoming after a medium pause (lines 3–4). The name of the fish is pre-modified by a positively valenced adjective. The modifier and the compound noun are delivered with dense articulation. This kind of prosodic contextualisation upgrades the positive attribution and connotation of the phrase and thus invites an evaluative response. There follows a long pause in which a recipient response is noticeably absent (line 5). In line 6, this response is finally produced in the form of a sound object *ooh*, which is lengthened, done in the lower range of the speaker's voice and has a rising-falling contour. Furthermore, the object is softer than the same speaker's prior talk and comes in delayed (cf. Figure 15 below). Its voice quality is breathy.

In line with 'high and pointed' *ooh*, this sound object, albeit produced with different prosodic-phonetic packaging, receipts an unqualified, positively valenced assessment. The lengthening and low pitch seem to show heightened affective involvement. The rise-fall may treat the content of the prior turn as exceptional, which might explain why the object is heard doing some kind of satisfaction mixed with pleasure, as if to say: "Yummy!". Again, the prior linguistic context is not designed to elicit an orientation towards the exceptionalness of the informing. For this and other reasons explained in the previous sections, the contour is treated as a staged production.

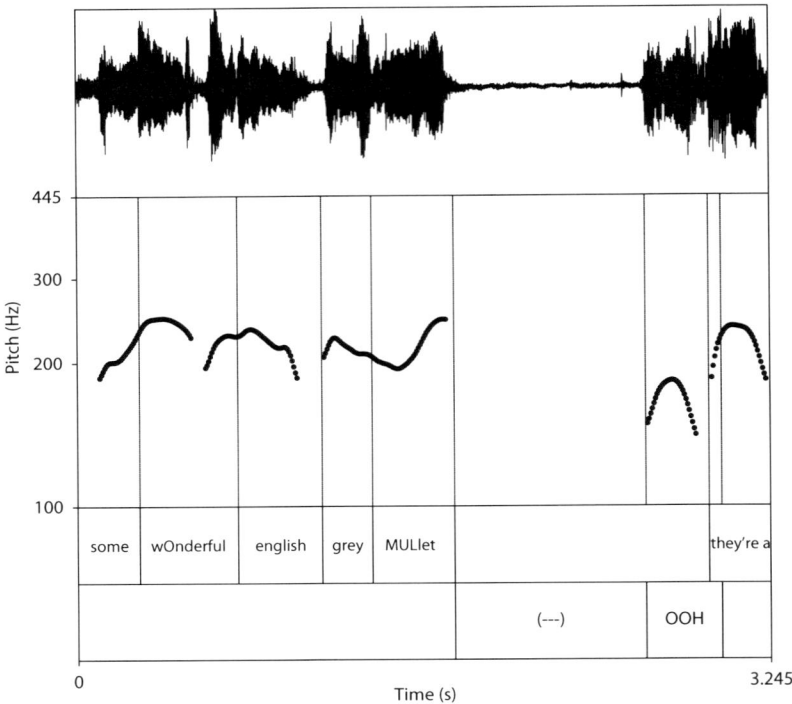

Figure 15. Acoustic analysis of Excerpt 15 ("on your slab this morning"), lines 3–7

Thus, the object affiliates with the prior evaluation in a staged, affect-laden manner. The receipt acknowledges lines 3–4 as informative and complete, while appreciating their evaluative dimension.

The smooth transition to line 7 indicates orientation to a TRP following the object. Resuming his talk, the expert next adds more detail to the nature of the dish. This provides evidence that the sound object is treated as sequence-expanding. Generally, the prepared nature of the interaction may result in an orientation towards progressivity and passive recipiency: the first speaker, i.e. the chef, is permitted to retain the floor (cf. Beach (1993: 341) for a discussion of *okay* with respect to this point). What is more, the use of the adjective phrase *vEry seasonal* verbalises a special, exceptional aspect of the dish. The verbalisation may be treated as orienting towards *ooh*. This may support the interpretation that *ooh* appreciates the exceptionalness of the dish.

To sum up, the sound object *ooh* with low pitched, rising-falling prosody can be used as a response token which acknowledges the prior assessment in passive recipiency and leaves the floor to the expert in post-production space. It appreci-ates the positive exceptional nature of assessment through a display of pleased satisfaction. The affect-laden sound object makes more talk related to the content of the prior assessment relevant and is in this way continuative. The interpretation that the sound object orients towards the exceptional nature of the prior assess-ment is supported by the subsequent topicalisation of a special, exceptional aspect by the first speaker.

7.8   'High' *ooh* in response to highly detailed informings in mundane complaints and troubles telling

While the sections above concentrated on variants of *ooh* in radio interactions, this section deals with *ooh* with high pitched prosody in everyday telephone con-versations. Here the object is very infrequent and is only used in order to receipt negatively valenced actions, as delivered in complaints and troubles telling. The low frequency of *oohs* in the conversational data set does not permit a more general account of the *activities* they are deployed in. Despite this, the analysis provides valuable insights when the use of *ooh* as a complaint or troubles receipt is contrasted with that of other sound objects in the same activity type, e.g. *click* as a complaint receipt (cf. Chapter 9) or 'low-falling and tailed' *ah* as a troubles receipt (cf. Chapter 8). Furthermore, the following discussion complements the findings on the use of high pitched *ooh* as an assessment receipt in radio phone-ins, where such sound objects were primarily found to respond to positively va-lenced assessments.

The actions that *ooh* responds to in everyday complaint and troubles se-quences have the format of unqualified statements which detail an aspect of topical talk in a drastic fashion. To give the exact details of a state of affairs is not typical of everyday interactions, where participants tend to display more "tolerance for imprecision and exaggeration" (Drew 2003: 922), although they also show an orientation towards "standards of relevant precision" (ibid: 937). It is rather characteristic of institutional interactions such as e.g. courtroom interactions and medical examinations that extreme or exaggerated claims may be questioned and producers of such claims may be asked to be more precise (Drew 2003).

Given these practices, informings which give exact details about some state-of-affairs are treated as deviations from the norm and therefore achieve a drastic effect in the everyday telephone interactions examined here.

7.8.1   'High' ooh *as a complaint receipt*

Drew (1998) observes that complaints about third parties' moral transgressions
and misconduct are formulated in rather "explicit" and "overt" terms (ibid: 306).
In other words, complaining parties do not usually mince words about such matters. He observes that recipients of such complaints can display their "moral indignation" through response cries (ibid: 310). In the everyday data examined in
the present study, high pitched *ooh* is deployed in sequential slots following a
complaint which details (cf. also Drew (1998: 318) for the observation that complainants can make "*overdetermined* descriptions of actions", italics in the original) and thereby 'objectifies' an aspect of the on-going topical talk. Such detailings
and objectifications are treated as rhetorical resources to upgrade the interactional
thrust of the complaint (cf. Pomerantz (1986).

The following fragment is an example of an *ooh*-receipt (line 31) of such a
highly detailed statement, which implements an account for a complaint about
housing prices.

```
(16)   [HOLT:M88:2:4] "telephone number"
1       Hil:   anyway they've got this vEry nice house in
2              ↓well they've fOUnd this vEry nice house in ↑GUILDford;
3       Mar:   YE:S,
4              (-)
5       Hil:   so: uhm[:
6       Mar:          [.hhh
7              which is the WAL[polston area of gUIldford,=
8       Mar:                  [hhh
9       Hil:   =(i[t is) vEry
10      Mar:     [yeah,
11      Hil:   on a vEry nice
12      Hil:   it's a ↑bIg eSTATE;=
13             =but it's VERy very NICE,
14      Mar:   h YEAH,
15             (--)
16      Hil:   uh::
17             but ↑quIte HONestly;
18             the prIces that (they've had to)
19             they've to pay up here is absolutely hor↑RIFic;
20             you KNO:[W,
21      Mar:          [yeah:- hh
22             sO i GATHer;=
23  →          =i mEAn the?
24  →          .hhh they they're fan↑TAStic;
```

```
25  →              Aren't [they;=
26  →                     NOW,
27  →   Hil:            [(that's ri:ght)
28  →              they're tal?
29  →              they're pAYing a hundred and TEN;
30  →              MARK;=
31  →   Mar:   =()87 ↑´`[?u:↓];.hh
32  →              (.)
33  →              GEE::;=
34  →              =<<all>hOw do they DO it>?=
35  →              =is it=
36  →              =you're ↑sUre that's not the TELephone ↓number;
37  →              HILla[ry,
38      Hil:           [NO: dea[r;=
39      Mar:                   [.hhh
40      Hil:   =but it mAkes you CRINGE, ((turn continues))
```

The turn which is receipted by the sound object *ooh* is delivered in lines 28–30: It details the price of the house in that it gives the exact sum rather than referring to it in more genral terms, such as *absolutely hor↑RIFic*, as was done in line 19. In terms of action, the turn thus accomplishes an account for a previous general complaint.

The negative valence of the sum, which would be – out of context – no more than neutral information, is gradually built up in the talk prior to it: After mentioning the positive aspects of the house (lines 1–2, 11–13),[88] the complainant contrasts them – signalled by the connector *but* in line 17 – to its price (lines 18–19). In closing so, she performs a complaint, which can be paraphrased as "The house is very nice but its price is absolutely horrific". The negative evaluation is lexically framed in an upscaled way in that the highly negative evaluative adjective *hor↑RIFic* is upgraded through an intensifying adverb *absolutely*. The local meaning of the discourse marker *you KNO:[W,* (line 20) invites a response. The recipient shows an orientation towards this by signalling agreement and producing a second assessment in next turn (lines 21–24). The tag question (lines 25–26) yields epistemic authority to the complainant (Raymond and Heritage 2006), to

---

87. The sound recorded at this point and transcribed as '.tlok' by Gail Jefferson cannot be clearly identified as a mechanical or a human one.

88. It is open to conjecture whether the mentioning of *the WAL[polston area* (line 7) constitutes another positive aspect of the house.

the effect that the sequence is subsequently expanded. In this way, the recipient turn thereby carries out a double action: First, it serves as a second assessment, which has been made relevant by the prior turn (Pomerantz 1984). Second, it leaves the epistemic authority over this assessment to the complainant.

In response, the complainant produces an account, the one which will subsequently be receipted by the sound object *ooh*. Remember that the price of the house was presented as "horrific" and agreed to be "fantastic" (in the negative sense of the word): Thus, the sum is prepared for as being negatively valenced (line 29).

At the same time, the overt statement of the house price functions as a highly detailed, evidential account which invites an affect-laden response. Its interactional thrust is additionally intensified through the turn-final personal address form (line 30).

The sound object used in response is phonetically different from the other variants of *ooh* in that it constitutes an ingressive sound. Prosodically, it is lengthened and higherpitched than prior talk by the same speaker. Moreover, it is delivered with high pitch register (in absolute terms) and produced with a lengthened, flat rise-fall to mid. The contour begins at 230 Hz, reaches a maximum of 277 Hz and falls to 230 Hz. The object is not louder than the same speaker's prior talk, has breathy voice quality and fades out into a hearable inbreath.

Given that the account is implicitly negative, highly detailed and unmitigated and to some extent comes as news to the *ooh*-producer – one reason why he does not make an upgraded assessment in line 31 may be that he is simply not aware of the current real estate prices in this area –, the sound object can be treated as serving multiple functions: It functions as a news receipt and at the same time treats the prior informing as inviting an affect-laden response: The lengthening and the extra high pitch display heightened affective involvement. The ingressive and in this sense reverse articulation can be taken as a contextualisation cue which upgrades the signal of heightened involvement even more. Assuming that the display orients towards the highly detailed, implicitly negative nature of a newsworthy account, it can be analysed as doing a mixture of 'indignation', 'shock' and 'disbelief'.

In what follows, the *ooh*-producer gradually seeks to mitigate his initially strong response: After delivering another display of heightened affective involvement (line 33) (following a short pause, line 32), he expands his turn with a rhetorical question which signals 'disbelief' (line 34). He then produces a question, this time jocular, which treats the account as a laughable (line 36). Thus, these moves from showing strong affect, to displaying 'disbelief' to a finally changing in the interactional mode can be seen as a gradual working towards 'getting back to business as usual'.

However, the complainant orients towards the light-hearted work-up of the complaint in a rather stoic manner: Maintaining a non-jocular modality, she first disconfirms the question (line 38) and then again displays a negative stance towards the housing prices (line 40). The phrase *it mAkes you CRINGE* constitutes a bodily metaphor for the physical experience of 'fear' or 'shock'. The complainant thus reconstitutes the serious mode of the interaction, which terminates the local sequence but allows for an expansion of the global complaint sequence in turn expansion (not shown here).

We have seen that 'high' *ooh* is used as a recipient resource in response to a highly detailed, unmitigated account in a complaint sequence. It acknowledges the account which substantiates a previous complaint, appreciating its extremely negative affective implications, and thus functions as an affect-laden complaint receipt.

Whereas such overt references to complainables are common in complaint activities, troubles talk is characterised by a tension between attending to the trouble and attending to business as usual. As a result, the kind of highly detailed, unmitigated formulations typical of complaints and receipted by 'high' *ooh* in the example above are not what are expected in troubles talk. The next section examines such a rare case.

7.8.2   *'High' ooh as a troubles receipt*

A general observation of our study on affect has been that if speakers bring forth an informing which is potentially negatively valenced, they usually do so in a dispreferred fashion: Using multiple linguistic resources, they delay, hedge and/or downtone their informing such that its negative dimension is mitigated (cf. also Freese and Maynard (1998) on deliveries of bad news). Holt (1993) in her study on death announcements finds that participants even tend to highlight the *positive* aspects of this event ("she was very poorly", "she died very peacefully"), thus mitigating the negative implications for the party affected by the death.[89] Interestingly, a single case analysis of 'high' *ooh* in troubles talk shows the opposite: In Excerpt 17 this kind of sound object responds to an action whose negative dimension is *not* mitigated or qualified, be it phonetically-prosodically or lexically (For comparison, cf. Chapter 8 on *ah* in troubles talk/deliveries of bad news). This may account for the infrequency of such cases in the present corpus, since participants tend to avoid doing topical talk in troubles talk in an overtly negative manner.

---

89. Her data only included news deliveries where the death of elderly people was announced. It is up to future research whether death announcements of people at a younger age would be handled in a different fashion.

The turn is constructed as a non-extreme yet unqualified declarative statement, which informs the recipient of a state of affairs in a highly detailed fashion. In the post-production context, the affective implications are further dealt with and worked up.

The troubles talk between Leslie and a tradesman Coupland is elicited by Leslie's enquiry about her interlocutor's recent stay in hospital (line 1). Coupland subsequently explains that he has fallen and broken his spine.

```
(17)   [HOLT:2:7] "fractures at the vertebrae"
1       Les:   cause <<h>you were in HOSpital> [i think;
2       Cou:                                    [well that's RIGHT;
3              <<all>Everything is it's such a long time aGO>;
4              <<all>it's very good of you to> reMI(h)ND me;
5       Les:   (WOW);=
6       Cou:   =i i have (0.26)
7              that's right;=
8              =i (0.30) i had a bad FALL;
9              (0.20)
10      Les:   did YOU?
11      Cou:   YE:S;=
12             =[i
13      Les:    [what did you DO;
14      Cou:   (so) i fe? i
15             you know i specialise in CLIMbing wor:k,=
16             =and[.hh
17      Les:       [YES;
18      Cou:   this is one of these where (0.24) the mighty was FALlen
19             i'm afr(h)ai(h)d;=
20      Les:   =´`OH::;
21  →   Les:   and di[d you ↑BREAK Anything;
22      Cou:         [(it was)
23  →   Cou:   well i've gOt (some) stable frActures at the VERtebrae;
24             (-)
25  →   Les:   <<pp>[hʊʔ↑´`[u:]>;
26  →   Cou:        [<<all,p,>(*) well (***)>
27  →             it sOUnds AWful;=
28             =(%i %bet).hh
29             but it
30             .hh / (--)
31             i:t's uh:
32             (-)
33             it's jUst gonna be a:
34             (-)
```

```
35        a lO:ng TI?
36        <<all>uh well i've gOt another fOUr weeks before i
37        shOUld be:>
38        (.) sort of reasonably FI:T.
```

The highly detailed, unqualified informing of analytic interest (line 23) implements an exposition of the trouble announced in lines 8 and 18–19, presenting
the consequences of the trouble teller's accident. To understand the interactional
thrust of this kind of informing, which leads to the production of 'high' *ooh*,
one has to reconstruct the build-up of the trouble announcement (lines 18–19)
immediately prior to the highly detailed, unqualified troubles informing: After
a pre-telling in line 15, which secures common ground about the trouble teller's
occupation, the trouble, that is, Coupland's fall, is (once more) referred to in
a self-ironic fashion (lines 18–19). The change-of-state token (Heritage 1984)
which the recipient produces next (line 20) has a lengthy, low-pitched rise-falling
contour with a final long glide to mid; it is monophthongised towards the end.
This prosodic make-up suggests that the recipient adopts the ironic modality;
as indicated by a smile voice, the light-hearted stance is maintained when the
next enquiry is made in turn expansion. The *and*-prefacing further shows an
orientation towards the broader agenda. In return, the troubles teller provides
a highly detailed description of the exact nature of his injuries. It is delivered in
the medical register (*stable frActures at the VERtebrae*), which marks a contrast
to the vernacular wording in the troubles recipient's enquiry (*di[d you ↑BRE]AK
Anything*). The use of medical vocabulary constitutes a resource for detailing
and at the same time objectivising in this context (line 23), which allows the
troubles teller to state the mere, "objective" facts in an unmitigated, unadorned
and thus drastic fashion.[90] In this manner, the lexical design of the turn achieves
a fairly abrupt change of interactional style or register. This kind of turn design
and placement make an affiliative response relevant, which is forthcoming next:
After a medium pause, the recipient responds with two sound objects (line 25).
The first object is cut off by a glottal stop. It is followed by a second object, which
contains a lengthened vowel close to the quality of cardinal vowel 8 ([u]). Prosodically, the vowel is accompanied by a step up to high and a flat rising-falling contour with a final fall to mid. The sound is delivered in a very weak, soft
fashion (thus making a weak gesture), has breathy voice quality and fades out

---

90. As pointed out by one of the anonymous reviewers, "[t]his medical term is not only more
objective but also more precise, indicating a less serious injury than an 'instable fracture' or a
'broken spine' (the latter of which could mean paralysis)."

towards the end.[91] What comes off as a bisyllabic object can be analysed as an instance of self-initiated self-repair, with the first element, i.e. the repairable, being cut off by a glottal stop (Schegloff 1979). It is then repaired in terms of a 'high' *ooh*-receipt: Consequently, the repair performs a re-orientation in terms of affective involvement and intensifies the affiliation displayed. This re-orientation has been made relevant by the unqualified and highly detailed nature of the prior informing, whose implementation the recipient did not anticipate. This can be seen by the format of her initial question, which is conducive to a response in a vernacular register.

In terms of function, 'high' *ooh* acknowledges the highly detailed troubles informing, appreciating its affective implications as extreme and affiliating with it. The sound object thus serves as an affiliative affect-laden troubles receipt. Unlike the troubles receipt *ah*, however, it orients towards the negative informing with an affective quality which may be described as 'shock' in everyday terms.

In what follows, the troubles teller resumes his talk with an early incoming (line 26), showing orientation to the affect-laden troubles receipt by backing down from its highly negative thrust. Despite the overlap, the use of the initial discourse marker *well*, which marks a concessive construction, evidences that the troubles teller responds to the way his informing was receipted. After some self-repair the troubles teller next ascribes negative valence to the informing through the negative evaluative adjective *AWful* (line 27). Note that he uses the copular verb *sOUnds* instead of e.g. *Is* in the assessment, which signals a mitigated epistemic stance. The epistemic marker in line 28, which post-modifies the assessment, works toward the same effect. The outbreath on post-completion in the same line can be heard as soundless laughter signalling 'trouble-resistance' (Jefferson 1984b). This trouble-resistance is further displayed by the adversative construction projected by the adversative marker *but*: The potentially lengthy process of recovery is constructed as something positive (lines 29–38). The troubles teller thus retracts the implications of his highly detailed negative informing (line 23) and resumes his orientation to business as usual (Jefferson 1988).

We have seen that 'high' *ooh* can be deployed to receipt unqualified negative troubles informings, which highly detail and objectify a state of affairs. A linguistic formatting of this sort is not so common for troubles informings, because troubles tellers tend to be aim for the right balance between an orientation towards the trouble and to business as usual in their talk. Like the troubles receipt *ah*, the sound object examined acknowledges the informing as troubles-informative. In contrast to this type of *ah*, it does not, however, treat the troubles informing with empathy (cf. Section 8.4) but seems to display 'shock' or 'horror'.

---

91. Due to the poor quality of the recording, no Praat analysis can be made.

Comparing the complaint receipt and the troubles receipt examined above, they are both high pitched and have a flat rising-falling contour with a final pitch movement to mid. For this reason they are formally categorised as the same kind of object, namely 'high' *ooh*. Although their function is *sequentially* different, with one object implementing a complaint receipt and the other a troubles receipt, they do similar things *interactionally*: Both display affective involvement and affiliation in response to highly detailed, objectifying informings with drastic affective import. However, the affective connotations slightly differ, with the affective dimensions displayed by the complaint receipt potentially being described as 'indignation', 'shock' and 'disbelief' and those by the troubles receipt as 'horror' and 'shock'. In this way, *ooh*-producers comply with the interactional relevancies in such sequential positions. In contrast to institutional interactions such as news interviews (Heritage 1985), displays of non-commitment and non-affiliation would constitute highly dispreferred actions with a corresponding impact on the further interactional development.

In the post-production context, first speakers can either further maintain their negative, unmitigated stance or back down from its negative implications. Both strategies support the observation that 'high' *ooh* is perceived as conveying the recipient's highly negatively valenced stance.

7.9 *Ooh* – a marker of extreme and dramatic affect?

In this section, it has been argued that the variants of the response token *ooh* serve to appreciate the prior informing as intense, extreme and/or dramatic (apart from showing some orientation to its exceptional nature). This was supported by the claim that it responds to unqualified assessments and highly detailed informings which implement rhetorically strong actions and make an equally strong response relevant. Excerpt 18 supports this interpretation by exemplifying a case where the production of an *ooh*-prefaced turn, that is, an *ooh*-token which forms part of a larger intonation phrase in initial position, is questioned in terms of its appropriateness. We will argue that this is done because the *ooh*-prefacing lends extra intensity to the response. Generally, the following discussion should only be seen as a footnote to the discussion on the variants of *ooh*, since the *ooh* examined here– in contrast to the ones analysed above – does not have prosodic prominence. This means that the sound object does not implement an independent action but provides – to borrow Heritage's (1998: 327) term – a "colouring" of the subsequent elements in the unit. Moreover, the example further substantiates the general claim made throughout this study that sound objects are perceived and treated as distinct conversational objects by participants in talk-in-interaction.

Excerpt 18 is taken from a radio phone-in where listeners call to give their answer to a riddle. Before the callers propose their solution, questions about the caller's biographical background are part of this programme's regular agenda.

```
(18)  [Brain teaser] "a bit young"
 1  →   M1:     <<all>have you got a BOYfriend>?
 2          (-)
 3  →   C1:     <<h>↑[ʔu] NO>;
 4          (-)
 5  →   M1:     <<h>↑[ʔu] NO>;
 6  →   M1:     <<h>whY do you say ↑[ʔu:] NO>;
 7          (.)
 8      M1:     i [MEAN; (.)
 9      C1:       [<<p>NO:>;
10  →   M1:     why why shOUldn't you have a ↑BOYfriend;=
11              =you sOUnd a lovely GIR:L?
12          (.)
13      C1:     i'm a bit YOUNG; i thInk;
14          (.)
15      M1:     how OLD are yOU?
16          (-)
17      C1:     nineTEEN,
```

The *ooh*-prefaced turn of interest is in line 3. It implements a response to the pre-senter's question whether the caller has got a boyfriend (line 1). The short initial delay of the turn points to a dispreferred turn format; the lexical item *no* indicates that the answer is negative. In terms of vowel quality, the sound object is similar to that of the cardinal vowel 8 ([u]). Prosodically, the entire turn has high global pitch. The sound object is produced on a high step-up in pitch and with a rising-falling contour. It is slightly lengthened and slightly louder than the prior talk. The global high pitch and the fall are maintained on *NO*. The two elements are integrated in one single TCU, with *NO* bearing the primary accent.

In his next turn, the presenter delivers a copy of the caller's turn. He also comes in with a short delay (line 4). Again, the vowel quality of the initial sound object is in the region of cardinal vowel 8 ([u]) and the sound object is followed by the negative marker *NO*. The presenter's voice indicates that this is not a random copy: By shifting into falsetto, the presenter adopts a pitch outside his normal range.[92] Hence the copy comes close to the original's pitch height. Thus, even though the copy does not perfectly match the original in terms of tempo and contour, in terms of pitch register, it forms an almost absolute match of the caller's turn in line 5 (cf. Figure 16).

---

92. For M1's overall pitch range, see Table 3.

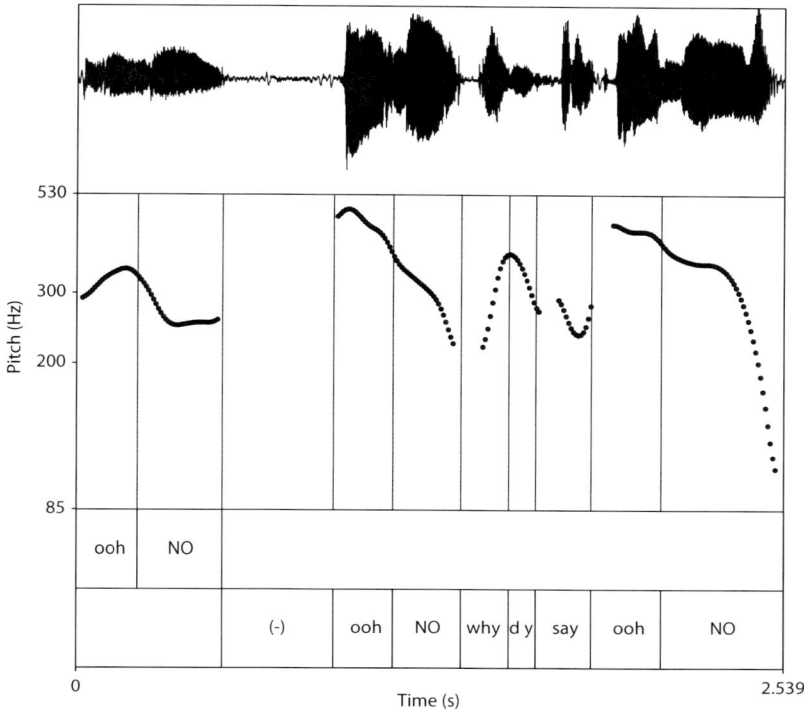

Figure 16. Acoustic analysis of Excerpt 18 ("a bit young"), lines 3–6

According to Couper-Kuhlen (1996) and Svennevig (2004), such other-repetitions do not represent random phenomena; they constitute a participant resource for various interactional purposes. Couper-Kuhlen (1996) examines repetitions of callers' answers which match in absolute pitch height on the basis of the same audio recordings. She argues that "by imitating his caller's words *and* pitch, the presenter can be heard to draw attention to and indirectly criticise the guess to and/or the way it is produced." (ibid:391, emphasis in the original). Similarly, Svennevig (2004) shows for Norwegian that speakers may display an affective stance of various sorts towards the content of prior talk through lexical other-repetition. This means that other-repetition, whether merely lexical or both lexical and prosodic, does not occur at random: It represents an orientation towards the unit repeated and a resource for the expression of (affective) stance towards it.

A closer examination of the subsequent interaction supports this interpretation: In line 6, the presenter produces another lexical repetition of the caller's *ooh*-prefaced response. In terms of prosody, it is not a good copy. This time he frames it as a direct quotation of the caller's *ooh*-prefaced turn in reported speech. The reported speech is embedded in a *wh*-question which solicits an account for line 3. In orientation to a short pause, which signals the relevant absence of response on the part of the caller, the presenter expands his turn. The use of the discourse marker *i MEAN* (line 8) projects that what is to come (lines 10–11) makes the presenter's previous talk more explicit and specific (Imo 2005). The use of the modal verb *shOUld* in line 10 conveys that the presenter interprets the caller's response as treating it as unlikely or improbable for her to have a boyfriend. This suggests that as opposed to a plain *no* or *no, I haven't*, the *ooh*-prefaced *NO* is heard to have done more than just disconfirming. Also, the caller's account which is forthcoming next (line 13) does not indicate that the presenter's understanding was wrong: It orients towards the (un)likelihood of her having a boyfriend.

This finding corresponds to Heritage (1998) on *oh*-prefaced responses to enquiries, that is, turns situated in the same sequential position as the *ooh*-prefaced turn here. He concludes: "Oh-prefacing can thus be a practice through which a speaker indicates a problem about a question's relevance, appropriateness, or presuppositions" (ibid: 295).

It is argued that the *ooh*-prefaced response in our example implies such a proposal as well: The presenter's question whether the caller has a boyfriend may be treated as inappropriate since the caller does not consider it a likely state of affairs that she should have a boy-friend because of her age. In addition, however, the choice of *ooh* over *oh* indicates an additional affective dimension, which adds an extra intensity to the action.

The excerpt has shown that the *ooh*-prefaced turn is perceived as a distinct formal entity which can be reproduced and imitated. This means that the vowel quality of the initial sound object is not delivered at random but treated as a meaningful element. From the way the *ooh*-prefaced turn is dealt with, it can be inferred that it conveys a specific meaning, i.e. it does more than mere disconfirming in that it signals an extreme affective stance towards the inappropriateness of the question.

7.10 Summary and conclusions

This chapter has examined the forms and functions of variants of *ooh* in response to unqualified, positive assessments and repair turns in radio phone-ins as well as in response to highly detailed informings in everyday conversation. Specifically, the analysis has focused on variants of *ooh* when produced under an independent contour with subsequent turn expansion. A summary of the main findings can be seen in Table 7.

To discuss, the prosodic cluster accompanying the variants of *ooh* is not an absolute, context-free pattern: It has been shown that speakers can increase the

Table 7. Variants of the sound object *ooh*: Forms and functions

Sound object		High and pointed *ooh*	High *ooh*	High *ooh*	Midrange *ooh*
obligatory prosodic-phonetic properties	segmental substance	close to cardinal vowel 8 (rounded, unrounded or ingressive)			
	duration	lengthened			
	pitch register	higher than prior speech by same speaker			lower than prior speech by same speaker
	pitch movement	wide ranging rise-fall	rise-falling		wide ranging rise-fall
	voice quality	breathy			
sequential placement		A: unqualified positive assessment B: affect-laden acknowledgement of the assessment (high and pointed *ooh*)	A: highly detailed troubles informing B: affect-laden troubles receipt (high *ooh*)	A: highly detailed complaint B: affect-laden complaint receipt (high *ooh*)	A: affectively valenced repairable B: initiation of repair (dealing with a trouble in understanding) A: (affectively valenced) repair B: affect-laden repair receipt (midrange and pointed *ooh*)
sequence-organising function		acknowledgement of assessment (assessment receipt)	acknowledgement of trouble (troubles receipt)	acknowledgement of complaint (complaint receipt)	acknowledgement of repair (repair receipt)
interactional function		(staged) display of 'pleasure'/'enthusiasm' about something exceptional, affiliation	display of 'horror'/'shock', affiliation		(staged) display of 'appreciation', affiliation
if turn expansion		positive assessment	–	mitigation of the negative implications of the affect-laden complaint receipt	('appreciative' formulation)
if stand-alone		–	retracting of the negative implications of the highly detailed troubles informing	–	–

affective involvement signalled by the object by modifying its vowel quality and increasing its prominence and pitch height.

In radio-phone-ins, 'high and pointed' *ooh* constitutes a presenter's resource. The accomplishment of such affective receipts makes the affective loading of the assessment available to the audience. As Couper-Kuhlen (1996: 391) notes, a programme's success relies heavily on audience interest. To perform staged displays of affect which may be labelled as doing 'enthusiasm' and 'positive excitement' may be one strategy to secure listeners' affiliation, to entertain them and to keep their interest in the radio broadcast alive. *Ooh*s in radio phone-ins also tend to be deployed close to interactional closings, which are always solicited by the presenter. This points to the fact that the presenter deploys the sound object to reward callers for their contribution and thereby legitimises a transition to the next item of the agenda. This transition is, however, not achieved by the sound object, but by the assessment implemented in turn expansion.

Ooh was rarely found to be followed by other speaker's resumption of talk. The cases found were characteristic of prepared speech situations.

Further, the analyses of 'high and pointed' and 'high' *ooh*s have shown that sound objects with similar shape can be used both in response to positively and negatively valenced informings. This corresponds to Local and Walker (2008), who find that the prosodic design of the response token *wow* is not linked in any way to the valence of the informing receipted: "[W]e find that instances of 'wow' which are hearable as the same object occur as unproblematic responses to both positive and negative informings: there is no straightforward mapping between *valence* and phonetic design." (ibid: 735, emphasis in the original)

This suggests that the particular valence of *ooh*-objects is constructed in context and time. In other words, affective labels such as 'shock' or 'pleasure' and 'excitement' cannot be associated with *ooh* in a context-free way. Affective meaning of this sort is contextually constructed, i.e. the cluster of prosodic-phonetic properties which comes with the sound object does not signal a particular valence. Its meaning must always be interpreted in relation to a specific sequential environment and the evaluative valence interactively established by participants.

CHAPTER 8

Types of affect-laden *ahs* in troubles talk and deliveries of bad news[93]

*Ah*s with different prosodic packaging represent fairly common sound objects in English. Their functions have been compared to that of the 'change-of-state token' *oh* (Aijmer 2002) but have also been analysed as signalling affective meaning, especially 'disappointment' but also 'sympathy' (Couper-Kuhlen 2006, 2009). In contrast to the types of *oh* and *ooh* examined, *ah* is not gradable but comes with fixed prosodic-phonetic packaging. Another differing aspect, the two packaged *ah*s ('low-falling and tailed' *ah* and 'flat-falling and low' *ah*) to be discussed in the following sections are restricted solely to receipting informings with negative valence.

The chapter will be structured as follows: After a literature review on the interjection *ah* in dictionaries and in interactionally informed studies (Section 8.1), we will be concerned with the affective dimensions of 'empathy', 'sympathy' and 'disappointment' in the conversation analytic/interactional linguistic literature (Section 8.2). We will then turn to the prosodic-phonetic packaging, with which two types of the sound object *ah* could be discerned in the present data: 'low-falling and tailed' *ah* and 'flat-falling and low' *ah* (Section 8.3).

Section 8.4 will examine 'low-falling and tailed' *ah* as an affect-laden troubles receipt, both with turn expansion (Section 8.4.1) and with subsequent other-speaker talk (Section 8.4.2). An additional section will analyse this kind of sound object as a resource for a mock display of affect (Section 8.4.3). Section 8.4.4 will summarise the findings on 'low-falling and tailed' *ah* as a troubles receipt. The next section (Section 8.5) will deal with 'low-falling and tailed' *ah* as an affect-laden receipt of bad news in activities where the consequential figure is the news *teller*. Section 8.6 will present a small study on 'flat-falling and low'*ah* in radio-talk rejection contexts and in response to bad-news reports with the news *recipient* as the consequential figure in the scenario. Section 8.7 discusses the interactional pay-off of using the response token *ah* in an environment where formal and functional differences between 'low-falling and tailed' and 'flat-falling and low' *ah*s are blurred. The analysis is wound up by a brief comparative discussion of these two types of *ah* (Section 8.8).

---

93. The section includes an excursus on a type of affect-laden *ah* in rejection contexts.

8.1   Previous accounts in the literature: *Ah* in English

8.1.1   Ah *in English dictionaries*

According to English dictionaries, interjections with a segmental substance represented as /ɑ:/ are spelled *ah* or *aah*. This phonological word constitutes a standard lexical entry in monolingual dictionaries.

The Cambridge International Dictionary classifies *ah/aah* as an exclamation, "used to express understanding, pleasure, pain, surprise or the fact that you have noticed something". According to this definition, *ah* can be deployed to signal cognitive as well as affective states. All example sentences show *ah* in sentence-initial position, as for instance "*Ah yes, now I see what's wrong – the wires have come loose*", "*Ah, it's wonderful to see you again*", or "*Ah, that's terrible, you must have been in such a pain*" (Procter 1995: 28, italics in the original). The first two examples seem to exemplify "understanding" and "pleasure" respectively. The meaning of *ah* in the last sentence, however, does not correspond to any of the definitions in a straightforward way. A look into The American Heritage Dictionary of the English Language (Morris ²1973) reveals a more extended list of emotion words: It states that apart from pain and surprise, the interjection *ah* indicates delight, satisfaction and dislike (ibid: 26).

This short overview illustrates that *ah* is to some extent taken to be synonymous with *ooh*: Both lexical items are described as expressions of surprise, pleasure, and pain by English dictionaries. As to the differences in usage, however, the reader is left in the dark.

8.1.2   *English* ah *in empirical studies*

As far as existing research on the uses and forms of *ah* in talk-in-interaction is concerned, most of the work at hand (with the exception of Couper-Kuhlen (2009) only touches roughly on prosodic issues. From a computer-linguistic perspective, Ward (2006) e.g. states that the non-lexical conversational sound /a/ [sic!] in American English indicates "that the speaker is fully on top of the situation and 'ready to act'" (ibid: 155). In contrast to *oh*, *ah* does not treat the contents of the prior utterance as new (ibid: 156), a view shared by Collier (2005: 188). Interestingly, Ward's (2006) transcriptions suggest that /a/ may come with a creak and has a variant /ao/ (ibid: 155–156). In addition, Collier (2005: 187) claims that *ah* is primarily used for two discourse functions: assessing and acknowledging, with the latter function especially being served when *ah* is realised in an independent unit.

In a corpus-linguistic study, Aijmer (2002) states that the 'core meaning' of *ah* is linked to pleasure or satisfaction, although *ah* serves "to receive new information, to signal remembering or the realization of something" in a way similar to *oh* (ibid: 145). Interestingly, she points out that *ah* tends to form an independent contour more frequently than *oh*, from which she concludes that *ah* has not yet been grammaticised as a "general intensifier" (ibid: 147). Also, falling intonation made up the majority of cases (79%), overriding the rise-fall (19%) (ibid: 147). Collocations include "*good, great, marvellous, what a pity*, which express pleasure, interest or sympathy." (ibid: 146, italics in the original). She points out that *ah I'm sorry* as opposed to *oh I'm sorry* conveys "a more serious apology" and comes across as more formal (ibid: 149). All in all, *ah* is identified in positions similar to *oh*, where, however, it signals slightly different meanings due to different collocations and depending on the level of politeness (cf. also Aijmer (1987).

From an interactional linguistic perspective, Couper-Kuhlen (2006, 2009) links *ah* to *oh* by suggesting that both objects can be deployed in the same sequential slot, that is, in response to the rejection of a request.

Rejections of requests or proposals create an environment which does not further the requester's or proposer's earlier assumptions or hopes and which bear negative implications for them. Couper-Kuhlen (2006) found that the rejection of requests can be receipted by *ah* in everyday British English telephone conversation as part of the following structure:

A: request
B: rejection of request
A: acceptance of rejection (rejection finaliser)

Excerpt 19 (Couper-Kuhlen 2009: 101) reflects this structure. The transcript sets in with the beginning of the recording. Keith (requester) is a friend of Leslie's daughter Kathrine. The requester is the caller.

```
(19)  [HOLT 1:4] "Not in at the moment"
1                    ((opening unrecorded))
2        Kei:   (hell-)o missiz FIE:LD;
3        Les:   YE:S-
4        Kei:   this is KEITH.
5               can i speak to KATHrine plea[se.
6        Les:                               [oh KEITH;
7               she's not IN at the moment,
8   →    Kei:   AH. ((subdued))
9               (0.9)
10       Kei:   what-
11              (.)
12       Kei:   [do you know what ti-
13       Les:   [do do you want to give me a MESSage;
```

The sound object is deployed to receipt the rejection of a request or proposal and functions as a rejection finaliser. Moreover, the object comes with a specific prosodic-phonetic cluster, i.e. 'subdued' prosody. In comparison to *ah*, *oh* with 'subdued prosody' may constitute a more common realisation of the rejection finaliser (ibid: 102).[94] Couper-Kuhlen (2006, 2009) argues that in a rejection setting, which prepares for a certain type of response, a 'subdued' tone of voice can be interpreted as what is commonly called 'disappointment' in lay terms. The rejecter's attempts to "console or conciliate the party whose proposal has been rejected and to make amends for the rejection" (Couper-Kuhlen 2009: 100) display that 'subdued' *ah* (or *oh*) is oriented to as making 'disappointment' relevant.

In some rather popular scientific work dealing with American English, it is suggested that *ah* (or *aw*) may signal "an acknowledgment of a specific sub-set of touchingness, viz, cuteness" (Yagoda undated). While we have found some similar evidence in our American English data base, the British English collection in focus does not contain instances which would clearly point to such usage.

To summarise, we have seen that *ah* has been related to *oh* by most empirical studies because they occur in similar or the same sequential positions in talk. Moreover, *ah* has been associated with both negative and positive affective dimensions, such as helplessness, 'sympathy', 'disappointment' but also 'pleasure' and 'satisfaction'. However, apart from Couper-Kuhlen (2009), these previous studies do not provide comprehensive descriptions of the various types of sound packaging of *ah*, thus showing a tendency to define *ah* by its segmental design alone.

In the following analytic account, we will focus on negatively valenced affective displays implemented by two types of *ah*, since the variants of the sound object examined were found to be primarily used in activities where such affective displays are made relevant by the recipient. These negatively valenced affective dimensions include what would be conceptualised as 'empathy', 'sympathy', 'disappointment', 'sorrow', or even 'frustration' in lay terms. The next section (8.2) will deal with such notions in the previous conversation analytic/interactional linguistic literature. Furthermore, we will address differences to affect-laden *oh*s when deployed in activities of the same type. However, this discussion must remain rather hypothetical for reasons of time and space.

---

94. The collection includes *ah, alright, oh, oh dear, oh I see, oh not to worry, oh right, oh well, oh well never mind, okay, okay never mind, okay then.* (ibid: 102).

8.2   'Empathy', 'sympathy' and 'disappointment' in talk-in-interaction

In our corpus, the types of *ah* examined can implement affect-laden recipient responses in troubles talk, bad-news deliveries and rejection contexts.

Jefferson (1988) in describing mundane troubles talk observes 'empathy' as an affective dimension coupled with recipient actions in specific slots ('announcement response', 'affiliation'), which "commits recipient as, now, a troubles-recipient" (ibid: 425). Additional interactional concepts which serve to capture the processes in which the troubles teller and the recipient negotiate and manage potentially affect-implicative topical talk are 'troubles-receptiveness' and -'resistance' (Jefferson 1984b, cf. Section 4.2.1) and 'affiliation' (Jefferson 1988): The so-called "Affiliation Response" refers to a recipient action where the activity of troubles talk reaches its affective climax: The troubles teller produces emotionally heightened talk (whose quality is not further specified), by "'letting go' and/or turning to or confiding in the troubles/recipient [sic!]". In this way, the affiliation response "constitutes the topical and relational heart of troubles talk, an intense focussing [sic!] upon the trouble and upon each other" (ibid: 428). Interestingly, this move was only identified in Jefferson's American data but was absent in British English interactions (ibid: 430, footnote 2).

To turn to troubles talk in institutional interaction, Hepburn (2004) in her study of crying in phone calls to a British child protection helpline treats the caller's crying as one among other affective displays (ibid: 287), for which whispering, sniffs, wobbly voice, high pitch, aspiration, sobbing and silence are typical features. While she does not label the affective dimension displayed by callers' crying, she notes that the child protection officer's, that is, the troubles recipient's, "high pitch may be one feature of doing sympathy" (ibid: 270). Similarly, Ruusuvuori (2005) suggests in her study of Finnish doctor-patient interactions that 'empathy' and 'sympathy' are actions on the part of the troubles recipient, i.e. the medical professional, which are accomplished as situated practices and are sequentially generated. 'Empathy', treated as a preferred response, refers to an understanding of the patient's trouble, while 'sympathy', here a dispreferred response, involves a sharing of the trouble (ibid: 220, also 219). Also on the basis of medical interaction, Heath (1989) asserts that "sympathy or appreciation" are potential doctor's responses to cries of pain on the part of the patient (ibid: 115).

This brief overview suggests that in institutional interactions, 'sympathy' and 'empathy'/'appreciation' are treated as expectable recipient emotion displays in troubles talk, with displays of 'sympathy' tending to constitute dispreferred actions which interfere with the tasks of the institutional professional. In contrast, 'sympathy' in mundane troubles talk is treated as an action which constructs the recipient as a troubles recipient, aligning with the activity proffered by the teller in the first place.

As regards mundane deliveries of bad news, Maynard (1997) does not further specify the affective dimension involved in the activity. It is only in his co-authored follow-up study on prosodic features of news deliveries (Freese and Maynard 1998) that the 'negative valence' postulated for bad news is made concrete in terms of an emotion term, namely 'sorrow'. 'Sorrow' is understood as both a teller's and recipient's emotion because participants are observed to co-construct the valence of the news. In doing so, they orient towards the affective stance displayed by the 'consequential figure'. Further, it is stated that the prosody of news responses can be heard as surprise, which is consequently treated as a recipient emotion. Freese and Maynard's (1998) work provides empirical evidence for the observations made by Sacks (1995) earlier that 'surprise' precedes 'sorrow' and 'joy' in news deliveries in order to allow for an elaboration of the news announcement:

> [P]eople do "Did he really?" for all kinds of announcements. In any event, sorrow and joy are prefigured by the surprise thing. In a way then, the surprise thing can be treated as reserving rights to future expressions of emotion, saying "I see that this is the thing that I will express emotion about. Let me give you some more room to tell me about it. Then you'll hear me give me a wail."   (ibid: 574)

In more recent work, Couper-Kuhlen (2009) suggests that recipients of bad news who are not the consequential figures of the news can respond with displays of 'sympathy'.

In a complementary study about bad news in a medical context, Lutfey and Maynard (1998) provide further evidence to support the claim that the valence of some news is indeed co-achieved in a conversational project between participants. This co-achievement can be e.g. deferred or hindered by displays of stoicism on the part of the patient (ibid: 333). In this sense the nature of the responsive actions by terminal patients are decisive for the success or failure of accomplishing 'an unpackaging of the gloss' (ibid: 338), i.e. the news of the patient's imminent dying and death.

Like in troubles talk, the accomplishment of negatively valenced affective displays is thus the outcome of an interactive process. However, the affective notions used in association with bad news are often 'sorrow' (and 'surprise') rather than 'sympathy'.

As far as rejection contexts are concerned, Davidson (1984, 1990) does not go into the affective implications of either rejections or acceptances of invitations/offers/requests in her seminal work on the subject. In contrast, Couper-Kuhlen (2009) suggests that rejecting actions prepare for responses of 'disappointment'.

To conclude, it will be shown in the following analysis of the uses of 'low-falling and tailed' *ah* in mundane troubles talk and bad-news deliveries that unlike troubles receipts performed by such a sound object, productions of 'low-falling and tailed' *ah* in bad-news deliveries are commonly followed by idiomatic expressions of 'sympathy' in the same turn. In this sense the affective displays performed by the same formal item are treated as two different participant categories. To capture these differences and following Jefferson (1988), 'low-falling and tailed' *ah* in troubles talk will be treated as doing 'empathy', whereas 'low-falling and tailed' *ah* in bad-news sequences (with the news teller acting as the consequential figure) will be associated with 'sympathy'. Finally, the analysis of 'flat-falling and low' *ah* as a rejection finaliser in radio interaction will illustrate findings parallel to those made by Couper-Kuhlen (2009) for 'subdued' *ah* in everyday rejection contexts, which warrant a treatment of that sound object as display of 'disappointment'. Moreover, the analysis of a single case study in the same section will demonstrate that 'flat-falling and low' *ah* is also functional as an affect-laden bad-news receipt when the news *recipient* is affected by the news, i.e. it may serve here as a display of 'disappointment' by the consequential figure in the scenario.

8.3   The prosodic-phonetic packaging of *ah*

Accompanied by two distinctive sound patterns, *ah* can be used for affect-laden recipient responses in troubles talk, deliveries of bad news and in post-rejection contexts. In contrast to the sound objects with the segmental substances [u:] or [əʊ], instances of *ah* are always produced on an independent contour in the present corpus.

Their segmental substance has a vowel quality close to cardinal vowel 5 ([a]). Objects including an unrounded open back vowel which becomes slightly more closed during articulation are subsumed as variants of this sound object. Objects with a clearly diphthongal quality (i.e. with a noticeable glide from cardinal vowel 5 ([a]) to cardinal vowel 6 ([ɔ]) are treated as a different type within the scope of the present study.[95] In some rare cases, the object can be aspirated, i.e. [ha:].

As regards the prosodic-phonetic packaging which accompanies such sound objects in troubles telling, deliveries of bad news and on post-rejection, its main characteristic property is low pitch. However, the trouble-receipt *ah* and the bad-news receipt *ah* performed in participation frameworks where the recipient is *not* the consequential figure of the news (henceforth referred to as bad-news receipt *ah* (1) differ from rejection finalisers and bad-news receipts enacted by the consequential figure himself/herself (henceforth referred to as bad-news receipt *ah* (2) in terms of their contour. For this reason, the latter two will be considered separately in the following descriptive account.

---

95. It will be left to future research to answer the question whether such diphthongal objects are variants of *ah* or should be categorised as a different sound object.

8.3.1   *The prosodic-phonetic packaging of* ah *in troubles telling and*
in bad-news deliveries (with the teller as the consequential figure)

The prosodic-phonetic packaging of *ah* in troubles telling and in bad-news delivery sequences with the consequential figure as the news teller consists of a set of stable and of variant properties.

Stable properties of the troubles receipt *ah* include lengthening and a contour which begins in the mid range of the speaker's voice and falls on a glide to the lower range, ending as a level tail (cf. Figure 17).

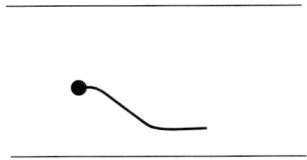

Figure 17. 'Low-falling and tailed' contour of *ah*

The articulatory force of the troubles receipt is stronger than that of 'flat-falling and low' *ah* deployed as a rejection finaliser (see below).

Variant properties include loudness – troubles-receipt *ah* can be as loud as or softer than the same speaker's prior talk, and timing – troubles-receipt *ah* can be early or late. Furthermore, 'low-falling and tailed' *ah* is sometimes accompanied by breathiness in troubles talk.

When deployed as a bad-news receipt, *ah* exhibits the same stable cluster of properties as do troubles-receipt *ah*s: The vowel is lengthened and is produced with the same low-falling tailed contour. It is also characterised by stronger articulatory force than *ah* in rejection contexts. Variant properties include loudness: Bad-news receipt *ah* 1 can be as loud as or softer than the same speaker's prior talk. In contrast to troubles-receipt *ah*, bad-news receipt *ah* 1 may be produced on time or late, and can be accompanied by creak.

8.3.2   *The prosodic-phonetic packaging of* ah *in rejection contexts and*
in bad-news deliveries (with the recipient as the consequential figure)

Ah as a rejection finaliser and as a bad-news receipt *ah* 2, realised in radio interaction, exhibit the same kind of properties in terms of duration and pitch as Couper-Kuhlen's (2009) 'subdued *ah*' in mundane conversation. Duration and pitch have been found to constitute two stable properties of the package. Consequently, the contour can be depicted as shown in Figure 18.

In contrast to 'subdued *ah*' in mundane conversation (Couper-Kuhlen 2009), 'flat-falling and low' *ah* in rejection contexts in radio interaction can sometimes

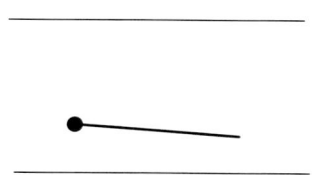

Figure 18. 'Flat-falling and low' contour of *ah*

be produced early. Furthermore, it can be accompanied by creak *or* breathiness and does not always end in a trail-off. A possible explanation could be that creak as well as the stronger articulatory force which goes along with it impart more interactional thrust to the affective display, which may not be preferred in common everyday contexts when receipting a rejection. In radio programmes, however, where such displays are staged for a split audience, creak may be used to achieve an (additional) dramatic effect.

To sum up, *ah* has been found to be produced with the same stable packaging ('low-falling and tailed') in everyday troubles talk and bad-news delivery sequences (1), including increased duration and a glide from mid to low with a level tail. The stable packaging identified for *ah* in rejection contexts and in bad-news delivery sequences (2) in radio interaction ('flat-falling and low') is also characterised by greater duration and low pitch but involves a different contour: Here the object is accompanied by a slight, narrow fall in the lower range of the speaker's voice. From this observation we can first conclude that the practice analysed by Couper-Kuhlen (2009) for mundane rejection contexts finds further application in more institutional environments. Secondly, we can see that the affective work required in the two types of bad-news delivery sequences depends on the corresponding participation frameworks and for this reason differs to a great extent.

8.4   Affect-laden *ah* in response to troubles talk

Ah can form a recipient response in the sequential environment of troubles talk, an activity involving negatively valenced tellings concerning the teller or a third party. The analysis will show that in such contexts, 'low-falling and tailed' *ah* functions as an affiliative troubles receipt in response to the announcement or the exposition of the trouble. This troubles receipt treats the prior informing as being informative about a trouble and as complete, but it makes more talk related to the trouble relevant. In that it appreciates the negative affect shown in the troubles informing by displaying heightened affective involvement, which could be labelled 'empathy', it accomplishes affiliation.

In troubles talk the troubles teller and the recipient manage "a tension between attending to the 'trouble' and attending to the 'business as usual'" (Jefferson
1988: 153). It will be illustrated that 'low-falling and tailed' *ah* can be used as a
recipient resource to deal with the relevancies of orienting towards a trouble and
of displaying affiliation when made relevant. Troubles talk can further emerge in
terms of "big packages" (Sacks 1995: 354). However, because troubles talk is as all
other conversational activities interactively constructed between participants in
time, the floor is constantly subject to negotiation.

We will show that recipients can use 'low-falling and tailed' *ah* to actively co-
construct troubles talk: Depending on the sequential position, it can form (1) the
first unit in a multi-unit construction ['low-falling and tailed' *ah* + assessment], i.e.
the affective dimension of the prior telling is further addressed in turn expansion
subsequent to the sound object; in what follows, the informing sequence is closed
locally but following a topic shift, the global troubles sequence is further expanded;
or the closing of the local sequence means a termination of the global activity and
a new sequence is initiated. (2) When used as a stand-alone, *ah* is followed by
the current troubles teller expanding their talk. (3) Furthermore, 'low-falling and
tailed' *ah* can be deployed to display a 'mock emotion' (Sandlund 2004, 2005).

8.4.1   Ah *as a troubles receipt + turn expansion*

When recipients respond with 'low-falling and tailed' *ah* to a troubles informing,
the sound object always forms a unit of its own in the present data. The turn can,
however, be expanded with an assessment which further shows an orientation towards the affective loading of the prior troubles informing. Such turn expansions
are carried out in specific sequential places in that they are situated at sequential
and topical boundaries. Excerpt 20 exemplifies a case where subsequent to turn
expansion, a topic shift is initiated and a new local informing sequence within the
larger package of troubles talk is occasioned. Here the phone has just been handed
over to Linda by her daughter. Leslie is the caller. Lord Geoff is the nickname of
Linda's husband.

```
(20)   [HOLT:M88:l:2] "Lord Geoff"
1      Lin:   helLO?
2      Les:   helLO; .h
3             <<hh>how did lor:d> ([!]) GEOFF: get on;
4      Lin:   =(<<muffled>Oh he's>) not ↓too BA:D;
5             not too BA:D,
6      Les:   .hhh
7             (.)
8      Lin:   gOt him HOME alright;
9             about uhm:=
```

```
10                =<<all>one o'clOck i supPOSE>.=
11                =[()
12      Les:       [oh ↓GOOD;
13                he made good ↓TIME the[n;
14      Lin:                            [↑YES;
15                he DID,hh
16                [(*)
17  →   Les:       [<<h>and is he fEEling BETter now a little bit>?
18  →   Lin:       <<muffled>MHM>,
19  →              <<muffled>not REALly,
20  →              <<muffled>N:O:,=
21      Les:       =NO:;
22                poor CHAP;hh
23  →   Lin:       <<all>no he's not fEEling very WELL>.
24  →   Les:       .hh %`[hɑ:]. h
25  →              stIll it's ↑all: Over with;
26      Lin:       [hm: YES;
27      Les:       [(***)
28                <<h>will he have the reSULT yet>;
```

To appreciate the interactional processes which finally generate the production of 'low-falling and tailed' *ah*, an analysis of the prior sequential context will be provided:

The sequence at whose boundaries 'low-falling and tailed' *ah* is produced is occasioned by Leslie, the potential troubles recipient, with an enquiry about how Linda's husband Geoff got on (line 3). The turn design conveys social intimacy: The speaker uses a nickname for the referent and pre-supposes the background knowledge shared by the interlocutors that Geoff has undergone some medical treatment earlier in the day. Linda responds with a 'downgraded response', which can be treated as 'trouble-premonitory' (Jefferson 1980), foreshadowing the presence of a trouble (lines 4–5): The fact that someone is not too bad does not mean that he is well. The assessment indicates a trouble and signals that it may be addressed later in the conversation (Jefferson 1980). Heritage (1998) argues that an initial *oh* in downgraded assessment turns, which come in response to how-are-you-inquiries, reinforces the downgraded nature of the action ("super-downgraded responses", ibid: 322). In this way, the local function of the assessment turn is enhanced to point of foreshadowing troubles talk. Heritage notes further that recipients often make an orientation towards 'super-downgraded responses' visible by enquiring about the trouble in the next turn (ibid: 322). However, this is not the case in the present excerpt: The (filled) pause in lines 6–7 indicates the noticeable absence of an affiliative response from Leslie. Lines 8–10 can be treated as an orientation towards this absence: The speaker expands her turn, by showing 'troubles resistance' (Jefferson 1984b). She mentions positively valenced events (*gOt him HOME alright*), which are related to her husband's treatment. This display of troubles resistance is ratified by the recipient (lines 12–13).

It is not until line 17 that Leslie orients towards the implications of the downgraded response in lines 4–5: This turn elicits talk about the referent's well-being in the here and now, as signalled by the present progressive, and implies that the referent was *not* feeling well earlier on.

The enquiry in line 17 is answered in the negative (18–20), which can be treated as a troubles announcement. The turn is designed with a dispreferred turn shape (Pomerantz 1984, Schegloff 2007), indicated by hedging (achieved by the muffled delivery of the entire turn), turn initial delay (accomplished by the turn-initial bilabial nasal sound object) (line 18), and lexical mitigation (negation of the adverb *REALly* (line 19).

In response, Linda's turn is acknowledged next (line 21) and assessed in terms of a [poor + N]-construction (line 22), which represents an idiomatic expression of 'sympathy'. By orienting towards the negative dimension of the prior turn, the speaker now affiliates with her interlocutor – unlike in lines 6–7, where such a response is noticeably absent. The next line supports this interpretation: The troubles teller reformulates lines 18–20 in terms of an explicit assessment and a full sentence. The negation of the predicate and the flat prosodic contour contextualise the turn in a negative and affect-laden fashion. Line 23 thus does an upgrade of lines 18–20 and invites an equally upgraded affective response.

The recipient responds to this affect-laden, negatively valenced, upgraded troubles announcement with the production of an aspirated version of *ah* ([haː]) (line 24). The initial fricative marks the object as a variant of the segmental prototype [aː]. The vowel quality of the object is close to that of cardinal vowel 5 ([ɑ]). The prosody of the sound object can be described as 'low-falling and tailed': The syllable is lengthened and produced in the low range of the speaker's voice. It falls from low-mid to low (from 294 Hz to 140 Hz), has the same volume as the same speaker's prior talk and displays creaky voice quality. Furthermore, the object is produced in a timely manner. The acoustic analysis supports this description as is illustrated by Figure 19.

The creaky voice quality of the object intensifies the display. Through the prosodic-phonetic make-up of the sound object, the recipient thus signals heightened affective involvement regarding the negative implications of the troubles announcement, an affective quality which has been described as 'empathy' by Jefferson (1988). In this way she constructs affiliation. At the same time, the announcement is treated as informative and complete. In contrast to the change-of-state token *oh* (Heritage 1984), however, the recipient response signals an orientation towards the affective dimension of the informing and thus functions as an affect-laden troubles receipt.

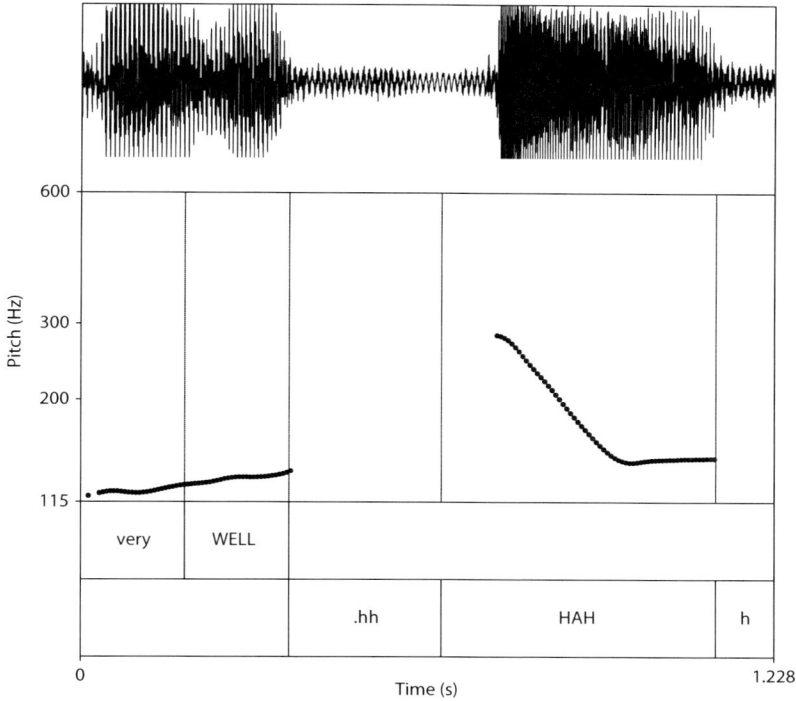

Figure 19. Acoustic analysis of Excerpt 20 ("Lord Geoff"), lines 23–24

The affective dimension of the sound object is furthermore evidenced by the action that follows: In the next sequential slot, the troubles recipient expands her turn with an assessment which downtones and qualifies the affective display performed by the sound object. The adverb *stIll* establishes a semantic link to the sound object (line 25).[96] Thus, the speaker treats the object as an affect-laden item, i.e. as a display of her affiliative and affective stance towards the troubles announcement. This provides evidence that the affective meaning of the sound object is not only an analyst's construct but also constitutes a participants' category.

At the same time, the assessment accomplishes an action which is often due before the termination of troubles talk: 'making light of the trouble' (Jefferson 1988). It highlights the good side of the situation, namely that the operation has been successfully completed.

---

96. If *stIll* referred to the prior turn of the troubles teller (line 23), the recipient would signal lack of agreement with the assessment made and in this manner perform a disaffiliative action. An interpretation of this sort is not displayed in the subsequent interaction.

'Making light of the trouble' is an action having 'close implicature' (Jefferson 1988), in the sense that it offers to close the sequence and move out of troubles talk to another activity. As line 28 indicates, this is not entirely true for the present excerpt: The troubles recipient does not begin a new sequence but expands the prior sequence by shifting the topic to the results of the operation. There are prosodic cues to support such an analysis: The turn is not delivered with an *extra* high onset, which would signal the beginning of a new sequence (cf. Couper-Kuhlen 2004b), but is cued as taking up the next item on the agenda of the troubles talk. This becomes particularly visible when comparing line 28 to line 3, which opens up an entirely new sequence, namely the reason for the call, and to line 17, the preceding item on the agenda. What line 28 thus accomplishes is to mark a transition from talk about an item on the agenda which displayed an orientation to the trouble-premonitory action, to the next item, which marks a shift from talk about the present situation to talk about the treatment's results. In this sense, the assessment can be seen as closing down a local informing sequence.

To sum up, 'low-falling and tailed' *ah* can receipt troubles announcements, acknowledging them as informative and complete. At the same time the prosodic-phonetic design of the sound object contextualises the receipt as affect-laden: The object appreciates the negative affective loading of the announcement in that it also signals heightened affective involvement, which may be labelled 'empathy', and achieves affiliation.

When the turn initiated with *ah* is expanded, the speaker can modify and qualify the affective display achieved by the sound object. This shows that the affective meaning of the object is a participants' category. The expansion may contain a closing implicative action typical for troubles talk such as 'making light of the trouble' (Jefferson 1988). It can signal the closing of the local informing sequence and mark a transition to the next item on the agenda in the troubles talk (here the outcome of the medical treatment).

Excerpt 21 illustrates another case where the turn is expanded subsequent to the production of an affect-laden troubles receipt *ah*. The troubles receipt is deployed in response to a troubles informing in the exposition of the telling. Thus, it is positioned later in the sequence than the troubles receipt in Excerpt 20. Here the closing of the local troubles informing sequence is followed by the resumption of a pending complaint sequence (line 17). The troubles talk is about a divorced woman, Helen, who now lives in a second and happy marriage with a man called Rob and is being treated for terminal cancer.

The analysis will focus on the excerpt from line 9 onwards; an account of the use of *ah* in line 8 is given below.

```
(21)    [Holt:Oct88:1:8] "even the kids"
1       Lin:    and the kids .hhh
2               you know she's got a gIrl i suppose about (.) FOUR
3               teen,=
4               =and a boy about .hh TWELVE maybe,
5               .hhh AN:D uh,
6               ↑even the kIds she said are so happy with ROB-
7               %you %KNOW-
8   →   Les:    <<breathy>[a::]>;hh
9   →   Lin:    they look such a nice FAMily,=
10              =they were in church this MORning-
11  →   Les:    <<breathy>`[a::]>; ⊙
12  →   Lin:    .h[hh
13  →   Les:      [oh i ↑hOpe it shall be alRIGHT,h[h
14  →   Lin:                                       [oh: ↑YES,
15  →           <<all>so do I>;=
16      Les:    =´`HM:.
17      Lin:    <<all>but going back to NANcy>; ((turn continues))
```

The sound object in line 11 responds to the turn in lines 9–10, which consists of an assessment and an evidential account. Despite the positive valence signalled by the positive evaluative adjective "happy", the assessment serves to give an implicit account of the sad situation of the consequential figure. The assessment is constructed from the perspective of the troubles teller and summarises prior statements about the family concerned in a final assessment. The credibility and authenticity of the assessment is strengthened through the evidential account in the next line. Because of its implicit negative valence, the turn makes an affect-laden affiliative response relevant next.

This now comes in the form of the sound object *ah*. The object has the same shape as *ah* in line 8, with its vowel quality being close to cardinal vowel 5 ([ɑ]). The unrounded vowel is closed further during production. It is lengthened and produced in the lower part of the speaker's pitch range, falling from low-mid (298 Hz) to low (178 Hz). It is as loud as the same speaker's prior talk and comes in neither too early nor too late. The object has breathy voice quality. The acoustic analysis as provided in Figure 20 below supports the description of duration, pitch and loudness.

Like the sound object *ah* ([hɑ:]) in Excerpt 20, *ah* ([ɑ::]) in line 11 acknowledges the troubles informing as informative and complete, with the low pitch signalling heightened affective involvement. Due to this kind of affective contextualisation, the object can be interpreted as an affiliative troubles receipt. In post-completion, the troubles recipient next produces a bilabial click and expands the turn with an *oh*-prefaced TCU, which expresses hope for a positive outcome. According to

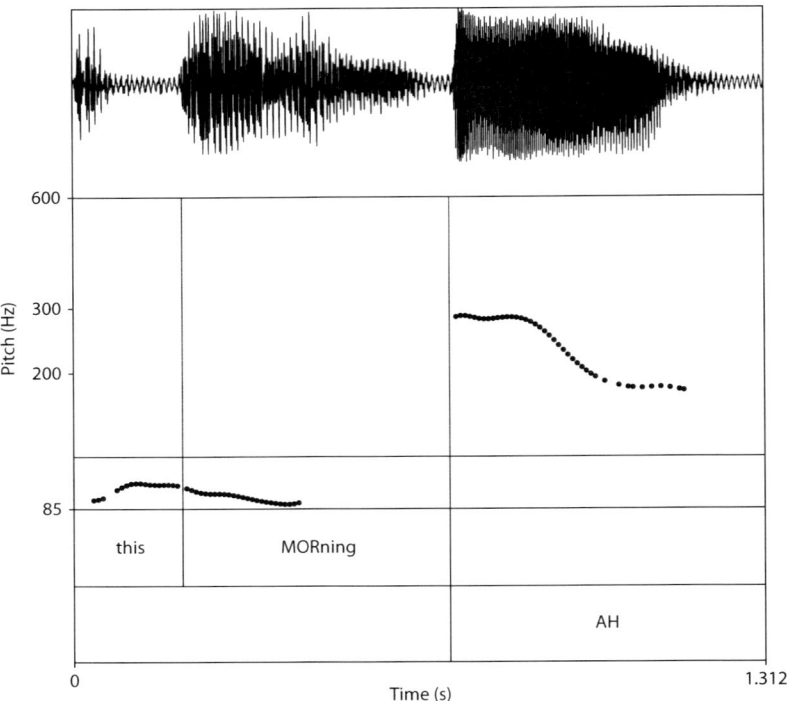

Figure 20. Acoustic analysis of Excerpt 21 ("even the kids"), lines 10–11

Jefferson (1988), such an 'optimistic projection' can accomplish a closure-implicative action in troubles talk in the same way as 'making light of the trouble'. Note that this turn expansion is co-achieved with the teller: She does not come in in the transition space following the sound object and the click. Furthermore, the turn expansion can be treated as an orientation towards the summarising character of the assessment in line 9 in that it carries out a closure-implicative action.

In response, the troubles recipient shows agreement with the optimistic projection (lines 14–15) and next resumes a pending complaint sequence (cf. Mazeland and Huiskes 2001 on Dutch *maar* (but) as a sequential conjunction). This shows that the optimistic projection is treated as sequence-terminating. In contrast to Excerpt 20, not only the local informing sequence but the entire troubles talk sequence is now closed down. With the initiation of the complaint sequence (line 17), the troubles talk is abandoned and the sequence closing is in retrospect ratified.

To sum up, recipients can use 'low-falling and tailed' *ah* ([a:] or its variant [ha:]) as affect-laden troubles receipt in order to respond to informings made in troubles talk. Such informings can either function as announcements of a trouble or be delivered in the exposition of a trouble. Troubles receipts performed with 'low-falling and tailed' *ah* treat the prior turn as complete and informative of a trouble. They orient towards the negative affective loading of the troubles informing in that their sound pattern displays heightened affective involvement. By appreciating the nature of the trouble in this way, they perform an action that affiliates with the troubles informing. After a pause, the turn can be expanded by the same speaker. This is usually done in terms of an assessment which further relates to the trouble by 'making light' of it or which expresses hope for a positive outcome. The respective sequential structures can be outlined as follows:

A: troubles announcement
B: affect-laden troubles receipt (realised through 'low-falling and tailed' *ah*)
     (filled) pausing
B: troubles assessment
A: troubles exposition
B: affect-laden troubles receipt ('low-falling and tailed' *ah*)
     (filled) pausing
B: troubles assessment

The turn expansion subsequent to 'low-falling and tailed' *ah* can accomplish a closure-implicative move on the local level (to the effect that a topic shift and a transition to the next item on the agenda in the troubles talk follows) or on a more global level (in that a new activity is resumed or initiated in what follows). The observation that *ah* is usually followed by a closure-implicative action when the turn is expanded suggests that *ah* constitutes a recipient response in troubles talk which is used when the troubles tellers have reached a good degree of social closeness and a maximum of affiliation is being accomplished. After this participants can go back to 'business as usual'.

However, it is not the troubles receipt *ah* which brings s sequential shift or closure about, but the assessment in turn expansion. This view will be expanded in the following section on 'low-falling and tailed' *ah* followed by other-speaker talk.

8.4.2   Ah *as a troubles receipt + subsequent other-speaker talk*

When the troubles teller engages in a type of troubles talk where they have secured the floor for a longer stretch of time, recipients may orient towards this by responding with 'low-falling and tailed' *ah*, after which they again leave the floor to the troubles teller for the latter to continue with their talk.[97]

---

97. The data also contain a few instances of diphthongal tokens (with a glide from an unrounded open back vowel to a more rounded and closed back vowel) in such positions. It will be an empirical question, which cannot resolved in this study, whether they are functionally different.

Excerpt 22 illustrates the use of 'low-falling and tailed' *ah* in response to a troubles informing that comes in the exposition towards the end of a larger troubles talk sequence (the ending of which was shown in Excerpt 21).

Line 1 resumes topical talk about the consequential figure which was suspended for an inserted 'second story'.

```
(22)   [Holt: Oct88:1:8] "so happy"
1      Lin:   and VIVian says (*) she looks DESperate;=
2             =↑but uhm .hh
3             she wEnt to see the specialist last WEEK,=
4             =and .hh he SAYS;
5             you KNOW;
6             goo? decEmber the %FOURTH.
7             cOme and see ME,=
8             =<<ll>(you've)> .hhh
9             had your last TREATment;=
10            =(and) ↑NOW:, hhh
11            you KNOW,
12            all you can do is keep your FINGers crossed; .hhh
13     Les:   oh: dear dear ↑DEAR;
14            [! hm:
15     Lin:   [.hh so i do HOPE she survives,
16            .hh [↑very SAD;
17     Les:       [hm;
18     Lin:   cause she had this the (b) a sa:d .hhh
19            you know an unhappy first MARriage,=
20            =<<all>and [the:n> .hh uhm: met this: (.)
21     Les:              [hm;
22     Lin:   she's a teacher at uhm: .hh ⊙
23            ↑YEOvil;
24     Les:   o[h YES;
25             [(at the) COLlege;
26     Les:   YES,
27            (-)
28     Lin:   a:nd then she met this: <<len>chap ROB> at yeovil
29            college,
30            who was also a TEACHer,
31            .hhh and HE was divOrced,
32     Les:   [OH:;
33     Lin:   [and of course they've: MARried,
34            an:d .hh
35            well they've been married two YEARS,
```

```
36            and they're ↑SO: hAp[py;
37    Les:                  [.h OH;
38            ↑what a SHAME;
39    Lin:    ↑so: HAPpy;
40            and the kids .hhh
41            you know she's got a gIrl i suppose about (.)
42            FOURteen,=
43            =and a boy about .hh TWELVE maybe,
44            .hhh AN:D uh,
45            ↑even the kIds she said are so happy with ROB-
46            %you %KNOW-
47  →  Les:   <<breathy>[a::]>;hh
48  →  Lin:   they look such a nice FAMily,=
49            =they were in church this MORning-
```

The sound object of interest, 'low-falling and tailed' *ah*, is used in line 47. The analysis will first describe the context which precedes and, on a local level, generates the sound object, illustrating the linguistic resources and practices with which the participants display heightened affective involvement and construct affect-laden troubles talk. It will then analyse the function of the recipient response 'low-falling and tailed' *ah* on the basis of its treatment by current speaker.

The troubles talk is partly delivered as a narrative, that is, part of it contains passages in which a chronological sequence of events is recounted. It thus constitutes a 'bigger package' where the teller has secured the floor for a larger stretch of talk. Throughout the telling, both the teller and recipient show heightened affective involvement (One indication is the recipient's heavy breathing throughout the excerpt; it is not notated in the transcript).

The excerpt is structured in two major chunks: Lines 1–12 link up to the previous talk about the consequential figure and bring the narrative to a close. In lines 13–17 recipient and teller assess and work up its negative implications. Line 18 resumes the troubles talk, which adds further detail and takes an evaluative-affective stance to it.

To begin with lines 1–12, the teller's speech is prosodically contextualised as negatively loaded through low pitch and reduced pitch movement (cf. Freese and Maynard 1998: 198). Lexically, the teller ascribes a negative affective state to the main character (*she looks DESperate*, line 1). The reported speech (indicated and introduced by a verbum dicendi in line 4 and a discourse marker in line 5) enacts the current state of affairs and diagnosis through the doctor's voice, that is, through a medical authority. The quoted speech is only contextualised as such through a change in voice quality and in register (in lines 6–7). Lines 8–12 are done in the teller's 'usual' voice.[98] Reported speech is a common practice for tellers to show heightened affective involvement and to signal their stance towards the narrative recounted (Günthner 1997), thereby inviting an affective recipient response. Here the teller presents the question of whether the consequential figure will recover and thus ultimately survive as being on a knife-edge. This is only conveyed implicitly; however, line 15 can be seen as making this stance explicit.

The recipient displays an orientation towards the negative affective implications of the telling by producing an *oh*-prefaced assessment (line 13). The multiple production of *dear* make it come off as a non-routinised variant of the standardised phrase *oh dear*. This and the step-up in pitch on the last instance of *dear* contextualise the turn as highly affect-laden.

When the teller resumes talk in line 16, she does so with a summarising negative assessment, which serves at the same time as an abstract: it secures the floor for an account (indicated by *cause* in line 18) of how very sad the consequential figure's situation is: After an unhappy first marriage, the consequential figure is now happily remarried (lines 18–36). The datum shows nicely how the development of the telling and its newsworthiness and valence are interactively constructed by the teller and recipient.

Using the continuers in lines 21, 24, and 26, the recipient does not treat the telling as "anything newsworthy, interesting or assessable" (Schegloff 1982:86). Positioned following potential TRPs, they lead to turn expansion. The teller shows an orientation towards this by continuing with her turn (particularly visible in response to line 26; lines 21 and 24 are produced in overlap, and are therefore not such clear cases, since the teller might not have heard them).

In lines 32 and 37 the recipient produces two – affect-laden – change-of-state tokens. While line 32 is again positioned in overlap and it is unclear whether the current speaker hears it, the *oh* in line 37 is positioned in the clear. It responds to the teller's assessment that Helen and her second husband are ↑SO: hAp[py;. The positive assessment has the structure [X be + intensifier + evaluative adjective]. It is upgraded through lexical (the intensifier ↑*so*) and prosodic cues (lengthening of the vowel in ↑*so*, pitch accent on ↑*so*), which further add affective loading to the assessment, inviting an affect-laden uptake. Although the assessment is positively

---

98. It is for this reason that they can be heard either as a continuation of the direct quote or as the teller's evaluation. However, since only the pronoun *you* in line 12 can be treated as generic, it would appear that only lines 10–12, if at all, can be interpreted as not belonging to the quote.

valenced, it serves as an account for the sad nature (line 16) of the consequential figure's situation: Given that she may be fatally ill, late marital bliss is constructed as an account for how sad the situation is. The recipient response must be understood as addressing these implications: Line 37 comes off as 'low-falling and tailed', which shows an orientation towards the negative implications of the prior informing and the displayed heightened involvement. The turn is expanded with the exclamation ↑*what a SHAME;*. This idiomatic expression for 'sympathy' can be understood as an additional explicit display of affect. In carrying out an affect-laden recipient response, the recipient affiliates with the teller's assessment. When the latter now resumes with her talk, she recycles the evaluative adjective phrase ↑*so: HAPpy;* (line 39) before producing the next tellable. This matches the heightened affective involvement just displayed and allows her to affiliate with the recipient's affective display.

The analysis makes visible that an affective recipient response is generated at specific places in the interaction, namely when heightened affective involvement has been made relevant. The 'low-falling and tailed' *ah* in line 47 is generated in a similar fashion in the sense that it comes in after the TRP of a TCU in which the teller signals an affective stance towards its content. This assessment represents an upgrade of the previous assessments in lines 36 and 39. It can be paraphrased as follows: "Not only is Helen extremely happy with Rob but even the kids are extremely happy with him". The affective loading of the assessment is emphasised and intensified through various linguistic resources: The adverb ↑*even* places focus on the subject *the kIds*. Again, the meaning of the evaluative adjective *happy* is intensified through the adverb *so*. In addition, in presenting the assessment as something the consequential figure has said, the teller "substantiate[s] and authenticate[s]" her assessment (Couper-Kuhlen 2007b: 99). The local affective quality and valence of the assessing turn is inferred from its function in the telling. It serves as an account for the initial assessment *[it's ↑very] SAD.* The turn thus invites an affect-laden response.

Responding with 'low-falling and tailed' *ah*, the recipient treats the unit as complete and informative about a trouble. By signalling heightened affective involvement, which could be labelled as 'empathy' in Jefferson's (1988) terms, the object shows affiliation with the assessment. An acoustic analysis can be seen in Figure 21.

When the teller comes in in the next sequential slot, she delivers a summarising assessment. This TCU (line 48) is delivered in smooth transition, which shows that 'low-falling and tailed' *ah* is treated as having a TRP and as yielding the floor. Its effect is to encourage the development of the on-going troubles talk.

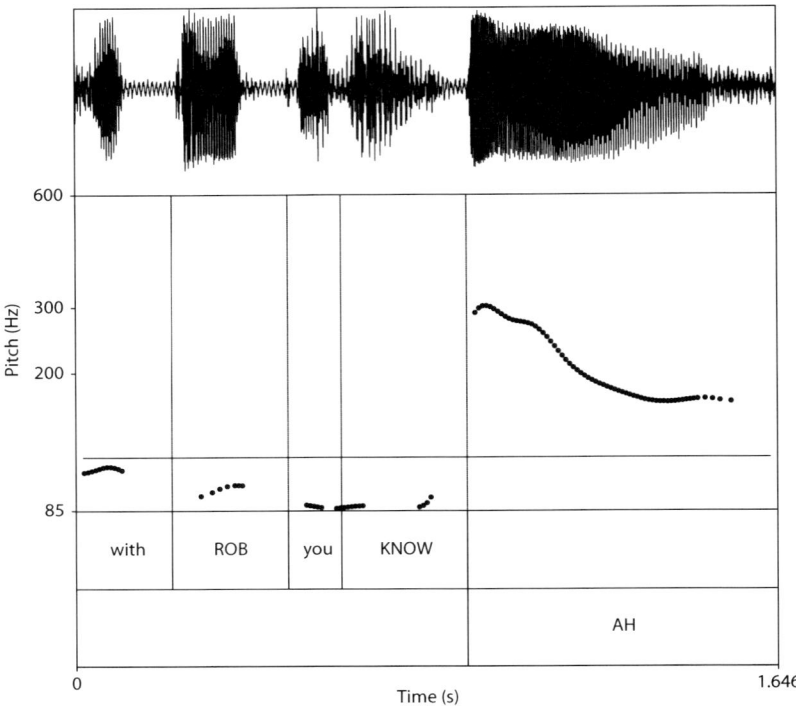

Figure 21. Acoustic analysis of Excerpt 22 ("so happy"), lines 45–47

To sum up, when the teller has secured the floor for a longer stretch of troubles talk, the recipient can display an orientation to this by responding with 'low-falling and tailed' *ah* without turn expansion at possible TRPs. She thereby leaves the floor to the teller, while treating the informing as complete and as a piece of troubles talk, orienting towards the negative affective loading of the local evaluative informing and affiliating with it. The observation that a floor switch can occur subsequent to 'low-falling and tailed' *ah* provides evidence that the object is oriented to as having a TRP and as constituting a TCU.

By producing a summarising assessment subsequent to the troubles receipt *ah*, the troubles teller makes a move which works towards closing the sequence. This kind of move runs parallel to the actions found in the same speaker's turn expansions, which were characterised as 'closure-implicative'. Thus we can conclude that while 'low-falling and tailed' *ah* does not seem closure-implicative itself, its post-production context is highly sensitive to such types of actions. Jefferson (1988) notes that after mutual focus on the trouble and affiliation have been achieved, speakers tend to move out of the activity and re-engage in business as usual. The production of 'low-falling and tailed' *ah* seems to represent a recipient resource to achieve such mutual focus on the trouble and affiliation, with the result that the sequence is brought to an end in subsequent talk.

Nevertheless, this kind of sequential development is not achieved through the troubles receipt alone: The actions that finally lead to sequence termination are an interactional achievement, accomplished by both conversational parties in concert.

The following sections will examine 'low-falling and tailed' *ah* as used to display a 'mock emotion' (Sandlund 2004, 2005). The mock display shows that speakers have a kind of metacommunicative knowledge concerning how and when to use 'low-falling and tailed' *ah* in troubles talk.

8.4.3   Ah *as a mock troubles receipt*

We have seen on the basis of Excerpts 20–22 that troubles recipients can use 'low-falling and tailed' *ah* as a troubles receipt in order to show their heightened affective involvement and affiliation with an informing about a trouble. This use of 'low-falling and tailed' *ah* may also be observed in Excerpt 23.[99] The excerpt provides evidence moreover that the affective dimension displayed by 'low-falling and tailed' *ah* is a members' category and that it can be deployed for strategic ends: Here the troubles recipient receipts a troubles announcement with 'low-falling and tailed' *ah*. The object is then mimicked and mocked by the troubles teller, which displays a re-orientation to business as usual.

The sequence starts near the beginning of a conversation between the troubles teller, Leslie, and the recipient, Rob, who is the vicar in the parish. The topical talk of this (brief) troubles talk sequence deals with Leslie missing her son Gordon, who has recently gone off to college in the North of England.

```
(23)   [HOLT SO88II:2:2] "lonesome"
1      Les:   helLO:?
2             (---)
3      Rob:   <<all>helLO leslie>,=
4             =it's rob MILler here,
5      Les:   <<h>oh helLO:>,[hh
6      Rob:                  [HOW are you.
7      Les:   OH::-
8             ALright;
9             MISSing GORdon;.hhh
10     Rob:   what's happening to GORdon.=
11     Les:   =well he's in Nor? in=ehm::
```

---

99. The transcript has been adopted from Couper-Kuhlen (2001a) and partly modified.

```
12              .hhh [!] ↓oh where IS he now;
13              .hhh <<smile>uh::m::::>
14              <<smile,h>UP in the NORTH>;
15              <<smile,h>NEWcastle>.
16              huhn huhn .hh
17      Rob:    is his college NEWcastle.
18      Les:    YES.
19              (.)
20              <<p>YES>.
21      Rob:    so (.)
22  →           THAT means you're all on your LONEsome.
23  →   Les:    <<h,acc>YES yEs:>;
24  →           un[FORtunately.
25  →   Rob:       [`%[a::].
26  →   Les:      `[a::].
27      Rob:    ↓NEVer mind.
28      Les:    eh huh huhnh .hhh
29      Rob:    ↑uhm::-
30      Les:    <<all>we're ↑hOping to come Over now that we're lEss
31              uhm: BUSy>;
```

The production of the 'low-falling and tailed' *ah* sound object in line 25 is generated in a slot following a local display of troubles receptiveness by the teller. The sound object which comes next (line 26) mimicks 'low-falling and tailed' *ah* and re-establishes troubles resistance on the teller's part. All in all, as will be analysed in what follows, the sequence is generally marked by a constant negotiation between troubles receptiveness and resistance among teller and recipient.

The sequence is initiated through Rob's how-are-you question in line 6. This question is positioned in the slot subsequent to mutual greetings (lines 3 and 5) in the opening of the telephone conversation, where such enquiries about each other's well-being are usually standardised routines. However, Leslie does not treat Rob's enquiry as routine: She first responds with an *oh*-prefaced (Heritage 1998) 'downgraded conventional response' (Jefferson 1988), which signals the presence of a trouble. As mentioned above, *oh*-prefaced downgraded conventional response point especially strongly to the presence of trouble and the possibility of some troubles talk. The prosodic design of the turn additionally indicates a non-routine action: The prosodic cluster of features accompanying ↓*OH*::; includes increased duration, a downstep in pitch and a flat, rising falling contour. The speaker then uses the subsequent slot to address the reason for her trouble (line 9) and thus to initiate troubles talk.

In response, the recipient embraces the topic by enquiring about Gordon (line 10). In doing so, he initiates sequence expansion, yet does not show an orientation towards the negative implications of the verb *MISSing*. The trouble teller's next informing that her son is in Newcastle (lines 11–15) can be treated as troubles-implicative: Leslie lives in the southern part of England, while Newcastle is situated in the North. What is more, with Gordon being the youngest child in the family, all the children have moved from home, which leaves Leslie and her husband alone (cf. also line 22). The delivery is, however, contextualised as an orientation to 'business as usual' (Jefferson 1988). Cues to this orientation are self-repair (line 11), pausing (lines 11–13), a parenthesis (line 12) which conveys word finding difficulties, and a smile voice in parts of the turn. The laughter which follows (line 16) further signals troubles resistance (Jefferson 1984).

The vicar next initiates repair (line 17), by providing a candidate understanding concerning the college, which is briefly confirmed in line 18. The falling final pitch movement of the confirmation signals turn yielding. This can be taken as another indication that the potential troubles teller is displaying troubles resistance: She does not expand on the affective implications involved in her son's move to the North. When a recipient response is noticeably absent in what follows (line 19), the confirmatory token is recycled in self-repair (line 20). Now Rob comes forward with a candidate interpretation of how his interlocutor is feeling (line 22). The matrix clause (*THAT means*) conveys that *you're all on your LONEsome* was inferred from Leslie's informing in lines 11–15. Gordon's attending college away from home is thus treated as a reason for the problem teller's loneliness. At the same time, the idiomatic expression "being all on your lonesome" modulates the other-attribution of affect in a playful, jocular tone. It indicates the speaker's alignment with the troubles teller's troubles resistance. In return, Leslie briefly confirms the candidate attribution (line 23). However, this time, her accelerated, high-pitched delivery can be taken as a display of heightened affective involvement, signalling troubles receptiveness. The turn is expanded with a negative assessment (line 24), signalling the teller's stance (i.e. 'regret') towards Rob's prior attribution. Although the assessment is also done with a short idiomatic formula, this time it does not come off as playful. The affect-laden display makes an affective response by the other speaker relevant.

In overlap with the assessment, the troubles recipient produces 'low-falling and tailed' *ah*. This acknowledges Leslie's confirmation as being trouble indicative and complete and functions as an affiliative, affect-laden troubles receipt. This charateristic is common to low-falling and tailed' *ah* found in other sequential contexts of this kind.

The troubles teller now produces an *ah* in return (line 26). Produced in smooth transition, its fomat matches exactly the lengthening of the vowel in the prior 'low-falling and tailed' *ah*. The overlap makes pitch analysis difficult but it is heard as having the same falling contour as Rob's sound object and as being performed with relative register matching (Leslie's sound objects falls from 314 Hz to 169 Hz. The F0 of Rob's sound object cannot be measured because of the overlap). It can be heard as mimicking Rob's display of affect as if to say "poor me" (cf. Couper-Kuhlen 1996). According to Sandlund (2004), an enactment of this sort is typical of mock displays of affect. "[C]onversationalists are skilled in both enacting and analyzing feigned emotions so that co-interactants can hear *which* emotional stance their contributions are designed to display and that they are offered playfully/non-seriously" (ibid: 266, emphasis in the original).

The troubles teller's production of the sound object and the mock display which comes along with it can thus be seen as a rhetorical resource which is used in a very accomplished manner: The troubles teller distances herself from the 'empathy' shown by the troubles recipient, taking a troubles-resistant stance towards his troubles receptiveness and affiliation.

In "topicalising"/making an issue of the affective dimension of Rob's turn, the sound object is treated as a display of affect. It can thus be concluded that the affective meaning of *ah*s of this kind is not only an analyst's concept but constitutes a members' category.

Furthermore the smooth transition after unit completion in line 26 shows that the sound object is followed by a TRP. The sound object thus forms a TCU, an action of its own which is oriented to as such (cf. Couper-Kuhlen (2001b: 20) for a similar argument).

In what follows, Rob responds to Leslie's mock display with the fixed formula ↓*NEVer mind*. It could be paraphrased as "don't let it trouble you" (Couper-Kuhlen 2004a: 213), and in this sense acknowledges the trouble resistance displayed by the mock display. This kind of orientation to business as usual anticipates the closing of the activity (Jefferson: 1988), which is further ratified by Leslie's subsequent laughter (line 28), an indicator of troubles resistance. Her turn in lines 30–31 now terminates the sequence: According to Jefferson (1988), a 'reference to getting together' constitutes a common practice to exit troubles talk.

To summarise, the topicalisation of the sound object's affective meaning through the responding mock display provides evidence that the sound object's affective dimension is a members' category rather than an analytic construction. Moreover, the mimicking shows that the participants must have some communicative metaknowledge both in terms of the form and the function of the 'low-falling and tailed' *ah*. However, a mimicked production of the sound object achieves just the opposite of a 'serious' one: Instead of displaying trouble-receptiveness, it performs troubles resistance.

8.4.4 *Summary and conclusions*

In summary, the basic findings related to 'low-falling and tailed' *ah* are:

1. When deployed by recipients of troubles talk, the sound object 'low-falling and tailed' *ah* functions as a *troubles receipt*: it treats the prior informing as informative of a trouble and complete; by making a *display of affective involvement*, it further appreciates the affective dimension of the prior informing and shows *affiliation* with it.

2. 'Low-falling and tailed' *ah* can receipt an expository informing in the delivery of a trouble (Excerpts 21 and 22, 23) or respond to the troubles announcement itself (Excerpt 20), leading to a more telescoped structure. Such troubles informings are accompanied by low pitch (either in absolute terms of the speaker's voice range or in relation to same speaker's prior unit); they are delivered in the present tense, which makes them come off as immediate and having high priority.

3. In the present data, 'low-falling and tailed' *ah* functioning as a troubles receipt is always produced in an independent intonation phrase. Subsequent to its production, the speaker can expand the turn or the other speaker can resume their talk. When the turn is expanded, this tends to be done with an assessment which modifies and qualifies the affective display performed by the sound object ('making light of the trouble') or expresses the hope of a good outcome ('optimistic projection'). Such actions are treated as sequence closing with the result that transition to a new sequence is accomplished. On the other hand, 'low-falling and tailed' *ah* can be oriented to as encouraging further elaboration of the delivery of the trouble when the *ah*-producer does not use the post-completion space for turn expansion.

4. The troubles receipt 'low-falling and tailed' *ah*, as opposed to *oh* accompanied by a comparable sound pattern, for example as in Excerpt 22, line 37, represents a recipient resource to achieve maximal mutual focus on the trouble and affiliation with the result so that the sequence now reaches its affiliative climax and is brought to an end in subsequent talk. Nevertheless, this does not mean that the troubles receipt is closure implicative in the same way as the assessments which typically follow in turn expansion.

5. The affective meaning of 'low-falling and tailed' *ah* is a members' category and may be mocked for specific communicative aims. Following Jefferson (1988), it may be associated with the dimension of 'empathy'.

The next section will be concerned with 'low-falling and tailed' *ah* as a bad-news receipt 1. Such sound objects are always followed by turn expansion.

8.5 Affect-laden *ah* in response to deliveries of bad news (with the teller as the consequential figure)

In response to announcements of bad news, 'low-falling and tailed' *ah* can be used as a bad-news receipt, appreciating the negative affective valence of the news told by (or about) the consequential figure. In the present data, the sound object always forms an independent contour and has a turn expansion, which commonly contains an idiomatic expression of 'sympathy'. This turn expansion is frequently occasioned by the news teller's noticeable absence of talk.

The analysis considers news sequences of the structure enquiry–news announcement–'low-falling and tailed' *ah*. It is argued that the post-completion space of *ah* is a position where the elaboration of the news sequence is negotiated and further affective work-up of the news is managed.

Recipients can deploy 'low-falling and tailed' *ah* in order to respond to the announcement of a negatively valenced piece of news. If the bad-news announcement is elicited by the recipient, this is usually done by an enquiry about the mental/physical state of the the potential news teller or a third party, i.e. the consequential figure.

Excerpt 24 illustrates a case where 'low-falling and tailed' *ah* receipts a news announcement which is elicited as an account in post-expansion. Subsequent to the production of the sound object, the status of the sequence is negotiated. It will be argued that the bad-news receipt signals possible completion of the sequence. After the turn is expanded by an assessment in orientation towards a noticeable absence of talk, the sequence develops further into news delivery.

The example is taken from a telephone conversation between two teenage friends Susan (caller, news teller, and consequential figure) and Gordon (recipient). In the talk prior to this excerpt, Susan has asked Gordon whether he is free in the evening but he announces that he already has other plans (not shown here).

```
(24)   [HOLT:SO88:1:5] "just bored"
1      Sus:   [Okay;
2             (.)
3             hh well that's All i wanted to KNOW;
4             (-)
5   →  Gor:   WHY's that.
6             (---)
7      Sus:   ↑hm::::
8             (.)
```

```
 9              NOTHing; h[h
10     Gor:            [.hhhh
11              yOU're just (.) BO:RED, [hhh
12     Sus:                            [mh: NO::;
13              (-)
14  →  Sus:     WELL-
15              i dIdn't pass my DRIving test;
16  →  Gor:     `%[a::]. h
17              (--)
18  →  Gor:     oh THAT's a pIty;
19              (.)
20              wAs it toDAY;
21              (--)
22     Sus:     <<p>NO:>,
23              <<p>it wAs YESterday>;
```

The sequence of concern starts in line 5: By asking why Susan wanted to know whether he was free in the evening, speaker Gordon solicits an account. This results in 'non-minimal post-expansion' (Schegloff 2007) of the prior sequence (not shown in full here). Susan's response is delayed by filled and unfilled pauses (lines 6–8), which cue the turn as dispreferred. The delay can be seen as iconic of the evasiveness conveyed by the word *NOTHing* (line 9). Her interlocutor orients towards this by implementing a candidate B-event question (Labov and Fanshel 1977, Pomerantz 1988). It enquires about her mental state, suggesting she is bored (line 11). Local and Walker (2008) have shown that questions about the psychological state of the co-participant are used as a strategy to solicit talk about their prior conduct. Thus, the question does not come out of the blue; it is potentially prepared for by and related to the interlocutor's prior action (Schegloff 2007, Koole 2007).

The response which follows is again delivered in a dispreferred turn shape (filled pausing, hedging). It announces that the speaker failed her driving test (line 15). While elicited by the offer of a candidate answer in line 11, the news announcement forms an action made relevant by the initial enquiry in line 5. The announcement presents the news teller as being negatively affected by an event whose negative valence is cued through lexical and prosodic resources: Lexically, it is indicated through the negation of the verb *pass*. Prosodically, delayed timing, low pitch level and narrow pitch range frame the informing as bad news (Freese and Maynard 1998). The negative affective loading of the news invites an equally affect-laden response; furthermore, it confronts the recipient with the delicate task of how to handle the announcement of bad news which directly affects the teller.

The recipient receipts this negatively valenced announcement with 'a low-falling and tailed' *ah*. It is extremely lengthened, low-falling and comes with heavy creak.[100] The object treats the announcement as informative and brings the sequence as was initiated in line 5 to a possible point of completion. At the same time, the signalling of heightened affective involvement through the low pitch implements an affective display, which appreciates the affective loading of the news and affiliates, that is sides, with it. The creak seems to lend even more interactional thrust to the object.

The medium pause which follows indicates the relevant absence of talk in a position in which both participants could self-select. The noticeable absence of talk on the news teller's part can be heard as withholding (cf. Heritage 1984:333–335). It treats the *ah*-receipt, which proposes a termination of the local informing sequence, as opaque with regard to what it is doing.

In turn, the *ah*-producer orients towards this by expanding his turn with an assessment which has been idiomatised as a lexical display of 'sympathy' (line 18). In verbalising his 'sympathy', the recipient once more affiliates with the consequential figure. On the one hand, the verbalisation of his affective stance can be seen as an upgrade of what was done by the sound object because it conveys his affective stance in a way that makes it accountable. On the other hand, it can be seen as weaker action in that it does not show his affective stance but tells about it. Furthermore, the *oh*-prefacing (Heritage 2002) signals the speaker's epistemic independence with regard to this assessment.[101] In fact, in data not shown here it becomes apparent that Gordon has also failed his driving test in the recent past.

In what follows, by enquiring about further details of the event referred to in the announcement, the speaker proposes a topic shift with the result that an elaboration of the news and sequence expansion are solicited.

The sequence in Excerpt 24 is thus structured as follows:

A: enquiry
B: bad-news announcement
A: affect-laden bad-news receipt ('low-falling and tailed' *ah*)
B: pausing
A: *oh*-prefaced assessment

---

100. Because of the heavy creak with which the sound object is delivered, no Praat analysis can be provided.

101. That means that his assessment "is based on a judgement that, rather than being constructed in immediate response to [the informant's] assessment, was formed earlier and in independence from it." (Heritage 2002:201)

To summarise, 'low-falling and tailed' *ah* can serve as a bad-news receipt. As in troubles talk sequences, such an *ah* performs an affect-laden and affiliative action. As is indicated by the following silence, an elaboration of the sequence is negotiated. A closing at this point could indicate the *ah*-producer's orientation towards progressivity (Heritage 2007) to the effect that the local sequence is brought to a close. The affective display and a subsequent closing at this point may, however, be treated as premature by the teller. In orientation towards the silence, the *ah*-producer expands his turn with an *oh*-prefaced assessment conveying 'sympathy' with an idiomatic expression. In contrast to troubles receipts, the turn is thus expanded through an assessment which does not qualify the affective display done by the sound object but verbalises it. This has the effect that an elaboration of the news sequence, not its closing, is solicited.

The next excerpt provides further support for the observation that in the post-production space of 'low-falling and tailed' *ah* the development or curtailment of the sequence is negotiated. In addition, the excerpt shows that the affect-laden bad-news receipt does indeed treat the informing as newsworthy.

As in Excerpt 24, Excerpt 25 exemplifies an informing about the mental/physical state of a person (the consequential figure) elicited in post-expansion. Its status is, however, not so clear (news announcement or account), as it is treated differently by the informant and informee. We will argue that the speaker's and recipient's different orientations towards the informing as a piece of news or as an account become visible in the post-completion space of 'low-falling and tailed' *ah*.[102] The informant, Steve, has called the home of informee, Leslie, to ask Leslie's husband Skip to apologise for Geoff, the consequential figure, for not being able to attend a meeting scheduled for the next day.

```
(25)   [HOLT:M88:2:3] "wretched gout"
1      Les:   helLO:,
2             (--)
3      Ste:   oh (.) LESlie,
4             sOrry to (.) b? to BOTHer you,.h[h
5      Les:                                   [oh: RIGHT;
6      Ste:   could you a:sk SKIP:;
7             ↑if .hh at when you gO to this meeting toMORrow, .h
8             could he give gEOff: haldan's apologies through
9             SICKness?
```

---

102. This observation modifies Maynard's analysis of this excerpt (cf. Maynard 1997:96–97), which suggests that the turn consisting of *ah plus* an assessment should be taken as *one* unified action rather than – as I will argue – two independent actions.

```
10              (.)
11      Les:    ↑YES yes;
12              <<h>oh[↑DEAR>;=
13      Ste:        [(*)
14      Les:    =<<h,all>whAt's [the ↑matter with GEOFF>;
15      Ste:                    [i (met)
16              (-)
17      Ste:    well he ( ) he's gOt this wretched uhm (.) .hh he's gOt
18              this wretched (.)
19      Les:    !G[OUT!; hh
20      Ste:      [GOUT; (.)
21      Les:    ↑oh: yE[s; .hhhh
22  →   Ste:           [and he he: he's (right flat) on his BACK-
23  →   Les:    `[a::].
24              [pOO:r GEOFF;
25      Ste:    [but if skip COULD give his apOlogies,=
```

Lines 6–9 constitute the reason for the call, a request to give a third party's apol-
ogies due to sickness, which is acknowledged and ratified by the interlocutor
(line 11). The recipient's *oh*-prefaced assessment (line 12) in response displays an
orientation towards the request as implying bad news. She next solicits an account, framed as an enquiry about the third party's situation. The response is
produced with a dispreferred turn shape (delay (i.e. pause in line 16), hedging
(*well*), disfluent speech connected with repeated self-repair). The co-completion
of the teller's word search (lines 19–20) makes it clear that the recipient is aware
of the referent's illness (cf. also Maynard (1997: 126, footnote 1). This is further
indicated by the use of an *oh*-prefaced continuer, which signals 'epistemic independence' (Heritage 2002) and further does not pick up on the negative loading
cued by lexical cues (*wretched* and *GOUT*) in the informing.

The teller then elaborates on his telling, informing his recipient about the
consequential figure's current condition at the moment of speaking (line 22). This
time, the unit is receipted with a 'low-falling and tailed' *ah*. It orients towards the
informing as newsworthy and complete, at the same time appreciating its affective
loading and affiliating with it.

The formal properties of the sound object are similar to those in Excerpt 24
("just bored"): The unrounded open back vowel is lengthened, has low pitch and
falls on a long glide to low (from 233 Hz to 124 Hz) (cf. Figure 22).[103] It has lower
volume than the same speaker's prior talk and slightly creaky voice quality.

---

103. Steve's voice range is between ca 75–360 Hz.

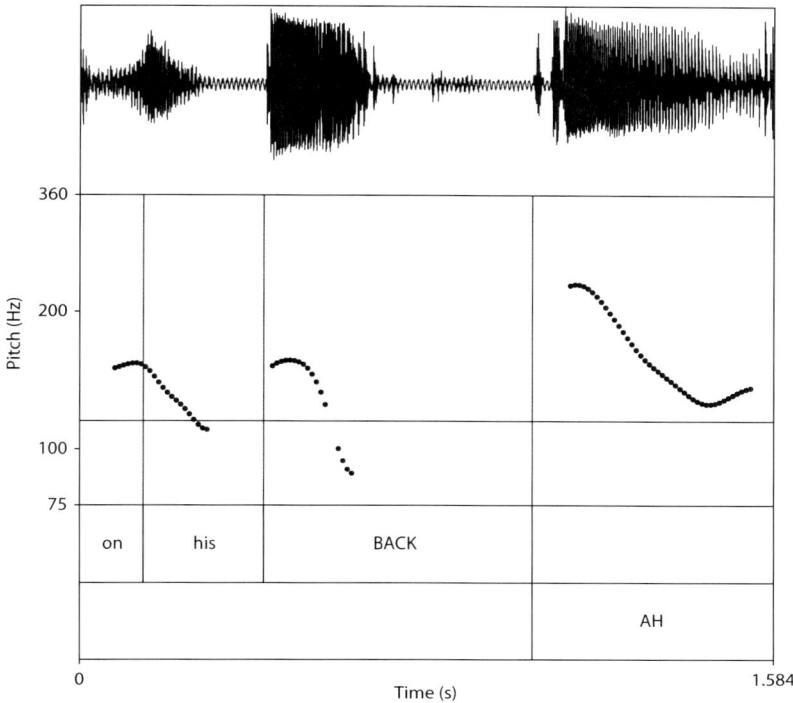

Figure 22. Acoustic analysis of Excerpt 25 ("wretched gout"), lines 22–23

The news teller orients towards the sound object as sequence-terminating by resuming the base sequence, i.e. his request, as indicated by the turn-initial re-sumptive *but* (cf. Mazeland and Huiskes (2001) on Dutch *maar*) (line 25). The non-minimal post expansion sequence is thereby closed. In this sense, 'low-falling and tailed' *ah* is locally treated as the receipt of an account.

Expanding her turn with an assessment, the *ah*-producer, however, signals a different orientation: The assessment, whose form [poor + X] constitutes a routine for displays of 'sympathy', may be taken as making the affective meaning of the prior sound object concrete. Example 24 has shown that *ah*-producers can elabo-rate their turn and further address the affective loading of the prior informing, a practice which usually occasions more related topical talk and an expansion of the sequence. Line 24 can thus be treated as an orientation towards an expansion of the sequence into a full-fledged news delivery sequence. From this perspective, 'low-falling and tailed' *ah* serves as a bad-news receipt 1.

Maynard (1997:97) summarises the structure of the sequence as fol-lows: "[S]ickness of a mutual acquaintance is initially offered as an account, is momentarily retrieved for treatment as (bad) news, and then is reembedded in a request-response sequence to once more account for the request." The analysis shows that the final treatment of the informing in line 22 is negotiated and settled in the post-completion space following the *ah*-receipt. It can therefore be concluded that 'low-falling and tailed' *ah* is not only interactionally functional in that its affective meaning performs an affiliative action; in acknowledging the account for the consequential figure's apology, it serves to organise the local sequence with the result that it is potentially closed. It is only in the post-completion that a development can be further encouraged. Furthermore, a high degree of newness in the informing seems to foster the possibility of the production of 'low-falling and tailed' *ah* and perhaps of an affect-laden response in general. If speakers inform a recipient about a state of affairs the informee is at least distantly aware of, the latter seem not to orient as readily towards its affective dimension.

In the excerpts above we presented cases where the bad-news receipt directly responds to the news announcement. In contrast, we will now turn to a case where, before dealing with its negative implications through 'low-falling and tailed' *ah*, the recipient responds to the news announcement with an initiation of repair. Here the news teller, Philip, is immediately affected by the event talked about and hence may be considered the consequential figure in the scenario; he has recently lost his mother. The bad-news sequence, which constitutes the reason for the call, is occasioned in line 1 by the potential news recipient, Leslie. The turn-initial *but* links up line 1 to the prior activity, in which Leslie accounts for not having called the day before (not shown here).

```
    (26)  [HOLT: X(C)1:1:3] "your mother"
1         Les:   but we were ↑vEry sorry to HEA:R,
2                that uh:
3                <<p>your ↑mOther had DIE:D>,=
4                =<<all,p>is that rIght PHI[Lip>?
5     →   Phi:                            [yeah yeah:
6                <<pp,all>[(that's right)> <<p>yEsterday MORning;=
7         Les:          [ye:s;
8     →   Phi:   =YES>;
9                (.)
10    →   Les:   o[h ↑YESter[day morning;
11    →   Phi:    [hm        [hm
12    →                hm hm [hm.
13    →   Les:               [`[a:].
14    →                (-)
15    →   Les:   `[a:];=
16                =i'm ↑so ↓SORry-
```

```
17    Phi:   .h <<f>well:> it was (.) uh: (.)
18           <<all>you know she was ↑very ↓POORly>;
             ((turn continues))
```

The enquiry which occasions the news announcement here is framed as a display of 'sympathy', addressing the recent death of the interlocutor's elderly mother (lines 1–3). At the same time, it is presented as seeking confirmation about the event in question (line 4). This makes it apparent that the information that the teller's mother passed away is not new as such. At the same time, the negative connotation of the verb *die* and the low volume and pitch with which the TCU <<p>your ↑mOther had D:IED>,=, contextualise it as talk about a negatively valenced event.

There follows a confirmation (line 5–6). Note that Leslie responds with a mere acknowledgement token (line 7, in overlap), which does not orient towards the affective implications of her interlocutor's response. The confirmation is next expanded through a "free constituent" (line 6) (Couper-Kuhlen and Ono 2007: 525), which announces the time of the speaker's mother's death. Its meaning, which can be paraphrased as "she died yesterday morning" can only be inferred from the prior context; its negative affective loading is thus only conveyed implicitly. It makes an affect-laden response relevant next.[104]

By repeating the time of the death in an *oh*-prefaced turn (line 10), the recipient implements a next turn repair initiation. Since the turn containing the trouble source is repeated at full length and without delay, the repair initiation cannot be motivated by problems of hearing or understanding. Instead, the repair initiator seems to claim that the speaker had other expectations or assumptions as to the time of the mother's death. The display treats the informing as newsworthy, while neither encouraging nor discouraging a development of the news (Maynard 1997). Coming in in overlap, the teller carries out the repair with a repeated production of weak confirmatory tokens (lines 11–12).

The recipient responds with a 'low-falling and tailed' *ah*, which ratifies the repair (line 13, cf. Figure 23 for an acoustic analysis).

---

104. Compare the following excerpt taken from Wilkinson and Kitzinger (2006: 158): The free constituent *Ten:: pou:nds* refers to the weight of the new-born baby. Wilkinson and Kitzinger (2006: 157) argue that it is treated as a surprise source by the other speaker (line 2).

```
[RT30: TG: 19:08]
01    Bee:   She had it yestihday. Ten:: pou:nds.
02    Ava:   °Je:sus Christ.° ←
03    Bee:   She ha[dda ho:(hh)rse hh .hh]
```

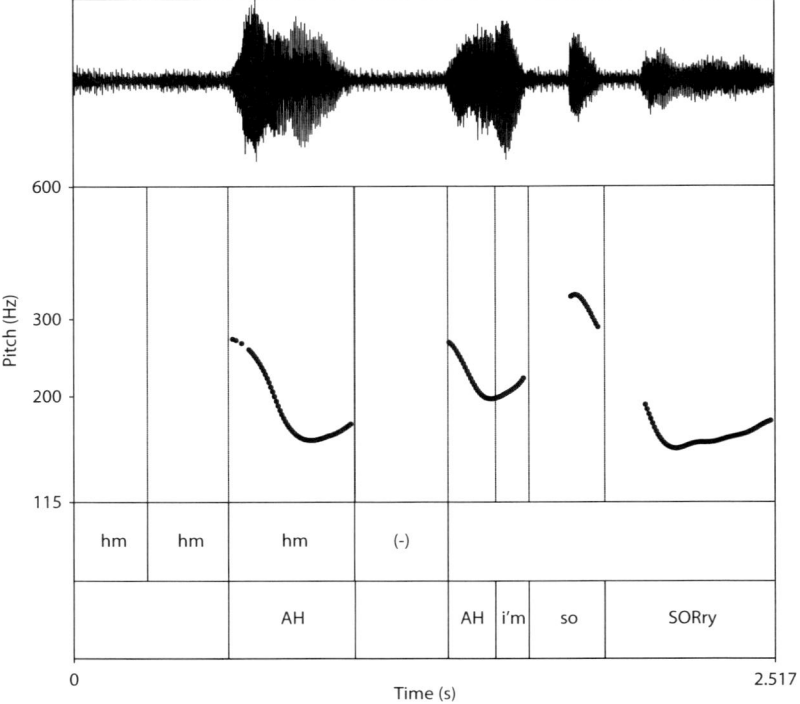

Figure 23. Acoustic analysis of Excerpt 26 ("your mother"), lines 11–16

In addition, it orients towards its affective loading by equally displaying affect and affiliation, i.e. it shows her siding with and 'feeling with' the consequential figure. 'Low-falling and tailed' *ah* thus serves as an affect-laden repair receipt which closes down the repair sequence.[105] As indicated by the short pause (line 14), there is next a noticeable absence of response. The news recipient orients towards this by the production of another 'low-falling and tailed' *ah*-receipt (line 15). It is followed by a latched self-assessment (intensified by the adverb ↑*so*) which performs an explicit, routine display of 'sympathy' (line 16). This turn expansion is iconic of an upgrade in accountability. Heritage (1984: 326) notes that affect-laden *ohs* can be treated by interlocutors as "opaque" in terms of meaning, which becomes visible in the absence of relevant uptake in the next slot. The [*ah* + assessment]

---

105. Wilkinson and Kitzinger (2006) describe such sequences (surprise source, display of ritualised disbelief, weak confirmation, display of surprise) as surprise sequences.

construction can in this sense be seen as doing self-repair of line 13. It is argued, however, that the [*ah* + assessment] construction performs an affiliative response to the news announcement in line 6, which is still relevantly missing. Lines 15–16 can thus be treated as a return to the base sequence, which was suspended on repair initiation.

Such an interpretation is supported by the next speaker's action: He elaborates on the news announcement by addressing the circumstances of his mother's death. His turn also displays an orientation towards his interlocutor's display of 'sympathy' in that it downplays the negative sides of his loss (lines 17–18), a kind of mitigating behaviour.

As in Excerpts 24 and 25, the news sequence is developed after an assessment conveying 'sympathy' is inserted by the *ah*-producer in the post-production space of the bad-news receipt. This time, however, the turn expansion is implemented without delay. Moreover, the latching suggests that it was planned in one go. This may be explained by the fact that it does not come as a direct response to the news announcement. Instead, the repair sequence allowed the *ah*-producer to process the affective implications of the news and find words for it.

To sum up, the structure of the news sequence can be outlined as follows:

A: bad-news announcement
    B: NTRI
    A: repair
    B: affect-laden repair receipt ('low-falling and tailed' *ah*)
B: bad-news receipt ('low-falling and tailed' *ah*) + assessment

To summarise, in this excerpt, 'low-falling and tailed' *ah* was found to be used in two functions:

On the one hand, the recipient uses 'low-falling and tailed' *ah* in order to ratify and appreciate the affective loading of an affect-implicative repair by displaying affect and affiliation. On the other, 'low-falling and tailed' *ah* is deployed to perform a bad-news receipt 1 which orients towards the negative loading of the consequential figure's announcement in an affect-laden and affiliative way and treats it as informative and complete. A self-assessment displaying 'sympathy' in subsequent turn expansion addresses the affective implications of the news in a more explicit fashion and is oriented to by the news teller as eliciting more topical talk, leading to an expansion of the news sequence.

Finally, the NTRI can be analysed as a strategy for treating the announcement as newsworthy, while at the same time deferring a direct response to its negative loading.

Sequential structure and setting

The analysis of news delivery sequences shows that the sound object 'low-falling and tailed' *ah* can be deployed as an affect-laden news receipt. The analysis has included sequences of the type

> enquiry
> (pre-announcement)
> news announcement
> (repair sequence)
> affect-laden news receipt
> (assessment)

Here the enquiry commonly addresses the mental/physical state of the other speaker or a third party i.e. the consequential figure in the scenario. The announcement is negatively valenced; it presents the current speaker or a third party as being highly negatively affected by an event, situation or state of affairs and invites an affect-laden response. The negative valence is achieved through lexical and prosodic cues. 'Low-falling and tailed' *ah* is deployed in order to treat the announcement as newsworthy, informative and complete. Its 'low-falling and tailed' contour appreciates the negative affective loading of the news announcement by displaying heightened affective involvement and affiliation with it. Furthermore, it can potentially curtail the news sequence. For these reasons, it has been described as a bad-news receipt.

The turn initiated with *ah* can be expanded through an assessment which commonly constitutes an idiomatic expression for 'sympathy'.[106] This can be taken as making what the sound object was conveying more concrete but still not accountable. Such expressions of 'sympathy' are done with idioms and, like sound objects, are not accountable in the same way as utterances produced on the fly (cf. Couper-Kuhlen (2004a), Drew and Holt (1988), Kitzinger (2000).

When the turn is expanded through an assessment conveying 'sympathy', more topical talk and sequence expansion is occasioned. When the post-completion space of 'low-falling and tailed' *ah* is used for transition to next speaker, the local news sequence is terminated and the pending activity is resumed.

The sequential structure shown above can emerge as a base sequence or in a side sequence, e.g. when accomplishing an account. In the post-completion space of 'low-falling and tailed' *ah*, sequence elaboration or termination can be negotiated, and in this sense the base sequence may or may not be returned to.

---

106. There seems to be a strong bias for expressions of 'sympathy' in the data examined; they are even produced in scenarios where the consequential figure and the *ah*-producer are socially only loosely connected.

8.6 Excursus: Affect-laden *ah* in radio-talk rejection contexts and bad-news deliveries (with the recipient as the consequential figure)

The following analysis will look at the use of 'flat-falling and low' *ah* in radio phone-ins and talk. The small study aims to complement that by Couper-Kuhlen (2009) on 'subdued' *ah* in everyday interaction by showing that displays of 'disappointment' in rejection contexts may be handled with similar resources in semi-institutional radio interaction (Section 8.6.1). Furthermore, it will illustrate that the management of affectivity in news delivery sequences depends on the participation framework: When the news recipient is the consequential figure in the scenario (as opposed to Excerpts 24–26), displays of 'disappointment' on his/her part in response to the announcement of bad news may be made relevant (Section 8.6.2). The following discussion also intends to complement findings from the present study made elsewhere that repair initiation is also used in bad-news sequences by the consequential figure in order to strategically defer a ratification of the bad news. Beyond this, the observation is again made that if instances of *oh* and *ah* with comparable sound shapes are used in one and the same sequence of sequences, *ah* is placed in a later position.

In contrast to turns containing 'low-falling and tailed' *ah* in troubles talk and news delivery sequences where the teller of bad news is the consequential figure, producers of 'flat-falling and low' *ah* in rejection contexts and in bad-news sequences where the *recipient* of the news is the consequential figure do not further assess the affective implications of the rejection/bad news on post-completion. Instead, turn expansions – if implemented – deal with alternatives to the rejection/bad news.

8.6.1 *Rejections of proposals in radio interaction*
In the following paragraphs we will shortly provide evidence that 'flat-falling and low' *ah* is deployed in rejection contexts in radio phone-ins to show 'disappointment'.

Excerpt 27 is taken from a radio programme, where callers have the task of solving a riddle. M is the presenter, C the caller.

```
(27)   [Brain teaser] "old-fashioned bird"
1      M:      RIGHT;
2              this Old-fashioned bird looks Anxiously for an
3              enterTAINer.
4              (.)
5              what do you reckon the ANSwer is;
6      C:      well i've got TWO answers. h
7      M:      hm=M?
8      C:      can i do them BOTH.
9              (.)
```

```
10    M:     go ON then;
11    C:     .hh UHM-
12           (.)
13  →        the first one is glen CAMPbell;
14           because of the film by the time i get to PHOEnix,
15  →  M:    yeah which is WRONG,
16           (.)
17  →  C:    `[a:].
18           .hh [and the SECond one;
19    M:         [he he
20    C:     for a bit of a (wuffy);
21           is cluck BERry.
```

We see that the example exhibits the same sequential structure as was identified by Couper-Kuhlen (2009) for mundane rejection contexts. In line 13, the caller proposes his solution to the riddle, which is rejected by the presenter (line 15). After a micro pause, the caller produces a 'flat-falling and low' *ah* (cf. Figure 24), which treats the rejection with heightened affective involvement and as having negative implications for himself.

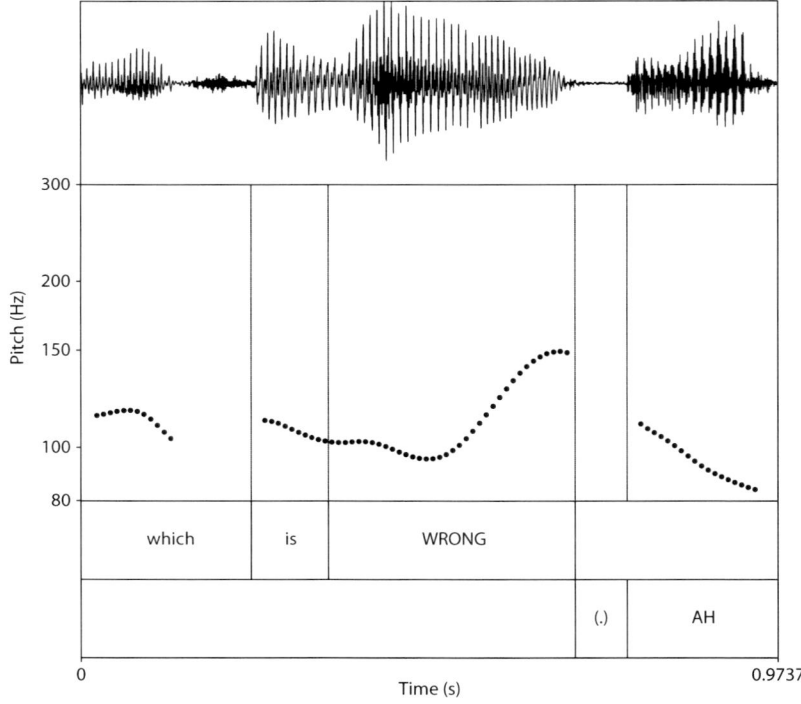

Figure 24. Acoustic analysis of Excerpt 27 ("old fashioned bird"), lines 15–17

In turn expansion, the caller makes a second try (lines 18, 20–21). This means, he uses the turn expansion in order to make an amendment to his rejected proposal. 'Flat-falling and low' *ah* in this kind of rejection context is rare in this set of radio data. Instead, callers use *oh* accompanied by a cluster of prosodic features comparable to that of 'flat-falling and low' *ah* and combinations of it as rejection finalisers. This points to 'flat-falling and low' *ah* making more affectivity relevant, which may not be preferred in radio phone-ins. Interestingly, the presenter uses strategies similar to those of rejecting parties in mundane conversation to make up for the rejection. For reasons of time and space, this observation cannot be further explicated.

8.6.2 News delivery sequences in radio interaction

Excerpt 28 illustrates that 'flat-falling and low' *ah* can also be used as an affect-laden receipt of bad news, this time as a resource of the consequential figure for displaying 'disappointment'. As will be shown, the recipient does not immediately accept and ratify the bad news. Instead he delays the finalising action in a strategic way. What is more, 'flat-falling and low' *ah* is positioned later than *oh* in the sequence.

The example is taken from a radio programme where a test of the local public transport system is being documented: The reporter is given the task of getting from A to B by public transport and reporting on how he gets by. In this excerpt, he faces problems when changing from train to bus and asks a passer-by for his connection. The report is broadcast live and commented on by the in-studio presenters (their interspersed laughter is not represented in the transcript).

```
   (28)  [Sadie Nine] "missed it"
1         Rep:   helLO
2                MAdam,
3                (--)
4    →           i'm lOOking for the seventy three A:,=
5    →           =i need to get to HAYbridge;
6    →    MA:    you've just MISSED it;
7                (.)
8         REP:   i ↑WHAT;
9         MA:    you've just MISSED it;
10   →           (-)
11        REP:   i ↑MISSED it;
12        MA:    YES;=
13               =you've (*) by;
14               and just MISSED it;
15   →           (.)
16   →    REP:   but in MY bit of paper;=
```

```
17              <<all>if you LOOK at my bit of paper there;>=
18              <<all>↑whAt's your NAME?>
19      MA:     SALly;
20      REP:    SALly;=
21              =<<all>are you from>
22              ↑Are you from the PUB;
23              (.)
24      MA:     NO,
25              i'm from the (**[*)
26      REP:                [were you LIStening;
27      MA:     i WA[:S;
28      REP:       [<<all>and you [RUSHED out>,
29      MA:                        [YEAH,
30      REP:    <<all>(*) look at (*****)>
31              .hh and it SAYS,
32              (--)
33              HATfield peverell to (**)
34              ↑OPposite,
35              (--)
36              take the BUS,
37              (.)
38              towards MALden;
39              (-)
40      MA:     yeah no that goes back to CHELMSfort;
41      REP:    OH:;
42      MA:     you should be ↑thIs side of the ROAD,
43              And the [bUs should stop up THERE,
44      IN1:            [oh DEAR];
45  →   MA:     and you've MISSED %it.
46              (.)
47  →   REP:    %`[ɑ:].
48              (--)
49              whAt do i do NOW;
```

The sequence is elicited with the reporter's enquiry about bus nr. 73A (line 4).
The informing in response (line 6) is bad news for the reporter in the sense that
he has missed his connection. In return, the reporter, that is, the consequential
figure of the bad news, does not ratify and finalise the informing; instead, he
initiates repair on it: first in line 8 and, when the repair is performed (line 9), a
second time (line 11). The NTRIs can be treated as enacting instances of 'pre-
disagreement' (Schegloff 2007). As was shown in the sections on 'extra high and
pointed' *oh* and on 'low-falling and tailed' *ah*, recipients can use next turn repair
initiation in order to defer an affective appreciation of their interlocutor's prior

action (cf. also Wilkinson and Kitzinger (2006) on suprise). Note that an acceptance of the repair is noticeably absent in lines 10 and 15 to the effect that the
bad news is not ratified.

The reporter next accounts for his enquiry, making his disagreement visible
(lines 16–17, 30–38). It is disconfirmed (line 40) in a turn with a dispreferred
shape (marked by the delay in line 39 and the initial weak agreement token *yeah*
in line 40). This time, the informing is ratified in terms of an *oh* with a 'flat-falling
and low' contour (line 41). While the low pitch displays an orientation towards its
negative implications, its rising-falling contour indicates an orientation towards
the unexpectedness of it. In accounting for the negatively valenced informing
(line 42–43), the passer-by deals with the affective loading of the *oh*-receipt. She
then recycles her initial announcement of bad news (line 45), which is now ratified and finalised by her interlocutor with a 'flat-falling and low' *ah* (line 47, cf. the
acoustic analysis in Figure 25).

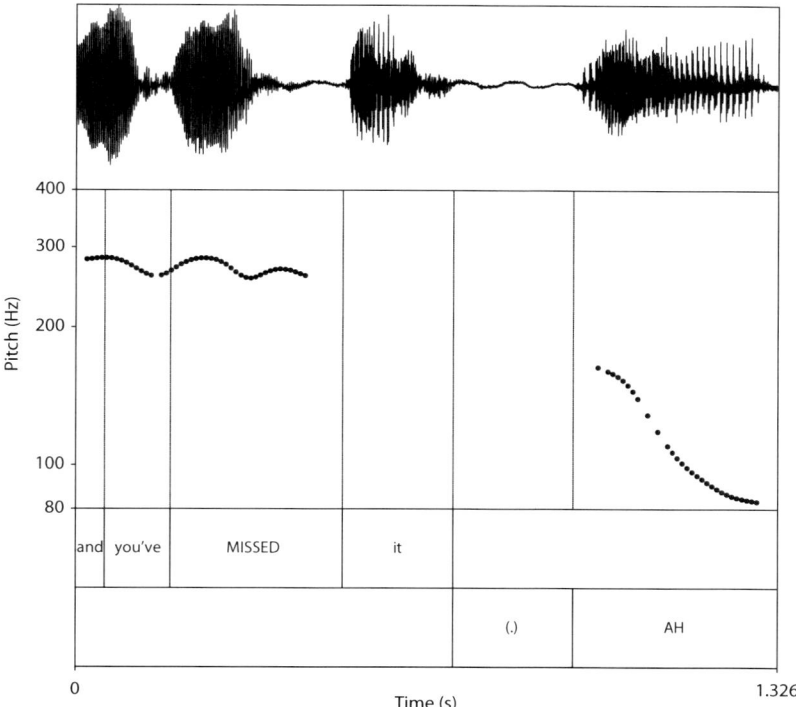

Figure 25. Acoustic analysis of Excerpt 28 ("missed it"), lines 45–47

The local news sequence initiated in line 4 is thus closed down on an affect-laden note, whose quality can be compared to that of 'flat-falling and low' *ah* in rejection contexts, 'disappointment'. This is further supported by the reporter initiating a new sequence, by enquiring for an alternative (line 49).

To summarise, the data shows that in bad-news sequences in radio interaction where the *recipient* acts as the consequential figure in the scenario, recipients can make displays of the same affective quality as in rejection contexts when ratifying the news, that is, show 'disappointment'. Next turn repair initiation may furthermore function as a strategic rhetorical resource in order to find out whether the bad news was warranted by objective facts (e.g. bus timetables) in the first place. Finally, it is noteworthy that like the recipient in troubles talk (Excerpt 22, "so happy"), the consequential figure and recipient of the bad news deploys *oh* with a 'flat-falling and low' contour in a slot before producing an *ah*-object.

8.6.3   Summary and conclusions

In addition to everyday interaction, 'flat-falling and low' *ah* can be used as a rejection finaliser in radio interaction. In radio quiz programmes, it serves to receipt the rejection of a proposal made by the caller in terms of the right answer to a riddle. As opposed to its use in mundane conversation, 'flat-falling and low' *ah* may be produced with creak, which points to a more emphatic, if not staged, production. The sequential structure matches that identified for everyday interaction:

> proposal
> rejection
> rejection finaliser ('flat-falling and low' *ah*)

In response to the rejection of a proposal, the sound object treats the rejection as informative and complete and thereby finalises it. At the same time, the low pitch signals heightened affective involvement. For this reason it can be treated as appreciating the negative affective implications for the rejectee and as making this kind of affect-laden appreciation available for the producer of the rejection. Note that this is in contrast to troubles talk and news delivery sequences when the news teller is the consequential figure. Here such displays of heightened affective involvement perform an affiliative move siding with a consequential figure other than self. In rejection contexts, a display of this kind is self-directed.

All in all, there is no instance in the data where the *ah*-producer implements an assessment in turn expansion which further addresses the negative implications of the rejection.

In a news sequence between a reporter and a passer-by in a radio live coverage, an analogous usage of 'flat-falling and low' *ah* was observed. Here the sound object is deployed by the consequential figure, that is, the news *recipient*, to ratify the bad news and appreciate its negative implications. Like in rejection contexts, the news receipt is followed by an action dealing with an alternative to the bad news. In line with the analysis of rejection contexts proposed above (cf. also Couper-Kuhlen (2009), the affective dimension displayed by 'flat-falling and low' *ah* can be labelled 'disappointment'. In contrast to the news sequences in Excerpts 24–26, the affect-laden display is thus self-directed.

Similar to the news sequence in Excerpt 26, the recipient defers the acceptance of the bad news by performing next turn repair initiation. It further elicits an account for the bad news. The structure of such a sequence can be described as follows:

> enquiry
> bad-news announcement
>> repair sequence
>> account sequence
> bad-news receipt ('flat-falling and low' *ah*)

Here the next turn repair initiation on the part of the bad-news recipient performs pre-disagreement. The disagreement is made visible through the recipient's eliciting an account of the rejection.

8.7 The interactional pay-off of the variants of *ah*: Do they signal discrete emotions?

In the preceding sections, we discussed variants of the sound object *ah* with the same segmental substance but different prosodic-phonetic packaging which are related to four functions: 'low-falling and tailed' *ah* in the function of a troubles receipt, a bad-news response 1 ('sympathy'), and a repair receipt, as opposed to 'flat-falling and low' *ah* as a rejection finaliser and bad-news response 2 ('disappointment') in radio interactions. Despite their variant properties, such as different contours in particular, both sound patterns can be heard as rather similar (cf. also Couper-Kuhlen (2009) because of their common vowel lengthening and low pitch. Nevertheless, distinct emotion labels were used as shorthand to refer to and differentiate the affect-laden displays made by the variants of this sound object. The following discussion of an excerpt taken from a radio interaction will be used to more clearly articulate the position taken in the present study. It will be argued that the packaging of *ah* tends to index – together with other contextual cues – whether the affective display is addressed to other (which would point to affective dimensions such as 'sympathy', 'empathy', 'commiseration', 'compassion' and the like) or to self (which would point to affective dimension such as 'disappointment', 'frustration', 'dissatisfaction' and the like). However, when being produced in short temporal succession and in a complex participation framework, the distinction between the two packagings may become blurred, especially if the prosody does not come off in a discrete fashion. And especially so if the turn initiated by the sound object is not expanded with an assessment or some other unit which verbalises a specific affective quality and makes the meaning of the initial sound object concrete. We will show that this kind of ambiguity may be exploited for interactional goals.

Excerpt 29 is a good example of this. It sets in in the last line of Excerpt 28. Remember that it is taken from a live radio broadcast where the reporter (REP) has the task of testing how well things go when using public transportation to get from A to B. His journey is followed and commented on by two in-studio presenters (IN 1 and IN 2).

```
(29)  [Sadie Nine] "another one"
1   REP     whAt do i do NOW;
2   ( ):     .h
3   MA:     you can take (.) aNOTHer o[ne.
4   REP:                              [`[a::].
5           [oKAY,
6   MA:     [**
7           how about CHELMSfort,
8   REP:    YEAH,
9           (-)
10  MA:     and get another bus from chelmsfort to ↑MALden.
11          (-)
12  REP:    `[a:].
13          thank you ↑so MUCH;
14  MA:     you're WEL[come;
15  REP:              [THANK you-
16  IN1:    he [he
17  MA:        [you don't get one here for two HOURs.
18  (MA):    two
19  IN1:    `[a[:].
20  REP:       [<<all>i beg your PARdon>?
21  MA:     two HOURs;
22  REP:    two HOURs,
23          (---)
24  IN1:    [oh NO.
25  REP:    [`[a:].
26  IN2:     `[a:[:];
27  REP:         [thank you MADam;
28          (.)
```

```
29 IN2:   R[ON;
30 REP:    [<<smile>what am i gonna DO(h)>;
31 IN2:   R[ON;
32 REP:    [hehehe[hehe
33 IN2:          [do you KNOW;
34        when ↑you said you're outside (*) swanIN,
35 (REP): YE[AH;
36 IN2:     [i lOOked into the instructions and it quite clearly
37        SAYS;
38        hAtfield pEverel to swanIN;
39        in brackets ↑!OPP!?
40        as in o p P;
41        [OPposite to s[wanin.
42 REP:   [YEAH;
43                     [OPposite;
44        (.)
45        oh that's exactly where i ↑WAS;
46 IN2:   what were you on the same ↑SIDE of the road to swanin
47        or were you-=
48 REP:   =↑NO;
49        i was on the ↑OTHER s[ide (**);
50 IN2:                   [↑oh: THAT'S okay then;
51 IN1:   YE[S;
52 IN2:     [YES;
53 REP:     [<f>SO>;
54        ↑thIs lady says the bus i wanted was the one i just
55        SAW;
56        t[hat was on the same side as (*) swanIN,
57 IN2:    [YES;
58 IN2:   `[a[:].
59 REP:      [and she's RIGHT;
60        having THOUGHT about it,
61        (.)
62 IN2:   `[a[:].
63 REP:      [this way does go towards MALden.
64        (---)
65 REP:   and i [haven't really thought for (where on) eArth
66 IN2:         [<<sigh>hhh>
67 IN1:         [oh DEAR.
68 REP:   <<smile>am i go(h)ing to be NOW>; [hihi
69 IN2:                                     [two HOURs;
70        (--)
71 IN2:   i don't know i think we might have to consult (-)
72        uh madam prodUcer what should he do [NOW;
73 REP:                                       [he he he
```

There are several instances of *ah*-objects in this excerpt, used as response tokens in different types of activities. While some sound objects clearly fall under one or the other type of contour (either 'flat-falling and low' or 'low-falling and tailed'), for some it cannot be determined whether the displays are self-directed (connected to 'flat-falling and low' prosody) or other-directed ('low-falling and tailed' prosody).

Lines 1–27 represent the interaction between the reporter and the lady on the street, with the two in-studio presenters acting as bystanders. Here the reporter and the lady are still engaged in amending her announcement of bad news in response to the reporter's enquiry for information about a bus connection (shown in Excerpt 28).

The sound objects in lines 4, 12 and 25 are produced by the reporter, i.e. the recipient of the bad news which was performed earlier in the conversation (cf. line 6 of Excerpt 28, "missed it"). [107] The reporter's sound objects receipt informings of various kinds as part of the lady's making amendments, an activity which can be called "looking for an alternative bus connection". The 'flat-falling and low' prosody of the *ah*-objects signals that the recipient receipts these informings as having negative implications for self (cf. Figures 26 and 27 for Praat pictures of lines 4 and 12, showing acoustic analyses of amplitude and F0 over time. Due to the overlap with which line 25 was delivered no acoustic analysis could be made). In this kind of interactional context, these objects may be characterised as doing self-directed 'sorrow', i.e. as 'disappointment' or 'self-pity'.

Lines 19 and 26, on the other hand, can be heard as objects with 'low-falling and tailed' prosody (The overlap does not permit an acoustic analysis of the two objects). Being produced by the in-studio presenters, they respond to the same kind of informings as did the reporter's sound objects (especially line 26). However, it can be assumed that they cannot be heard by the reporter's interlocutor in the street but only by himself and the radio audience. On the basis of the tone of voice with which they are produced, and the participation framework, we argue that the affect-laden displays performed by the in-studio presenters' sound objects are addressed to other, that is, to the reporter.

The sound objects in lines 58 and 62 produced by the in-studio presenters, however, are not such clear cases: At least line 58 comes with 'flat-falling and low' prosody.[108] Both serve as recipient responses to an account in which the reporter

---

107. Note that the sound object in line 25 represents one of the rare cases where *ah* is placed in turn-final position, here in an incremental turn expansion.

108. Due to the overlap, no acoustic analysis of the object can be made.

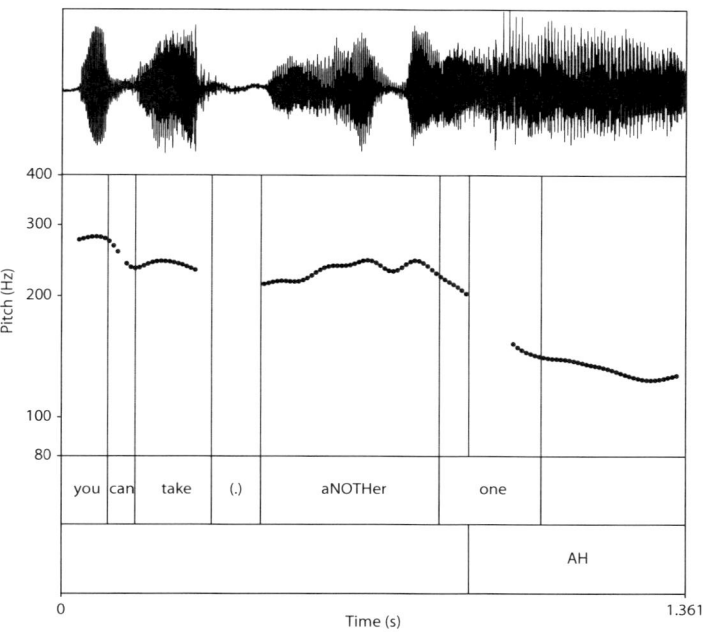

Figure 26. Acoustic analysis of Excerpt 29 ("another one"), lines 3–4

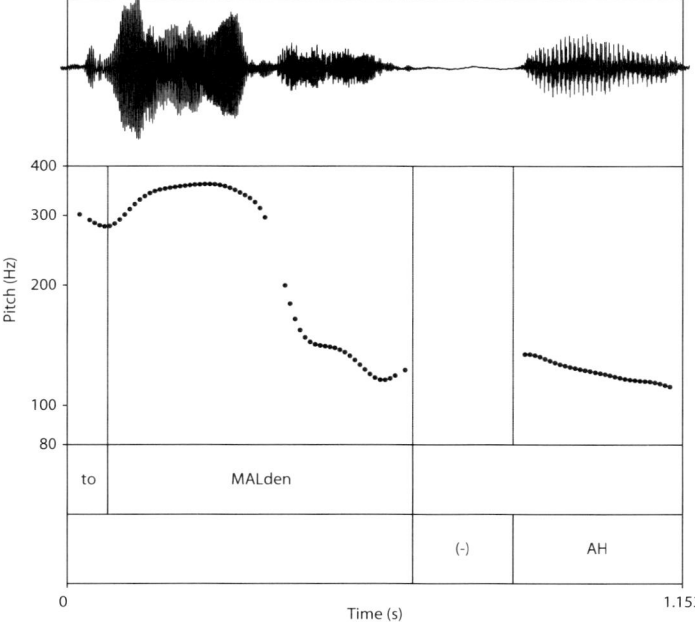

Figure 27. Acoustic analysis of Excerpt 29 ("another one"), lines 10–12

explains to the in-studio presenters why he had trouble finding his bus. This little troubles telling follows on an account for missing the bus, which is elicited by in-studio presenter 2 from line 29 onwards, implying that the reporter did not follow his instructions. When the account is ratified, the reporter further extends it with a little troubles telling from line 53. By eliciting the account, in-studio presenter 2 changes the footing and constructs herself as a ratified participant.

On the one hand, lines 58 and 62 could be addressed to other and do affiliation with the troubles teller and his trouble. Such affect-laden, affiliative responses are made relevant by the negative implications of the telling. Here the trouble would be treated as the 'reporter's trouble' alone. Alternatively, the affective displays (cf. also the loud sighing in line 66) could be self-directed. This latter interpretation is supported by line 72, where the troubles recipient (in-studio presenter 2) shifts the participant framework by initiating talk with the producer of the programme and seeking instructions on how to proceed. From this request it can be inferred that the troubles teller's missing the bus and the unforeseen two hours' delay has consequences for the course of the live broadcast. This makes visible that 'troubles teller's trouble' is also 'recipient's trouble'.

On the basis of lines 58 and 62 we can see that the attribution of the affective display is not always clear. What is more, the fact that explicit reference to affective states is avoided by the producer on post-production may indicate that the ambivalence of the sound object is interactionally exploited. Note that through the reporter's missing the bus the success of the live broadcast has been put at risk. When the in-studio presenter leaves it open whether to treat this extralinguistic problem as the 'reporter's trouble' or the 'in-studio presenter's trouble' in the ongoing interactional project, she avoids potentially "face-threatening" acts toward the reporter.

To conclude, the ascription of clear-cut affect labels may not always be warranted by the data. While *ah*-producers may make systematic formal distinctions packaging the object with specific sound patterns, they do not always actually make the meaning of these objects concrete. Without verbalisations in turn expansion which further address the affective dimension at play, the affective meanings of *ah*-objects remain rather vague. This can be exploited in participation frameworks where the participants' status is ambiguous. We think that it is exactly this vagueness which makes sound objects powerful tools for affect display in interaction. This vagueness becomes especially visible when the distinction between negatively valenced affect with heightened involvement directed at *self* (which could be labelled as e.g. 'disappointment' or 'self-pity')' or *other* (which could be labelled as e.g. 'sympathy' or 'empathy') becomes formally and interactionally blurred.

Table 8. Variants of the sound object *ah*: Forms and functions

Sound object		Low-falling and tailed *ah*		Flat-falling and low *ah*	
obligatory prosodic-phonetic properties	segmental substance	close to cardinal vowel 5 (sometimes aspirated)			
	duration	lengthened			
	pitch register	low			
	pitch movement	begins in the mid range of the speaker's voice and falls on a glide to the lower range, ending as a level tail		slight, narrow fall in the lower range of the speaker's voice	
	articulatory force	stronger than that of flat-falling and low *ah*		weaker than that of low-falling and tailed *ah*	
sequential placement		A: troubles announcement/-exposition; B: affect-laden troubles receipt (low-falling and tailed *ah*)	A: enquiry about mental/-physical state of the recipient or a third party; B: announcement of bad news; A: affect-laden bad-news receipt (low-falling and tailed *ah*)	A: proposal; B: rejection; A: affect-laden rejection finaliser (flat-falling and low *ah*)	A: enquiry; B: announcement of bad news for recipient; B: affect-laden bad-news receipt (flat-falling and low *ah*)
sequence-organising function		acknowledgement of trouble (troubles receipt)	acknowledgement of bad news, potentially sequence-terminating (bad-news response)	(staged) ratification of rejection (rejection finaliser)	acknowledgement of bad news by the consequential figure, potentially sequence-terminating (bad news response)
interactional function		display of 'empathy'; affiliation	display of 'sympathy'; affiliation	display of 'disappointment'	
if turn expansion		expressions addressing the positive aspects of the present situation or more positive future prospects	idiomatic expressions of 'sympathy'	amendment of proposal	enquiry about alternatives
if stand-alone		continuation of activity	–	proposals of alternatives/compensation for rejection	–

8.8   Summary and conclusions

Speakers use *ah* in a variety of contexts and functions: The analysis included the use of 'low-falling and tailed *ah*' as a mundane troubles and news/account receipt 1 and of 'flat-falling and low' *ah* as a rejection finaliser and bad-news receipt 2 in radio interactions. These findings are summarised in Table 8.

The formal distinctions identified suggest that speakers make a conceptual difference between affect-laden displays directed to other (e.g. 'empathy', 'sympathy', 'compassion') and to self ('disappointment', 'self-pity'). However, these formal differences may be blurred, which may be exploited for specific interactional goals.

Nevertheless, the discussion of different sorts of news sequences revealed that the management of such displays does not only depend on the activity in question but also on the participation framework.

The analysis further shows that recipients may use the post-production slot of the variants of *ah* in order to do further work on the affective dimension displayed by the sound objects and verbalise aspects of their affective dimension. Depending on the activity, these verbalisations in turn expansion are systematically different. For instance, the display done by a troubles receipt *ah* may be modulated and qualified through assessments. Bad-news receipts 1, followed by an idiomatic assessment, can in retrospect be contextualised as signalling 'sympathy'. In rejection contexts and when the recipient of the bad news is at the same time the consequential figure, the slot may be used in order to make amendments. This shows that as in the case of the variants of *ooh*, the post-production slot of the sound object is a position sensitive to affective work and management.

CHAPTER 9

More affect-laden sound objects

To round out the present study of sound objects, this section presents sound objects with sound patterns which have been traditionally described as outside the standard British English sound system (cf. Ladefoged (2001):[109] Alveolar and bi-labial clicks, [!] and [☉], and whistling, [ʍ]. Like the variants of the vocalic sound objects *oh*, *ooh* and *ah*, they are deployed as recipient responses to affect-laden speaker actions.

The frequency of such sound objects in this kind of interactional environment is rather low in the present corpus (but compare Wright (2005) for the uses of clicks in other activities). The following accounts should therefore be treated as exemplary (single) case studies. In Section 9.1 we will examine the use of clicks in complaint sequences. We will finally be concerned with the sound object [ʍ] in news delivery sequences in Section 9.2.

9.1   The affect-laden sound object *click*

In the data examined, clicks can be deployed as recipient responses to complaints. Their production can either be followed by a turn by the next speaker or the current speaker can expand their talk, often with more sound objects.[110] Clicks

---

109. The sound object [ʊx] represents another "anomalous" type found in the data. The segmental substance is made up by an initial vowel close to the quality of the cardinal vowel 13 ([ʊ]) plus a voiceless velar fricative. The consonant is commonly treated as a "Scottish" sound (Giegerich 1992) and not as part of the regular standard British English system. The sound object is used as a responsive action in proposal sequences and deliveries of good news in the present data and can be related to affective dimensions such as pleasure in lay terms. Since the data sample is too limited and sequentially too heterogenous, it cannot be considered for the purposes of the present study. Despite this sequential heterogeneity, the sound object is accompanied by a fairly stable cluster of prosodic properties: increased duration, noticeably higher pitch than prior speech by same speaker, rise-falling pitch movement and greater loudness than prior talk by the same speaker.

110. Clicks do not as a rule have enough prosodic prominence to qualify them as forming independent intonation phrases. In cases where the click is followed by more elements by same speaker, these will therefore generally be noted in the same line as the click. Nevertheless, the

responsive to complaints include bilabial [⊙] or alveolar clicks [!]. Whether these formal differences are coupled with functional ones is a question, however, which remains for future research. Wright (2005), for example, suggests that bilabial and alveolar clicks may be used interchangeably.

Complaints have been described as activities where complainant and recipient do the interactional work of 'moral indignation' (Drew 1998, Günthner 2000, cf. also Section 4.2.3). We will argue that clicks constitute a recipient resource which performs this kind of affective work in a very minimal fashion, although it may sometimes be ambiguous. Clicks are functional at the terminal boundaries of narrative and non-narrative sequences.

9.1.1 Previous accounts of clicks in dictionaries, phonetic text books and talk-in-interaction

Clicks are stops articulated on a velaric ingressive airstream (Ladefoged and Maddieson 1996: 246, Laver 1994: 131, 174). This is in contrast to the vowels and consonants of the English phonemic system, which are all made on a pulmonic egressive airstream (cf. Ladefoged and Maddieson (1996: 246–280) for a comprehensive outline of the articulatory and acoustic properties of clicks). In contrast to English, clicks have phonemic function in languages such as, for instance, the Khoisan languages of Southern Africa (e.g. Bushman, Nama, !Xóõ and !Xũ, cf. Laver (1994: 174) for an overview of click-languages). For English, clicks are traditionally categorised as paralinguistic sounds which serve as emotional interjections. In what follows, an outline of descriptions of clicks in dictionaries, grammar books and phonetic handbooks will be provided before coming to a brief review of, to our knowledge, the only interactional study on clicks so far available (i.e. Wright (2005).

The Collins Cobuild English Language Dictionary lists the graphemic expression *tut* as having the sound structure of a click, roughly characterised by a tongue position behind one's teeth and insuction of air. From this rough articulatory description it cannot be determined whether *tut* stands for a dental or alveolar click. The exclamation is described as expressions of annoyance, frustration or disapproval in speech (Sinclair 1987: 1574). In contrast, The Cambridge International Dictionary of English represents the phonemic structure of *tut* as /tʌt/, indicating its emotional meaning as that of disapproval. It is added that an exact reduplication, i.e. *tut tut*, constitutes a humorous variant of the exclamation, as in e.g. *You're*

---

question whether productions of clicks followed by other speaker's talk actually constitute *full* turns is an issue associated with sound objects in general (cf. Schegloff (1982: 92). In any case, clicks are treated as being followed by TRPs in the present data. This observation points to an interesting difference between TCUs and intonation phrases.

late again – tut tut! (Procter 1995: 1572, italics in the original). Again providing the most comprehensive information, the dictionary further lists a derivational verb *tut*, which means "to say sth. disapprovingly" (ibid: 1572). Also, it gives *tsk* (or *tsk tsk*) as another graphemic symbol of /tʌt/ (ibid: 1566).

Similarly, phonetic handbooks and grammars stereotypically acknowledge the use of a double voiceless dental click [ǀ], a so-called interjection spelled *tut tut* or *tsk tsk* for English. Quirk et al. (1985: 853) point to the 'spelling pronunciation' /tʌt/. The interjection is generally treated as a paralinguistic sound expressing affective states of 'exasperation' and 'impatience' (Laver 1994: 175) or 'mild regret' and 'disapproval' (Quirk et al. 1985: 853).

To sum up, according to English dictionaries, grammars and phonetic text books, clicks are spelled as *tut* and serve as interjections/exclamations in English. There are two kinds of pronunciations possible: that of a dental/alveolar click or the 'spelling pronunciation' tʌt/. Clicks serve as expressions of such manifold inner states as 'exasperation', 'impatience', 'mild regret', 'disapproval', 'annoyance' or 'frustration' (cf. Section 6.1 for a criticism of the confusing polysemy of such dictionary entries).

As far as the use of clicks in talk-interaction is concerned, there is still a lot of work to be done. One rare account from an interactional linguistically informed perspective is Wright (2005) on clicks in conversational British English. In her view, "clicks can be regarded as functioning linguistically, as they are part of the meaning of talk; that is, as being part of the linguistic system of English rather than only the 'paralinguistic'" (ibid: 241). Furthermore, she argues against the widespread view in the traditional literature that clicks are associated with expressions of negative feelings, such as e.g. 'annoyance' or 'irritation'. Instead, she claims that they are solely functional at sequential boundaries for sequence organisation (that is, for indicating a new, disjunctive sequence) and in word search for turn construction (that is, for the achievement of turn-holding). As mentioned above, Wright (2005) does not assign different functions to the different formal types of clicks found in the data, which include mainly alveolar and bilabial clicks.

Even though one could regard it as an empirical question whether affectivity may at times play a role in the two sequential/turn-constructional environments examined by Wright (2005), her study provides evidence that clicks are functional for sequence-organisation and turn-construction. It also suggests that they may be extremely versatile and highly context-bound in terms of their interactional functions and meaning.

To sum up, according to traditional accounts, clicks constitute paralinguistic interjections which express emotions such as e.g. exasperation, impatience etc. From an interactional linguistic point of view, clicks are used as systematic linguistic resources at specific sequential places, without affective meaning. Furthermore, no form-function relationship between different types of clicks and functions is found. The same is true for the clicks found in the complaint sequences presented in the following sections. They can be bilabial [⊙] or alveolar [!]. However, we argue that in complaint sequences, clicks serve affective functions albeit in a very minimal and weak fashion.

9.1.2   'Moral indignation' and 'disapproval' in talk-in-interaction

As outlined in Section 4.2.3, the type of affect often associated with complaint activities in English talk-in-interaction is 'moral indignation' (Drew 1998). Interestingly, the same is stated for German (Günthner 2000). However, not all studies dealing with complaints make such a link: More generally, complaints are often merely associated with negative assessments (e.g. Barnes and Moss (2007), Couper-Kuhlen (2006), Halonen and Sorjonen (2008). Furthermore, Barnes and Moss (2007) point out that complaining can be done in an ironic fashion as well. Edwards and Potter (2005), examining marital counseling sessions, associate the stance displayed in a husband's responses to his wife's complaints about him with "anger and resentment" (ibid: 258).

One aspect appears to be of special importance in the analysis of clicks as recipient responses in third-party complaint activities: First, complaints make affiliative responses relevant on the part of the recipient in mundane interactions (Halonen and Sorjonen 2008: 42). Disaffiliative responsive moves may be followed by concessive actions on the part of the complainant (ibid: 42–43). For this reason, we can expect that in contrast, recipient actions which display a *concordant* stance should *not* require extra interactional work. This observation becomes especially significant when examining clicks whose meaning is not verbalised or explicitly spelled out by participants.

9.1.3   Clicks in response to complaints

The following account will discuss the use of responsive clicks in their function as affect-laden complaint receipts in narrative and non-narrative complaint sequences. First, we will see that the click receipts the climax of the complaint story. We will then turn to an example of a non-narrative complaint sequence, where the click arguably serves the same kind of function. In both sequential environments, a click alone does not accomplish the affective appreciation made relevant on the part of the recipient in this slot. For this reason, we argue that the clicks serve to display a weaker affective stance than that displayed by the complainant. In terms of affect labels, a click may be treated as doing 'disapproval' rather than a co-display of 'indignation', which would be treated as an interactionally stronger action.

Nevertheless, it has been observed in the present data that (lengthy) narrative sequences tend to prepare for more affectively and morally appreciative work on the part of the recipient than a non-narrative complaint.

9.1.3.1 *Clicks in response to climaxes in complaint stories.* Recipients of narrative complaints use clicks at the boundary of such stories, i.e. in response to the story climax. Following the click, the complainant can come in with a further complaint with the result that the activity is expanded. Alternatively, the complaint recipient can produce further signals of affective appreciation and affiliation so that the narrative is abandoned.

Case 1 (activity expansion subsequent to a click) is illustrated by Excerpt 30. Here the click responds to the climax of a complaint story episode about the misconduct of the complainant's friends. The excerpt is taken from a telephone interaction between two teenage friends Dana, the complainant, and Gordon. The complaint story episode is preceded by some troubles talk on the part of the complainant. In the talk prior to the excerpt shown, Gordon has apologised for having called Dana late the night before. Line 19 seems to make reference to this call.

```
(30)   [HOLT:U88:1:4] "talking for another hour"
1      Dan:   [BUT uhm- (--)
2      Gor:   [.hhh
3      Dan:   all moʔ this MORning;
4             (--)
5             uh[:m (--) i: (-)
6      Gor:      [hhh
7      Dan:   my EYE's been really [itching bAdly;=
8      Gor:                        [.hhh
9      Dan:   =and hh we've been: (.) throwing boiling water in it
10            and STUFF;=
11            =<<pp>and [it (.) itches a> LOT; hh
12     Gor:             [<<breathy>oh DEAR>; hh
13            (-)
14     Dan:   .hh SO [uhm- (--)
15     Gor:          [.hhh
16     Dan:   <<all>uh and [it's rEAlly NICE>;=
17     Gor:                [hhh
18     Dan:   =AND uhm- (.)
19            lAst night i got off the PHONE,
20            (.)
21     Gor:   h ´`YEAH; hh[h
22     Dan:               [and I was having MASS[fits;=
23     Gor:                                     [hhh
```

```
24      Dan:    =and ↑Everybody could SEE th[at,
25      Gor:                                [hhhhhh
26  →   Dan:    so whAt did they ↑DO?
27  →           they %stayed ↑TALKing for another hOUr.
28  →           (--)
29  →   Gor:    [⊙]
30              (.)
31      Dan:    <<acc>apArt ↑from the fact [my mother (had been) having
32      Gor:                               [hhh
33      Dan:    fits about where i was uh cause i hadn't RUNG her>,
34      Gor:    hhh
35      Dan:    SO-
```

The click responds to a complaint (lines 26–27) which constitutes the affect-laden climax of a story episode about the complainant's friends (lines 18–25).

The global sequence begins with a bit of troubles talk about Dana's eye (lines 1–16). The recipient responds to the troubles telling with a routine response to bad news (line 12). As an 'oh-prefaced assessment', its functional orientation is ambiguous in that it can solicit sequence-expansion or termination (Maynard 1997: 109). Furthermore, "standardized" routines such as oh dear and oh good are described as having a "laconic and abstract quality". They allow the recipient "to align to announced good or bad news without being overly committed or distanced in displaying their appreciation of the newsworthiness and valence so far displayed" (Maynard 1997: 109). This is visible in the present excerpt as well: Using the oh-prefaced assessment, the recipient shows orientation towards the negative implications of the trouble without displaying much affective involvement. Following the absence of more talk on the part of the recipient (line 13) and a summarising, ironic assessment by the teller (line 16), the troubles talk is closed down.

Line 18 signals a return to the ongoing global activity (Local 2004). The story episode which is now told has a four-part structure: (1) I got off the phone, (2) I was having mass fits (3) everybody could see that (4) they stayed talking for another hour. The third element bears the traits of an extreme case formulation, a practice typically observed in complaint activities: By claiming that ↑Everybody was involved, the number of agents is set as absolute and the complaint strengthened. The fourth element is delayed by a rhetorical question. This delay is strategic in that it dramatises the contents of the fourth element, which conveys a violation of socio-cultural norms: For guests to stay when the hostess is not feeling well is not acceptable. In this manner, the rhetorical question plays up the complainable in a climatic move. The first two elements (lines 19 and 22) are prosodically cued as an expansion of the troubles talk: They are also delivered with relatively low pitch and a compressed pitch range, however with fewer disfluency markers (i.e. pauses, break-ups). Lines 24, 26–27 mark a shift in prosodic contextualisation: The high pitch peaks – particularly when done on the primary accents on ↑*DO* (402 Hz) and ↑*TALKing* (378 Hz) – indicate a heightened level of affective involvement. This kind of prosodic contextualisation, together with the lexical, rhetorical and sequential format of the story can be treated as doing 'indignation'. The kind of affective stance signalled makes these TCUs come off as complaints. This action format and type make an affiliative and affect-laden response by the recipient relevant.

After a medium pause, the recipient of the complaint produces a bilabial click (line 29) (cf. the acoustic analysis in Figure 28. Here the pitch floor and ceiling values determined correspond to the Dana's voice range (ca 80–440 Hz) because the sound object does not have an F0).

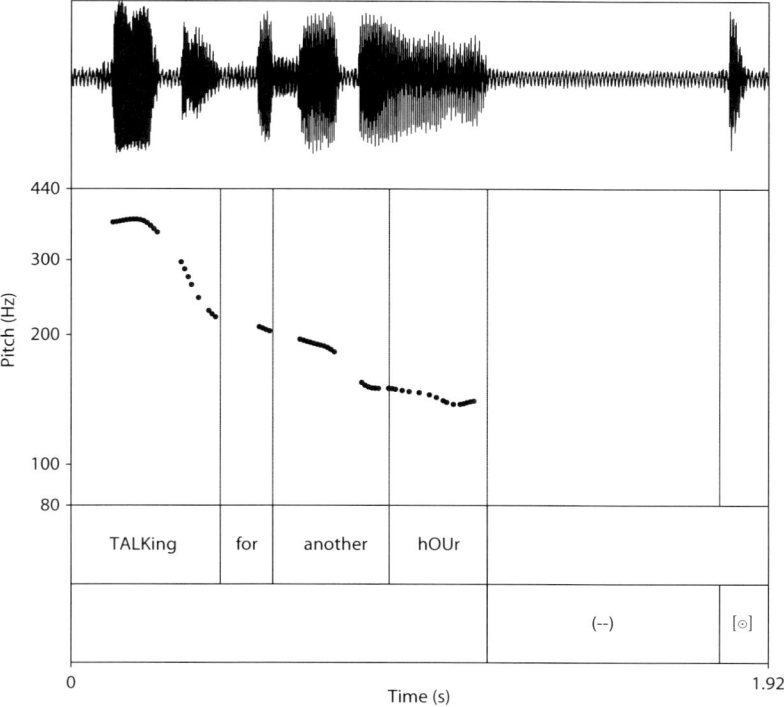

Figure 28. Acoustic analysis of Excerpt 30 ("talking for another hour"), lines 27–29

The click is rhythmically aligned with the complaint, which cues an affiliative recipient response (for illustration, cf. the rhythmic analysis in Excerpt 30').

```
(30')   Rhythmic analysis of Excerpt 30 ("talking for another hour"), lines 27–29
1   →   Dan:   /↑TALKing for another /
2   →          /hOUr.
3   →                            (--)=/
4   →   Gor:   /=[◦]
```

The complainant next orients towards the click as being followed by a TRP: With
early timing she comes in with her next turn. Delivered with increasing tempo and high pitch peaks, this turn is delivered in an indignated tone of voice
similar to that used in the complaint receipted by the click. The prepositional
phrase *apArt ↑from the fact* can be paraphrased as *not considering*. The turn thus
performs a complaint which is presented as adding more to and topping the
complaint receipted by the click. The complaint sequence is thereby expanded.
We can conclude from this that the click is treated as sequence-expanding, even
though the complaint story episode is locally terminated through the topical talk
shift from the friends' misconduct to the mother's having fits. That the complaint
story is locally closed is further supported by the fact that the complainant does
not solicit another uptake of the complaint about her friends' misconduct but
delivers a new complaint. In this way the recipient's click is deployed at a topical,
if not sequential boundary. According to Drew (1998), the end of complaints is
sensitive for so-called "expressions of moral indignation". Formally, they can be
verbalised or done through 'response cries' (ibid: 310). The click thus comes in
a position where such affective, affiliative moves are made relevant. Since the
complainant does not treat the click as a departure from what is expected, it
can be concluded that the sound object aligns with the ongoing participation
framework: In this sense it seems to signal a concordant stance towards the complainable, albeit in a minimal fashion. Nevertheless, it may be open to conjecture
whether the click is not slightly ambiguous in terms of the stance signalled. Does
it signal a negative stance toward the content of the complaint or of the fact that
the first speaker is complaining? In any case, the minimal form of the recipient
response may be iconic of the weak force of the affective display. To capture this
notion, it is argued that the affective quality of the click should be described by
the lay concept of 'disapproval' rather than of 'indignation'.

In addition to single clicks, recipients may do clicks as part of clusters of sound
objects. Again, the click responds to the climax in initial position. Excerpt 31 illustrates such a case: Here the complainant Leslie tells the recipient Linda about
the misconduct of a mutual acquaintance, a so-called Mr. R. (cf. Drew (1998)

for an in-depth discussion of various aspects of the example). The sequence is introduced by a story abstract, in which the complainant announces that she is *broiling about something* (not shown here). The excerpt only shows the final part of the narrative.

```
(31)  [HOLT:C85:4] "dreadful"
 1        Les:  AND uh-
 2              ↑we were looking round the STALLS,=
 3              =and poking aBOUT-
 4              <<all>and he came up to me and he SAYS>;
 5              <<breathy>´`OH::>;
 6              ↑h(h)elLO leslie;
 7              (-)
 8    →        <<h>still trying to buy something for ↑NOTHing>;
 9              (-)
10    →  Lin:  [!] .hhh
11              (---)
12       Lin:  [ʋ[::] leslie;
13       Les:    [<<smile>↑[u::>]; he he ↑he
14              (--)
15       Lin:  <<p>is[n't>
16       Les:        [<<f,h>what]do y[ou SAY>;
17       Lin:                        [he
18              (-)
19       Lin:  <<l>oh=isn't he DREADful>.
20       Les:  <<p,h>YES>;
```

The click responds to the climax, which is constructed in direct reported speech. Introduced by a verbum dicendi (line 4), it conveys the acquaintance's insulting words – the complainable – in an idiomatic phrase for meanness (Drew 1998: 308) (lines 5–8). The insult is presented as coming right out of the blue and targeting innocent people (the personal pronoun ↑*we* (line 2) refers to Leslie and her husband). In the quote, the complainant is constructed as a penniless person who cannot afford things at the sale.[111] According to Drew (1998), reported speech represents a common rhetorical resource for the construction of the climax in complaint stories (cf. also Günthner (1997) for German):

---

111. The fact that Leslie was short of cash when she visited the sale was accounted for in an earlier part of the story not shown here.

> The complainant leaves the complained-about's words to 'speak for themselves,' as it were: the particular respect in which what the other said was reprehensible is displayed, implicitly, through the collective lexical, prosodic, and pragmatic features of the reported speech itself. Hence, the complained-about behaviour is animated in such a way that the recipient can appreciate how rude, unjust, and thoughtless the other was without the complainant needing to categorize the particular offense that was thereby committed.   (Drew 1998: 320)

Climaxes to complaint stories invite "collaborative" displays of 'indignation' on the part of the recipient (Drew 1998: 311, cf. further Goodwin (1984), Selting (1994) on affective recipient responses of story climaxes). The recipient response in the present example orients towards this: She produces an alveolar click followed by an audible inbreath.[112] More clearly than in Excerpt 30 ("talking for another hour"), the click seems to perform an appreciation of the 'indignation' displayed in the climax. From the abruptness and noise with which the airstream is inhaled, the inbreath can be heard as doing similar interactional work as the click. In this way, the recipient displays that she sides with the complainant, i.e. affiliates with her. However, this is done in formally minimal terms: Again the minimal form of the click stands iconically for the implicit and opaque fashion with which the recipient stance is conveyed. The explicit evaluation of the complainable (line 19) does not come until more sound objects are delivered (lines 12–13) and is ultimately solicited by the complainant (line 16). In the subsequent talk not shown here, the recipient delivers more explicit displays of 'moral indignation'. Thus it follows that the click was produced in a context where such displays are made relevant on the part of the recipient. However, the click is merely treated as a minimal, weak signal. As in the excerpt discussed above, it is for this reason that we argue that the click is doing something less than 'indignation', an affective dimension which may be captured by the lay concept of 'disapproval'.

Moreover, the subsequent talk (not shown here) provides evidence that an explicit commitment to the stance taken must be elicited. The post-complaint context is characterised by a development from implicit displays of 'disapproval' through sound objects of various sorts to explicit evaluative attributions through lexical means. This suggests that explicit expressions of stance, which can be held accountable, are treated as showing more commitment than sound objects. Furthermore, explicit expressions have the interactional force to close off the complaint sequence. Sound objects, on the other hand, come off as more spontaneous and affect-laden because they are placed in the next slot right after the story boundary.

---

112. Due to the poor quality of the recording, the analysis of the click cannot be backed by a Praat picture. In Jefferson's original transcript, the ascription of the click is unclear. On the basis of the present material, it can, however, be heard as recipient response (Richard Ogden, p.c.).

9.1.3.2 *Clicks in response to non-narrative complaints.* Complaints can also be performed in the course of non-narrative sequences and with less affective loading. This is shown in Excerpt 5' ("polyester mostly"), which for convenience is reproduced in full length. Here the click receipts a repair embedded in the complaint sequence.

```
 (5')   [HOLT:M88:1:2] "polyester mostly"
1       Les:    .hh but the ↑thIng was i cOUldn't get uhm: [⊙]
2               i couldn't get a (.) cotton: (-) petticoat or (.) k?
3               cotton SLIP;
4               ↑ANywhere;
5       Lin:    COUL[Dn't you[:,
6   →   Les:        [.hhh     [NO;
7               they're all this polyESter mOstly,
8               .h[hh
9   →   Lin:      [!]  ´`[ʔəʊ[:];
10      Les:               [so ↑in the end i bought a white hh
11              cotton SKIRT;=
12              =and i hOpe it won't be too FULL;=
13              i'll just have to SEE;h .hh
14      Lin:    ´`[əʊː];
15              ´`YES.
16              <<l>THERE's a point>,
17      Les:    YES. .hh
18              ↑ANYway;
19              (.)
20              SO:- hh
21              there we ↑ARE?
```

The complaint sequence is delivered in a non-narrative structure and with less affective involvement than e.g. Excerpt 30 ("talking for another hour"). The lower degree of involvement shows up through the absence of extreme pitch peaks and the disfluency of the complainant's speech: While the pitch accent in line 1 signals a new beginning (Couper-Kuhlen 2004b), that in line 4 functions as an affective display, yet the pitch height signals only moderate involvement.[113] The repair, performed after an enactment of 'ritualised disbelief', has a moderately high pitch peak on the initial TCU (line 6) but is otherwise located in the middle and lower parts of the speaker's range. In addition, the non-narrative nature of the complaint provides little room for a substantial build-up of an affective stance, potentially 'indignation'.

---

113. The bilabial click in line 1 has a turn-holding function (Wright 2005).

The recipient's response addresses the two actions implemented by the complainant's prior turn, that is, the complaint and the repair. First, following a slight delay, the alveolar click appreciates the complaint and affiliates with the 'indignation' made relevant by the complainant. Secondly, *oh* orients towards the repair by signalling a slow realisation of what was conveyed by the complainant. Thus, the affective implications of the complaint are not further dealt with in the post-production context of the click and other dimensions of the turn are focused on.

The first speaker does not expand on the complaining activity but next treats the affective implications of the complainable in a bit of troubles talk (cf. the sigh-like filled pause in line 10). In this way the complaint activity is abandoned. Lacking any further sign of affective involvement, the recipient response in lines 14–16 shows an orientation towards a non-affective treatment of the topical talk.

9.1.4 Summary and conclusions

Recipients may use alveolar or bilabial clicks in order to receipt complaints in the mundane data examined. They may be produced as single sounds or be followed by more sound objects, they occur in response to both narrative and non-narrative complaints.

Clicks serve as minimal complaint receipts which acknowledge the other speaker's complaint and display the recipient's affective stance toward the complainable. Albeit in a weak way, their affective stance seems concordant and affiliative with that of the complainant's, yet at the same time remains somehow ambiguous. Does the recipient display 'disapproval' over the content of the complaints or the action side of complaining?

It was argued that the minimal form of the response is iconic of the weakness of the stance displayed. For this reason, it is proposed that the click does something less than moral 'indignation', conveying an affective quality which may be captured by the lay concept of 'disapproval'. In this way, clicks become a powerful recipient resource in complaint activities: By showing 'disapproval' the recipient signals a concordant and hence affiliative stance, yet without bringing in too much affective involvement.

In both narrative and non-narrative complaint sequences, recipients of complaints produce clicks in response to turns which are negatively valenced and are delivered with high pitch peaks signalling heightened affective involvement. When used in narrative complaint sequences, the click receipts the climax of the story. These findings are summarised in Table 9.

Table 9. Variants of the affect-laden sound object *clicks*: Forms and functions

Sound object		*Click*	
obligatory prosodic-phonetic properties	segmental substance	alveolar [!] or bilabial [⊙] stops articulated on a velaric ingressive airstream (clicks)	
sequential placement		A: climax of a complaint story B: affect-laden acknowledgement of the climax (click)	A: non-narrative complaint B: affect-laden acknowledgement of the complaint (click)
sequence-organising function		acknowledgement (complaint receipt)	acknowledgement of the complaint (complaint receipt)
interactional function		minimal display of 'disapproval', affiliation	minimal display of 'disapproval', affiliation

The post-production space of clicks is a place where further treatment of the 'indignation' signalled by the complainant can take place or not. The data suggests that the form of the post-production context depends on to what extent this kind of treatment was made relevant in the complaint on sequential (narrative or non-narrative) and linguistic grounds (prosodic, lexical). A lengthy narrative sequence which shows 'indignation' through explicit and implicit devices on various linguistic levels seems to prepare for more affective and moral work than a complaint which comes as part of a repair in a non-narrative environment and where a co-display of 'indignation' is invited in an interactionally weaker fashion. However, these observations can only be considered tentative and must be checked on the basis of a larger sample of clicks in complaint sequences.

9.2   The affect-laden sound object *whistle*

The sound object *whistle* ([ʍ]) is used to respond to an informing which makes reference to a numerical figure. It appreciates the affective loading which is implied in such an action without ascribing any valenced stance to the informing.[114] The section will first address general phonetic aspects of whistling as documented in the previous literature (Section 9.2.1) and then present a single case analysis of the sound object *whistle* (Section 9.2.2).

---

114. There are surely other contexts where whistling is used to display a valenced stance.

9.2.1 *The sound object* whistle *in previous phonetic accounts*
The sound object *whistle* represents a labial whistle, i.e. a 'hole tone'. The tongue and lips are in a w-position and protrude. As is the case with whistles in general, there is no vibration of the vocal folds (Shosted 2006: 168).[115] The sound object *whistle* is classified as a type of 'recreational' whistling (Shadle 1997: 53, Shosted 2006: 168). 'Recreational' whistles have "very little frication noise", and may have "a frequency range from 500 to 4,000Hz" (Shadle 1983 in Shadle (1997: 53), italics in Shadle 1983). They are distinct from 'whistly fricatives' (cf. Shadle (1997: 53–54) for a more general account of the articulation of the whistly fricatives [s z ʃ] identified for human languages) and 'whistle languages', in which the prosodic pattern of a language is whistled (Busnel and Classe 1976, cf. further Laver (1994: 481–482), Shadle (1997: 53–54).[116] In this sense 'recreational' whistling constitutes a kind of non-lexical sound which has not been found to be a phoneme in any known human language.

9.2.2 *The sound object* whistle *in response to an informing*
      with reference to a numerical figure
In the present data, the sound object whistle is deployed as a recipient resource in response to an informing in which the news teller makes reference to a numerical figure, e.g. to a sum of money.[117] By whistling the recipient appreciates the news teller's contextualisation of the figure as extremely large without committing themselves to the display of a valenced stance.

Excerpt 32 exemplifies this particularly well. Here the news teller, Hilary, is telling her cousin Mark that her future son-in-law Mark is going to save 1800 pound by doing his own conveyancing.

```
(32)   [HOLT:M88:2:4] "conveyancing"
1      Hil:    [(oh:) DWAYNE said-
2      Mar:    [.hhh
```

---

115. It has not been possible to identify a typical prosodic cluster (specifically a typical contour) accompanying the sound object on the basis of the present corpus. Whether this is a typical property of [ʍ] must be left to future research.

116. Cf. further Shosted (2006: 167, 168) for an overview of languages with whistly fricatives and in particular for /ʂ ʐ/ of Southern Bantu, cf. also Ladefoged and Maddieson (1996: 171), Laver (1994: 252) for accounts of whistly fricatives of Shona.

117. Even if whistling seems constrained to respond to this very specific type of informing, it is not the only type of sound object which receipts talk in which reference is made to figures and numbers (cf. Excerpt 19, "telephone number").

```
3               (well) stormy courtship [a good ENDing;=
4     Mar:                             [.hhh
5     Hil:  =you KNOW,hh
6     Mar:  YE[S-
7     Hil:    [at the ↑mOment they're sort of hAnging on %eh on
8           thrEAds of a HOUSE;=
9           =they've (-)
10          they've vIrtually GOT it;=
11          =but it's all this .h exchanging PA[(pers);
12    Mar:                                     [hoh YES:-
13    Hil:  <<p>and mike's qui[te> (--)
14    Mar:                     [.hhh
15    Hil:  quite a brainy CHAP;=
16          =<<p>he's> .hh
17          he's doing his own con↑VEYanci[ng;
18    Mar:                                [.h <<f>↑oh YEAH>,=
19 →  Hil:  =because it's gonna ↑sAve them <<f>Eighteen hUndred
20 →        ↑POUND>;
21    ( ):  tch
22 →  Mar:  ´`↑[w];
23          (-)
24    Hil:  ((clears her [throat)) and as ↑far as mike's
25 →  Mar:               [´`CRUMBS;
26    Hil:  conCERNED,=
27          =it's (--)
28          a good you know i mean i? it is a lot [of ( )
29    Mar:                                        [well of COURSE
30          it [Is;
31    Hil:     [well ↑WORTH it.=
32          =well he ↑bought this book MARK-=
33          =called .hh
34          the conveyancing ↑FRAUD. h
```

The news sequence is built up in such a way that it ultimately prepares for the news informing which elicits the sound object *whistle* (lines 19–22). The informing implements an account which is presented as a kind of high point in the telling.

In the pre-telling, Mike is valenced in positive terms (lines 13, 15). This is achieved through the positive connotation of the adjective *brainy*. With Mike being the teller's son-in-law to be, the positive attribution can be considered a bit of self-praise. The use of the adverb *quite* qualifies the meaning predicated. It can thus be seen as an orientation to social norms according to which self-praise and self-complimenting are dispreferred.

The teller next delivers an evidential account (lines 16–17), which is treated as a news announcement by the recipient: In slight overlap, he produces an announcement response (line 18), whose prosodic form indicates heightened involvement: It is higher-pitched, slightly louder and faster than prior talk by the same speaker. The announcement response is treated as a news mark by the teller: She elaborates on the news, giving financial reasons for Mark's initiative (lines 19–20). The account conveys the precise sum of money to be saved in an explicit fashion. In contrast to lines 13 and 15, the turn makes an unqualified claim and is framed as affect-laden: Lexically, the verb ↑sAve indicates a positive stance towards the money. Prosodically, the dense accentuation and increased loudness on <<f>EIghteen hUndred ↑POUND>; display heightened involvement. Its contextualisation function can be compared to Uhmann's (1996: 339) findings for German: "[…] beat clashes [i.e. dense accentuation, E. R.] are useful devices which provide for the speaker's affect display and which secure an immediate subsequent assessment". The turn's final pitch movement to low furthermore signals turn-yielding and solicits an uptake of the turn.

With a slight delay, the recipient delivers the sound object whistle ([w̥]) (line 22).[118] The whistling sound, a gliding rise-fall, fades out towards the end. With a peak at 776,57 Hz, its pitch exceeds the speaker's regular voice range markedly (cf. Figure 29).[119]

---

118. On completion of the teller's turn there follows a barely audible sound (indicated by * in the acoustic analysis) which Jefferson assigns to the recipient and notes as *tch* in the original transcript. By ear analysis the sound can be described as a click. Due to the quality of the recording, however, it cannot be established what type of click it is, nor which of the speakers actually produced it. Since the whistle follows in such a close temporal succession, we have doubts whether it would have been physically possible for the recipient to articulate both the click and the whistle in such a short period of time. Given that these issues cannot be ascertained with the auditory and technical resources at hand, the click will not be included in the present analysis.

119. Even if an acoustic measurement and auditory description of the sound [w̥] is possible, such an account may be problematic since prosody is concerned with the study of *linguistic* sounds. Accordingly, the analysis of duration, loudness and pitch is assessed relative to talk produced by participants. In such a framework, it can be stated that the pitch of the [w̥] examined here is considerably higher than a male adult's voice range and is louder than prior talk. The same applies for duration, as this parameter is related to syllabic units which do not exist in whistling.

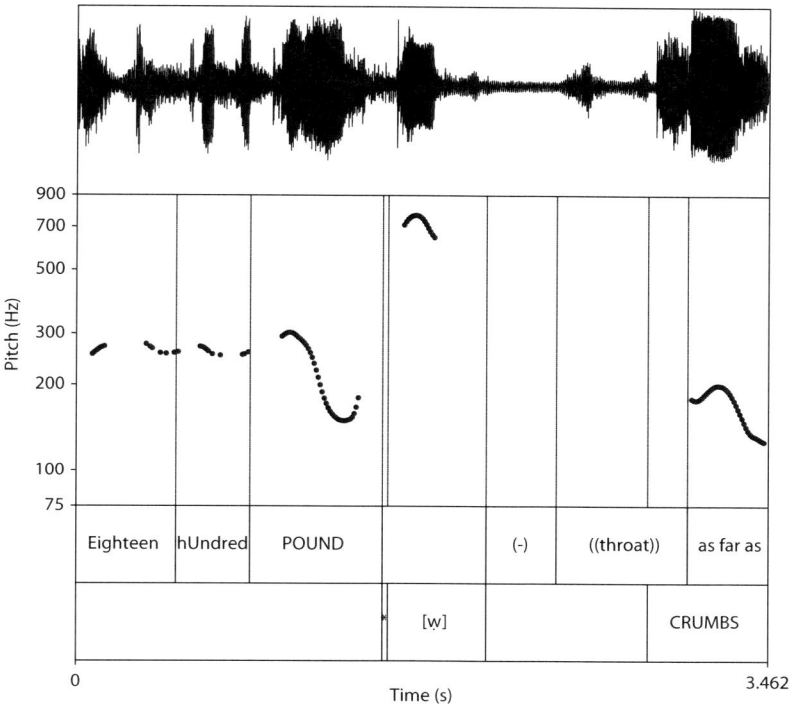

Figure 29. Acoustic analysis of Excerpt 32 ("conveyancing"), lines 19–25

Furthermore, the whistle is rhythmically integrated into a structure established in the turn the sound object receipts. It comes right on the next beat following the turn (cf. Excerpt 32').

```
(32')   Rhythmic analysis of Excerpt 32 ("conveyancing"), lines 19–22
1       Hil:    /<<f>Eighteen    /
2               /hUndred         /
3    →          /↑POUND>;=        /
4       ( ):    tch
5    →  Mar:    /=´`↑[ʍ];         /
```

Like a change-of-state token, the sound object acknowledges that the prior turn is informative. In addition, it appreciates the affective loading of the news. Nevertheless, it does not display any overt valenced stance to what was said but merely responds to the heightened involvement signalled in the teller's talk.

Next follows a medium pause during which neither party takes a turn. This suggests that the teller treats the whistling as too weak an uptake of the piece of news to be sequence-expanding. When the teller finally produces a signal by clearing her throat, this may be interpreted as another (filled) pause, i.e. as withholding.[120] The whistler orients towards this by resuming his talk with a formulaic expression, a so-called 'secondary interjection'. It displays affective involvement and thereby appreciates the account in a way similar to the sound object: Note that the lexical expression does not evaluate the piece of news in the sense of ascribing a specific affective valence to it. Like the whistle, it merely appreciates the news. With its initial velar plosive and the vowel being stretched, it is produced in a marked fashion. This may be iconic of the extra interactional weight being attached to the phrase.

A split second later, in an almost simultaneous start with the formulaic expression, the news teller herself offers an evaluation of her news (lines 27–28, 31). The evaluation is presented as Mike's stance (lines 24, 26). Though the end of line 28 is not hearable or may be curtailed, it could be completed by the noun "money". After weak agreement on the recipient's part (lines 29–30), the evaluative subject complement is repaired in more general terms (*a lot of money* becomes *[well ↑WORTH it.)*. In this way, the teller herself makes the positive valence of the piece of news explicit and thereby relevant. As can be seen in lines 32–34, this evaluative work-up is sequence-terminating.

We have seen that the sound object *whistle* is deployed to respond to news in which a numerical figure, e.g. a sum of money, is presented as having some affective value. Through the sound object, the recipient appreciates the heightened involvement displayed but does not take an evaluative stance (on a positive-negative scale) to the news. In terms of sequence organisation, the whistling is treated as sequence-expanding. In the post-production context, the affective implications of the news can be further dealt with. These findings are summarised in Table 10.

To conclude, whistling enables the recipient to appreciate the heightened involvement displayed by the news teller, without committing themselves to taking

---

120. The corpus examined for the present study indeed suggests that speakers may deploy 'clearing their throat' or 'cough' in a well-timed and interactionally relevant manner (cf. also (Roach et al. 1998:87). The observation that even 'clearing the throat' or 'cough' can be communicatively meaningful supports the argument that non-lexical signals such as whistling can be subsumed with vocalic sounds under the label of sound object. Similarly, Local and Walker (2008) suggest that "even presumed physiologically determined phonetics resulting from transient physical states (coughs and colds) may be manipulable and interactionally deployable." (ibid:728).

Table 10. Forms and functions of the affect-laden sound object *whistle*

Sound object		Whistle
obligatory prosodic-phonetic properties	segmental substance	labial whistle/hole tone: [ʍ]
sequential placement		A: news informing which makes reference to a figure B: affect-laden news response (*whistle*)
sequence-organising function		acknowledgement of the news (news response)
interactional function		display of 'appreciation'

a valenced stance towards the news. This makes whistling a powerful recipient resource when dealing with socially delicate or even taboo topical talk, such as talk about money. It has been suggested that whistling is used as a "speech surrogate" in certain types of interactions, where speakers can exclusively rely on the exchange of whistled melodies for communication (e.g. when bargaining for and selling goods) (Laver 1994: 481). Such practices can be observed both for speakers of 'whistled' languages, where the whistled melody is connected to the prosodic pattern of the language, and for speakers of non-tonal languages, where the whistled melody does not match the intonation of the native language (Laver 1994: 482). We do not think that the sound object *whistle* forms a 'speech surrogate' in this sense. While whistling is clearly deployed in place of a linguistic sign and its use is restricted to certain contexts, it is not used in a sequence of whistled "turns". It rather performs a response to a unit of speech and is followed by more speech which orients towards the production of the sound object. Moreover, it serves interactional functions which cannot be fulfilled by verbal speech in the same way. Having no semantic content, it is non-accountable. In this way the observation that a non-lexical vocal sign can be used in spoken interaction for tasks that cannot be fulfilled in the same way by linguistic signs adds to our understanding of vocal communication.

9.3   Summary and conclusions

The tentative analytic account of clicks and recreational whistling as response signals in affect-laden activities has shown that from a functional perspective, non-lexical vocal signals are used in a fashion similar to 'linguistic' sound objects.

Like the types of *ah*, *ooh* and *oh* examined, clicks and recreational whistling acknowledge affect-laden informings and appreciate their affective loading. This observation confirms the approach of interactional linguists, who take an unbiased view of all phenomena which are vocally produced in talk-in-interaction and treat them as potentially meaningful. At the same time, the non-lexical character of clicks and whistling involves the signalling of a meaning dimension which seem to capture even less than that of vocalic sound objects. Especially in the case of clicks, their minimalistic form appears as minimalistic as their affective meaning.

PART IV

Summary and conclusions

Taking an interactional linguistic perspective, the present study has shown that if affect-laden interjections are examined in their primordial habitat of *talk*-in-interaction, that is as *sound* objects, they can be found to be used in formally and functionally systematic, context-sensitive ways. The parallel findings made for paralinguistic signals such as responsive whistling and clicks further expands our view of the use of vocal resources in talk-in-interaction as potentially functional devices in dynamic processes of meaning-making.

The following sections will first offer a summary of the main assumptions and results of the present study and then draw conclusions from these findings.

Summary

The methodological procedure of the present study largely follows an interactional linguistic approach. It illustrates that the contextualisation potential of sound objects is made up by their prosodic-phonetic shape as well as their context-specific use. Moreover, sound objects evoke prismatic meaning clusters which are methodically left unstated by participants. In this way, the affect labels used by the analyst to differentiate between the affective meaning(s) signalled by sound objects are shorthand terms which are not meant to convey fixed referential meanings. However, the affective quality of recipient responses in the activities examined (i.e. troubles talk, news delivery sequences, complaint sequences, assessments, repair and rejection contexts) is potentially constrained.

To outline the specific findings made for each affect-laden sound object examined, *oh* may come with a stable package of prosodic-phonetic properties which can be heard as 'extra high and pointed'. The set of obligatory properties includes noticeable lengthening, high pitch in absolute terms and a rise-falling contour, which begins on a high onset, rises to a peak at the top of the speaker's range and falls on a glide to mid. *Oh* with this kind of packaging is used in the following environments: (1) in response to repairs which are initiated in an affect-laden way in order to clarify a prior incongruent context and (2) in response to a piece of news which is constructed as being exceptional, i.e. as forming a contrast to the regular case. In these positions, 'high and pointed' *oh* serves as an affect-laden repair receipt and news response respectively and can be interpreted as doing so-called 'surprise', 'astonishment' or 'amazement'. Since displays of 'surprise' implemented by 'extra high and pointed' *oh* do not signal any valenced stance, it is argued that they act as 'pro forma' affect-laden displays. This is supported by the data which shows that 'extra high and pointed' *oh* may be deployed in order to (1) avoid affiliation, (2) defer a valenced uptake, and (3) leave the evaluation of the news to the other speaker, i.e. the speaker with greater epistemic rights.

What is commonly referred to by the graphemic expression *ooh* are sound objects coming with a range of prosodic packaging in response to unqualified, positive assessments, and to repair in radio phone-ins, and in response to highly detailed negatively valenced utterances in mundane complaint activities and troubles talk.

The prosodic bundles with which these kinds of *ooh* are produced are not as stable or distinctive as those of extra high and pointed *oh* and of *ah* in the present data. It is suggested that the lexicalisation of *ooh* may still be emergent. Nevertheless, a first distinction between instances of *ooh* with high or midrange pitch and with rising-falling contours of various shapes is made:

Ooh with a 'high and pointed' contour is produced with lengthening, in high register, with a rising-falling contour and often with breathy voice. This sound object is used by the presenter in order to receipt unqualified, positive assessments on the part of the caller/expert. The presenter thereby ratifies assessments of this kind, signalling high involvement and treating their content as exceptional. This kind of contextualisation in a positive, evaluative context suggests the interpretation of affective dimensions such as 'enthusiasm'/'positive excitement'. Since the prior talk does not give any cues which would warrant a treatment of the contents conveyed as exceptional, it is concluded that this kind of orientation is 'staged' by the presenter. This staging may serve to reward the interlocutor more intensely and thereby to increase the audience rate. 'High and pointed' *ooh* is always followed by turn expansion. The positive assessment in turn expansion makes a transition to the next item on the agenda relevant.

Ooh functioning as repair receipt in radio interaction is done with a midranged, rising-falling contour. The turn expansion, which was always produced, occasions a return to the base sequence.

Responsive *ooh*s which are followed by the first speaker's resumption of talk constitute a category in their own right: Being very rare in the corpus, they are only found in prepared speech.

In everyday interaction, *ooh*-objects with high pitch and a flat, rising-falling contour are observed as affect-laden receipts of highly detailed, negatively valenced informings in complaint sequences and trouble talk. Such informings invite an equally drastic response on the part of the recipient. The prosodic contextualisation which signals high affective involvement evokes affective dimensions such as 'indignation' or 'shock' in the complaint context and 'horror' or 'shock' in the environment of troubles talk. In the post-production context the negative implications of the highly detailed informing are further attended to. Generally, it is concluded that *ooh* is deployed to ratify the prior action in an affiliative and affect-laden fashion and to treat its contents as conveying something extremely positive or negative. An additional wide ranging rising-falling contour treats the prior informing as exceptional.

The chapter on the affect-laden variants of *ah* concentrated on *ah* with a 'low-falling and tailed' and 'flat-falling and low' packagings. 'Low-falling and tailed' refers to a cluster of obligatory properties which includes lengthening and a contour which begins in the lower mid-range of the speaker's voice and falls on a glide to the lower range, ending as a level tail. It has a rather strong articulatory force. 'Flat-falling and low'*ah*s on the other hand are marked by a slight, narrow fall in the lower range of the speaker's voice and a weaker articulatory force than that of 'low-falling and tailed' *ah*.

'Low-falling and tailed' *ah* may be used by troubles recipients in response to troubles announcements and to the exposition of a trouble and is related to affective dimensions of 'empathy'. By showing heightened involvement, it treats the prior informing as being informative about a trouble and as complete, while signalling affiliation. When the turn is expanded, this is done in terms of assessments which are closure-implicative on the local or on a more global level. 'Low-falling and tailed' *ah* followed by other-speaker talk makes more talk related to the trouble relevant, thereby paving the way for sequence expansion. Similarly, it is used in sequential positions where maximal affiliation is accomplished. In a single case study, 'low-falling and tailed' *ah* as a display of mock affect (Sandlund 2004, 2005) is discussed.

'Low-falling and tailed' *ah* in response to bad-news announcements where the teller is the consequential figure in the scenario functions as a bad-news receipt, appreciating the negative affective valence of the news. In the present data, the turn is always expanded by the *ah*-producer, often in orientation towards a noticeable absence of talk on the part of the news teller. This is commonly done in terms of an assessment which constitutes an idiomatic expression of 'sympathy'. This is taken as an indication that 'low-falling and tailed' *ah* displays concordant dimensions of affect (i.e. 'sympathy', 'commiseration', 'compassion' and the like). It was argued that the post-completion space of *ah* is a position where the elaboration of the news sequence is negotiated and managed. Here an idiomatic expression of 'sympathy' invites more talk related to the bad news and thus paves the way for a sequence expansion.

In a brief excursus, 'flat-falling and low' *ah* in response to rejections in radio phone-ins and in response to bad news with the recipient as the consequential figure is examined. This small study provides the background for a discussion whether 'low-falling and tailed' *ah* and 'flat-falling and low' *ah* may be treated as the same object, as has sometimes been suggested. It is concluded that the formal distinction made by participants points to it being interactionally relevant, i.e. the two formal types are perceived as doing different things: This means 'low-falling and tailed' *ah* is treated as doing an other-directed display (of 'empathy', 'sympathy' etc.), and 'flat-falling and low' *ah* as doing a self-directed display (of 'disappointment' etc.). Nevertheless, there may be cases where the participant framework and a certain formal fuzziness lead to these distinctions becoming blurred. Again, this formal and functional vagueness may be exploited interactionally for specific communicative goals.

Chapter 9 explores the use of clicks in complaint sequences and of recreational whistling in response to informings which make reference to a numerical figure in two small studies. Clicks constitute recipient resources at the boundaries of narrative and non-narrative complaint sequences. In both cases, it is argued that they represent a minimal recipient response which only weakly appreciates the 'moral indignation' signalled by the complainant. In narrative sequences they may receipt the story climax. Following the click, the complainant may expand the sequence with an additional complaint which in terms of content marks a topic shift. Alternatively, the complaint recipient may add further signals of affective appreciation and affiliation subsequent to the click which terminates the complaint story and occasions an evaluative summary of the story. Similarly, clicks in non-narrative complaint sequences seem to do weak affective appreciation of the complaint. All in all, the higher the degree of affective involvement conveyed by the complaint (cued by negatively valenced lexis and high pitch peaks), the less minimal the affective response seems to be.

Finally, recreational whistling constitutes another resource for performing a 'pro forma' display of affect. It receipts informings which contain a numerical figure with heightened involvement, albeit without the attribution of any valence to it. This may signal that to introduce a figure may be a socially delicate act. For this reason the recipient may leave the evaluation to the first speaker who introduced it and has the greater epistemic rights.

Conclusions

In the present study, we explored the hypothesis that affect-laden sound objects can represent a recipient practice to respond to affect-laden informings (and informings which were initiated by an affect-laden action). The data analysis provided evidence for this hypothesis by showing that sound objects may contextualise affective dimensions of various sorts in this position. From this, we can infer a number of insights, both methodological and theoretical, concerning sound objects, prosody and affectivity in interaction, which will be introduced in what follows:

a.   A catalogue of criteria for the analysis of sound objects

On the basis of the present study, a catalogue of analytic criteria for sound objects is proposed. It is schematically illustrated in Table 11:

Reber and Couper-Kuhlen (2010) further suggest that phonation and final voicing along with visual-spatial aspects contribute to the formation of sound objects. To our knowledge, the co-ordinated organisation of vocal, sequential and

Table 11. Scheme for the analysis of sound objects

Sound object		
segmental substance		
prosodic-phonetic properties	duration	
	pitch register	
	pitch movement	
	volume	
	rhythmic integration	
	articulatory force	
sequential placement		
sequence-organising function		
interactional function		
subsequent turn expansion/ other-speaker talk		

visual-spatial resources in the production of sound objects is largely unexplored (but see e.g. Barth-Weingarten (in print a). A first examination suggests a distinction between visual-spatial resources which are (1) physiologically inherent to the articulation of sound objects and those which (2) (by convention) build part of an embodied gestalt in which the sound object is performed. To illustrate the former point (1), even without having a video recording available, it can be assumed, for example, that the producer of the whistle in Excerpt 32 will have pursed lips on production (Reber and Couper-Kuhlen 2010: 86). Regarding the latter (2), the production of a 'pained sound' in rejection sequences may for example be accompanied by the participant averting her head and lowering her gaze (Reber and Couper-Kuhlen 2010: 84).

b. **Segmental substance and prosodic features of sound objects:**
    Two intersecting contextualisation systems

As mentioned above it was found that the affective meaning of each object is co-constructed through the prosodic-phonetic shape of the object and the sequential position it is situated in. In the case of interjectional objects, the types of prosodic-phonetic packaging with which the objects are produced are constitutive for their meaning in the sense that they distinguish one object from another (e.g. 'low-falling and tailed' *ah* versus 'flat-falling and low' *ah*). Despite being heard as one object, the data warrants at the same time *a differentiation between the segmental and prosodic levels in sound objects*, at least analytically: For instance, the data suggest that different segmental substances with similar prosodic packaging (e.g. 'extra high and pointed' *oh*, 'high and pointed' *ooh*, and *hi* with such a contour, cf. Schegloff (1998: 244) are interactionally and function-ally different. These divergences point to the presence of two intersecting con-textualisation systems, a segmental and a prosodic one, even if the objects may be perceived as single gestalts.

The differentiation between the segmental and prosodic levels in sound ob-jects further motivates the approach taken in the present study to treat sound objects with an identical segmental substance but different types of prosodic packaging as variants of one type. In other words, what is represented by one graphemic expression may be realised in speech by various sound forms. The question as to whether the commonalities between these variants should be conceptualised as a family resemblance structure of a prototypical category or whether such variants are stored as individual items as proposed by Exemplar theory must be addressed in future (experimental) research. Along the same lines, more research is needed to clarify the status of (these variants of) sound objects as "constructions" (Croft 2001).

c.   Both high and low pitch register may cue heightened affective involvement
The prosodic analysis also provides valuable insights for our understanding of the contextualisation of affectivity in talk-in-interaction: In line with Bolinger's (1986) proposal concerning the iconicity of prosodic cues in the expression of affect, studies such as Selting (1994) stand for a common understanding that high pitch register is linked to heightened affective involvement. The present study modifies this kind of understanding by showing that both high *and* low pitched sound objects represent participant resources for displaying heightened affective involvement (cf. e.g. 'high and pointed' *ooh* and 'low-falling and tailed' *ah*). Rath-er than equating high register with strong affective displays, the findings suggest that pitch accents on sound objects which noticeably deviate from the speaker's mean pitch level, together with other prosodic cues, come off as signalling height-ened affective involvement. In other words, deviations from what is treated as the normal voice of the speaker may be heard as cues for heightened affective involve-ment in contexts sensitive for such displays.

d.   Sound objects perform non-accountable actions
The analysis of sound objects has provided evidence that affectivity may be dis-played in highly implicit, gradual and vague ways by participants. The prismatic, affective dimensions signalled by sound objects are rarely made explicit, with turn expansions also commonly consisting of highly idiomatic and/or evaluative expressions (cf. e.g. Section 8.5 on 'low-falling and tailed' *ah* in bad-news reports). This also means that when talking about affect-laden events or situations, par-ticipants in everyday talk-in-interaction rarely make explicit reference to affective

states and experiences – in other words, participants avoid using emotion words such as disappointment, anger, etc. when doing affect-laden topical talk in the mundane activities examined.[125]

In contrast, affect-laden sound objects are characterised by a lack of or only underspecified referential meaning in contrast to emotion words, whose meaning, being content words, is fully referential (Figure 30).

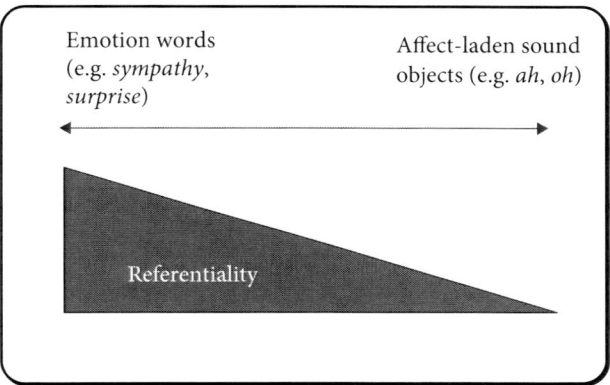

Figure 30. Referentiality of emotion words and affect-laden sound objects

In this way, sound objects enable the speaker to convey affective meaning dimensions in implicit, gradable and vague ways. This kind of prismatic meaning-making has the advantage that the interactional thrust of sound objects may not be unequivocally understood or recognised by co-participants as would be the case when emotion words are used. In other words, affect-laden displays performed through sound objects are packaged in such a way that their producers cannot be held fully 'accountable' (Garfinkel 1967, Garfinkel and Sacks 1970) (cf. Figure 31), a strategy which can be an advantage in socially delicate situations. This also confirms the theoretical assumption of the conventional nature of affective displays made at the outset of the study.

---

125. This is in contrast to e.g. doctor-patient interactions where following the patient's narrative reconstructions of past experiences it is the doctor's task to instigate an explicit labeling of the affective dimensions made relevant in the telling (Fiehler 1990: 241).

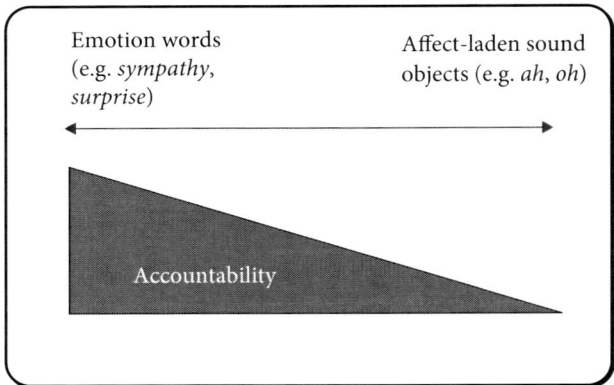

Figure 31. Accountability of emotion words and affect-laden sound objects

e.   Affect-laden sound objects have different contextualisation potentials
Affect-laden sound objects are used by recipients with an orientation towards different relevancies: The three packaged types of *ah* and the clicks examined serve exclusively to respond to negatively valenced informings, which in turn make a negatively valenced affect-laden display relevant, whereas the variants of *ooh*, 'extra high and pointed' *oh* and recreational whistling serve as recipient responses to informings of positive and negative valence in the data. This means that the contextualisation potential of the former group of objects is more constrained than that of the latter, even though that all are context-bound.

f.   Interjectional and paralinguistic sound objects may serve similar functions
Figure 32 shows that certain interjectional and paralinguistic sound objects may be used to perform similar functions, e.g. as news responses or complaint receipts.

Although they are not synonymous in their affective meaning potential and fulfil different interactional relevancies in news and complaint sequences, the fact that interjectional and paralinguistic sound objects may appear in the same context makes them members of the same functional class. This has consequences for our conceptualisation of language use in interaction: Participants may deploy paralinguistic sound objects in the same systematic ways as objects which are fully lexicalised (e.g. types of *oh*s or *ah*s) or are on their way to lexicalisation (types of *ooh*s). This means that we cannot only assume a formal continuum of interjection-like expressions between animal sound and linguistic articulation as proposed by Pompino-Marschall (2004), but also a functional continuum in the sense that non-linguistic sounds may be used for similar conversational tasks

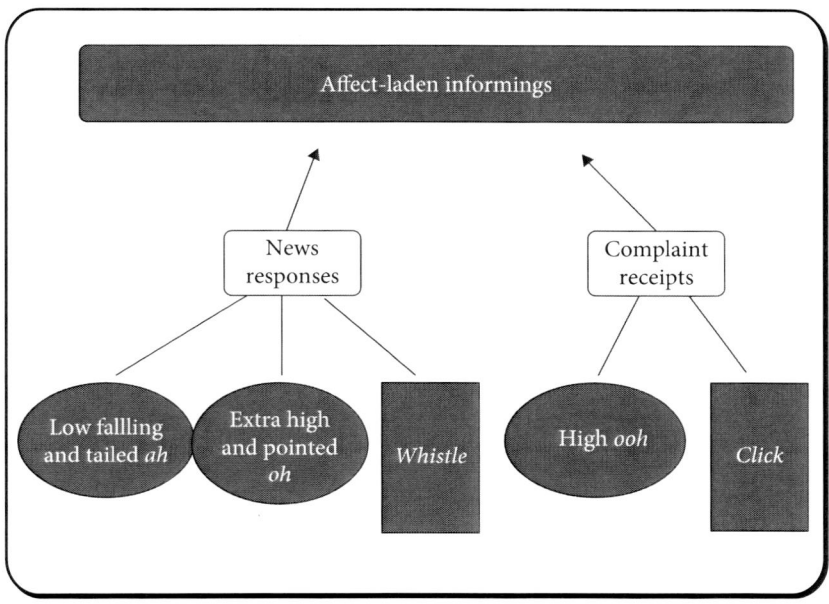

Figure 32. Functional similarity of sound objects

as linguistic signs. On this basis, the uses and shapes of sound objects become conventionalised in language use as do constructions in emergent grammar (Hopper 1987) (cf. also Reber and Couper-Kuhlen (2010: 89–90).

g.   **Sound objects may be deployed for 'pro forma' displays of affect**
With respect to 'extra high and pointed' *oh* and recreational whistling it was claimed that they perform 'pro forma' displays of affect because they do not ascribe any valence to the prior informing, but only signal heightened involvement. This suggests that what is treated as affect-laden in talk-in-interaction may not always correspond to common psychological models of emotion, such as e.g. Appraisal Theory (Roseman and Smith 2001), which include aspects of valence. An interactional linguistic approach to affectivity in talk-interaction may thus provide valuable insights into how affectivity is displayed and managed in social interaction.

h.   **Sound objects are typical of conversational interaction**
The fact that the corpus of the study cuts across a range of discourse types offers valuable insights into how affect-laden sound objects are deployed. For example, such objects appear less frequently in the face-to-face interactions examined.

Since we have had to rely on audio recordings for the face-to-face data used here, it can only be speculated that participants deploy visual rather than vocal signalling systems to perform non-verbal affective displays in these interactions. If this observation proves valid, it would furnish evidence for the significance of visual cues in face-to-face communication in constructing interactional, interpersonal meanings. Furthermore, it would illustrate the context-sensitivity of communicative signalling systems.

Another finding concerns the institutionalisation of interaction. Affective sound objects in the corpus tend to be used more frequently in non- or semi-institutionalised interaction. Whether the frequency of affective sound objects can be actually regarded as an indicator of institutionalisation must, however, be left to further research.[126]

i.   Sound objects are not *per se* affect-laden

Even though the present study is exclusively concerned with the use of affect-laden sound objects, it is generally assumed that sound objects are not *per se* affect-laden. This assumption was exemplified in a single case study on two formats and uses of *oh* embedded in the same global sequence. Here a 'surprised' *oh* (extra high and pointed) was compared to an *oh* which performed a more matter of fact display. The two treatments were further evidenced by the participants' orientations in the subsequent talk. In this sense, the data warrant the view that at least in the case of *oh*, depending on the sound pattern and context, sound objects with the same segmental substance may function to signal a variety of mental and affective states and processes. This view is corroborated by other interactional work which observes a variety of non-/affect-laden meanings and contexts for *oh* (cf. e.g. Heritage (1984), Couper-Kuhlen (2009).

j.   Affect-laden sound objects are minimal practices of response positioned on a functional continuum between continuers and assessments

The form and function of affect-laden sound objects is invited by the linguistic, sequential and/or functional design of the prior turn. Thus they constitute neither random nor absolutely spontaneous productions. Although minimal in form, the sound objects analysed represent a full-fledged practice to receipt and

---

126. Heritage (1995) makes a similar claim for the change of state-token *oh*: The absence of *oh* in news interviews, court room hearings etc. is accounted for by the institutional, i.e. non-conversational, nature of these interactions, while the occurrence of *oh* is related to 'conversational' types of interaction or conversational passages of otherwise institutional interaction (ibid: 401–402, 404).

signal affective displays. By virtue of this function they may receipt and ratify the prior action. At the same time they make more talk related to the affective dimension at stake relevant. This puts them in a functional position between continuers and assessments (cf. Goodwin (1986) for a distinction between the latter two action types).

More commonly the turn is, however, expanded by an additional TCU following the sound object. This may point to the fact that the affect-laden sound objects analysed may not be sufficient to receipt affect-laden informings alone, but that additional, verbal elements are relevant in order to manage the affective work invited from the recipient.

References

Abraham, Werner (ed.). 1991. *Discourse Particles. Descriptive and theoretical investigations on the logical, syntactic and pramatic properties of discourse particles in German and English.* Amsterdam: John Benjamins.

Aijmer, Karin. 1987. "Oh and ah in English conversation." In *Corpus Linguistics and Beyond*, Willem Meijis (ed.). 1987, 61–86. Amsterdam: John Benjamins.

Aijmer, Karin. 2002. *English Discourse Particles. Evidence from a corpus*, Amsterdam/Philadelphia: John Benjamins.

Aijmer, Karin. 2004. "Interjections in a contrastive perspective." In *Emotion in Dialogic Interaction*, Edda Weigand (ed.). 2004, 99–120. Amsterdam/Philadelphia: John Benjamins.

Ameka, Felix (ed.). 1992a. Special Issue on "Interjections." *Journal of Pragmatics* 18(2/3).

Ameka, Felix. 1992b. "The meaning of phatic and conative interjections." *Journal of Pragmatics* 18(2/3): 245–271.

Antaki, Charles. 2002. "'Lovely': Turn-initial high-grade assessments in telephone closings." *Discourse Studies* 4(1): 5–23.

Antaki, Charles, Houtkoop-Steenstra, Hanneke and Rapley, Mark. 2000. "'Brilliant. Next question…': High-grade assessment sequences in the completion of interactional units." *Research on Language and Social Interaction* 33(3): 235–262.

Arndt, Horst and Janney, Richard W. 1987. *InterGrammar. Toward an integrative model of verbal, prosodic and kinesic choices in speech.* Berlin et al.: Mouton de Gruyter.

Atkinson, J. Maxwell and Heritage, John (eds). 1984. *Structures of Social Action. Studies in Conversation Analysis.* Cambridge et al.: Cambridge University Press.

Auer, Peter and diLuzio, Aldo (eds). 1992. *The Contextualisation of Language.* Amsterdam/Philadelphia: John Benjamins.

Auer, Peter and Uhmann, Susanne. 1982. "Aspekte der konversationellen Organisation von Bewertungen." *Deutsche Sprache* 1(82): 1–32.

Barnes, Rebecca and Moss, Duncan. 2007. "Communicating a feeling: The social organization of 'private thoughts'." *Discourse Studies* 9 (2): 123–148.

Barth-Weingarten, Dagmar (in print a). "Response tokens in interaction – prosody, phonetics and a visual aspect of German JAJA." *Gesprächsforschung – Online-Zeitschrift zur verbalen Interaktion.* [www.gespraechsforschung-ozs.de]

Barth-Weingarten, Dagmar (in print b). "Double sayings of the response token JA in German interaction – some additional observations on their phonetic form and alignment function." *Research on Language and Social Interaction.*

Battacchi, Marco W., Suslow, Thomas and Renna, Margherita. ²1997. *Emotion und Sprache: Zur Definition der Emotion und ihren Beziehungen zu kognitiven Prozessen, dem Gedächtnis und der Sprache.* Frankfurt/Main et al.: Peter Lang.

Beach, Wayne A. 1993. "Transitional regularities for 'casual' 'Okay' usages." *Journal of Pragmatics* 19(4): 325–352.

Bergmann, Jörg. 1991. "Über Erving Goffmans Soziologie des Gesprächs und seine ambivalente Beziehung zur Konversationsanalyse." In *Erving Goffman – ein soziologischer Klassiker der zweiten Generation*, Robert Hettlage and Karl Lenz (eds). 1991, 301–326. Bern/Stuttgart: UTB Haupt.

Betz, Emma and Golato, Andrea. 2008. "Remembering relevant information and withholding relevant next actions: The German token *achja*." *Research on Language and Social Interaction* 41(1): 58–98.

Biber, Douglas, Johansson, Stig, Leech, Geoffrey, Conrad, Susan and Finegan, Edward. 1999. *Longman Grammar of Spoken and Written English*. Harlow: Longman.

Bolden, Galina B. 2006. "Little words that matter: Discourse markers 'so' and 'oh' and the doing of other-attentiveness in social interaction." *Journal of Communication* 56(4): 661–688.

Bolinger, Dwight. 1986. *Intonation and Its Parts: Melody in spoken English*. Stanford: Stanford University Press.

Brinton, Laurel. 1996. *Pragmatic Markers in English: Grammaticalization and discourse functions*. Berlin/New York: Mouton de Gruyter.

Bühler, Karl. 1999. *Sprachtheorie*. Unabridged reprint of the Jena 1934 edition. Stuttgart: Lucius und Lucius.

Busnel, René-Guy and Classe, André. 1976. *Whistled Languages*. New York: Springer-Verlag.

Caffi, Claudia and Richard W. Janney. 1994. "Toward a Pragmatics of emotive communication." *Journal of Pragmatics* 22(3/4): 325–73.

Cantor, Joanne. 1994. "Fright reactions to mass media." In *Media Effects. Advances in theory and research*, Jennings Bryant and Dolf Zillmann (eds). 1994, 213–245. Hillsdale, NJ: Lawrence Erlbaum.

Carter, Ronald and McCarthy, Michael. 2006. *Cambridge Grammar of English. A comprehensive guide. Spoken and written English. Grammar and usage*. Cambridge et al.: Cambridge University Press.

Clayman, Steven E. 1993. "Booing: the anatomy of a disaffiliative response." *American Sociological Review* 58: 110–130.

Collier, Nikolinka. 2005. *DiSPEL- Discourse Particle Model*. Unpublished Thesis. University College Dublin.

Colombetti, Giovanna. 2005. "Appraising valence." *Journal of Consciousness Studies* 12 (8–10): 103–126.

Couper-Kuhlen, Elizabeth. 1983. "Intonatorische Kohäsion. Eine makroprosodische Untersuchung." *Zeitschrift für Literaturwissenschaft und Linguistik* 49: 74–100.

Couper-Kuhlen, Elizabeth. 1986. *An Introduction to English Prosody*. London: Edward Arnold.

Couper-Kuhlen, Elizabeth. 1993. *English Speech Rhythm. Form and function in everyday verbal interaction*. Amsterdam/Philadelphia: John Benjamins.

Couper-Kuhlen, Elizabeth. 1996. "The prosody of repetition: On quoting and mimicry." In Elizabeth Couper-Kuhlen and Margret Selting (eds). 1996a, 366–405.

Couper-Kuhlen, Elizabeth. 1998. "Coherent voicing. On prosody in conversational reported speech." *InLiSt – Interaction and Linguistic Structures* 1. [http://www.ub.uni-konstanz.de/handle/urn:nbn:de:bsz:352-opus-4538, last accessed 04/05/11]

Couper-Kuhlen, Elizabeth. 2001a. "Constructing reason-for-the-call turns in everyday telephone conversation." *InLiSt – Interaction and Linguistic Structures* 25. [http://www.ub.uni-konstanz.de/handle/urn:nbn:de:bsz:352-opus-6856, last accessed 04/05/11]

Couper-Kuhlen, Elizabeth. 2001b. "Intonation and discourse: Current views from within." In *Handbook of Discourse Analysis*, Deborah Schiffrin, Deborah Tannen and Heidi Hamilton (eds). 2001, 13–34. Oxford: Blackwell.

Couper-Kuhlen, Elizabeth. 2004a. "Analyzing language in interaction: The practice of *never mind*." *English Language and Linguistics* 8(2): 207–37.

Couper-Kuhlen, Elizabeth. 2004b. "Prosody and sequence organization: The case of new beginnings." In Elizabeth Couper-Kuhlen and Cecilia E. Ford (eds). 2004, 335–376.

Couper-Kuhlen, Elizabeth. 2006. "A sequential approach to affect. The case of 'disappointment'." Paper presented at the 9th International Conference on Conversation Analysis, Helsinki, May 10–14, 2006.

Couper-Kuhlen, Elizabeth. 2007a. "Relatedness and timing in talk-in-interaction." Paper presented at the 10th International Pragmatics Conference, Göteborg, July 8–13, 2007.

Couper-Kuhlen, Elizabeth. 2007b. "Assessing and accounting." In Elizabeth Holt and Rebecca Clift (eds). 2007, 81–119.

Couper-Kuhlen, Elizabeth. 2009. "A sequential approach to affect: The case of 'disappointment'." In *Talk in Interaction: Comparative dimensions*, Haakana, Markku, Minna Laakso and Jan Lindström (eds). 2009, 94–123. Helsinki: Finnish Literature Society (SKS).

Couper-Kuhlen, Elizabeth. in print. "On preference in responses to rejection." Special Issue on "Stance and Affect in Interaction: Sequential and dialogic perspectives." *Text and Talk*, Elise Kärkkäinen and John W. Du Bois (eds).

Couper-Kuhlen, Elizabeth and Ford, Cecilia E. (eds). 2004. *Sound Patterns in Interaction. Crosslinguistic studies from conversation*. Amsterdam/Philadelphia: John Benjamins.

Couper-Kuhlen, Elizabeth and Ono, Tsuyoshi. 2007. "'Incrementing' in conversation. A comparison of practices in English, German and Japanese." *Pragmatics* 17(4): 513–552.

Couper-Kuhlen, Elizabeth and Selting, Margret (eds). 1996a. *Prosody in Conversation: Interactional Studies*. Cambridge: Cambridge University Press.

Couper-Kuhlen, Elizabeth and Selting, Margret. 1996b. "Towards an interactional perspective on prosody and a prosodic perspective on interaction." In Elizabeth Couper-Kuhlen and Margret Selting (eds). 1996a, 11–56.

Couper-Kuhlen, Elizabeth and Selting, Margret. 2001. "Introducing Interactional Linguistics." In Margret Selting and Elizabeth Couper-Kuhlen (eds). 2001, 1–22.

Couper-Kuhlen, Elizabeth and Thompson, Sandra A. 2005. "A linguistic practice for retracting overstatements: Concessive repair." In Auli Hakulinen and Margret Selting (eds). 2005, 257–288.

Croft, William. 2001. *Radical Construction Grammar: Syntactic theory in typological perspective*. Oxford: Oxford University Press.

Cruttenden, Alan. 1986. *Intonation*. Cambridge et al.: Cambridge University Press.

Curl, Traci. 2004. "'Repetition' repairs. The relationship of phonetic structure nd sequence organization." In Elizabeth Couper-Kuhlen and Cecilia E. Ford (eds). 2001, 273–98.

Davidson, Judy. 1984. "Subsequent versions of invitations, offers, requests, and proposals dealing with potential or actual rejection." In J. Maxwell Atkinson and John Heritage (eds). 1984, 102–128.

Davidson, Judy A. 1990. "Modifications of invitations, offers and rejections." In George Psathas (ed.). 1990, 149–179.

Deppermann, Arnulf. 2001. "Gesprächsanalyse als explikative Konstruktion – Ein Plädoyer für eine reflexive ethnomethodologische Konversationsanalyse." In *Gesprächsforschung: Tendenzen und Perspektiven*, Zsuzsanna Iványi and András Kertész (eds). 2001, 43–73. Frankfurt/Main et al.: Lang.

Deppermann, Arnulf. 2006. "Construction Grammar – Eine Grammatik für die Interaktion?" In *Grammatik und Interaktion*, Arnulf Deppermann, Reinhard Fiehler and Thomas Spranz-Fogasy (eds). 2006, 43–65. Radolfzell: Verlag für Gesprächsforschung. [http://www.verlag-gespraechsforschung.de/2006/pdf/gui-deppermann.pdf, last accessed 04/05/2011]

Dersley, Ian and Wootton, Anthony. 2000. "Complaint sequences within antagonistic argument." *Research on Language and Social Interaction* 33(4): 375–406.

Drescher, Martina. 1997. "Emotions in discourse. French interjections and their use in discourse." In Susanne Niemeier and René Dirven (eds). 1997, 233–46.

Drescher, Martina. 2003. *Sprachliche Affektivität. Darstellung emotionaler Beteiligung am Beispiel von Gesprächen aus dem Französischen*. Tübingen: Niemeyer.

Drew, Paul. 1984. "Speakers' reportings in invitation sequences." In J. Maxwell Atkinson and John Heritage (eds). 1984, 152–64.

Drew, Paul. 1987. "Po-faced receipts of teases." *Linguistics* 25: 219–253.

Drew, Paul. 1998. "Complaints about transgressions and misconduct." *Research on Language and Social Interaction* 31(3/4): 295–325.

Drew, Paul. 2003. "Precision and exaggeration in interaction." *American Sociological Review* 68(6): 917–938.

Drew, Paul. 2005. "Is *confusion* a state of mind?" In Hedwig te Moulder and Jonathan Potter (eds). 2005, 161–183.

Drew, Paul and Heritage, John (eds). 1992a. *Talk at Work: Interaction in institutional settings*. Cambridge: Cambridge University Press.

Drew, Paul and Heritage, John. 1992b. "Analyzing talk at work: An introduction." In Paul Drew and John Heritage (eds). 1992a, 3–65.

Drew, Paul and Holt, Elizabeth. 1988. "Complainable matters: The use of idiomatic expressions in making complaints." *Social Problems* 35(4): 398–417.

Drew, Paul and Wootton, Anthony (eds). 1988. *Erving Goffman: Exploring the interaction order*. Cambridge: Polity Press.

Du Bois, John W. 2007. "The stance triangle." In *Stancetaking in Discourse: Subjectivity, evaluation, interaction*, Robert Englebretson (ed.). 2007, 139–182. Amsterdam: John Benjamins.

Duranti, Alessandro and Goodwin, Charles (eds). 1992. *Rethinking Context: Language as an interactive phenomenon*. Cambridge: Cambridge University Press.

Durst, Uwe. 2001. "Why Germans don't feel 'anger'." In *Emotions in Crosslinguistic Perspective*, Jean Harkins and Anna Wierzbicka (eds). 2001, 115–148. Berlin/New York: de Gruyter.

Eckert, Hartwig and Barry, William. ²2005. *The Phonetics and Phonology of English Pronunciation. A coursebook with CD-ROM*. Trier: Wissenschaftlicher Verlag.

Edwards, Derek. 1995. "Two to tango: Script formulations, dispositions, and rhetorical symmetry in relationship troubles talk." *Research on Language and Social Interaction* 28(4): 319–50.

Edwards, Derek. 1999. "Emotion discourse." *Culture and Psychology* 5(3): 271–291.

Edwards, Derek. 2000. "Extreme case formulations: Softeners, investment, and doing nonliteral." *Research on Language and Social Interaction* 33(4): 347–373.

Edwards, Derek and Potter, Johnathan. 2005. "Discursive psychology, mental states and description." In Hedwig te Moulder and Jonathan Potter (eds). 2005, 241–259.

Eerdmans, Susan, Prevignano, Carlo and Thibault, Paul J. (eds). 2003a. *Language and Interaction. Discussions with John. J. Gumperz.* Amsterdam/Philadelphia: John Benjamins.

Eerdmans, Susan, Prevignano, Carlo and Thibault, Paul J. 2003b. "Preface." In Susan Eerdmans, Carlo Prevignano and Paul J. Thibault (eds). 2003, vii–xi.

Egbert, Maria and Bergmann, Jörg. 2004. "Angst – Von der Phänomenologie zur Interaktion." *ZiF:Mitteilungen* 4: 11–23.

Ehlich, Konrad. 1986. *Interjektionen.* Tübingen: Niemeyer.

Ekman, Paul. 1999. "Basic emotions." In *The Handbook of Cognition and Emotion,* Tim Dalgleish and Mick Power (eds). 1999, 45–60. Sussex, U.K.: John Wiley and Sons.

Endo, Tomoko. 2007. *Sharedness in Comprehension and Alignment: A::: in Japanese conversation.* Qualification paper submitted to UCLA in Winter 2007. Asian Languages and Cultures, UCLA.

Fiehler, Reinhard. 1990a. "Emotionen und Konzeptualisierungen des Kommunikationsprozesses." *Grazer Linguistische Studien* 33/34: 63–74.

Fiehler, Reinhard. 1990b. *Kommunikation und Emotion. Theoretische und empirische Untersuchungen zur Rolle von Emotionen in der verbalen Interaktion.* Berlin/New York: de Gruyter.

Fiehler, Reinhard. 2002. "How to do emotions with words: Emotionality in conversations." In *The Verbal Communication of Emotions. Interdisciplinary perspectives,* Susan R. Fussell (ed.). 2002, 79–106. Mahwah, NJ/London: Lawrence Erlbaum Associates.

Firth, Alan. 1995. "Ethnomethodology." In *Handbook of Pragmatics,* Jef Verschueren, Jan-Ola Östman and Jan Blommaert (eds). 1995, 269–278, John Benjamins: Amsterdam.

Fischer, Kerstin. 2000. *From Cognitive Semantics to Lexical Pragmatics: The functional polysemy of discourse particles.* Berlin/New York: Mouton de Gruyter.

Fischer, Kerstin (ed.). 2006. *Approaches to Discourse Particles.* Amsterdam: Elsevier.

Ford, Cecilia E. and Couper-Kuhlen, Elizabeth. 2004. "Conversation and phonetics. Essential connections." In Elizabeth Couper-Kuhlen and Cecilia E. Ford (eds). 2004, 3–25.

Ford, Cecilia E., Fox, Barbara and Thompson, Sandra A. (eds). 2002. *The Language of Turn and Sequence.* Oxford: Oxford University Press.

Freese, Jeremy and Maynard, Douglas W. 1998. "Prosodic features of bad news and good news in conversation." *Language in Society* 27(2): 195–220.

Fries, Norbert. 1996. "Grammatik und Emotionen." In *Sprache und Subjektivität* I, Wolfgang Klein (ed.). 1996, 37–69. Stuttgart: Metzler.

Fussell, Susan R. and Moss, Mallie M. 1998. "Figurative language in emotional communication." In *Social and Cognitive Approaches to Interpersonal Communication,* Susan R. Fussell and R. J. Kreuz (eds). 1998, 113–141. Mahwah, NJ: Lawrence Erlbaum Associations.

Gardner, Rod. 2002. *When Listeners Talk: Response tokens and listener stance.* Amsterdam: John Benjamins.

Garfinkel, Harold. 1967. *Studies in Ethnomethodology.* Englewood Cliffs, NJ: Prentice-Hall.

Garfinkel, Harold. 1988. "Evidence for locally produced, naturally accountable phenomena of order, logic, reason, meaning, method, etc. in and as of the essentially quiddity of immortal ordinary society (I of IV): An announcement of studies." *Sociological Theory* 6: 103–109.

Garfinkel, Harold and Sacks, Harvey. 1970. "On formal structures of practical action." In *Theoretical Sociology: Perspectives and developments,* John C. McKinney and Edward A. Tiryakian (eds). 1970, 338–366. New York: Appleton-Century-Crofts.

Gehweiler, Elke. 2008. "From proper name to primary interjection: The case of *gee!*" *Journal of Historical Pragmatics* 9(1): 71–88.

Giegerich, Heinrich. 1992. *English Phonology: An introduction*. Cambridge: Cambridge University Press.

Goffman, Erving. 1959. *The Presentation of Self in Everyday Life*. Garden City, New York: Doubleday.

Goffman, Erving. 1978. "Response cries." *Language* 54(3): 787–815.

Goffman, Erving. 1981. *Forms of Talk*. Philadelphia: University of Pennsylvania Press.

Golato, Andrea. 2003. "Studying compliment responses: A comparison of DCTs and recordings of naturally occurring talk." *Applied Linguistics* 24(1): 90–121.

Golato, Andrea and Betz, Emma. 2008. "German *ach* and *achso* in repair uptake: Resources to sustain or remove epistemic asymmetry." *Zeitschrift für Sprachwissenschaft* 27(1): 7–37.

Goodwin, Charles. 1984. "Notes on story structure and the organisation of participation." In J. Maxwell Atkinson and John Heritage (eds). 1984, 225–246.

Goodwin, Charles. 1986. "Between and within: Alternative treatments of continuers and assessments." *Human Studies* 9(2/3): 205–217.

Goodwin, Charles. 2007. "Participation, stance, and affect in the organization of activities." *Discourse and Society* 18(1): 53–73.

Goodwin, Charles and Goodwin, Marjorie Harness. 1987. "Concurrent operations on talk: Notes on the interactive organization of assessments." *IPrA Papers in Pragmatics* 1(1): 1–54.

Goodwin, Charles and Goodwin, Marjorie Harness. 1992. "Assessments and the construction of context." In Alessandro Duranti and Charles Goodwin (eds). 1992, 147–190.

Goodwin, Marjorie Harness. 1980. "Processes of mutual monitoring implicated in the production of description sequences." *Sociological Inquiry* 50(3/4): 303–317.

Goodwin, Marjorie Harness. 1996. "Informings and announcements in their environment: Prosody within a multi-activity work setting." In Elizabeth Couper-Kuhlen and Margret Selting (eds). 1996a, 436–461.

Goodwin, Marjorie Harness and Goodwin, Charles. 2001. "Emotion within situated activity." In *Linguistic Anthropology. A reader*, Alessandro Duranti (ed.). 2001, 239–257. Malden, MA et al.: Blackwell.

Gove, Philip Babcock et al. (eds). 1986. *Webster's Third New International Dictionary of the English Language, Unabridged*. Springfield, MA: Merriam Webster Inc.

Günthner, Susanne. 1996. "The prosodic contextualization of moral work: An analysis of reproaches in 'why'-formats." In Elizabeth Couper-Kuhlen and Margret Selting (eds). 1996a, 271–302.

Günthner, Susanne. 1997. "The contextualization of affect in reported dialogues." In Susanne Niemeier and René Dirven (eds). 1997, 247–276.

Günthner, Susanne. 2000. *Vorwurfsaktivitäten in der Alltagsinteraktion. Grammatische, prosodische, rhetorisch-stilistische und interaktive Verfahren bei der Konstitution kommunikativer Muster und Gattungen*. Tübingen: Niemeyer.

Gumperz, John. 1982. *Discourse Strategies*. Cambridge: Cambridge University Press.

Gumperz, John. 1992. "Contextualization and understanding." In Alessandro Duranti and Charles Goodwin (eds). 1992, 228–252.

Haakana, Markku. 1999. *Laughing Matters. A conversation analytical study of laughter in doctor-patient interaction*. Väitöskirja. Helsingin yliopiston suomen kielen laitos.

Haakana, Markku. 2007. "Reported thought in complaint stories." In Elizabeth Holt and Rebecca Clift (eds). 2007, 150–78.

Hakulinen, Auli and Selting, Margret (eds). 2005. *Syntax and Lexis in Conversation: Studies on the use of linguistic resources in talk-in-interaction*. Amsterdam: John Benjamins.

Halonen, Mia and Sorjonen, Marja-Leena. 2008. "Using niin-interrogative to treat the prior speaker's action as an exaggeration." *Discourse Studies* 10(1): 37–53.

Heath, Christian. 1989. "Pain talk: The expression of suffering in the medical consultation." *Social Psychology Quarterly* 52 (2): 113–125.

Heinemann, Trine. 2009. "Participation and exclusion in third party complaints." *Journal of Pragmatics* 41(12): 2435–2451.

Hepburn, Alexa. 2004. "Crying: notes on description, transcription, and interaction." *Research on Language and Social Interaction* 37 (3): 251–290.

Heritage, John. 1984. "A change-of-state-token and aspects of its sequential placement." In J. Maxwell Atkinson and John Heritage (eds). 1984, 299–345.

Heritage, John. 1985. "Analyzing news interviews: Aspects of the production of talk for an 'overhearing' audience." In *Handbook of Discourse Analysis*. Vol.3, van Dijk, Teun (ed.). 1985, 95–117. London: Academic Press.

Heritage, John. 1995. "Conversation analysis: Methodological aspects." In *Aspects of Oral Communication*, Uta M. Quasthoff (ed.). 1995, 391–418. Berlin: de Gruyter.

Heritage, John. 1998. "Oh-prefaced responses to inquiry." *Language in Society* 27(3): 291–334.

Heritage, John. 2002. "Oh-prefaced responses to assessments: A method of modifying agreement/disagreement." In Cecilia E. Ford, Barbara Fox and Sandra Thompson (eds). 2002, 196–224.

Heritage, John. 2005. "Cognition in discourse." In Hedwig te Molder and Johnathan Potter (eds). 2005, 184–202.

Heritage, John. 2007. "Intersubjectivity and progressivity in person (and place) reference." In *Person Reference in Interaction: Linguistic, cultural and social perspectives*, Tanya Stivers and Nick J. Enfield (eds). 2007, 255–280. Cambridge: Cambridge University Press.

Hochschild, Arlie Russell. 1979. "Emotion work, feeling rules, and social structure." *The American Journal of Sociology* 85(3): 551–575.

Holt, Elizabeth and Clift, Rebecca (eds). 2007. *Reporting Talk: Reported speech in interaction.* Cambridge: Cambridge University Press.

Holt, Liz. 1993. "The structure of death announcements: Looking on the bright side of death." *Text* 13(2): 189–217.

Hopper, Paul. 1987. "Emergent grammar. General session and parasession on grammar and cognition." *Berkeley Linguistic Society* 13: 139–157.

Huddleston, Rodney and Pullum, Geoffrey K. 2002. *The Cambridge Grammar of the English Language*. Cambridge et al.: Cambridge University Press.

Hutchby, Ian. 1996. *Confrontation Talk: Arguments, asymmetries and power on talk radio.* Mahwah, NJ: Erlbaum.

Hutchby, Ian. 2006. *Media Talk: Conversation Analysis and the study of broadcasting.* Maidenhead: Open University Press.

Hutchby, Ian and Wooffitt, Robin. ²2008. *Conversation Analysis: Principles, practices and applications.* Cambridge: Polity Press.

Imo, Wolfgang. 2005. "A Construction Grammar approach to the phrase 'I mean' in spoken English." *InLiSt – Interaction and Linguistic Structures* 42. [http://kops.ub.uni-konstanz.de/handle/urn:nbn:de:bsz:352-opus-15607, last accessed 04/05/2011]

Jefferson, Gail. 1974. "Error correction as an interactional resource." *Language in Society* 3(2): 181–199.

Jefferson, Gail. 1978a. "What's in a 'nyem'?" *Sociology* 12(1): 135–139.

Jefferson, Gail. 1978b. "Sequential aspects of storytelling in conversation." In *Studies in the Organization of Conversational Interaction*, Jim Schenkein (ed.). 1978, 219–248. New York, NY: Academic Press.

Jefferson, Gail. 1979. "A technique for inviting laughter and its subsequent acceptance/declination." In *Everyday Language: Studies in ethnomethodology*, George Psathas (ed.). 1979, 79–96. New York, NY: Irvington Publishers.

Jefferson, Gail. 1980. "On 'trouble-premonitory' response to inquiry." *Sociological Inquiry* 50(3/4): 153–185.

Jefferson, Gail. 1984a. "On stepwise transition from talk about a trouble to inappropriately next-positioned matters." In J. Maxwell Atkinson and John Heritage (eds). 1984, 191–222.

Jefferson, Gail. 1984b. "On the organization of laughter in talk about troubles." In J. Maxwell Atkinson and John Heritage (eds). 1984, 346–369.

Jefferson, Gail. 1985a. "Notes on a systematic deployment of the acknowledgement tokens 'Yeah' and 'Mmhm'." *Papers in Linguistics* 17(2): 197–216.

Jefferson, Gail. 1985b. "An exercise in the transcription and analysis of laughter." In Teun van Dijk (ed.). 1985, 25–34.

Jefferson, Gail. 1988. "On the sequential organization of troubles talk in ordinary conversation." *Social Problems* 35(4): 418–442.

Jefferson, Gail. 1990. "List construction as a task and resource." In George Psathas (ed.). 1990, 63–92.

Jefferson, Gail. 2002. "Is 'no' an acknowledgment token? Comparing American and British uses of (+)/(−) tokens." *Journal of Pragmatics* 34(10/11): 1345–1383.

Jefferson, Gail. 2004. "A note on laughter in 'male-female' interaction." *Discourse Studies* 6(1): 117–133.

Jefferson, Gail and Lee, John R. E. 1981. "The rejection of advice: Managing the problematic convergence of a 'troubles telling' and a 'service encounter'." *Journal of Pragmatics* 5(5): 399–422.

Jefferson, Gail, Sacks, Harvey and Schegloff, Emanuel. 1987. "Notes on laughter in the pursuit of intimacy." In *Talk and Social Organisation*, Graham Button and John R. E. Lee (eds). 1987, 152–205. Clevedon: Multilingual Matters.

Jespersen, Otto. 1922. *Language. Its nature, development and origin*. London: Allen and Unwin.

Jespersen, Otto. 1924. *The Philosophy of Grammar*. London: Allen and Unwin.

Jones, Daniel. 1917. *An English Pronouncing Dictionary*. London: Dent.

Jones, Daniel. 1918. *An Outline of English Phonetics*. Cambridge: Heffer.

Jovanović, Vladimir Ž. 2004. "The form, position and meaning of interjections in English." *Facta Universitatis: Linguistics and literature* 3(1): 17–28 [http://facta.junis.ni.ac.rs/lal/lal2004/lal2004-02.pdf, last accessed 04/05/11].

Kehrein, Roland. 2002. *Prosodie und Emotionen*. Tübingen: Niemeyer.

Kelly, John and Local, John. 1989. *Doing Phonology. Observing, recording, interpreting*. Manchester, New York: Manchester University Press.

Kitzinger, Celia. 2000. "How to resist an idiom." *Research on Language and Social Interaction* 33(2): 121–154.

Kockelman, Paul. 2003. "The meanings of interjections in Q'eqchi' Maya: From emotive reaction to social and discursive action." *Current Anthropology* 44(4): 467–490.

Kövecses, Zoltán. 1987. *Metaphors of Anger, Pride and Love: A lexical approach to the structure of concepts*. Amsterdam: John Benjamins.

Kövecses, Zoltán. 1990. *Emotion Concepts*. New York et al.: Springer Verlag.

Kövecses, Zoltán. 2000. *Metaphor and Emotion: Language, culture, and body in human feeling*. Cambridge: Cambridge University Press.

Koole, Tom. 2007. "Introduction to the panel 'Relatedness as an interactional acomplishment'." Paper presented at the 10th Interactional Pragmatics Conference, Göteborg, July 8–13, 2007.

Kryk, Barbara. 1992. "The pragmatics of interjections: The case of Polish *no*." *Journal of Pragmatics* 18(2/3): 193–207.

Labov, William and Fanshel, David. 1977. *Therapeutic Discourse: Psychotherapy as conversation*. New York: Academic.

Ladefoged, Peter. 2001. *Vowels and Consonants. An introduction to the sounds of languages*. Malden, MA/Oxford: Blackwell.

Ladefoged, Peter and Maddieson, Ian. 1996. *The Sounds of the World's Languages*. Oxford, UK/ Cambrigde, MA: Blackwell.

Lakoff, George and Johnson, Mark. 1980. *Metaphors We Live by*. Chicago/London: The University of Chicago Press.

Laver, John. 1994. *Principles of Phonetics*. Cambridge et al.: Cambridge University Press.

Linell, Per. 2005. *The Written Language Bias in Linguistics: Its nature, origins and transformations*. London/New York: Routledge.

Local, John. 1996. "Conversational phonetics: Some aspects of news receipts in everyday talk." In Elizabeth Couper-Kuhlen and Margret Selting (eds). 1996a, 175–230.

Local, John. 2004. "Getting back to prior talk: And-uh(m) as a back-connecting device." In Elizabeth Couper-Kuhlen and Cecilia Ford (eds). 2004, 377–400.

Local, John and Kelly, John. 1986. "Projection and 'silences': Notes on phonetic and conversational structure." *Human Studies* 9(2/3): 185–204.

Local, John, Kelly, John and Wells, Bill. 1986. "Towards a phonology of conversation: Turn-taking in Tyneside English." *Journal of Linguistics* 22(2): 411–437.

Local, John and Walker, Gareth. 2005. "Methodological imperatives for investigating the phonetic organization and phonological structures of spontaneous speech." *Phonetica* 62(2–4): 120–130.

Local, John and Walker, Gareth. 2008. "Stance and affect in conversation: On the interplay of sequential and phonetic resources." *Text and Talk* 28(7): 723–747.

Locke, Abigail. 2003. "'If I'm not nervous, I'm worried, does that make sense?': The use of emotion concepts by athletes in accounts of performance." *Forum Qualitative Sozialforschung/Forum: Qualitative Social Research* 4(1): 50 paragraphs. [www.qualitative-research.net/fqs-texte/1-03/1-03locke-e.htm, last accessed 04/05/2011]

Lutfey, Karen and Maynard, Douglas. 1998. "Bad news in oncology: How doctor and patient talk about death and dying without using those words." *Social Psychology Quarterly* 61(4): 301–320.

Maynard, Douglas. 1997. "The news delivery sequence: Bad news and good news in conversational interaction." *Research on Language and Social Interaction* 30(2): 93–130.

Maynard, Douglas. 2003. *Bad News Good News: Conversational order in everyday talk and clinical settings*. Chicago: University of Chicago Press.

Mayor, Michael (ed.). 2002. *Macmillan English Dictionary*. Oxford: Macmillan.

Mayor, Michael (ed.). ⁵2009. *Dictionary of Contemporary English*. Harlow: Pearson Educated Limited.

Mazeland, Harrie. 2007. "Parenthetical sequences." *Journal of Pragmatics* 39(10): 1816–1869.

Mazeland, Harrie and Huiskes, Mike. 2001. "Dutch 'but' as a sequential conjunction: Its use as a resumption marker." In Margret Selting and Couper-Kuhlen (eds). 2001, 141–169.

Montes, Rosa Graciela. 1999. "The development of discourse markers in Spanish interjections." *Journal of Pragmatics* 31(10): 1289–1319.

Monzoni, Chiara Maria. 2008. "Introducing direct complaints through questions: The interactional achievement of 'pre-sequences'?" *Discourse Studies* 10: 73–87.

Morris, William (ed.). ²1973. *The American Heritage Dictionary of the English Language*. Boston et al.: American Heritage Publishing Co., Inc. and Houghton Mifflin Company.

Müller, Frank Ernst. 1996. "Affiliating and disaffiliating with continuers: Prosodic aspects of recipiency." In Elizabeth Couper-Kuhlen and Margret Selting (eds). 1996a, 131–176.

Nenova, Nikolinka, Joue, Gina, Reilly, Ronan and Carson-Berndsen, Julie. 2001. "Sound and function regularities in interjections." In *Disfluency in Spontaneous Speech (DiSS'01)*, ISCA Tutorial and Research Workshop (ITRW), Edinburgh, Scotland, UK, August 29–31, 2001, ISCA Archive, 49–52. [http://www.isca-speech.org/archive_open/archive_papers/diss_01/dis1_049.pdf, last accessed 04/05/2011]

Niemeier, Susanne and Dirven, René (eds). 1997. *The Language of Emotions. Conceptualization, expression, and theoretical foundation.* Amsterdam: John Benjamins.

Nübling, Damaris. 2001. "Von *oh mein Jesus!* zu *oje!* Der Interjektionalisierungspfad von der sekundären zur primären Interjektion." *Deutsche Sprache* 1(1): 20–45.

Nübling, Damaris. 2004. "Die prototypische Interjektion: Ein Definitionsvorschlag." *Zeitschrift für Semiotik* 26(1/2): 11–45.

Ochs, Elinor and Schieffelin, Bambi. 1989. "Language has a heart." *Text* 9(1): 7–25.

Ochs, Elinor, Thompson, Sandra and Schegloff, Emanuel (eds). 1996. *Interaction and grammar.* Cambridge/New York: Cambridge University Press.

O'Connor, J. Doc and Arnold, Gordon F. 1961. *Intonation of Colloquial English. A practical handbook.* London: Longmans.

Ogden, Richard. 2006. "Phonetics and social actions in agreements and disagreements." *Journal of Pragmatics* 38(10): 1752–1775.

Pawlowska, Adela, Pajak, Anna and Raczaszek, Joanna. 2002. "The cross-culture differentiation of *anger.* Wierzbicka's *Natural Semantic Metalanguage* as a research tool: Problems with implementation, limitations and ways of modification." In *Cognitive Linguistics Today*, Barbara Lewandowska-Tomaszczyk and Kamila Turewicz (eds). 2002, 109–122. Frankfurt/Main: Lang.

Peirce, Charles S. 1955. "Logic as semiotic: The theory of signs." In *Philosophical Writings of Peirce*, Justus Buchler (ed.). 1955, 60–73. New York: Dover.

Peräkylä, Anssi and Ruusuvuori, Johanna. 2006. "Facial expression in an assessment." In *Video analysis: Methodology and methods*, Hubert Knoblauch, Bernt Schnettler, Jürgen Raab and Hans-Georg Soeffner (eds). 2006, 127–142. Frankfurt/Main et al.: Lang.

Pomerantz, Anita. 1984. "Agreeing and disagreeing with assessments." In J. Maxwell Atkinson and John Heritage (eds). 1984, 57–101.

Pomerantz, Anita. 1986. "Extreme case formulations. A way of legitimizing claims." *Human Studies* 9(2/3): 219–229.

Pomerantz, Anita. 1988. "Offering a candidate answer: An information seeking strategy." *Communication Monograph* 55(4): 360–373.

Pompino-Marschall, Bernd. 2004. "Zwischen Tierlaut und sprachlicher Artikulation: Zur Phonetik der Interjektionen." *Zeitschrift für Semiotik* 26(1/2): 71–84.

Potter, Jonathan. 2006. "Cognition and conversation." *Discourse Studies* 8(1): 131–140.

Potter, Jonathan and Hepburn, Alexa. 2003. "'I'm a bit concerned' – Early actions and psychological constructions in a child protection helpline." *Research on Language and Social Interaction* 36(3): 197–240.

Procter, Paul (ed.). 1995. *Cambridge International Dictionary of English*. Cambridge et al.: Cambridge University Press.

Psathas, George (ed.). 1990. *Interaction Competence*. Washington, DC: University Press of America.

Pudlinski, Christopher. 2005. "Doing empathy and sympathy: Caring responses to troubles tellings on a peer support line." *Discourse Studies* 7(3): 267–288.

Pullum, Geoffrey K. and Ladusaw, William A. 21996. *Phonetic Symbol Guide*. Chicago/London: The University of Chicago Press.

Quirk, Randolph, Greenbaum, Sydney, Leech, Geoffrey and Svartvik, Jan. 1985. *A Comprehensive Grammar of the English Language*. London/New York: Longman.

Rasoloson, Janie N. 1994. *Interjektionen im Kontrast – Am Beispiel der deutschen, madagassischen, englischen und französischen Sprache*. Frankfurt/Main et al.: Peter Lang.

Raymond, Geoffrey. 2004. "Prompting action: The stand-alone 'so' in sequences of talk-in-interaction." *Research on Language and Social Interaction* 37(2): 185–218.

Raymond, Geoffrey and Heritage, John. 2006. "The epistemics of social relationships: Owning grandchildren." *Language in Society* 35(5): 677–705.

Reber, Elisabeth. 2009. "Zur Affektivität in englischen Alltagsgesprächen." In *Theatralität des sprachlichen Handelns. Eine Metaphorik zwischen Linguistik und Kulturwissenschaften*, Mareike Buss, Stephan Habscheid, Sabine Jautz, Frank Liedtke and Jan Schneider (eds). 2009, 193–215. München: Fink-Verlag.

Reber, Elisabeth. 2010a. "Interjections in the EFL classroom: Teaching sounds and sequences." *ELT Journal*. [doi: 10.1093/elt/ccq070]

Reber, Elisabeth. 2010b. "Double function of prosody: Processes of meaning-making in narrative reconstructions of epileptic seizures." In *Prosody in Interaction*, Dagmar Barth-Weingarten, Elisabeth Reber and Margret Selting (eds). 2010, 295–301. Amsterdam: John Benjamins.

Reber, Elisabeth and Couper-Kuhlen, Elizabeth. 2010. "Interjektionen zwischen Lexikon und Vokalität: Lexem oder Lautobjekt?" In *Sprache intermedial: Stimme und Schrift, Bild und Ton*, Arnulf Deppermann and Angelika Linke (eds). 2009, 69–96. Berlin/New York: de Gruyter.

Reisigl, Martin. 1999. *Sekundäre Interjektionen*. Frankfurt/Main: Peter Lang.

Roach, Peter, Sibbard, Richard, Osborne, Jane, Arnfield, Simon and Setter, Jane. 1998. "Transcription of prosodic and paralinguistic features of emotional speech." *Journal of the International Phonetic Association* 28: 83–94.

Roseman, Ira J. and Smith, Craig A. 2001. "Appraisal Theory: Overview, assumptions, varieties, controversies." In *Appraisal Processes in Emotion. Theory, methods, research*, Klaus R. Scherer, Angela Schorr and Tom Johnstone (eds). 2001, 3–19. Oxford et al.: Oxford University Press.

Ruusuvuori, Johanna. 2005. "'Empathy' and 'sympathy' in action: Attending to patients' troubles in Finnish homeopathic and general practice consultations." *Social Psychological Quarterly* 68(3): 204–222.

Sacks, Harvey. 1984. "Notes on methodology." In J. Maxwell Atkinson and John Heritage (eds). 1984, 21–27.

Sacks, Harvey. 1995. *Lectures on Conversation*. vol. 1 and 2. G. Jefferson (ed.), Oxford, U.K.: Blackwell.

Sacks, Harvey, Schegloff, Emanuel A. and Jefferson, Gail. 1974. "A simplest systematics for the organisation of turn-taking for conversation." *Language* 50: 696–735.

Sandlund, Erica. 2004. *Feeling by Doing: The social organization of everyday emotions in academic talk-in-interaction*. Karlstad: Karlstad University Studies.

Sandlund, Erica. 2005. "On words and their interactional power: How to accomplish social goals with 'mock' states-of-being." In *The Power of Words. Studies in honour of Moira Linnarud*, Solveig Granath, June Miliander and Elisabeth Wennö (eds). 2005, Karlstad: Karlstad University Press.

Schegloff, Emanuel. 1968. "Sequencing in conversational openings." *American Anthropologist* 70(6): 1075–1095.

Schegloff, Emanuel. 1979. "The relevance of repair for syntax-for-conversation." In *Syntax and Semantics 12: Discourse and syntax*, Talmy Givón (ed.). 1979, 261–288. New York: Academic Press.

Schegloff, Emanuel. 1982. "Discourse as an interactional achievement: some uses of 'uh huh' and other things that come between sentences." In *Analyzing Discourse: Text and talk*, Deborah Tannen (ed.). 1982, 71–93. Washington, D.C.: Georgetown University Press.

Schegloff, Emanuel. 1987. "Analyzing single episodes of interaction: An exercise in Conversation Analysis." *Social Psychology Quarterly* 50(2): 101–114.

Schegloff, Emanuel. 1991. "Conversation Analysis and socially shared cognition." In *Perspectives on Socially Shared Cognition*, Lauren Resnick, John Levine and Stephanie Teasley (eds). 1991, 150–171. Washington, D.C.: American Psychological Association.

Schegloff, Emanuel. 1993. "Reflections on quantification in the study of conversation." *Research on Language and Social Interaction* 26(1): 99–128.

Schegloff, Emanuel. 1996a. "Confirming allusions: Toward an empirical account of action." *American Journal of Sociology* 102(1): 161–216.

Schegloff, Emanuel. 1996b. "Turn organization: One intersection of grammar and interaction." In Elinor Ochs, Sandra Thompson and Emanuel Schegloff (eds). 1996, 52–133.

Schegloff, Emanuel. 1998. "Reflections on studying prosody in talk-in-interaction." *Language and Speech* 41(3/4): 235–263.

Schegloff, Emanuel. 2000. "When 'others' initiate repair." *Applied Linguistics* 21(2): 205–243.

Schegloff, Emanuel. 2005. "On complainability." *Social Problems* 52(3): 449–476.

Schegloff, Emanuel. 2006. "On 'uh' and 'uhm' and some of the things they are used to do." Paper presented at *brandial*, Potsdam, September 11–13, 2006.

Schegloff, Emanuel. 2007. *Sequence Organization in Interaction. A primer in Conversation Analysis*. Vol. 1, Cambridge et al.: Cambridge University Press.

Schegloff, Emanuel, Jefferson, Gail and Sacks, Harvey. 1977. "The peference for self-correction in the organization of repair in conversation." *Language* 53(2): 361–382.

Schiffrin, Deborah. 1987. *Discourse markers*. Cambridge: Cambridge University Press.

Schmitt, Reinhold. 2003. "Inszenieren: Struktur und Funktion eines gesprächsrhetorischen Verfahrens."*Gesprächsforschung –Online Zeitschrift zur verbalen Interaktion* 4: 186–250. [http://www.gespraechsforschung-ozs.de/heft2003/ga-schmitt.pdf, last accessed 04/05/11]

Schnieders, Guido. 2002. "Verärgerung in Reklamationsgesprächen. Zur Analyse von Emotionsmanifestationen im Diskurs." In *Unternehmenskommunikation*. Michael Becker-Mrotzek and Reinhard Fiehler (eds). 2002, 115–144. Tübingen: Gunter Narr Verlag.

Schourup, Lawrence. 1982. *Common Discourse Particles in English Conversation*. Ann Arbor, Mich.: University Microfilms.

Schwarz-Friesel, Monika. 2008. "Sprache, Kognition und Emotion: Neue Wege in der Kognitionswissenschaft." In *Sprache- Kognition- Kultur. Sprache zwischen mentaler Struktur und kultureller Prägung*, Heidrun Kämper and Ludwig M. Eichinger (eds). 2008, 277–301. Berlin/New York: Walter de Gruyter.

Searle, John R. 1979. *Expression and Meaning*. Cambridge: Cambridge University Press.

Selting, Margret. 1994. "Emphatic speech style – with special focus on the prosodic signalling of heightened emotive involvement in conversation." *Journal of Pragmatics* 22(3/4): 375–408.

Selting, Margret. 1995. *Prosodie im Gespräch. Aspekte einer interaktionalen Phonologie der Konversation*. Tübingen: Niemeyer.

Selting, Margret. 1996. "Prosody as an activity-type distinctive cue in conversation: The case of so-called 'astonished' questions in repair initiation." In Elizabeth Couper-Kuhlen and Margret Selting. (eds). 1996a, 231–270.

Selting, Margret. 2003. "Lists as embedded structures and the prosody of list construction as an interactional resource." *InLiSt – Interaction and Linguistic Structures* 35. [http://kops.ub.uni-konstanz.de/handle/urn:nbn:de:bsz:352-opus-11416, last accessed 04/05/11]

Selting, Margret, Auer, Peter, Barden, Birgit, Bergmann, Jörg, Couper-Kuhlen, Elizabeth, Günthner, Susanne, Meier, Christoph, Quasthoff, Uta, Schlobinski, Peter and Uhmann, Susanne. 1998. "Gesprächsanalytisches Transkriptionssystem (GAT)." *Linguistische Berichte* 173: 91–122.

Selting, Margret, Auer, Peter, Barth-Weingarten, Dagmar, Bergmann, Jörg, Bergmann, Pia, Birkner, Karin, Couper-Kuhlen, Elizabeth, Deppermann, Arnulf, Gilles, Peter, Günthner, Susanne, Hartung, Martin, Kern, Friederike, Mertzlufft, Christine, Meyer, Christian, Morek, Miriam, Oberzaucher, Frank, Peters, Jörg, Quasthoff, Uta, Schütte, Wilfried, Stukenbrock, Anja and Uhmann, Susanne. 2009. "Gesprächsanalytisches Transkriptionssystem 2 (GAT 2)." *Gesprächsforschung* 10: 353–402. [http://www.gespraechsforschung-ozs.de/heft2009/px-gat2.pdf, last accessed 04/05/11]

Selting, Margret and Couper-Kuhlen, Elizabeth. 1996. "Introduction." In Elizabeth Couper-Kuhlen and Margret Selting (eds). 1996a, 1–10.

Selting, Margret and Couper-Kuhlen, Elizabeth. 2000. "Argumente für die Entwicklung einer interaktionalen Linguistik." *Gesprächsforschung – OZS* (1): 76–95. [http://www.gespraechsforschung-ozs.de/heft2000/ga-selting.pdf, last accessed 04/05/11]

Selting, Margret and Couper-Kuhlen, Elizabeth (eds). 2001. *Studies in Interactional Linguistics*. Amsterdam: John Benjamins.

Shadle, Christine. 1983. "Experiments on the acoustics of whistling." *The Physics Teacher* 21(3): 148–154.

Shadle, Christine. 1997. "The aerodynamics of speech." In *The Handbook of Phonetic Sciences*, William J. Hardcastle and John Laver (eds). 1997, 33–64. Oxford, UK/Cambridge, MA: Blackwell.

Shosted, Ryan K. 2006. "Just put your lips together and blow? The whistled fricatives of Southern Bantu." [http://www.cefala.org/issp2006/cdrom/articles/shosted.pdf, last accessed 04/05/11]

Sinclair, John (ed.). 1987. *The Collins Cobuild English Language Dictionary*. London/Glasgow: Collins.

Sinclair, John (ed.). 1995. *Collins Cobuild English Dictionary*. London: Harper Collins Publishers.

Sorjonen, Marja-Leena. 2001. *Responding in Conversation. A study of response particles in Finnish*. Amsterdam/Philadelphia: John Benjamins.

Sorjonen, Marja-Leena. 2002. "Recipient activities. The particle *No* as a go-ahead response in Finnish conversations." In: Cecilia E. Ford, Barbara Fox and Sandra Thompson (eds). 2002, 165–195.

Sorjonen, Marja-Leena and Hakulinen, Auli. 2009. "Alternative responses to assessments." In *Conversation Analysis. Comparative studies*, Jack Sidnell (ed.). 2009, 281–303. Cambridge: Cambridge University Press.

Stein, Jess et al. (eds). 1966. *The Random House Dictionary of the English Language*. New York/Toronto: Random House.

Svennevig, Jan. 2004. "Other-repetition as display of hearing, understanding and emotional stance." *Discourse Studies* 6(4): 489–516.

Sykes, J. B. (ed.) [7]1983. *Concise Oxford Dictionary of Current English*. Oxford: Clarendon Press.

Szczepek Reed, Beatrice. 2006. *Prosodic Orientation in English Conversation*. Basingstoke et al.: Palgrave Macmillan.

te Moulder, Hedwig and Potter, Jonathan (eds). 2005. *Conversation and Cognition*. Cambridge et al.: Cambridge University Press.

ten Have, Paul. 2001. "Seconds to troubles talk: The case of radio counseling." Draft prepared for "Language and Therapeutic Interaction: International Conference in Discourse Analysis", Brunel University, Uxbridge 30–31 August 2001. [http://www.paultenhave.nl/stt.htm, last accessed 04/05/2011]

ten Have, Paul. 2002. "The notion of member is the heart of the matter: On the role of membership knowledge in ethnomethodological inquiry." *Forum Qualitative Sozialforschung/Forum: Qualitative Social Research* 3(3): 53 paragraphs. [http://www.qualitative-research.net/index.php/fqs/article/view/834/1812, last accessed 04/05/11]

Terasaki, Alene. 1976. "Pre-announcement sequences in conversation." *Social Science Working Paper* 99. School of Social Sciences. University of California, Irvine.

The Oxford English Dictionary. 1933; reprinted 1970. Oxford: Oxford University Press.

Thornborrow, Joanna. 2001. "Questions, control and the organization of talk in calls to a radio phone-in." *Discourse Studies* 3(1): 119–143.

Uhmann, Susanne. 1996. "On rhythm in everyday German conversation: Beat clashes in assessment utterances." In Elizabeth Couper-Kuhlen and Margret Selting. (eds). 1996a, 303–365.

van Dijk, Teun (ed.). 1985. *Handbook of Discourse Analysis*. Vol. 3. London: Academic Press.

Vöge, Monika. 2010. "Local identity processes in business meetings displayed through laughter in complaint sequences." *Journal of Pragmatics* 42(6): 1556–1576.

Ward, Nigel. 2006. "Non-lexical conversational sounds in American English." *Pragmatics and Cognition* 14(1): 129–182.

Wehmeier, Sally (ed.). [7]2005. *Oxford Advanced Learner's Dictionary*. Oxford et al.: Oxford University Press.

Wells, Bill and Macfarlane, Sarah. 1998. "Prosody as an interactional resource: Turn-projection and overlap." *Language and Speech* 41(3/4): 265–294.

Whalen, Jack and Zimmerman, Don H. 1998. "Observations on the display and management of emotion in naturally occurring activities: The case of 'hysteria' in calls to 9-1-1." *Social Psychological Quarterly* 61(2): 141–59.

Wharton, Tim. 2003. "Interjections, language and the 'showing-saying' continuum." *Pragmatics and Cognition* 11: 39–91.

Wierzbicka, Anna. 1992. *Semantics, Culture and Cognition. Universal human concepts in culture-specific configurations*. New York/Oxford: Oxford University Press.

Wierzbicka, Anna. 1996. *Semantics. Primes and universals*. Oxford: Oxford University Press.

Wierzbicka, Anna. 1997. *Understanding Cultures Through Their Key Words. English, Russian, Polish, German, and Japanese*. New York/Oxford: Oxford University Press.

Wiggins, Sally. 2002. "Talking with your mouth full. Gustatory *Mmms* and the embodiment of pleasure." *Journal of Language and Social Interaction* 35(3): 311–336.

Wilce, Jim. 2003. "Comment on 'The meanings of interjections in Q'eqchi' Maya: from emotive reaction to social and discursive action' by Paul Kockelman." *Current Anthropology* 44(4): 481–482.

Wilkins, David P. 1992. "Interjections as deictics." *Journal of Pragmatics* 18(2/3): 119–158.

Wilkinson, Sue and Kitzinger, Celia. 2006. "Surprise as an interactional achievement: Reaction tokens in conversation." *Social Psychology Quarterly* 69(2): 150–182.

Wright, Melissa. 2005. *Studies of the Phonetics-Interaction Interface: Clicks and interactional structures in English conversation*. Doctoral thesis, University of York. [http://www.tropic.org.uk/~melissa/, last accessed 04/05/2011]

Yagoda, Ben. undated. "Pardon the Interjection. The Internet and the rise of *awwa, meh, feh*, and *heh*." [http://www.slate.com/id/2159929/pagenum/all/#page_start, last accessed 04/05/11]

Yang, Li-chiung. 2006. "Integrating prosodic and contextual cues in the interpretation of discourse markers." In Kerstin Fischer (ed.). 2006, 266–298.

Yoon, Kyung-Eun. 2007. *Complaint talk in Korean Conversation*. Unpublished doctoral dissertation. University of Illinois at Urbana-Champaign.

Appendix

Figures

Tables

Excerpts

(17) [HOLT:2:7] "fractures at the vertebrae"
(18) [Brain teaser] "a bit young"
(19) [HOLT 1:4] "Not in at the moment"
(20) [HOLT:M88:l:2] "Lord Geoff"
(21) [Holt:Oct88:1:8] "even the kids"
(22) [Holt: Oct88:1:8] "so happy"
(23) [HOLT SO88II:2:2] "lonesome"
(24) [HOLT:SO88:1:5] "just bored"
(25) [HOLT:M88:2:3] "wretched gout"
(26) [HOLT: X(C)1:1:3] "your mother"
(27) [Brain teaser] "old-fashioned bird"
(28) [Sadie Nine] "missed it"
(29) [Sadie Nine] "another one"
(30) [HOLT:U88:1:4] "talking for another hour"
(30') Rhythmic analysis of Excerpt 34 ("talking for another hour"), lines 27–29
(31) [HOLT:C85:4] "dreadful"
(5') HOLT:M88:1:2] "polyester mostly"
(32) [HOLT:M88:2:4] "conveyancing"
(32') Rhythmic analysis of Excerpt 36 ("conveyancing"), lines 19–22

GAT-Transcription conventions (Selting et al. 1998, 2009, modified)

i.   Basic transcription conventions

Sequential structure

[	overlap
[	
=	latching

Pauses

(.)	micro-pause
(-), (--), (---)	short, middle or long pauses of ca 0.25–0.75 seconds, up to ca. 1 second
(2.85)	measured pause (measured to hundredths of a second)

Other segmental conventions

and=uh	slurring within units
:,:`:,:::	lengthening, according to its duration
uh, er, etc.	hesitation signals, so-called "filled pauses"
ʔ	glottal stop

Laughter

so(h)o	laughing particles during speech
haha hehe hihi	syllabic laughing
((laughing))	description of laughter

Accents

ACcent	primary, or main accent
!AC!cent	extra strong accent

Final pitch movements

?	high rise
,	mid-rise
-	level pitch
;	mid-fall
.	low fall

Other conventions

((cough))	paralinguistic and non-linguistic actions and events
<<coughing> >	accompanying paralinguistic and non-linguistic actions over a stretch of speech
%WORD	creaky voice quality
(* *)	unintelligible passage, according to the number of syllables
(such)	presumed wording
al(s)o	presumed sound or syllable
(such/which)	possible alternatives
(( ))	ommission of text
→	specific line in the transcript which is referred to in the text

ii.   Detailed transcription conventions

Accents

Accent	secondary accent

Pitch step-up/step down

↓	pitch step down
↑	pitch step up

Change of pitch register

<<l> >   low pitch register
<<ll> >   extra low register
<<h> >   high pitch register

Pitch movement within an accent

'SO   rise
`SO   fall
^SO   rise-fall syllable
` 'SO   fall-rise

Volume and tempo changes

<<f> >   forte, loud
<<ff> >   fortissimo, very loud
<<p> >   piano, soft
<<pp> >   pianissimo, very soft
<<all> >   allegro, fast
<<len> >   lento, slow
<<cresc> >   crescendo, becoming louder
<<dim> >   diminuendo, becoming softer
<<acc> >   accelerando, becoming faster
<<rall> >   rallentando, becoming slower

Breathing in and out

.h, .hh, .hhh   breathing in, according to its duration
h, hh, hhh   breathing out, according to its duration

Rhythm

Each line represents a foot, i.e. an interval which consists of an accented syllable perceived as a rhythmic beat and subsequent unaccented syllables, ending on, but not including the following accented syllable (Selting et al. 2009: 387). Left-hand slashes indicate the beginnings, right-hand slashes the ends of such intervals (Couper-Kuhlen 1993: 74). Slashes lined up under one another indicate that the next beat, that is, the beginning of the next foot, is perceived rhythmi-cally on time. This is exemplified as follows:

```
1    Les:  /sOme i can    /
2          /wEAr under     /
3          /NEATH:;        /
```

Isochronous rhythmic structures (i.e. structures with perceptually equal stress-timing) "need at least three prominent syllables [i.e. beats, E. R.] at equal intervals in time to be whole, although these need not come from the same speaker" (Couper-Kuhlen 1993:70). If the next beat is produced earlier or later than expected, the rhythmic structure breaks off. For example, beats which are perceived as delayed are indicated as in line 5 of the following excerpt:

```
1 Les:    they've ↑pUt in: to wIn=uhm (1.38) an
2         /↑EXport a    /
3         /wArd;
4                   (-) /
5 Mum:        /<<h>´`[əʊː]>;
6 Les:   AND uhm:-
```

Latching marks (=) speaker change without a rhythmic break (ibid: 74).

Subject index

Name index